FOUR
FRIENDS

ALSO BY WILLIAM D. COHAN

The Last Tycoons: The Secret History of Lazard Frères & Co.

House of Cards: A Tale of Hubris and Wretched Excess on Wall Street

Money and Power: How Goldman Sachs Came to Rule the World

The Price of Silence: The Duke Lacrosse Scandal, the Power of the Elite, and the Corruption of Our Great Universities

Why Wall Street Matters

FOUR FRIENDS

PROMISING LIVES CUT SHORT

WILLIAM D. COHAN

FLATIRON
BOOKS
NEW YORK

FOUR FRIENDS. Copyright © 2019 by William D. Cohan.
All rights reserved. Printed in the United States of America. For information,
address Flatiron Books, 120 Broadway, New York, NY 10271.

www.flatironbooks.com

Illustrations by Randy Glass

The Library of Congress Cataloging-in-Publication Data is available upon request.

ISBN 978-1-250-07052-4 (hardcover)
ISBN 978-1-250-07053-1 (ebook)

Our books may be purchased in bulk for promotional, educational, or business use.
Please contact your local bookseller or the Macmillan Corporate and
Premium Sales Department at 1-800-221-7945, extension 5442, or by
email at MacmillanSpecialMarkets@macmillan.com.

First Edition: July 2019

10 9 8 7 6 5 4 3 2 1

To Quentin, Deb, and Teddy

Contents

In most lives there's a moment when people strip away all the branding and status symbols, all the prestige that goes with having gone to a certain school or been born into a certain family. They leap out beyond the utilitarian logic and crash through the barriers of their fears.

—DAVID BROOKS

Please remember that our time on this Earth is not guaranteed. Please tell those you love that you do. Right now. This very minute.

—SOPHIA BUSH

Not for Oneself

O NLY ONE AMERICAN HIGH SCHOOL has produced two presidents of the United States: Phillips Academy in Andover, Massachusetts, known simply as Andover. It was no surprise, really, that people emerged from Andover thinking they could do, or be, anything they wanted. That idea that we really were "*la crème de la crème de la jeunesse américaine*," as we were told regularly, or that we were part of some kind of young and invincible Delta Force, was intoxicating. The message seeped into our DNA whether we realized it or not.

Just like George H. W. Bush (Class of 1942) and George W. Bush (Class of 1964) before him, my Andover classmate Bruce MacWilliams (Class of 1977) wanted to be president of the United States. Bruce was tall, handsome, and outgoing. He was an athlete—he was on the varsity cross-country team, the cross-country ski team, and the lacrosse team—and was a fine photographer. He had fair skin, long wavy hair parted down the middle, and a vague aura of constantly being in a drug-induced state whether true or not. You know the type: All the Andover boys wanted to be like him and all the Andover girls wanted to sleep with him. "He was pretty cocky," remembered Hugh Jones, a friend of Bruce's from Cornell. "Bruce was pretty much the man and he pretty much was sure of that." Of course, this being Andover, Bruce had some serious competition on campus on the Big Dick Energy front. The late 1970s was when John F. Kennedy Jr.—the glamorous future "Sexiest Man Alive" with unassailable presidential DNA—was also a student at Andover.

MacWilliams's Andover pedigree went back to his great-grandfather

Mabie Crouse Klock (Class of 1899). Mabie Crouse Klock came from
wealth and made more. He was an avid yachtsman and once owned a
steamer that caught the attention of a young John Jacob Astor, who
promptly bought the boat from him. Klock was also one of the early
financial benefactors of what became the Crouse-Irving Hospital, in his
native Syracuse, New York. "My great-grandfather was like the Great
Gatsby of Syracuse," Bruce remembered.

Klock's grandson—Bruce's father—John J. MacWilliams also went
to Andover (Class of 1947). He later joined the Aetna Life and Casualty Company, in Hartford, where Bruce and his three siblings spent
part of their childhood. In 1968, when Bruce was in fourth grade, his
father was offered the opportunity to run the Colonial Penn Group,
a floundering life insurance company based in Philadelphia. Colonial
Penn was about to go bankrupt. MacWilliams took the job. "My dad
said, 'What the hell, I'm gonna give it a shot,' and went down there and
turned the company around," Bruce said. "Within like six, seven years,
he made it a Fortune 500 company. He was on the cover of all the
magazines, and he was kind of a darling for a while because he made a
lot of money." There were private planes, fancy country clubs, soirees
with Republican politicians, and lofty dreams.

It was the late Mad Men era, and the MacWilliamses took to it.
"They would put on their designer suits, and they would look really
great," Bruce explained. And they loved to drink. "Our parents were
all getting bombed at lunch, and having martini lunches, and my dad
was a CEO," he continued. "He was a successful guy, and he looked
fantastic. My mom looked fantastic, too. But they would go out to parties and they would have cocktail hour, and they would drink a lot. It
was the way they grew up, and they inherited it from their parents." As
had generations of MacWilliamses before him, Bruce said he inherited
from his parents the notion of drinking as a glamorous activity. In the
years before Bruce alighted at Andover, his father would encourage the
family to have wine with dinner, just as he found his business acquain-

tances did with their families in Italy, where John MacWilliams often traveled. "He expressed that that was a way to grow up fast, and to learn how to drink responsibly," Bruce said.

Andover was a family tradition. Two of Bruce's three siblings attended the school. At Andover, Bruce and I were in Nathan Hale House together, and I remember him well: his hair, his infectious demeanor, the time he spent palling around with the other hipster guys, Jamie Clark from Texas and two guys from New York City, Will Iselin, a descendant of John Jay, and Will Daniel, whose grandfather was Harry Truman. They were all my dorm mates, it's true, but we traveled in different circles. Nathan Hale West was part of Rabbit Pond cluster, one of six clusters comprising various student dorms and historic homes (where students also lived) that made it easier for Andover to feel like it was a manageable size, even with its twelve hundred students. Each cluster had a dean, responsible for administering discipline, among other duties. John "Jack" Richards II was the Rabbit Pond cluster dean. Richards, a history teacher, epitomized the WASPy Andover administrator. We referred to him, mostly affectionately, as "Jack Dick."

Like so many of the Andover students at the time, Bruce smoked a lot of marijuana. There was a famous cartoon in the *Pot Pourri*, the student yearbook, about how one Andover student was explaining to another that there was no drug problem at Andover: "We can get anything we want." Bruce and his Nathan Hale friends spent a lot of time together smoking pot. Two of his friends were expelled. "They caught them and threw them out, but they didn't catch me," MacWilliams recalled, "and Jack Richards brought me in and read me the riot act, said, 'Hey, listen, we haven't caught you yet, but we know you're doing it, and if we catch you, you're out, so shape up.'" After Richards spared MacWilliams, he claimed to have reformed his behavior.

In his senior year at Andover, MacWilliams served as the president of Rabbit Pond cluster (defeating me in the election) and ended up working closely with Richards. All these years later, I still remember the contours of the race between us. Alan Cantor, one of my closest friends at Andover, was the incumbent cluster president; he not only encouraged me to run for the position but also did his best imitation of making an inchoate political endorsement of my candidacy. By then, Bruce was living with his buddies in one of the small stately homes around the periphery of Rabbit Pond cluster, doing whatever cool guys did back then. We had little interaction with each other by that point in our Andover careers but we were always friendly enough when we bumped into each other on the campus pathways. Like almost everyone at Andover, I liked the guy. I was then living in the west side of Alfred E. Stearns House (named after a former headmaster), a late-1950s brick structure with an oddly Soviet countenance. We always thought Stearns was the locus of power in Rabbit Pond cluster given both its central location and the fact that many of the school leaders lived in the dorm. With my friend Alan's endorsement and a modest amount of retail campaigning on my part, I thought for sure I would win the election. Although the vote was close, I had miscalculated the appeal of Bruce's magnetic personality and his abundant charm.

Bruce found Andover to be seminal. "I absolutely loved Andover," he said. "I thought it was the best. It was like a party mixed up with friends, and I was learning a lot, and I became proud of myself because I was going to the best secondary school in the country. There was just so much that was really fantastic about it. I felt so lucky to be there, and to be given that opportunity, and to be able to turn it into something."

One thing Bruce hoped might come from his Andover experience was a political career. It was not a crazy thought. Andover had produced Henry Stimson (Class of 1883), Roosevelt's secretary of war, who held many other cabinet positions over the years. JFK's son was a fellow student, as was Harry Truman's grandson. George H. W. Bush was, at that time, both an Andover trustee and the director of the Central Intelligence

Agency. If you thought about it, the MacWilliamses of Gladwyne were not terribly unlike the Bushes of Kennebunkport or even the Kennedys of Hyannis Port. And Bruce was not particularly shy about sharing the thought that if things had turned out a little differently, his father might also have been president of the United States, instead of the CEO of a somewhat predatory insurance company. He had the looks. He had the brains. He had the money, and he had the connections. (He also thought his older brother, John, a former Wall Street banker, should have been Obama's secretary of state or chief of staff. "He's a guy you want behind you when you go out into battle," he said.)

When Bruce ran for Rabbit Pond cluster president, and won, he began to think the dream might be possible. "I even got sucked into that whole thing because I found out how easy it was," he said. "It's like, *Oh wow, you just need to show up and say a few kind words and get voted in, and you got a job.*" One minor hiccup for him came with the election of Andover school president, a school-wide ballot comprising the six cluster presidents. Bruce slept through the assembly where the candidates made their pitches. He still came in second.

The ambition persisted. When Bruce told his father he wanted to be president of the United States, he wasn't joking. "I said, 'Look at Andover. I've just been hanging out with John Kennedy, man.' I had tea with Jacqueline Onassis and John Kennedy at the Andover Inn. And Jacqueline Onassis leaned over and said, 'Oh, John, you know who your friend Bruce reminds me of? He reminds me of your father.' And I almost fell out of my chair."

He had come by his friendship with John Kennedy Jr. through his role as cluster president. For some odd reason, part of the role was to represent fellow students who lived in your cluster through a disciplinary procedure. The Secret Service decided that John Kennedy Jr. should be placed in Stearns House West (my dorm for my third and fourth years at Andover) because it was right next to the Andover Inn. John was an Upper when Bruce was a senior and the cluster president.

John always liked to push the disciplinary envelope at Andover, if in a charming way. He didn't intentionally flaunt the rules as much as sort of pretend they never really existed in the first place, since it was pretty clear from his own experiences in life that the rules of the road would never apply to him anyway. Whether it was staying out on campus beyond the 10 p.m. curfew, or getting high, or having girls in his room outside regular parietal hours, John brought a sly, infectious attitude toward his nocturnal activities. Who wouldn't want to be part of them, if invited?

On one of those occasions when John was out late, roaming the campus, he got caught. It fell to Bruce to defend him before the Andover disciplinary authorities. At first, Bruce wasn't so sure he felt comfortable representing the young prince, since at that point he didn't really like him. They were two alpha males competing over the same territory, particularly for the affections of the Andover women. Bruce thought, as a senior and the cluster president, he would be the Big Man on Campus. "I saw all the girls flock around this guy—'Who's this guy?'" Bruce remembered. "And then I saw the initials on his shirt, and it said JFK, and it wasn't even JFK JUNIOR. It was like one of his dad's shirts that he had kept. And I go, 'Oh my God, I'm never going to be able to compete with this guy.'" But the more he got to know John, the more Bruce liked him. And then he went to bat for John. "They wanted to throw the book at him," Bruce said. "And I said, 'Listen, you can't do that, because you're making an example out of him.' They said, 'We've got to make an example out of him.' I said, 'Yeah. You make him an example by not making an example. You have to treat him just like you treat everybody else; otherwise, you're giving him special attention. You can't do that. He's just a student, and any other student, you wouldn't do this to him, because he's not John Kennedy. So treat him just like you would every other student.' And they said, 'Bruce, you'd make a great lawyer.' But I got him off the hook, and they bought my argument, and then we became friends."

One time they spent the weekend in Boston and were having a beer together at a little bar around the corner from the downtown bus station. They were playing backgammon, passing the time. When it occurred to Bruce that they'd best return to Andover, he said, "John, we better get back, man. You're going to get back in trouble again, and I'm cluster president, I'm going to get in trouble." Kennedy told him not to worry so much. "I have a car."

"You have a car?" Bruce asked. "You dog. How'd you end up getting a car on campus? Where's the car?"

"Don't worry," John said. "Wait right here."

Suddenly a car pulled up, and out jumped two Secret Service agents. "We hop in the damn car and drive back to Andover and I thought to myself, *Oh yeah, I forgot who this guy is.*"

When Jackie Onassis told him he reminded her of John's father, Bruce said, "It's like someone whispering in your ear and telling you, 'Yeah, you should maybe give this a shot.'" He thought, *Hey I can do it, because my dad has the connections.* Jackie O was telling him he reminded her of JFK. Why not give it a shot? "Andover really is a factory for making presidents, if you look at it," he said. "It's so right for it, because it's 'the Best and the Brightest.' You've got an opportunity. You've got the intelligence. You've got the confidence. And then you've got the *Non Sibi*—Not For Oneself—so what are you going to do? You're going to go help everybody. And how are you going to help each other?" Well, if you were at Andover, among the best and the brightest, and you emerged relatively unscathed from it and from your wealthy, well-connected political family, then the logical thing to consider, if you were Bruce MacWilliams, was becoming president of the United States.

But sometimes things don't always work out as planned.

BRUCE GOT IN EARLY DECISION to the Cornell School of Architecture. There isn't a specific curriculum for how to become president of the United States, so in the meantime he decided to pursue one of his avocations. He had been interested in drawing at Andover, was captivated by architecture, and had enjoyed his one summer at the Harvard Graduate School of Design. In fact, a Harvard dean declared his summer project a "genius design" and had recommended him for the architecture school at Cornell. "For guys like me, who loved architecture and thought it was really neat, but wasn't totally committed to necessarily being an architect for the rest of my life, it was a little bit intimidating," he said. "They were expecting you to spend all-nighters in the studio, designing masterpieces." Politics, and a high-sloped political career, remained his primary ambition.

At Cornell, Bruce decided to room with David Buck, a classmate from Andover who was also in the architecture school. David grew up in Belmont, Massachusetts, near Boston. His father, Dudley Buck, a famous scientist at MIT, was part of the team that worked on designing and building the first computers. He was once featured in *Life* magazine (among many other publications) for developing the cryotron, a tiny switch that briefly seemed like it might be a quantum leap forward in computer development. (It was not to be, and then silicon came along and changed everything.) When David was three months old, his father died suddenly after handling some poisonous chemicals in his MIT lab. The papers disguised his mysterious death as due to a virulent form of pneumonia. But others, including his wife and David's older brother, thought the Russians deliberately poisoned him as part of the ongoing Cold War. Very few of us at Andover—and certainly not me—knew anything about David's father, or that he had died under mysterious circumstances, or that David was the product of a single-parent family. These were topics that simply weren't discussed.

But there was no missing David Buck at Andover. He wasn't an athlete, or a student leader, or a standout academically, or the most handsome or most likely to succeed. What I remember most about him was his magnetic and gregarious personality. His strawberry-blond hair, face full of freckles, and perpetual smile made him universally liked. One of our classmates, Richard Riker (whose family once owned what is now Rikers Island in New York Harbor), showed me a picture he had taken of David during a trip he and a bunch of his Andover friends took to Hollywood, Florida, during spring break of our senior year. They were staying at the modest Holly Hill Motel and having a blast. "I remember drinking a lot of Busch beer," Riker recalled. David, his hair still wet from a swim and a cheap towel wrapped around his shoulders, was on the phone making some arrangements. He looked slight and elegant but determined. He was a guy who got things done.

In the picture, as usual, Buck was wearing a starched red-striped Brooks Brothers button-down shirt, more or less matching his hair. It was his signature look. "Dave would always have that same uniform on," Bruce remembered. "He had seven Brooks Brothers shirts, and I can even see them right now. He had them all pressed, and he always pressed the shirts so that they were doubly pressed. Make them stiff so they'll stand up in the corner by themselves. And then he had like four pairs of khakis, and he would just wear those over and over again, one belt, one pair of shoes, two pair of shoes, and he wore that outfit every single day."

Bruce and David did not know each other particularly well at Andover. David was more in my circle of friends than Bruce's—people who were involved in the school radio station, WPAA, or the school newspaper, the *Phillipian*, or the *Pot Pourri*, the yearbook. But Bruce recalled, "Once we realized we were both going to Cornell, we decided, 'Hey, let's become roommates.'"

Bruce was a little ambivalent about actually becoming an architect, and that ambivalence started showing up early in his time at Cornell. Instead of putting in the requisite hours on his architectural studies, Bruce was spending a lot of time at night hanging out with his friends and playing varsity B lacrosse. David Buck, though, seemed very committed to architecture. He "was focusing all of his work, his attention on the architecture, and he was really good at it, too," Bruce said. There was no shortage of pressure to perform academically and socially. Dave used to stay up very late, designing buildings for his architecture classes. "He was living full-throttle at all times," Bruce said. "I never got the feeling that he had huge ambitions. It was just because he just wanted to do it to the fullest. He was so much fun to hang out with." He had joie de vivre. He had that ability to really live life to the fullest, that carpe diem sprit. They would literally go parachuting together, at night. "We were thrill seekers," Bruce said.

During his freshman year, Bruce drove a used BMW 2002 tii. He ended up crashing it and then getting a hot new car, a silver Volkswagen Scirocco. Actually, Bruce had been in five car accidents before he was nineteen. He was the driver in two of the wrecks, and his friends were driving in the other three. "We were all driving really fast, and racing each other on the streets," he said. "And then you add in there the alcohol and marijuana, and it's a prescription for a crash. I'm really lucky I'm here." But these near misses did not dissuade Bruce, or David for that matter, from fantasizing about being Grand Prix Formula One race-car drivers. They used to go over to Watkins Glen, twenty-four miles away from Cornell, to watch Niki Lauda race against James Hunt—the longtime Formula One racing rivals. In 1976, Lauda had suffered a horrific crash that almost killed him. He soon returned to Formula One racing despite suffering second-degree burns. His face remained deformed. "We didn't even really notice that part of it," Bruce recalled. "We just noticed how cool all of the Formula One race-car drivers were, and it was almost contagious. There were like four of us that all loved racing, and we loved street racing." Dave didn't have his own car. "But he used to love being my wingman," Bruce recalled.

Besides a love of driving fast, alcohol seemed to be David's main vice. Bruce remembered how Bucky, as David was affectionately known, would think nothing of downing a bottle of Gordon's gin. "He would just drink straight from the bottle, like, holy mackerel," Bruce said.

Their sophomore year at Cornell, Bruce switched out of the architecture program into liberal arts. His ambivalence about architecture was the cause of the switch, along with the realization that taking courses in history and political science would be a better way for him to get refocused on his dream of becoming president. He had already arranged to work the following summer, 1979, in New Hampshire to help elect his fellow Andover alum George H. W. Bush president. Politically, Bruce thought of himself as an independent, but he became excited about Bush's prospects for becoming president after his father encouraged him to study his résumé, which included being a congressman, heading up the CIA, serving as the US ambassador to the United Nations, and serving on the Andover board of trustees.

During their sophomore year, Bruce and David decided to join a fraternity and were soon living at Theta Delta Chi. They decided to buy two queen-sized waterbeds and install them in their room, leaving little space for anything else. "We put them side by side in the room, but they took up the entire room," Bruce recalled. "There was no place to dress . . . it was fun as hell. We basically slept in the same big huge waterbed together for a year."

Life seemed full of infinite possibilities for Bruce as a future president of the United States, and for David as an architect, designing important buildings. But their gauzy dreams, based on those infinite possibilities, turned into a frightening nightmare on the night of May 16, 1979. Classes at Cornell had ended for the school year, as had most of the exams. Bruce had finished his last exam. His plan was to pack up his Scirocco in two days, head back home to Gladwyne—the seventh richest zip code in the country—and then either drive or fly up to Nashua, New Hampshire, and "work all summer" for Bush. That night, Bruce and David decided to meet a friend, Justus O'Brien, over at Quill and Dagger, a secret club at Cornell that taps its members from the best and the brightest on campus.

David, Bruce, and Justus drank a bottle of tequila together. "Because why not?" Bruce said. "It was the last lacrosse game, it was summer, *Let's celebrate, it's a big night, we deserve to live to the fullest*, so we did. We drank a lot." Bruce remembered that Bucky then suggested they all go to Simeon's, a somewhat classy bar in town. "There's going to be some people there," David said. "It'll be really fun." The friends drove down the Cornell hill to Simeon's and drank some more. Then the plan was to continue the fun at Justus's house, a short ride back up the Cornell hill. David was in the front seat of Bruce's car. They were set to follow Justus to his house. That's when Bruce got in his head the idea that he could race Justus. It was 1:47 a.m. "We got in the car, and we chased him back onto campus, and we were on campus . . . and I came around the corner going really fast—much too fast, because I thought I was a Formula One race-car driver—and came around, and I saw the guy in front of me had his blinker on. And I could swear that he had his blinker on to the right, which means that he was pulling to the right to park along the side of the road." But Bruce was wrong: The driver of the car in front of him—his new friend Justus O'Brien—had his left blinker on, not his right one. "I came whipping around the corner to the left to pass him, and just at the last minute he pulled left instead," Bruce recalled. "So I saw his right blinker on, but he pulled left, and right in front of me, and I didn't even have enough time to put on the brakes. It just hit the front of the car, and my car flipped end-over-end twice, and then landed upside down over a telephone pole. And lights went out, and blood was everywhere, we were both unconscious. The engine came right up into my face. Thank God I was wearing my seat belt—nobody back then was wearing seat belts. That was before there was a law." (In 1984, New York State became the first state in the country to require that seat belts be worn by everyone in a car.)

JUSTUS O'BRIEN WATCHED THE SCIROCCO hit his Civic and then disappear. "Then I was the only one there," he said. "I got out of the car. I was stunned, absolutely stunned." He was uninjured. "Not a scratch," he continued. The Civic was totaled. He got out of the car and looked around for Bruce and David. He saw them in the flipped-over Scirocco. "The one really horrific memory I have from that evening is looking under and seeing if they were all right or alive and there was just this incredible deathly silence," he said. "It was just awful. All I could hear was like the drip of—presumably—their blood coming down from the accident. I couldn't tell the nature of their injuries. I mean obviously I heard afterward what had happened. They were both unconscious." He called out their names. "They couldn't respond," he said.

In short order, the police arrived on the scene. They gave O'Brien a blanket to wrap himself in. "They were afraid I was going to go into shock of some kind just from the trauma of the accident," he said. "I was really concerned about both Bruce and David. It wasn't easy getting them out of the car." The Jaws of Life were needed to extract them. "I was there for all that," O'Brien recalled. "They had the Jaws, they cut the door open." It turned out the injuries were so severe that the nearby Tompkins County hospital could not handle them. "It's too intense for us," the Ithaca hospital told the ambulance drivers. Bruce was transported to the Upstate Medical Center in Syracuse, fifty-seven miles away. The paper reported he had broken his leg and was in "satisfactory" condition. David was also transported by ambulance to Syracuse, to the Crouse Irving Memorial Hospital—the very hospital that Bruce's ancestors had endowed. The paper reported that the police said David had suffered head injuries and had broken his leg, too, and that the hospital said he was "in critical condition."

Bruce and David's fraternity brothers were reluctant to call their friends' parents to explain what happened. Bruce recalled that only one of his fraternity brothers—a cocaine dealer—had the guts to do it. "They were chicken," he recalled. "They didn't want to call our parents and tell them that we were almost dead, but he actually did. He called my parents and told them." (This same student was himself killed in a car accident a year later.) Bruce's father, John, called the Ithaca police, who told him that Bruce had "a fifty–fifty chance of living" and that David was in a coma "and we don't know if he's going to come out of it."

When Bruce woke in the hospital, he had no recollection of what had happened. This was not unusual. "It's like a short-circuit thing where your memory cuts off to protect you from what you went through," he said. "I didn't even know I was in a car accident. They told me I was in a car accident. They didn't tell me I was with Bucky. They kept it a secret that Bucky was in [the car], they said, 'Okay, you were in an accident with your roommate, and he's in the hospital, too, and he looks like he's going to recover,' but they didn't tell me any more. . . . In that moment all of a sudden I felt so bad about the accident, and the fact that I had put my [roommate's life in danger]—and I didn't even know how bad he was—and for one second, I had the thought, *Oh God, I don't want to be here right now.* And at that moment, I left my body, and died, and went to the tunnel of white light, and I saw little angels in the tunnel, and they were pulling me toward the light, further and further. And I said, *No, no, I don't want to. I want to go back and help the world.* And as soon as I had that thought, I came back into my body. And by the way, when you're in that place, it's so beautiful and so blissful you don't want to come back. It's the best feeling you've ever had. But I came back, and I came into my body, and I had tubes up my nose, my hands were tied down, and blood was all caked over my face, and I pried my eyes open and I saw my parents, my older brother, John, looking down at me. And I felt so high, higher than a kite, after that experience, but they were looking at me like I was—there were just tears in their eyes because I'm looking a mess. I used to be a handsome kid, and my face was all totally shattered, and I'm just almost dead."

Despite the extent of his injuries, Bruce healed quickly, within a month or so. He has a scar from below his navel to his neck. "They opened him all the way up," his friend Hugh Jones remembered. "He had the internal bleeding and just crushed everything." On the day he was to be released from the hospital, Bruce insisted on seeing David. Confined to his wheelchair, he was wheeled by nurses into David's room. "That was the first time I knew that he was in a coma, and he might not come back," he said. "And that's where I, you know . . ." He started crying as he recalled the memory. "I felt such shame, and such remorse, and I felt so bad, because I knew that I was responsible," he continued. "And we were both drinking, and we were both going crazy, but I was the one driving and it was my responsibility, and I was to blame."

He quickly realized he could not possibly spend the summer working for George H. W. Bush in New Hampshire. A life in politics no longer seemed right, or even possible. "That was the end of my political ambition," he said. "It just completely switched me in a different direction. I didn't even think about politics after that. I was like, *No, I'm done. That's not me.*"

DESPITE BRUCE'S WARM MEMORIES of his relationship with David, there were lawsuits. David sued both Bruce and Justus O'Brien in Tompkins County, New York. O'Brien recalled that David was seeking $2 million from the defendants. Bruce's father argued to let the lawyers fight it out with the insurance company. "Don't you fight it out with Bucky," his father told him. Bruce took his father's advice.

During the pendency of the lawsuit, Bruce and David weren't supposed to speak, per the instructions of their respective attorneys. "But Bucky and I never, ever had any animosity," Bruce said. "I said [to him], 'Hey, listen, tell your lawyers to get as much as they can. I hope you're treated well, and you can make some money off this. That's really not my concern. My concern as your friend and someone who cares about you [is] that you get 100 percent healthy, and you can do whatever you want to do with your life.' I have always believed that, and I never, ever had any kind of animosity toward him at all. And my dad was so supportive in that regard. And he believed exactly the same thing. He said, 'We will take care of it any way we can, and don't worry about the lawsuit stuff.'"

Bruce ended up being slapped with "driving while ability impaired," a lesser charge than "driving while intoxicated." He kept his driver's license. He said the police's evidence against him was hampered by the fact that they took a blood sample from him when he was unconscious and so he could not have given them his consent. In effect, he got off on a technicality. "I was obviously drunk by anybody's standards," he said. "But they had no case on me, I guess. I don't know. The lawyers figured it out."

Bruce said he doesn't recall much about the settlement with David, other than that the case was settled. "It was all fine," he said. "It was all good. My dad never even blinked. He just said, 'Don't worry about it.' My dad never even kept me apprised of the details." David Buck's brother, Doug Buck, had a different view of the fairness of the MacWilliamses' settlement. "Bullshit, their lawyers fought him tooth and nail and David was sick of the whole process and just wanted to end it," he wrote in an email. "He ended the lawsuit way earlier than he should have for a pittance. I believe he settled for $275,000 and the lawyer took his share. I believe that was the amount Bruce's lawyers first offered."

AFTER THE MAY 1979 CAR ACCIDENT, the lives of David Buck and Bruce MacWilliams quickly diverged. Bruce returned to Cornell that fall and continued his studies in the liberal arts program. The summer after his junior year at Cornell, he took a gig painting a house in Newport, Rhode Island. He met up there with Hugh Jones, his friend from Cornell who had also taken a year off from the college before returning. The two undergrads designed and built a Colonial-style home at 77 Thames Street, in downtown Newport. Jones could see that the accident had changed Bruce. "He never drank after that," he said. "He had meditated before that. He was into meditation, but he just really went full-on into the meditation after that."

Bruce then transferred to Columbia University, where he studied film. He recalled, "As soon as I started shooting with a motion picture camera, I said, *Oh my God, this is what I should do with the rest of my life. . . .* I've always been in film ever since." He ended up with a degree from Cornell, in 1984—he had a choice between a Columbia degree and a Cornell degree and chose Cornell—and then set about making his first movie, *Real Cowboy*, which was set in the South Bronx and Bisbee, Arizona. He was twenty-seven years old. He showed it around and people seemed to like it and urged him to move to Los Angeles if he was serious about filmmaking. He settled in Santa Monica, where he lives today. He pays the bills for his wife and teenage son by directing commercials. He can't say for certain whether he ever saw Bucky again. "I visited him once, I think, or twice," he said.

David Buck's recovery from the car accident was very different from Bruce's. He was transferred to Mass General Hospital, in Boston, to be closer to his mother. Our Andover classmate Phil Balshi remembered visiting David there. He remembered David being in the hospital for about a year. "I don't think he could speak very well on my first visit," Balshi recalled. On his second visit, Balshi said, David had regained some speech. He also thought, at that early point, his friend had trouble walking and difficulty remembering people and places. "Being the gregarious guy he was, womanizer, whatever you want to call him, and being in that physical condition, I think must have been incredibly depressing for him," he said. Eventually, David left Mass General and moved back home with his mother.

On a few occasions, Hugh Jones drove up from Newport to see his friend, outside of Boston. Bucky was still recovering. "He was really foggy," Jones said. "It was really hard seeing him then. He had to put it all back together. It was a lot." His vision was particularly affected by the accident. "His eyes were terrible," Jones continued. "He had these big funky glasses. He'd kind of lose his train of thought. A little bit of it was his personality because he was always a little—not spacy, but kind of nonchalant about things." He remembered David walked with a limp and used a cane. "He was hurting."

Eventually, David recovered sufficiently from his injuries to return to Cornell and to graduate. But he could no longer handle the curriculum at the architecture school. "It took a long time to get back on his feet," his brother explained, "and he couldn't walk without being steadied. He stayed positive but was never the same." One day, after she had graduated from Cornell, David's college friend Jamie Lustberg ran into him in the architecture school. She had returned to campus to play in an alumni squash tournament. She was walking through the drawing studios when she heard someone say, "Hey, Punky," the nickname David had given to her. She turned and saw him. "He was suffering, I could tell," she said. "It was very bittersweet. He was happy to see me but . . . something was missing, something was missing . . . It was almost like he had been rebuilt." Lustberg remembered he had scars on his face and that he just seemed generally frustrated—with the architecture school, with getting things done, with even walking around. "He was four years older, at least, than all his classmates," she said. "He was not doing well."

Doug Buck encouraged his brother to move to Seattle to live with him. He had a decent business buying, renovating, and selling homes as well as developing other buildings in and around Seattle, which was booming. David lived with his brother, who was still single, in a rundown house he bought in the Highlands, an exclusive gated neighborhood favored by some of Seattle's richest and most powerful families.

At first, David sold government-guaranteed investment contracts for Marsh & McLennan, the big insurance company. "But he didn't like being a salesman cold-calling," his brother said. They decided to fix up the house in the Highlands and then sell it. Their house had "great bones" and was big, another friend from Cornell, Beau Poor, recalled, and it was in a beautiful neighborhood. But they had little furniture. Hugh Jones thought David must have used some of the money he received from the MacWilliamses to fix up the house with his brother. "We were driving around," Jones said, "and I remember seeing like big freaking buildings, like a fifteen-story apartment building, and Bucky said, 'Yeah, we own that.' . . . These were not small buildings and there wasn't just one. And they're like, 'Yeah, we own that. We own that.' And it's like, jeez, okay." Jones was impressed that the brothers' business seemed to be going so well but was also wondering just what role David was actually playing in it, given his ongoing medical difficulties. Jones visited their house in the Highlands, and remembered driving through the gate into the enclave. "It was like a Bel Air mansion," he said.

David was also working at Boeing. Doug Buck explained that he worked in what was known as the offset program, which was a way for Boeing to sell its military aircraft to foreign countries. He worked closely with the Israeli military, which required David to get into the office early every day to speak with the Israelis during their working hours. But given that he was often out late drinking, he would show up late for work the next day or still a little drunk, or both. This behavior did not please his superiors at Boeing. Jones did not understand why Bucky was working at Boeing in the first place given how well it seemed the real estate business was going. "The real estate had gone so well . . . you know, buying up all these big buildings in Seattle in the 1980s," he said. Jones thought the Boeing program might be a special one. "I remember being really surprised when he told me that he was working for Boeing," he said. "I was wondering—I didn't say it—but I was kind of wondering if maybe Boeing had some program to help handicapped or disadvantaged people or people that had health problems or something that helped him get the job."

Jones was passing through Seattle with his fiancée. They had chartered a sailboat for a week out of the San Juan Islands, and David invited them to stay the night with him and his brother at their house in the Highlands. They all made dinner together that night and there was lots of drinking, of course. "Then something weird happened," Jones remembered, "which was that as we were leaving the next morning, my fiancée told me that Bucky was like hitting on her the night before and trying to basically, you know . . . We were having a good time and the next morning we're driving to the airport and Amy is sitting there like, 'He hit on me last night. I thought he was your friend.'" Understandably, that angered Jones. "It was a situation with Bucky where it was kind of hard to get pissed at Bucky about that, but yet I was like, 'You asshole. I've made a real effort to try to stay connected with you and this is the thanks I get.' I never looked him up after that."

Another friend of ours from Andover, Bill Van Deventer, whose nickname was BVD, ran into David in Seattle, at the Henry Art Gallery. Van Deventer had moved to Seattle after graduating from UVA and the Yale School of Architecture to try his hand at architecture. He had become the architect that David could not. BVD didn't know David had moved to Seattle, nor vice versa. They coincidentally met at the Henry, which was showing an exhibit of photographs from Andover's Addison Gallery collection. That's how BVD learned that David had been working at Boeing. They met up another time at the Seattle Art Museum, to which the Buck brothers had made a sizable donation. They had dinner a few times after that, drank a lot, and had a nice time. But during a brief serendipitous conversation they'd had years before at the San Juan airport, BVD had come to realize that the car accident had affected Dave far more than he was first able to discern. He learned that his friend had problems with both his short-term and long-term memory and that his job at Boeing, as Hugh Jones suspected, was designed for those with handicaps. "His personality was completely different from what I had ever remembered," he said. The last time he saw David was when he asked if he could borrow BVD's parallel-line ruler, an architect's tool.

In September 1991, at the Tokoriki Island Resort in Fiji, Doug Buck married a divorcée three years his senior whose father was a respected lawyer in Palm Beach. They were in the midst of a lengthy sailing adventure. "I was no longer able to interact with David on a daily basis," Doug explained.

Eventually, Boeing fired Dave and he put together his résumé. He bought a condominium in a plush, modernist high rise at 2201 3rd Avenue, in the Belltown neighborhood of Seattle. His apartment was on the eighteenth floor, giving him expansive views of the Seattle waterfront, west toward Bainbridge Island. "He was really on his own," his brother said. In 1998, David called his old Andover friend Marty Koffman, the secretary of our Andover class, who had the unenviable task of writing notes about the comings and goings of our classmates on a semiannual basis. (I'd had the job for years before ceding it to Marty.) "I got a message from David Buck, to which I responded but I got no answer," Koffman reported to us all that summer. "*David please call back. I must have a wrong number.*" The following spring David emailed Koffman. "David Buck blinked into my email and let me know he is alive and kicking in Seattle," Koffman wrote in the class notes that appeared that fall.

But alas, that was no longer true. David Buck died on August 10, 1998, most likely in his new apartment. The King County associate medical examiner pronounced him dead three days later. The immediate cause: "Alcoholic cirrhosis." His death certificate listed his occupation as an economist in the financial industry, but that seems misleading at best.

The consensus seemed to be that David Buck had drunk himself to death, although no one much wants to discuss what happened, especially since both his father and his paternal grandmother had been teetotalers. On August 19, he was buried next to his father in the Furnace Village Cemetery, in Easton, Massachusetts. He was thirty-nine years old, having outlived his father by seven years.

ONE MINUTE YOU THINK YOU ARE on a path to become the president of the United States. Or a great architect. Or you're just wondering how you will get through another day in your senior year of high school. But in another moment, that life can be over, or irredeemably altered beyond any recognition.

We all know people who died young and tragically. Occasionally, for reasons we often don't know, we think about them, wondering where they'd be now, if only. Sometimes I think about Brad Morrison, who was two classes ahead of me in grammar school, the tiny, private Shepherd Knapp School in central Massachusetts. His hobby was collecting glass insulators from the tops of telephone poles; the insulators attached the electrical wires to the pole. Nowadays these insulators are made of ceramic, painted an ugly brown. But back then, they were made of glass—mostly a translucent green, but other sublime colors, too—and they were made in a variety of different shapes and sizes and designs. They became collectibles. There were catalogs filled with the different kinds of glass insulators listing how much each was worth in the market. They were difficult to obtain, obviously. My friend Bobby Miller and I would study the catalogs for hours.

One morning at Shepherd Knapp we were informed that Brad had died after climbing up a telephone pole to try to get a glass insulator, only to have fallen off, breaking electrical wires along the way. It was never really clear to me whether he died from his fall or from being electrocuted. But it didn't really matter. Brad Morrison was gone, his life snuffed out in an instant, a victim of appallingly bad judgment.

Everyone has a version of a Brad Morrison story. These deaths loom so large that we are left only with stupefying bewilderment when, for instance, we stop to consider what might have been for the ten people at Santa Fe High School in Texas, the seventeen at Marjory Stoneman Douglas High School, the twenty-eight deaths at Sandy Hook Elementary School, the thirteen at Columbine High School, the fifty-eight people killed at the country music concert in Las Vegas, the forty-nine who died at the nightclub in Orlando, the fourteen people who died during the attack in San Bernardino, California, or the eleven worshippers gunned down on a Sabbath morning at the Tree of Life synagogue in Pittsburgh. And on and on.

But it was the slow, tragic death of David Buck following the sudden accident in which he was a drunken passenger that got me thinking about how the trajectory of one's life can change in an instant. You may think you are going about your business—supervising a deposition in San Francisco, crossing the street after coming home late from a party in Brooklyn, going for a weekend sail with your kids on Lake Michigan, or making your way to a wedding on Cape Cod—when suddenly you are confronted with the terrifying prospect of your own death, maybe even before you realize it. Not every one of these tragedies unfolded as did David Buck's, slowly but inexorably. And few of those responsible for them get the kind of redemption that Bruce MacWilliams was fortunate to receive. Such moments of grace can't be counted on. But when it happens, those left behind can't help but stop, even for a moment, and reflect upon the fragility of life.

Andover is a place where very big dreams are formed, nurtured, and encouraged without the slightest bit of irony. When they get snuffed out, whether in an instant or over time, the damage to the rest of the Delta Force can be substantial, if only because it reveals the stark truth that no one is exempt from the one unavoidable aspect of life: death. Not even those who have every privilege that life offers, right from the start, can escape the inevitable. It's one thing when death strikes at a ripe old age or after a long illness or when it seems better than the alternative.

But when lives are taken suddenly, with little warning, or changed in an instant at the end of one's sophomore year in college, it just doesn't seem fair, or right, or make a whole lot of sense. Even the religious begin questioning their faith at such moments, and rightly so.

In the years after David Buck's tragic death, which I first discovered only by reading Marty Koffman's class notes, I began thinking about my other Andover classmates and friends whose lives—once filled with nearly infinite promise—had similarly been extinguished far too early. There was Jack Berman, dead at age thirty-six; Will Daniel, dead at age forty-one; Harry Bull, like David Buck dead at thirty-nine; and John F. Kennedy Jr., once perhaps the most famous man alive—and my dorm mate in Stearns House West and close friend—who died on a hot August night at age thirty-eight, along with his wife and sister-in-law, after he piloted his own plane into the Atlantic Ocean, right off the coast of Martha's Vineyard.

The stories of these four friends of mine from Andover are not just the stories of their deaths. There's nothing much to that alone other than morose facts. Rather, as I became further and further immersed in the rich details of their short lives, I became increasingly fascinated the more I learned about how they happened to get to Andover, what they did afterward, and how they grew into husbands, fathers, and men of the world—and then, yes, how their lives ended just as they were getting going.

We had mostly lost touch, of course; this was the era before social media made keeping track of friends an easy click away. That made for a little sadness if only because we had all been pretty close for a few years before going our separate ways as our lives came into greater focus. On the other hand, it wasn't exactly a shock, either. In those days, before cell phones, the only way to keep in touch was by somehow getting the pay-phone number to a college dorm. Which wasn't likely. And let's face it, guys rarely write letters to other guys. So the inevitable separation that followed the Andover graduation, along with the losing touch, seemed like just another step on the path to achieving the goal of greatness that the school had thrust upon us.

To be sure, telling their stories was a reporting challenge, not just because they were not around to be interviewed but also because with one exception they were not famous or particularly well known. I relied—and am thankful for—the recollections of friends, relatives, wives, and children. In these pages, I've tried to report my friends' stories as honestly and responsibly as I've previously told the stories of Lazard, Bear Stearns, Goldman Sachs, and the Duke lacrosse scandal. I decided early on that the greatest gift I could give my old friends was sharing with others the truths of their lives, at least as best I could figure them, for as long as they were with us.

The End Depends
upon the Beginning

ANDOVER IS AS OLD AS AMERICA ITSELF, and has always been an unlikely combination of elite and ecumenical. Founded in April 1778 by a trio of austere Calvinist men from a wealthy New England family, Andover has long gone out of its way not only to nurture America's best and brightest but also to find "youth from every quarter"—young men and women who might likely benefit from an Andover education but who probably had never heard of the place, let alone considered paying for it. For more than 240 years, this academic and social alchemy has made Andover a bouillabaisse of rich and poor, of entitled and ambitious, of privileged and disadvantaged. But of course, there was no getting around the fact that Andover was started for the sole purpose of manufacturing, and nurturing, the future leaders of the country—as long as they were white, male, and Protestant.

Samuel Phillips Jr. was only twenty-six, and seven years out of Harvard, when he founded Andover, which was backed financially and philosophically by his wealthy father, who lived in town, and by his wealthy uncle, John, who lived nearly twenty-five miles away from Andover in Exeter, New Hampshire. (John Phillips started Phillips Exeter Academy three years later; the two schools have been friendly rivals ever since.) Samuel Junior was raised essentially as an only child—all his other brothers and sisters had died—and much was expected of him. When he was at Harvard, his father wrote him letters admonishing him to keep to the straight-and-narrow path of the teachings of their Calvinist Church. "Beware of Bold Company," he wrote his son. "Spread up your Bead [Bed] as soon as you are up. Two mornings I found it very much like a pig's nest. Find some place for your Tea Kettle out of sight."

After Harvard, newly married Samuel Junior moved back to Andover. He started buying land and became one of the area's most respected farmers. He was selected to represent Andover in the Provincial Congress, in 1775, after the Revolutionary War had started. He was an impassioned speaker at the congress, and was later asked to undertake the Herculean task of moving the books in the Harvard library to Andover for safekeeping during the conflict. According to Fritz Allis's exhaustive history of Andover, *Youth from Every Quarter*, one of the main reasons the Phillips family chose to start Andover, Allis believed, was to try to preserve a way of life they thought might be quickly slipping away from them. Paradoxically, while the Phillips men were advocates for some relief from British oppression, they were not big supporters of the war, or of the radical changes that a victory might portend for their very comfortable lives and lifestyle. The school was founded "as a bulwark against change," Allis wrote, "an agency for maintaining the virtues of the past."

The short Andover "Constitution," written in April 1778 by Samuel Junior and signed by his father and uncle, captured Samuel Junior's concern about the changes that he feared the American Revolution would unleash. Despite their revolutionary proclivities, he and his family had prospered under British rule. He wrote about "the prevalence of ignorance and vice, disorder and wickedness" afoot in the land. He and his family were starting the school, he continued, "for the purpose of instructing YOUTH not only in English and Latin grammar, writing, arithmetic, and those sciences, wherein they are commonly taught; but more especially to learn them the GREAT END AND REAL BUSINESS OF LIVING."

The first Andover class, in 1778, had about fifty students, a mixture of Abbots, Baldwins, Lowells, Lovejoys, Walkers, and Wards. No less a revolutionary figure than Paul Revere designed and engraved the Andover seal. Made of pure silver and embossed to a copper plate, the seal depicts a rather disproportionately large beehive, atop a pedestal, surrounded by a group of industrious buzzing bees. You get the picture. There are two Latin phrases on the seal. The first, NON SIBI, means "not for oneself." The other, FINIS ORIGINE PENDET, is translated into English as "the end depends upon the beginning."

Within five years, Andover had expanded its reach beyond the Massachusetts elite to those sons (and much, much later, daughters) of the burgeoning nation as a whole. George Washington's nephew and eight grandnephews attended Phillips Academy in its early years. In fact, in 1783, Howell Lewis, a Virginian and Washington's nephew, became one of the first students from outside New England to attend the school. In 1795, Washington used his pull to get his nephew's two sons into Andover. Andover graduated Samuel F. B. Morse, the inventor of the telegraph; Oliver Wendell Holmes, the doctor, poet, and father of the future Supreme Court justice; the very famous Henry Stimson; and Jack Lemmon, the movie star. Another movie star, Humphrey Bogart, did not graduate—in fact, he was expelled for throwing the headmaster into Rabbit Pond—yet managed to find some success in life nonetheless. President Andrew Jackson spent a night at the school in July 1833 and addressed the students the next morning on horseback. In 1913, President Theodore Roosevelt attended the graduation ceremony of his son Archibald. In 1921, former president William Howard Taft, then a professor at Yale Law School and soon to be a Supreme Court justice, was an honored guest and speaker. (His father was an Andover graduate.) In 1928, on the occasion of the school's 150th anniversary, President Calvin Coolidge addressed the students.

It's not exactly clear why the school was so successful so quickly, but it may have been the combination of educational and moral rectitude plus a determination to cater to the elites, both intellectually and financially, along with being open—again both intellectually and financially—to those who had promise but could not afford the place.

Whatever it was, the school has been a leader in secondary-school education from the start. In 1944, the school's endowment was $7 million; it is now around $1.1 billion (nearly as much as Exeter's) to which will be added another $400 million or so, thanks to an ongoing capital campaign based on the concepts of "knowledge" and "goodness" found in Samuel Junior's constitution.

IN 1933, CLAUDE FUESS, A BELOVED Andover teacher, became headmaster. Fuess was determined to fight the perception—by then well entrenched—that Andover was a snobby place, solely designed to further promote the advantages of America's elites and ruling class. Fuess lamented in a well-read essay that Andover and its private-school brethren had graduated "too many of the country club set . . . who feel they have performed their civic duty when they have grudgingly paid their taxes and when they have damned the Government." He continued, "If we do not reform ourselves, the state is likely to do it for us . . . Exclusiveness—at least in a social sense—cannot persist much longer. . . . The gravest perils to American independent schools will come from snobbishness . . . bigotry, provincialism, reactionarism, smugness, stupidity, and inertia—the seven deadly sins of our type of education." Fuess's other impulses were far less noble. He imposed a quota on the number of Jewish students who could attend Andover each year. Fuess was afraid that if Andover did not have a policy limiting the Jews on campus to around two percent of the school population—around fourteen Jews out of seven hundred students—then they would overrun the place, given their penchant for scholarly aptitude. "It is just too bad about the little Jewish boy," Fuess wrote in a 1935 letter, "but I can't very well blame Dean Lynde"—the dean of the academy at the time, in charge of admissions—"for trying to keep our school as predominately Aryan as possible."

Two national publications—*Fortune*, in May 1944, and the *Saturday*

Evening Post, in September 1947—visited Andover and tackled the thorny subject of Andover's ongoing efforts to try to shed its elitist image. It was a tough sell. "It has been said of Andover that it is not a boys' school," *Fortune* began, "but an institution of learning that boys are permitted—reluctantly—to attend," quickly noting that John Hancock himself had signed its articles of incorporation. Some 75 percent of the boys at Andover came to the school from "solid Republican homes," according to the *Saturday Evening Post*; half of the students said that their fathers were "businessmen," and a third were the sons of "professional" men. "Andover still draws most of its boys, as it has done for decades, from the great mercantile, upper middle classes of New England and New York," the magazine reported. "Yale, Harvard and Princeton, in that order, are the graduates' favorite colleges."

Andover was plenty rigorous: In the 1940s, nearly one-third of the students—some 250—flunked out before graduating. But those who prevailed more often than not seemed to go on to great success, a virtuous circle for the ages. In 1917, Thomas Cochran, Class of 1890, became one of the few partners at J.P. Morgan & Co. "If I ever get any money, it will go to Andover," he had said at the start of his banking career. He made good on that promise. He gave $100,000 to Andover after World War I. (Upon hearing of that gift, Yale—where Cochran went to college and was a member of Skull and Bones—wanted a slice of his beneficence as well; he responded with a check for $5,000.) "It's the preparatory school which really shapes the character of a boy," he continued. "The college can merely build on that. Andover comes first." Before Cochran's death, he donated a whopping $11 million to Andover. Cochran, more than any other person, transformed Andover into a school of "physical opulence," according to the *Saturday Evening Post*, adding—as have many since—that "[i]n appearance and in fact, it is more like a college than a boys' school." A million dollars was set aside to maintain the grounds, and an eighty-nine-acre bird sanctuary and arboretum was created. In 1928, Cochran donated fifty American

paintings to the school and called for the creation of an art museum—
"to enrich permanently the lives of the students"—that three years later
he endowed and named after his late friend, Keturah Addison Cobb,
the mother of a woman he admired. The Addison Gallery of American Art opened in May 1931. He also donated the money for what
became the Cochran Chapel, the neo-Georgian church that is one of
the first, and grandest, buildings to greet visitors to the campus. It was
dedicated to Cochran in 1932.

George H. W. Bush, fresh from Greenwich Country Day School,
was thirteen years old when he arrived at Andover in September 1937.
He got off to a poor start, as teacher Fred Stott noted in his reports
home. He was "not well measured in all respects," Stott wrote, in stark
impolitic language. "Parents of wealth and social position"—as if that
were unusual at Andover—"cocky and 'high hat' . . . very mediocre performance." Worse, Bush used an anti-Semitic slur to describe a Jewish
friend. He always remembered the incident, felt deeply ashamed by it,
and voluntarily revealed it some seven decades later to Jon Meacham,
his biographer. "Never forgotten it," Bush told him. But Bush also stood
up for another Jewish boy, Bruce Gelb, who was being bullied, and they
became lifelong friends.

The next year, Bush had shown some improvement. "Markedly a
gentleman," his counselor wrote. Bush was peripatetic at Andover: trying out for the baseball team, making friends—he was very popular—
and trying to overcome a chronic illness that put him in the infirmary
five times in his Upper (third) year at the school. In April 1940, his
parents moved him to Massachusetts General Hospital, in Boston, for
a few days after he came down with a staph infection. "Not a strong
boy," one teacher wrote of Bush in his letter of recommendation to Yale.
"Serious illness. Nice boy, popular, friendly, gets on well with adults,
very polite. Slow but hard worker. Illness put him at a great disadvantage
this year. Can analyze well [but] is slow in doing it. . . . Ambitious and
self-confident but perhaps not self-assertive enough. Real interests are

athletics . . . Always a gentleman, responsible, courteous, generous. WATCH: should not attempt too much outside work this year. Not a neat boy." He was of course admitted to the university.

The attack on Pearl Harbor changed things dramatically for Bush, and for many other Andover students. "I knew what I wanted to do," he told Meacham. "It was an easy call—no second guessing, no doubts." He enlisted in the war effort as soon as he possibly could. Both Fuess and alumnus Henry Stimson, who happened then to be Roosevelt's secretary of war, had argued that the Andover boys should get some college under their belts before enlisting, which would make them "more valuable" to the military effort later on. But Bush was not taking that advice. June 12, 1942, was Bush's eighteenth birthday and the day he graduated from Andover. Immediately thereafter, he went to Boston and enlisted in the navy, officially a seaman second class, with orders to report, in September, to flight training in Chapel Hill, North Carolina. In August, his father accompanied him to Pennsylvania Station in New York City to take the train to North Carolina and then to war. His father was in tears. "So off I went, scared little guy," Bush told Meacham. "Got on the train, didn't know anybody." A little more than two years later, over a remote Japanese island, the enemy shot down the navy plane Bush was piloting. As his plane was descending into the ocean, Bush completed the mission of eliminating a radio tower, parachuted out safely, and, along the way, became a bona fide war hero.

Bush returned often to Andover and was eventually made a lifetime member of the Andover board of trustees. In November 1989, about ten months after he was sworn in as the forty-first president of the United States, he gave a speech at Andover commemorating the two hundredth anniversary of George Washington's visit to the school. As he noted, "legend had it" that Washington kissed a girl at the Andover Inn and that she never washed the cheek again. "I can't bear living testimony to his visit, but I can speak very briefly of my time here," he said. "I loved those years. They did, indeed, teach the great end and real business of living. And even now its lessons of honesty, selflessness, faith in God—well, they enrich every day of our lives."

Three of Bush's four sons—George W., Jeb, and Marvin—also attended Andover, with two graduating (Marvin was there for two years in the early 1970s before transferring to another school). By the time George W. arrived in September 1961, it was clear that his family connections had been the key to his admission. His father was then a prominent oilman in Texas, although not a particularly successful one. But when George W. applied for admission to St. John's, supposedly the best private school in Houston, he was rejected. Fortunately for him, he had also applied to Andover.

At Andover, George W. Bush seemed to be immensely popular, providing ample evidence of his future political skills to those who would come looking for them later. In his senior year, he was head cheerleader and led his fellow cheerleaders in a drag skit making fun of Andover's rivals. (There are pictures.) He had lots of friends. But there were also those people who found him arrogant and condescending. "Governor Bush's student days were in most respects supremely undistinguished, and anyone hoping to find reassurance about his candidacy through signs of great intellect or gravitas in those years will be disappointed," Nicholas Kristof wrote years later in the *New York Times*. "There were many other students then who seemed far more likely to emerge as political leaders. . . . In an institution that respected brains and brawn, George seemed to overflow with neither. He was a mediocre student and no more than a decent athlete, and he paled in comparison with his father and namesake"—here Kristof engaged in more than a bit of revisionist history—"who had been brilliant at everything he did."

In fact, like his father, George W. had a tough time adjusting to Andover's academic rigor. On his first essay at Andover—about his sister's death from leukemia, at age seven—he reportedly received a grade of zero. The teacher had written, in red ink, the word "disgraceful" on the paper. (I was not aware that a grade of "zero" at Andover was even possible.) According to Clay Johnson, a fellow Texan who was also in Bush's Andover class (and whom George would appoint as deputy director of the Office of Management and Budget), the Texans were having trouble coping with the Andover academics. "It was a shocking experience," Johnson said. "It was far away from home and rigorous, and scary and demanding. The buildings looked different, and the days were shorter. We went from being at the top of our classes academically to struggling to catch up. We were so much less prepared than kids coming from Massachusetts or New York." But Bush's gregariousness and sense of humor were a winning combination. Donald Vermeil, his Andover roommate, recalled his year with Bush as "probably the funniest year of my life." Bush, he said, had a way of "keeping everything light and entertaining without offending people or getting out of line." Also like his father, George W. was messy. "School rules required boys to wear [a] jacket and tie during meals and classes," Kristof wrote. "He tested these rules by frequently wearing sneakers (without socks), ancient pants, a wrinkled shirt, a disastrously knotted tie and sometimes an army jacket. Friends say his aim was not just to rebel but also to remind everyone that he was a Texan, not a preppy."

After perusing his transcript and his test scores, the dean of students at Andover urged Bush to apply to the University of Texas. He had never made the honor roll at Andover. His College Board scores were 566 verbal, 640 math. He, of course, got into Yale. Kristof asked William Semple, one of Bush's Andover classmates, what would have been students' reaction in 1964 to the idea that thirty-six years later Bush would be a serious candidate for president of the United States. "The reaction," he said, "would have been gales of laughter."

In October 1962, *Time* magazine put Andover headmaster John Kemper on the cover. By then, Andover's endowment was $25 million. There were 841 boys enrolled from forty-four different states. Of the 208 graduating seniors, Harvard accepted 42 and Yale accepted 39. The curriculum was relentless. Four years of English, with an emphasis on writing. Three years of math. Three years of a foreign language, where no English was to be spoken in class; and lots of science, history, art, and music. The electives ranged from Russian to anthropology. "All this bespeaks the enduring Andover," *Time* gushed, "which is run on nothing more complicated than the primitive idea of ordeal. But the ordeal is far different from the one old grads remember." In 1962, a jock also had to be a good student. "The balanced hero is in," the magazine continued. "The snob is out." Compulsory daily chapel at 7:30 a.m. remained a fixture of the school, as did the dress code of jacket, tie, button-down shirt, plus "wrinkled khakis" and loafers or "ragged sneakers." There were no cars allowed, no bicycles allowed, and, of course, no liquor allowed. Seniors and Uppers could smoke cigarettes; others who smoked got "posted" and were confined to campus. "Otherwise rules are sparse," the story continued. "A boy can go for days without making his bed." (Samuel Phillips Sr. would not have been pleased.)

Independence, up to a point, seemed to be the mantra—along with hard work, discipline, and entrance to an Ivy League college. According to *Time*, "They work, work, work. The irony is that Andover's soaring standards may encourage the widespread notion summed up by one senior: 'We get good grades so we can get into a good college—a prestige college. That's why we're here.'"

But by the end of the 1960s, old verities seemed to be breaking down fast. A June 1969 article in the *New York Times* featured the "news" that Andover students had elected three "Negro" classmates "from the ghettos of Chicago and Oakland" to be class presidents for the following school year—the first two black students at Andover had arrived in the 1850s, and in 1865, Richard Greener became the first black student to graduate—and that unnamed "sources" in the Class of 1969 said that "at least 90 percent of the seniors use marijuana at least twice a week." The article also pointed out that over the Memorial Day weekend, Andover students "wearing antiwar armbands" had "clashed" with townspeople, who "denounced them as Communists." The Andover students, and their newly elected leaders, were also intent upon doing away with compulsory chapel services, the requirement of having to wear a coat and tie, and restrictions on the length of a student's hair. The so-called hair proposal, if approved by the faculty, would have banned beards and would have allowed Kemper to "rule" whether any student's sideburns or hair "appeared too long for proper decorum." This just wasn't going to fly anymore, and it didn't. Kemper's hair proposal was defeated.

In 1971, Kemper was diagnosed with cancer of the lymph nodes. Two months later, he was dead. He was fifty-nine years old. In 1972, Theodore Sizer, the progressive dean of the Harvard School of Education, was selected to replace Kemper. Sizer has been described as the John F. Kennedy of Andover: handsome, smart, ambitious, and visionary. He inspired years of Andover students. He was the kind of educator who would think nothing of quoting Tu Fu, a Chinese poet who lived during the Tang dynasty, in the school yearbook, or of chiding students about having too much fun the night before without making it into a disciplinary matter. Sizer's youthful, infectious energy was a breath of fresh air after years of Kemper's military rigor, and you could almost feel the school settling down and embracing, in its way, the liberalism that the 1960s unleashed but that places as conservative and "Establishment" as Andover had trouble processing, or comprehending.

Sizer changed Andover dramatically. He ratified the merger with Abbot Academy, a prestigious girls' boarding school founded fifty years after Andover—and down the hill from it—that made the school fully coeducational for the first time. Combining Andover and Abbot was a material step forward in the school's development and its ongoing appeal. The dress code was thrown out. There was no longer any compulsory chapel. Nobody said a peep about the length of someone's hair. There was a surprising amount of tolerance around the use—and misuse—of drugs and alcohol. Sizer seemed to strike the right balance between permissiveness and personal accountability at the very moment when a new paradigm was required. There was even a pub on campus for those seniors who were eighteen years old, then the legal drinking age. Indeed, my first cousin Bobby Cohan said the Andover that I entered in the fall of 1973 could not have been more different from the one that he had graduated from in 1967. "In six years the whole thing changed," he said. "That's like, not even close to where I went. I went to a completely different school than you."

I WAS BORN AND RAISED IN WORCESTER, Massachusetts, fifty miles and a world away from Andover. Worcester, the second largest city in New England, was—and remains—an amalgam of tight-knit neighborhoods of WASPs, Jews, and Italian, Portuguese, Irish, and other immigrants. It was always a city that seemed on the precipice of becoming something grander than it was but never quite made it. Maybe the new airport—atop one of Worcester's seven hills—would draw traffic away from Boston's overcrowded Logan Airport and revitalize the city? Nope. Maybe the Centrum, the civic center built in the 1970s, would draw new and diverse forms of culture to Worcester? Nada. Maybe the shopping mall—the Galleria, complete with a curved glass roof similar to one in Milan—would draw people downtown? Not really. The big hope for Worcester these days is the arrival of the WooSox—the Boston Red Sox farm team that the city managed to lure away from Pawtucket, Rhode Island. We'll see. Worcester was the kind of place that couldn't even retain its best asset: the El Morocco, a tiny, hole-in-the-wall restaurant, at 73 Wall Street, started by immigrants from Syria, which served the best salads, shish kebab, and rice pilaf this side of Damascus. It got mobbed up, moved to a big, expensive new site at 100 Wall Street, and promptly went out of business. (The new building has since been torn down. Worcester.)

My grandfather Joe was the patriarch of the Cohan family. Tall, patrician, and handsome, Joseph B. Cohan changed the family's name from Cohen to Cohan. My grandfather had started an accounting firm in Worcester, where both my father, Paul, and my uncle Herbert would work their entire professional lives. Joe thought the firm would blend better into the Worcester business community if people thought we were Irish, not Jewish. There was no need to call attention to our immigrant roots in Germany and Russia, even though we'd been in town since the 1880s. *Cohan*—as in George M. Cohan of "I'm a Yankee Doodle Dandy" fame—was an Irish name; *Cohen* was the ultimate Jewish name, the tribe of the great rabbis.

My extended family on my father's side all lived in Worcester's small but prosperous Jewish shtetl. My father's sister and her family lived next door; Herbert and his family—including Bobby—lived less than a mile away. (My mother's family lived in St. Louis, where they immigrated from Hungary.) Slowly but surely Assumption College, a nearby Catholic school, took control of most of the real estate on our street. There was a monastery at the top of the road and a paved pathway from our road down to the school's chapel. Eventually, a group of nuns affiliated with Assumption College bought our house and we moved to a new one on the hill above Herbert's house, in the more prosperous part of Worcester's shtetl.

Andover fit in perfectly with our family's aspiration for assimilation. By then, Fuess's ill-tempered plan to keep Jews out of Andover had been overcome—although meaningful change happened slowly, and there still weren't many Jews in the school. Still, among them were four Cohan sons from Worcester. (Maybe the spelling threw the admissions office off the scent?)

My cousin Bobby was the first person in our family to go to Andover. Bobby went to the Shepherd Knapp School through eighth grade, as did I, a small, private day school ten miles or so outside of Worcester founded in 1953 by Neil and Mary Halkyard and named after Neil's foster parent. It had once been a farm. Each grade had about ten students in it. The school's curriculum mirrored the times: It was traditional and then, in the late 1960s, it was progressive. After eighth grade, there weren't many good options in Worcester. The kids in the classes ahead of Bobby at Shepherd Knapp had applied to prep schools such as Deerfield and Choate. He had never even heard of Andover. He had no idea what it was or where it was. But the Halkyards thought he should apply there, and elsewhere. As best as he can remember, he got into two high schools: the nearby Worcester Academy and Andover. "They took me on a chance," he said. "They weren't sure I was going to make it."

He didn't know what it meant to have been admitted to Andover. But he clued in quickly. A few weeks later, he and his family went on vacation to the Diplomat Hotel, in Hollywood, Florida. There were a bunch of kids standing around, and one of them started talking about how he had just gotten into Andover. "He was trying to show off to some girls," Bobby said. So he asked him what dorm he was going to be in at Andover because he was going to be there, too. But the guy ignored Bobby's question and then later pulled him aside and told him that he wasn't really going to go to Andover. He had only said that to try to impress the girls. "Then I knew this was a big deal," Bobby recalled.

One thing Bobby Cohan had in common with the Bushes was that he found the adjustment to Andover pretty tough. "I was little," he said. "I wasn't a good athlete. I wasn't a cool guy." In his first year, he and his buddies formed the Rising Storm, a garage rock band. "I can't separate the band from my experience at Andover," he said. In the end, he mostly loved Andover, and described it as one of the best experiences of his life: "I made the closest friends." My older brother Peter—Class of 1975—seemed to mostly enjoy Andover, too, so it was no surprise that when Shepherd Knapp ran out of grades, I would follow in the footsteps of my brother and first cousin. (My younger brother, Jamie, followed me to Andover.)

I was always younger than my classmates because I skipped kindergarten and went directly to the first grade at Shepherd Knapp. By the time eighth grade rolled around, I had proven my academic skills. I was Andover-worthy. I had been on the "Plus List" for the two prior school years, which meant that I had been on the honor roll for the entire year. (When I was in sixth grade and Peter was in eighth, we both made the Plus List, the only two siblings in the school to do so. Accordingly, my parents were given the actual wood plaque with our names painted on it in gold-leaf lettering. They still have it stashed in a closet in their Florida condominium.)

I applied only to Andover and Exeter. It was time to move beyond our privileged, sheltered life in Worcester to a privileged, sheltered life at one or the other of the nation's most prestigious private high schools. On March 10, 1973, came the news that I had been accepted at both. There was no real decision to be made. Exeter seemed cold, austere, and rigid, as if the Calvinists were still running the place. Andover, by contrast, seemed laid-back, liberal-minded, and open. Besides, it was closer to Worcester, and my older brother was there to provide cover, and protection, as needed.

In my first year at Andover—ninth grade, a Junior in Andover parlance—at the time I was the youngest person in my class of about 125 students. And it showed in pretty much every way, every day. I was unable to compete athletically at Andover and twice failed a so-called Physical Aptitude Test, or PAT, and had to spend two trimesters running laps, lifting weights, and doing push-ups and pull-ups in a misguided attempt to whip me into shape. I was only a marginally better student, but I was a fun dorm mate, always eager for a laugh in my large room on the west side of Nathan Hale House, a new dorm set in the woods on the edge of Rabbit Pond. It housed ninth graders, all new to the school but at varying degrees of maturity. There was the fast New York crowd, from which I felt light-years removed. There were the athletes, from whom I also felt light-years removed. There were a few guys like me who had grown up here and there, and were nothing special except for a modicum of wit.

I was a young thirteen-year-old. John Cushing lived across the hall from me. From outside of Boston—there was always some vague sense that he was related to Cardinal Cushing—he was rambunctious, big, and strong. As a ninth-grader, he was the goalie on the varsity soccer team. He thought nothing of downing three cheesesteak subs, from a local delivery place, *after* dinner. He used to call me "fat turkey." Next door to me lived Eliot "Buzz" Tarlow, the senior proctor and an Andover legacy, whose chief attributes seemed to be an Amazonian athletic ability—he was on the varsity crew team—and a penchant for sadism, especially when it came to me. He also had glorious stereo equipment and was exacting about cleaning the vinyl before playing his Jim Morrison records at high volume. I always marveled how Tarlow got into Harvard but figured Harvard always needed new blood for its crew team.

In my first weeks at Andover, someone stole my bicycle, never to be seen again. I had lent it to Will Iselin, my dorm mate from New York City whose lineage dated back to the aforementioned John Jay, a Founding Father, the second governor of New York State, and the first chief justice of the US Supreme Court. Somehow the bike got stolen under Will's auspices. Will was "rather chastened and taken aback by the whole situation," our housemaster Fred Pease, the school's chaplain, wrote my parents, "and at a brief house meeting last night the situation brought home to the whole dormitory the point of my strictures"—Pease was a reverend, after all—"to them about being very careful with their own and other people's belongings." Pease was apologetic, on Will's and on Andover's behalf, as if to say, *Don't get the wrong first impression here.* More important, Pease continued, was the fact that I seemed to be "off to a good start" at Andover, that I seemed to be "enjoying the place and the routines and the people," and that I had "plenty of friends in the broader campus community." In any event, Pease concluded, he hoped that the theft of the bike did not "sour things too much" for me.

It did not.

At the end of the first trimester, somehow my housemates elected me their representative to the Rabbit Pond cluster council. I can no longer recall how it happened, or why, but it was a lovely honor just the same. "It is nice to see someone get deserved recognition," Pease wrote my parents, "and I think the dorm showed very good judgment." Along with summarizing my mediocre academic performance for them, Pease wrote my parents that I had "emerged" as a "very considerable person" at Andover—"honest, straight-forward and outspoken, friends, thoughtful and considerate of others and with a considerable sense of humor." I was thirteen, but would still gladly have that be my epitaph.

YOU DON'T NEED TO HEAR it from me, but high school is a difficult time for everyone, both academically and socially. That fact was as true at Andover as it was at Doherty Memorial High School (or at North Shore High School, of mythical *Mean Girls* fame). The adjustment was hard for Oliver Wendell Holmes, it was hard for both Bushes, and it was hard for me. (It was hard for my two brothers, too.)

Then, as now, Andover had around eleven hundred students spread out over four classes: The Junior, or freshman, class had around two hundred students, or about a hundred fewer than the others. On one hand, the school could seem big and impersonal: It was a beehive of activity, where more than a thousand students were darting around the large campus that was bifurcated by Massachussetts Route 28. On the far end of campus, toward Boston, were the playing fields, and on the other end, down the hill, was the old Abbot campus. The cluster system did an effective job of breaking the school into small living communities, and in short order, between the clusters and the classes and the camaraderie on the playing field, it was rare that you would be walking on the campus and not see a friend.

The hub of the campus, both geographically (more or less) and emotionally, was the dining hall, or Commons as it was known. If you think of Andover's campus as a bicycle wheel, Commons would be its hub, figuratively and metaphorically. The building was divided in four dining rooms—Lower Right, Upper Right, Lower Left, and Upper Left. Day after day, these dining rooms came to stand for the distinctly different types of students who would flock to them at each meal. Lower Right was where the jocks ate. Upper Right was where the nerds ate. Lower Left was where the student leaders, along with artistic, scholarly, and intellectual types, or those who thought they were, hung out. Upper Left was for the stoners and partiers. The only things that unified the four dining halls were their similarity in appearance, the poor quality of the food, and the fact that everyone—whether on scholarship or not—had to participate in "Commons duty," the charitable way of referring to spending a week working behind the scenes cleaning up after everyone else at each meal. The highlight of this unpaid service was getting to watch the whole milk and orange juice coagulate after half-consumed beverages were dumped.

LOWER YEAR AT ANDOVER (known to most of the world as sophomore year, or tenth grade) ratcheted up the academic intensity. Frank Bellizia, my English Competence teacher, was blunt. "Bill has problems," he wrote, "but he's working very hard." And then he added, "He'll be all right, but his writing will probably never be outstanding." Thank goodness for math. According to my math teacher Frank Eccles, although "quiet" and "modest," I was the "top student" in his class and "a very nice lad." He noted that I was a "good problem solver," had taken a high degree of interest in working with the new (late-1970s model) computers (such as they were), and was "perceptive, clear thinking and learns quickly." Again, though, it was the good Reverend Pease who appreciated me most. He wrote my parents that he saw me as "an influence for sanity and humanity" among my "fellow students" and as a result, the Peases "rejoice" in my "triumphs" and "commiserate" in my "agonies" and "enjoy him greatly."

In his final note home about me, at the end of my second year at Andover, Fred Pease could not possibly have been kinder. He managed to spin a bunch of mediocre observations about my academic performance into a view that I had had my best term of the year, which may technically have been true. But that was beside the point. You would have thought I was heaven-sent by Him to him. "I want to commend him as strongly as possible in every respect," he wrote my parents, "for his job at Phillips Academy this year and over two years. Bill has been a somewhat unofficial but very important student leader in the dormitory community for two years, and his quiet strength—his patience, tolerance and sense of humor and his high personal standards and expectations of himself as well as others—all these have been very important." In retrospect, I think his praise for me derived from the fact that I was one of the few people in the dorm who never gave him a moment's worry: I didn't drink or smoke, didn't play my music loudly, rarely had guests in my room, didn't break any rules, and always gave it my best shot academically even though that often was lacking. On the margins, I looked pretty good.

My last two years at Andover represented a different phase of my high school career. My time in Nathan Hale West had come to an end, and I moved to Stearns House West, on the side of Rabbit Pond. That's where the upperclassmen lived. I had a tiny single room on the first floor, and plenty of good friends. I was growing up, fast. By then, I had also become heavily involved in the school newspaper, the *Phillipian*, but not as a writer. I was focused on the business side of things.

Upper year at Andover was for all the marbles, the moment when one's academic performance and extracurricular activities needed to be alchemized into a transcript of da Vinci–esque proportions if there were to be any chance of admission to one of the Holy Trinity of Harvard, Yale, or Princeton. Fully half of our senior class of three hundred students would be admitted to one or more of these three universities. We just didn't know which half. Most of those spots were in play when the school year began in September 1975. Not surprisingly, given my own DNA and that of the school, I fully expected to get into one of them. Nobody wanted to be among the "losers" who didn't. But my academic record was only mediocre at best, as were my test scores. So gaining admission to one of them was a long shot for me, except in my own mind.

In January 1976 came an inevitable "little disciplinary difficulty," in the immortal words of cluster Dean Jack Dick in a letter home to my parents. On a whim and at around eleven o'clock on a wintry Friday night, three of us in my dorm—Alan Cantor, my dear friend and the cluster president; Chris Randolph, my dear friend and classmate; and I—went over to Stevens House, an all-girl dorm next door, to visit with Corky Harold in the television room of her dorm. Then (as now) Corky was an ebullient, effervescent woman with abundant charm and smarts. She was a quintessential preppy from tony Guilford, Connecticut, with a cool older brother who was also at Andover until he got kicked out. Not only did the risk seem minimal but it also seemed more than worth it, to spend some clandestine time with her. "Feeling somewhat bored and restless," Richards wrote, "they knocked on the girl's window and asked her to let them into her dorm, which she did. The quartet was sitting, engaged in innocent conversation, when they were apprehended by a member of our campus security police on a routine patrol, whereupon they were sent back to Stearns House and their names turned into me." Rules are rules, and it was against the rules to be out of the dorm past ten at night and against the rules to be in a girls' dorm to boot. "A bit of a lark it was," Richards continued, "and I ascribe no malicious intentions to any of the four, but the fact is that the three boys succeeded in breaking a major rule by being out of their dormitory without permission at such an hour, and perhaps more important, showed very poor judgment in entering a girls' dormitory. Technically, the three boys were eligible for dismissal from the Academy." I was petrified. Who knew where this seemingly minor infraction could lead, in Upper year no less? I was also fearful of the inevitable parental admonishment.

We were not raised to break the rules. But cooler heads prevailed "because of the innocence of the circumstances and the previously clean records of all three boys." We were "awarded," according to Richards, "a Censure" and "placed in two weeks of Restriction"—limited mobility around campus or off-campus—for our "illegal bit of nocturnal activity." My parents took it in stride.

Suddenly it was crunch time, spring of Upper year. The set of grades that would likely determine whether any of Cambridge, New Haven, or exurban New Jersey were in my future. If any were, I would be considered a statistically "successful" Andover graduate; otherwise I would be considered a "failure" by Andover's exacting standards. I was the business manager of the *Phillipian*, Andover's independent, student newspaper. Not only did *independent* mean editorially independent, but it also meant financially independent. Other than getting some free space in the basement of the science building for our offices, the paper got no financial support whatsoever from the school, although our finances were monitored on a regular basis by a school administrator. All the revenue we generated came from selling subscriptions and advertising. I was in charge of both, as well as of the weekly task of getting the paper printed in Cambridge, at the offices of the *Harvard Crimson*. It was a major responsibility, and a major sinkhole of time on a daily basis. I took it seriously, and loved it. It was my choice, of course, to take the job, and I had worked hard to get it in the previous few years. I had also run for cluster president, hoping to succeed Alan Cantor. (I lost to the aforementioned Bruce MacWilliams.) But, a little like Bruce, I often fantasized about being in public office, perhaps as a US senator. That dream quickly faded, though.

My college counselor, Marion Finsbury, was blunt and austere. She told me she really could not be the slightest bit encouraging about my chances of getting into Harvard, Yale, or Princeton. Or into any school in the Ivy League, for that matter. Or into Williams, Amherst, or Stanford. (Don't bother to apply, she said.) Schools such as Duke,

Northwestern, Cornell, and Penn were more my style, she suggested (yes, the latter two are in the Ivy League, but please). I applied to HYP anyway, and, as Finsbury predicted, I did not get in.

I did get into the schools she said I would—I think they made calls in those days to bolster the written applications—and I decided to go to Duke. It was a stunningly beautiful campus, with a handsome student body in bucolic Durham, North Carolina. It could not have been more different from Andover. It was a warm spring day when I visited the campus, from the northern Massachusetts tundra; the sights, sounds, and smells of the American South were intoxicating. I was ready for a geographic and ideological change. It seemed right. Still, I felt like a total failure; that somehow I had not fulfilled my mandate, or my destiny, by going to Duke instead of Harvard. Not only did I feel great disappointment deep in my core, but the ghosts of Andover made me feel like a loser, too. I was meant to go to Harvard and it hadn't happened.

The truth was, I was more devoted to the *Phillipian* and my other extracurricular activities than to my studies. I was also co-head of the Jewish Student Union, a cheerleader, a radio DJ, and an assistant of some kind in the athletic department. I was very good at my job as the paper's business manager. We made more money that year than ever before. We gave half of what we made—thousands of dollars—back to the school, another 25 percent to the school's two-hundredth-anniversary $50 million fund-raising campaign, and split the last quarter of our profits among the board members. I think we each walked off with something like $500, a not-insignificant amount in those days.

I believed a nice celebratory dinner was very much in order. I gave Fred Stott—by then the secretary of the academy and the person in the administration with whom I worked closely to make sure our bills got paid and our revenues were properly accounted for—a heads-up that I wanted to have a special dinner for the board the evening before we were meant to hand over the reins to the paper in a ceremony presided over by Headmaster Sizer. I remember he went to the shelf in his office in George Washington Hall and pulled down an ancient tome. Somewhere in its pages was a general directive that when the school's trustees visited the campus, they were to be provided with "adequate but not excessive" accommodation and entertainment. "Keep that in mind," Stott told me. But in my mind, "adequate but not excessive" could mean almost anything. So I decided we would celebrate at Locke-Ober, once upon a time the most expensive restaurant in downtown Boston. I reserved a private room, with an open bar, and arranged to pay for our meal with a check drawn on the *Phillipian* account. The fifteen or so members of the outgoing board showed up on time, and in some form of respectable attire. We ate and drank to our hearts' content. Anything anyone wanted, and as much again, was provided. At the end of the evening, I wrote out a check to the restaurant for something like $1,250.

By the time I showed up at Headmaster Sizer's house the next morning, nursing a considerable hangover (I am certain I was not alone in my condition), the meal at Locke-Ober had already become legendary. Sizer pulled me aside. "I heard you had quite the dinner last night," he said. I was shocked. How in the world had Sizer already heard about it? I'll never know. To his credit, though, he never pressed charges for what clearly was an evening of heavy off-campus drinking, although probably I was the only one under eighteen and drinking illegally.

The way Sizer handled our Locke-Ober celebration has always impressed me. It also further drove home the point that Andover was the kind of place that celebrated performance art and encouraged quirkiness and out-of-the-box thinking. That's an idea that had also occurred to Joshua Rothman, a culture editor at *The New Yorker*, who graduated from Exeter and then Princeton. One of his classmates at Princeton was Shamus Khan, who graduated from St. Paul's and wrote *Privilege: The Making of an Adolescent Elite at St. Paul's School*. Rothman credits Khan with articulating how prep schools have changed over the years to be slightly less elite but still manage to prepare their graduates with

exceptional real-world navigational skills. "It's about negotiating a relationship with the people who are older and younger than you are,"
Rothman said. "The way that our elite world is now, that's actually not
a relationship of straightforward admiration and emulation. It's actually like rebellion and skepticism and resistance are part of what's expected of younger people but in a certain way that is productive and
understood to be sort of creatively destructive or that's to their credit.
There's a certain way of relating to people who are older than you. We're
supposed to admire those people but also critique them." It gets even
more complicated, he suggested. "There's all these complexities around
your place in the world, like you're supposed to be pretty ironic and self-
aware about your own privilege," he continued. "You're supposed to be
pretty critical of your betters and people who are older than you. But
you're also supposed to be modifying institutions instead of rejecting
them and you're supposed to be cool and have youth culture, but you're
supposed to have the right amount of youth culture. . . . It's not something that just comes naturally. It's something you have to be immersed
in, an environment where you see it modeled for you by older kids and
you see it modeled by all these teachers, on what they expect and what
they reward."

Rothman believed that, as was the case with Khan's experience at
St. Paul's, Exeter taught him—as Andover had taught me—how to
strike the right balance between irony and respect, and taught him invaluable social skills. "It gives you this tool kit that allows you to wiggle your way into a space in the preexisting institutional hierarchy
that you encounter as you get older," he said. "That involves a certain
amount of antagonism as well as receptivity to what's above you. . . . It's
all about little ways of creating a sort of environment of trust in which
you can practice all that stuff until you get it exactly right." He observed
that a poor kid at a regular high school who acts up in class is more
likely to get into trouble than a kid at Andover or Exeter who is rambunctious. "It's like a theater," he said of the elite prep schools, "and

you're performing and everyone is getting their performance critiqued. It's much more of a sort of safe space to learn exactly how much you can be a jerk and exactly how much you should be kowtowing to the people who have power."

That's what we both learned of a lasting nature during our years at Andover and Exeter. "I didn't really learn much materially," he said. "I took Latin and I don't remember any of it. I remember getting to college and taking my first college-level history courses and I got my ass kicked by those classes. I thought going into them that I knew stuff. But I didn't know anything. What I did know was how to talk really well in class, how to take criticism, how to interact, how to go a professor's office hours—that was something I knew how to do that none of my peers knew how to do—all these skills about how to negotiate the learning environment. I was under the impression when I was at boarding school that I was working incredibly hard and that we were the Delta Force of high school students. But then one thing I discovered when I got to Princeton was that that wasn't really true. I mean everyone else from public high school also worked their asses off, and they'd all been working like maniacs. It's just that they didn't have this sort of esprit de corps idea that we were all destined for great things and we were the elite squadron."

He met his future wife at Princeton. She graduated from a public high school. "She pulled all the same all-nighters and had all the same crazy stuff that we did," Rothman continued. "It's just that she didn't have a whole environment that was creating a sense of manifest destiny around that. It's not that I learned study skills, it's that I learned social skills." Contrasting his professional experiences with those of his wife's puts his understanding of his years at Exeter into sharper focus. "I'm dramatically more comfortable than she is with navigating hierarchies and working with older people, and representing myself to people who are outside of my intimate circle," he said. "It's like I emerged sort of like a politician in a way that she did not from her high school. She emerged a worker bee and had to learn how to navigate. She worked at McKinsey for a while. She had to learn how to navigate that. Whereas I know if I worked at McKinsey, I would know exactly how to act with partners and with everyone. That would be just what I had done for my whole life when I was a teenager. One thing that always blows my mind, and which fascinates me, is when I contrast her experience of high school to mine, it's like two data points. Her experience of high school was like *Lord of the Flies*. It was all about other kids her age. She had all these clubs and all these study groups that she went to. She would leave for school at seven in the morning and she would come home at night and her parents would just see her right before bed. It was really not a parental time. There was all this stuff about getting away, having secret parties in some kid's house where the parents were on vacation. It really wasn't like this development of a childhood adolescent world. I would have thought that boarding school was like that but it wasn't. It was heavily oriented around adults. There was constant adult stuff. It was just everywhere. Things having to do with being observed by grownups and having that whole social life with them. If I think about the number of adults that I had friendly relationships with at boarding school versus the number of adults she had friendly relationships with in the regular public high school, just because of living at the school I had more intimate relationships with grown-ups than she did. I really think that's a huge part of it."

When I think of Andover, I like to think of that kind of tolerance for zany behavior, that idea that elite prep schools were like "a theater," in Rothman's articulation. Rothman's metaphor of the Delta Force also resonates with me. It was not literally true, of course—Andover was not training anyone for military special ops. The George H. W. Bush types at Andover were far and few between, even accounting for the unusual circumstances at the time of his graduation. But the idea that we, at Andover, were special—*la crème de la crème de la jeunesse américaine*, after all—whether we were or not, and that much was expected of us, whether it was possible or not, remained a powerful one. That's why the pathos is so palpable when things don't work out as expected.

For four friends of mine at Andover—Jack Berman, Will Daniel, Harry Bull, and John F. Kennedy Jr.—things didn't work out as expected. And that's why I wanted to tell their stories; I just couldn't get out of my mind that searing contrast between the infinite promise of youth and the harsh reality of adulthood.

Despite its size, Andover was really a very small and intimate place. Everyone knew of everyone else, even if we were not all close friends. So it was with me and Jack, Will, Harry, and John, all of whom I knew and was friendly with to varying degrees.

JACK WAS TWO YEARS AHEAD of me at Andover. I knew him best from the small Friday-night Shabbat services that a handful of the Jewish students on campus would attend, more for camaraderie and a sense of community than for anything particularly religious. Even then, Jack was a serious fellow who led the services with a befitting sense of solemnity and purpose. What I remember best from those weekly gatherings was the fact that we would meet in the Kemper Chapel, a grotto for the school's Catholic students in the basement of the soaring Cochran Chapel above. Each Friday night, either Jack, Alan Cantor, or I would remove the brass crucifix from the wall and lay it on a chair on one side of the room. And then the brief services would begin, followed by sips of cheap Mogen David wine and sponge cake.

I do remember the Passover seder during my second year at Andover. It was held in Cooley House, a small modernist gathering place by the athletic facilities. There was of course plenty of sweet red wine on hand, in keeping with the Passover tradition. But kids being kids, before long a whole lot of Mogen David was being consumed. "They didn't want to look like they were intolerant of our religion, and we just got so drunk," Cantor said. But not Jack.

That was typical of Jack. By all accounts, he was a serious student at Andover who rarely participated in the extracurricular shenanigans that his peers seemed to find so captivating. That meant he avoided the usual adolescent black holes of drinking, drugs, and sex. "I don't remember him ever talking about girls," Cantor said. "He was a grown-up and consequently wasn't a lot of fun." He said Jack reminded him of his first-year roommate at Harvard, Mike Kaplan, who wrote in his thirtieth-year Harvard reunion notes, "I finally am in chronological balance. I've always been a 52-year-old man."

I KNEW WILL A BIT BETTER THAN I knew Jack. Like me, during our first year he was in Nathan Hale House, named after the Revolutionary War martyr and built in 1966 in a style that married elements of a modern glass house with the brutalist architecture then in fashion. For the longest time during our ninth-grade year together, I had no idea that Will was Harry Truman's grandson or that his father was the *Times'* Washington bureau chief and the paper's former managing editor. While he seemed far more sophisticated than I did, I had no idea he grew up in New York City or that he came from such rarefied stock. To me, as to others, he seemed like a younger version of Gregg Allman. His skin was "so white and pasty," our friend Phil Balshi recalled, that Will looked "almost ghostly." We called him "Goldilocks."

He also seemed very smart, but also very ethereal, as if he were in a perpetual state of being high. He spoke slowly, quietly, and deliberately, and had a guttural laugh that seemed more like an ironic chuckle than anything else. Will was a smoker. The rules on smoking had evolved such that you could smoke cigarettes with your parents' permission, but two smokers could not room together. Of course, being allowed to smoke cigarettes was the perfect cover, smell-wise, for smoking pot, and lots of people in Nathan Hale seemed to indulge in both.

I remember times, after dinner, when Will would wander up to my large single room and just sit there giggling while I chatted away about something or other. Nothing I was saying was particularly humorous. I always got the sense that Will was just hanging out in my room for his own amusement, since there must have been something about my obvious naïveté—having grown up, sheltered, in the Worcester shtetl— that he got a tickle out of when he was in one of his altered states. I certainly never participated with him in his flights of fancy, and he never asked me to. Bruce MacWilliams remembered that they both would get stoned and then Will would come visit me. "When he was talking to you, Bill, he was stoned," Bruce said.

I KNEW HARRY MORE FROM TAKING CLASSES together—Gil Sewall's treacherous History 35 course and his delightful History of Art course— than any other way. I always found him to be whip-smart, making one insightful counterintuitive comment after another. I knew he was one of the few people from Chicago at Andover, but I did not know he was a legacy or that his family owned one of the oldest and most successful industrial companies in the Midwest. I knew he had conservative po- litical views that were diametrically opposed to those of nearly everyone else on campus—and certainly to mine—but he always delivered them in such a silken fashion—much the way William F. Buckley did or Bill Kristol does—that it was hard not be impressed, hard not to take what he said seriously. Although he lived in nearby Pine Knoll cluster, I didn't socialize with him much. He was more in the Will Daniel school of extracurricular experimentation than I was. Both Harry and Will were Upper Left types; I started out in Upper Right—the land of the nerds—but as my status on campus evolved, I shifted to Lower Left, the home of the student leaders and creative types. Still, I always felt a kinship with Harry, and we always greeted each other in class, or in Commons, as good friends would, even though we were not. Maybe it was my partial midwestern roots, maybe it was that after he arrived he was the youngest member of the Class of 1977 and I was the second youngest, I don't know.

John, well, we all knew John.

Jack

I F THE GERMANS HAD HAD their way during World War II, there would have been no Jack Berman. Neither Jack's father, Misha Berman, later known as Morris, nor his mother, Bluma Kamenmacher, should have survived their wartime experiences in Poland and Lithuania, let alone meet in a refugee camp in Germany, start a family, and move to America. But they did.

Jack's older brother Norman explained how when the Germans invaded Russian-occupied Lithuania in 1941, Bluma's family had tried to flee, but ended up stuck in the Vilnius ghetto in a small apartment with twenty-five others. Each day, Norman said, "they were marched to a factory and they worked, [then] they were marched back. They had their ration card. They ate. They didn't eat well. The ration was about five hundred calories a day."

Two years later, when the ghetto was liquidated in September 1943, only two thousand, or 5 percent, of the original occupants had survived. Among them, incredibly, were Bluma, her mother Feiga, and her sister Sarah (another sister, who had been smuggled out of the ghetto, wasn't so lucky and had been shot in a roundup of Jews in another town).

Their saga continued. After the Vilnius ghetto was closed, the Germans loaded the survivors onto trucks, shipped them north to Estonia, and put them in slave labor camps. The surviving Kamenmacher women left the Stutthof camp three weeks before it was burned to the ground because of a typhus infestation. In these camps, they were lucky if they ate. "What she described was just hair-raising," Norman said. "Walking barefoot in the snow carrying heavy railroad ties. Fixing railbeds with just one layer of clothing. It was real slave labor. . . . . Somehow, the three women survived." On May 8, 1945, when the Germans surrendered, the Russians liberated the Estonian slave labor camps. Bluma, Feiga, and Sarah were sent to Föhrenwald, a "displaced persons" camp south of Munich.

Misha Berman's path to Föhrenwald was equally harrowing. His father owned a grain mill in Ukraine. In 1936, when he was eighteen, Misha was inducted into the Soviet army, where he served for five years. When, in 2010, Norman visited the town where his father grew up, he encountered a place that time forgot. "The streets were muddy," he recalled. "It looked like 120 years ago. There are wagons being drawn by horses, just a couple of cars." He found a ninety-two-year-old man, supposedly the oldest person around, and asked him if he knew the Bermans. It turned out the man had worked for Norman's grandfather at the mill. He drove a team of horses and transported grain. "They had the general store over there," the man told Norman. "They had a beautiful house over here. These are his fields." Norman thought that sounded charming. Then the man told him a story of what happened in 1941. "One day the local police showed up with trucks. They had guns. They said, 'Everybody get on the trucks.' There was this panic and screaming and some people ran across the fields and they were shot, and the rest were gathered into the trucks and they took them away, all of them." To Norman, the man's demeanor was so matter-of-fact he could have been describing a fender-bender. "They were nice people," the man continued. "It's too bad."

Those murdered included Misha's mother and father, his two older brothers, and some cousins. "There was a whole network of his family that basically just was wiped out," Norman said. Misha was spared only because he was still serving in the Russian army. At one point afterward, he was given a leave from his service and returned home to find that his family was gone, strangers were living in his home, and the mill was confiscated. "When he started asking around," his son continued, "he was arrested and he ended up in a ghetto at the very next town over. He spent six months in that ghetto. He escaped and he spent the rest of the war pretty much in hiding. He was in the forests of Ukraine." After the Germans surrendered, Misha also found himself in Föhrenwald, the largest displaced persons camp in Europe.

Misha and Bluma were married in a Jewish ceremony on October 22, 1946. Between them, they could identify seventy relatives who were murdered. As part of starting over, Norman Berman was born in the Föhrenwald refugee camp on May 6, 1948. "When we were in the DP camp and I was born, I mean it was like the second coming of Christ," Norman said. "It was like there might as well have been halos—'Oh, I was able to conceive, I was able to give birth to a child. This child must be magic'—and that was a lot of my experience growing up. I would screw up, but I could do no wrong. Everything Norman did was wonderful."

To leave the camp, the choices narrowed down to two: Israel or the United States. Misha Berman's mother's sister had moved to New York City before the war and the two sisters had been in contact, by letter, after it, enabling the Berman family to get on the list for the United States. They took a retrofitted troop carrier to Boston, then a train to New York. They settled in a first-floor apartment in the Bronx. Misha worked in a luggage factory; Bluma again worked as a seamstress. He earned seventy-five cents per hour; she earned twenty-five cents per hour more because she was skilled labor.

Their lives were hard but they were alive. "They were overwhelmed," explained Norman. "They came off the farms. They couldn't speak English. They spoke Yiddish. . . . We're living in a slum. It was awful. . . . One night in fact the ceiling in the bathroom caved in. There was a gas leak." Not surprisingly, there was bitterness and resentment, despite the fact that they had survived Hitler's extermination efforts. "They cursed Hitler whenever they had a problem," Norman said. "My grandmother especially. She suffered from arthritis so she would have an ache or something and she would curse that Hitler. 'He did this to me.'"

AFTER A FEW YEARS OF LIVING in the Bronx, the Bermans were convinced that there was a better way of life awaiting them outside New York City. That was also the view of Baron Maurice de Hirsch, a wealthy industrialist, and the Jewish Agricultural Society, which he founded in 1900 to encourage Eastern European Jews to resettle themselves away from American cities into rural communities. Hirsch believed that part of why Jews ended up being persecuted was because they'd end up in the cities and become successful businessmen, resulting in inevitable envy and jealousy. Thanks to aid from the Jewish Agricultural Society, in 1953 Misha and Bluma bought a sixty-acre dairy farm in rural Moosup, Connecticut, with a brook running through it, and moved out of their tenement in the Bronx. There was a seventy-year-old farmhouse and an empty dairy barn. The idea was to convert the dairy barn to a chicken barn, buy day-old chicks, and go from there. At first it would be a chicken farm, and over time the Bermans would become egg farmers.

As the family settled into Moosup, Norman remembered how especially nervous his mother was. They were alone in the middle of nowhere. "The first night when they came it was almost dark and it was a little rainy and raw," Norman recalled, "and she walked out onto the field and she looked around and said to herself, *We don't know anybody . . . We don't know the language. We don't know the customs. We don't have any money. How are we ever going to survive?*" She was twenty-five, and scared to death.

At the chicken farm on Snake Meadow Road, they eked out a life. "They didn't take vacations," Norman said. "They didn't spend money. They didn't improve the house. They didn't buy clothes." In 1955, the three Bermans became naturalized American citizens in

Hartford. And they contributed to the creation of Temple Beth Israel, in nearby Danielson. The Bermans were not hugely religious but they observed the Sabbath and High Holy Days, and kept kosher. They were somewhat skeptical of the concept of God, especially given what they'd experienced during the Holocaust. A favorite mantra was: "There's a God? Where was He when we really needed Him?" Still, they believed the community needed its own synagogue. There was some concern about how their Yankee neighbors would react to the building of a Jewish temple in a rural Connecticut town—"They'll come and shoot us just like our neighbors did back in Poland," Norman recalled them thinking—but instead something surprising happened. "They found support from the neighbors," he said. "And when they put out the word that they were going to build a synagogue, churches got together and they said, 'Why don't we see if we can't raise some money to help you out?' Banks, businesses, chamber of commerce—they said, 'Yeah it would kind of be neat to help these people get back on their feet. We know what happened to them.' There was actually a coming-together within this community and they built this beautiful synagogue."

One day, a few weeks before Norman was to celebrate his bar mitzvah, he was outside after school, washing the family's car. Suddenly, he felt a sharp pain near his elbow. At first, he thought it was a bee sting. But that did not seem right. "It was piercing, piercing pain," he said. "I had no idea. There wasn't a lot of blood initially." His father took him to the local doctor. "He's examining and poking, and he says, 'You've been shot!'" Norman recalled. It turned out he had a big chunk of a twenty-two-caliber bullet lodged up against the bone in his forearm. To remove the bullet was a fairly involved surgery, and it left Norman was a large scar on his forearm. To this day, he still feels some numbness where the bullet entered. There was an investigation, naturally, and it revealed that the bullet came from the direction of his neighbor up on the hill. One of Norman's closest friends from the town had a twenty-two-caliber gun and was playing around with it. The friend explained to the police he was out target shooting. But he denied that he had deliberately fired the gun in Norman's direction when he saw Norman washing the car. The boy was from a prominent family in town, and he and Norman used to strip down old cars in the woods, get them running again, and race them around. Norman believed it was an accident. "I think he was trying to scare me and hit something near me that would frighten me," he said. "I don't think he was trying to hit me, I'm pretty sure he wasn't." Still, their friendship was a casualty of the incident, especially after Norman's uncle Izzy accused the boy's family of trying to cover up what Izzy thought was a deliberate act. "Things were pretty awkward," Norman said.

JACK WAS BORN IN 1957, when Norman was already almost ten. "As much as my birth was a miracle because here they are having lost everything, this was like the American dream," Norman said. "It was almost like my parents relaxed and had sex again." By the time of Jack's birth, the Bermans had ten thousand chickens. Norman said his parents were content. He said their thinking was, "We're fortunate to be independent. We're fortunate to be free. We're fortunate to live in this country." They voted in every election. They were proud citizens. They read the newspapers. They were very frugal, and were able to save a few thousand dollars each year for their retirement. They were uneducated farmers and at peace with that life. "Their highest grade was fourth grade," he explained. "That was their education." Norman essentially raised his younger brother since he was the only one in the family who could translate and interpret for Jack both the horrific experience of the Holocaust and the feeling of liberation being in America. "You have to understand," Norman explained, "we were on a farm in rural Connecticut. Our closest neighbor was one half mile away. Our closest Jewish neighbor was over three miles away. . . . We were isolated. So having a little brother was a gift. We were together always."

Norman mentored Jack and taught him the ways of the world. "He could do no wrong," Norman said. "He was just this magical child. He was sweet, sweet, sweet, earnest, honest. I don't know that he had a devious bone. What you saw was what you got." They played together. They fished together. From a young age, Jack seemed infinitely curious. He hung on every one of his brother's words about the way the world worked and always had more questions. "We would just go for hours," he said. It was obvious to Norman, his parents, and his teachers that Jack was gifted academically. Once he could read, Norman used to take Jack to the local library and check out books. He'd take out twenty books and read them all. Norman decided to up the ante. After each book that Jack read, Norman made Jack record details of the story on an index card and what meaning the book had for him. When Jack was in the fourth grade, the Moosup library gave an award to the student who read the most books over the summer. Jack read forty-two books. Norman made Jack write a report, on the index cards, on each book. "There is something about a little brother that brings out a sibling's sadism," Norman said. In fifth grade, Jack won first prize in the regional spelling bee. In sixth grade, he started a newspaper and served as its editor, reporter, and business manager. "It was a first for the school and a great success," Norman said. "The paper folded when Jack left."

UNLIKE HIS BROTHER, JACK didn't have to work in the barn collecting eggs. The proximate reason was that he seemed to be allergic to dust. But the real reason was that his parents wanted Jack to focus on his studies, not on farming. Norman explained, "My mother said, 'Look, it's enough that you're doing it. He's the real intellectual. Let him stay in the house. He can do music. He can study. He can read. He can write.'" This was a little frustrating to Norman. "On the one hand I felt I was getting a raw deal," he said, "but on the other it was like okay, he is the smart one."

After Jack completed sixth grade at the Moosup Elementary School, his parents decided to send him to the Hebrew Day School in Norwich, twenty miles away. Norman, by then a student at Boston University, wasn't consulted. (Norman later put himself through law school at night and is now a litigator in Boston.) The idea would be for Jack to spend half the day studying math, English, and science and the other half studying Torah, the Talmud, and other prayers. In an essay written when he was eighteen, Jack reflected back on the decision to go to the Hebrew Day School. "So began a period in my life during which arose a near-certainty that I would become a rabbi," he wrote.

At first, Jack seemed to be at a disadvantage at Norwich Hebrew. The other students had been together for six years, were close, and knew the ropes. Jack did not. He was an outsider, even among his own people. They "were well ahead of Jack," Norman explained. "Within one year, Jack had caught up and become the group's leader and spokesperson." He quickly mastered the translating of Hebrew texts. "The rabbis, the teachers, were just in awe of him," Norman continued. "He was running circles around some of the older kids in terms of memorizing portions of the Torah." All this study gave Jack headaches. His reward for excelling was more study. "Recesses and physical activity were not considered viable parts of the educational experience," Jack continued in the essay. "But to further occupy me through the cold mornings of winter I was stuck in the closet, and told to wade through the essays of rabbis and scholars that nobody else in the school got to read, on rattling subjects like assimilation and marriage, mixed marriage and heaven. Hell."

In February 1971, when he was in eighth grade, Jack reported in a school application that he was five foot five, weighed 135 pounds, was the son of parents neither of whom had gone to college, and was a straight-A student. But Jack displayed his natural talent for Judaism on nearly a weekly basis at Temple Beth Israel. Alan Cantor, a friend of

Jack's from rural Connecticut who also ended up at Andover with us, remembered how the synagogue could not afford a rabbi of its own, so each Friday night the Sabbath service was run by men from the congregation, including both him and Jack, after they both had had their bar mitzvahs. Here they were at fourteen years old leading the Friday-night service, singing the haftorah. Jack and Alan used to exchange letters when Alan was away at summer camp. "He used to write very ornate and funny letters," Alan said. "I always felt like he was way smarter than I was." He recalled how one time Jack felt the need to correct the way he pronounced the word *indict*, which of course is not pronounced the way it is spelled. "I think I might have been more intimate with him if he weren't so intimidating intellectually," Alan continued.

After two years at the Norwich Hebrew school, Norman, still away at BU, figured if Jack kept on this path, he would end up at a yeshiva and become a Hebrew scholar or a rabbi. He knew his brother had a broad range of intellectual interests and talents, and feared that the life of a Hebrew scholar was too narrow and isolated for him. "He needed to be doing other things as well," Norman said. "He needed sports. He was getting chubby."

There were family arguments about what was best for Jack. "I started fighting with my parents about it," Norman said. "There were a lot of family meetings and fights." Finally, Bluma wondered what Jack would do if he didn't go to a yeshiva. "He should go to the best school in the world," Norman blurted out. "He should enjoy and take advantage of the best that there could be." Norman contacted an association of secondary schools, in Boston. "I've got this genius brother and he's at a point where we need to find the right school for him," he said. The brothers decided Jack should apply to Andover, even though it was already February. "With my inexperienced guidance, Jack applied to Phillips Academy at Andover after admissions had closed and after financial aid had been allocated for the year," Norman said.

Norman returned to the farm, from Boston, and took Jack back up himself to Andover for his interview. "Not only do you have to let this kid in but you've got to help him pay for it, too," Norman told the admissions officer. Although the school was about as far removed from the Berman family's experience as could possibly be imagined, it still felt right to the two brothers, especially to Norman. "This was beautiful," he said. "We were in awe." Jack was a bit nervous about the whole thing but quickly came around, too. "We bought into the American dream," Norman said. "If you've got the smarts, then you should be able to write your ticket, the world should be at your feet . . . this is the land of opportunity. All you've got to do is work hard and be smart, and get your education. Obviously, the pedigree matters. If you can go to a school like Andover, then you can go to a good college. This is what we want. This is what we dreamed when we were in the barracks in Poland, in those god-awful work camps."

Or so went the theory of the case. In practice, Misha and Bluma were as nervous as ever about the prospect of Jack going away to Andover. There were long debates, in Yiddish, about the wisdom of the decision. Norman remembered his parents' logic: "This is not us. This is not for us. . . . How's this Jewish kid going to get kosher food? Or what's he going to do for the holidays? . . . Aren't they going to beat him up? Isn't it dangerous there? Are there any other Jews?" Norman told his parents everything would be fine. "If he can run circles around the other Talmud scholars and master chapters of Hebrew, I have a feeling he'll figure out what he needs to do at Andover," he explained to them.

JACK WAS FOURTEEN YEARS OLD. He would be attending Andover on a half scholarship. He had never lived away from home. "He was scared out of his wits at first," Norman said. He remembered the image of Jack being dropped off at his dorm at Andover with only a big green canvas duffel bag, filled with his belongings. "He's standing there on the sidewalk with this huge bag and my parents are saying goodbye to him," Norman said. "You know, 'Study hard. Be careful.'" The Bermans understood the import of the moment—how far the family had come in one generation, from the concentration camps in Poland to the steps of one of the most prestigious schools in the world—but what it would mean on a day-to-day basis for their son eluded them.

The moment also marked an important transition in the relationship between the two brothers. They remained close. But now there was a difference. Norman said, "I felt *Okay, I'm going to be glad to be your brother*—this is in my head, I don't think I told him this—*but this doesn't seem right to just be micromanaging your life*. I think I drew back. And I think he was aware of it. He was pissed. . . . We stayed close and everything but it felt like now that he was at Andover, my feeling was I needed to step back a little bit."

Jack got off to an extraordinary start academically at Andover. An English teacher wrote in a November 1971 report that "Jack is a high-powered lad with considerable verbal gifts. He is a sophisticated writer, though I am trying to rid him of the jargon habit: he uses 35% more words (usually big ones) than are necessary. Very good classwork—often over the head of other boys who sit back and ooh and aah. A very nice boy—but then, what do you expect from Moosup, Connecticut?" In Clement House, where he lived, the housemaster reported that Jack was "also a good citizen, quiet, well-organized and polite" who got along well with his peers and seemed to be enjoying his Andover experience. Jack continued to impress everybody throughout his first year at Andover, and ended up on the honor roll. "He got to Andover and just said, 'Wow, what a pool, I'm going to swim in it,'" said his Andover friend John Barber, who grew up in Middletown, Connecticut, fifty miles and a stratosphere away from Moosup. "He was quiet and scholarly and measured but he also had this sort of glorious kind of cackle of [a] laugh and at times [a] very wacky sense of humor, so he could surprise you."

His second and third years at Andover would not be as easy in the classroom. He seemed to have particular trouble with math and chemistry. By the first semester of his Upper year (eleventh grade), there was near-universal criticism of Jack's academic performance in letters sent home. "Two years ago Jack was one of my best students in History 10," Robin Crawford wrote after Thanksgiving 1973. "He was particularly notable for a very solid written expository style. All of that seems to have simply vanished." Harper Follansbee, Jack's biology teacher, was equally bewildered. "Somehow Jack gives the impression of being an honor student but then doesn't live up to that," he wrote.

It seems unlikely that Jack's parents would have sat Jack down in Moosup over Christmas vacation and read him the riot act for squandering a huge opportunity, especially since the fact that he was even at Andover in the first place was beyond their wildest imagination. They remained preoccupied with the egg farm and had developed no better an understanding of the nuances of the English language—and there were plenty of nuances in these academic reports, along with some clear-eyed warnings. Norman was in Boston, working on his law career and pursuing his own life. He had already decided to step back from his role parenting Jack. This was a challenge Jack would have to meet and overcome on his own, if he could. "What he realized was that maybe the sun didn't rise and set over him," Norman surmised.

By spring 1974, there was some improvement in history, and his biology teacher Follansbee also remarked on Jack's appearance—the era of post-1960s long-haired renegades must have startled some of the old guard—finding him to be "attractive, neat and clean in appearance, polite but very quiet and unobtrusive. I think he sets good standards for himself and tries to reach them. He seems to have the respect of his classmates but I am uncertain as to how wide his circle of friends is. He seems fairly self-sufficient to me." Math however continued to be a disaster, with Jack flunking the final exam.

Alan Cantor followed in Jack's footsteps to Andover, one year later.

"To a certain degree, it influenced my going," he said. On occasion, Alan used to ride back and forth with Jack to their homes in central Connecticut, but he did not spend a lot of time together with him at Andover. Despite his academic troubles, Jack gave off an impression that was serious and not all that much fun. "He wasn't a hang-around kind of guy," Alan said. "I think of him as someone who knew where he was going and he didn't feel a particular need to bring other people along on the ride. He was not unfriendly, but he didn't really seem to spend time with people on the way. He was working toward something. At that point in my life as an adolescent, I was just hoping a girl would occasionally smile at me. And Jack was figuring where he was going to go to college and grad school and make his career, and he was just sort of humming along on that track. He just sort of seemed to know where he was going. . . . He was not a backslapper. He also wasn't anyone you could possibly dislike. But back then he was like a thirty-year-old man. He had a certain quiet intensity to him."

Alan and Jack did, however, team up to start Andover's first Jewish student organization. The group sponsored bagel breakfasts on Sunday mornings and held Sabbath services on Friday nights in the basement of the imperious Cochran Chapel towering above. At that time, the faculty adviser to the Jewish Student Union, as it was known, was the school's protestant minister. (Andover's sole Jewish teacher, Jack Zucker, known around campus as "Fat Jack," was a poet from the Bronx. He had no interest in being the faculty adviser to the Jewish Student Union.)

Even though there were probably only around sixty Jewish students—out of a population of twelve hundred—there was rarely a feeling of anti-Semitism, or overt racism of any kind, at Andover. Indeed, Andover was then one of the more ecumenical school settings on the planet. Maybe it was the times or maybe it was, as Al Cantor postulated, that Andover's very few Jews, African Americans, Asians, and Hispanics were more like exotic species encased in dioramas—more like a source of wonderment for the WASP establishment—than anything else. I share Alan's observation about the school. I never felt the least bit of anti-Semitism or prejudice at Andover. Everyone seemed to feel kind of lucky to be there in the first place, and my class-mates were an endless source of wonderment, especially their intelli-gence, their creativity, their senses of humor (and in some cases, their seemingly bottomless capacity for drugs and alcohol).

Besides the Jewish Student Union, Jack's activities outside the class-room included the school newspaper and rowing crew, the latter about as unlikely an avocation as there could be for someone once a tick or two away from becoming an Orthodox rabbi. A teammate, his friend John Barber, remembered that Jack was "not overly athletic and grace-ful, but highly committed" to the sport and to the team. Jack handled the so-called seven position in the boat of eight rowers with some aplomb. "Number seven is actually the toughest spot of all because you have to follow stroke and you have to lead the starboard side," accord-ing to Barber.

Barber said Jack was "clearly a scholarship kid but he had [none of] what the British would call chippiness. He was just thrilled to have the opportunity. . . . I can still remember him saying, 'I never want to see another chicken in my life. I never want to smell chicken shit in my nostrils again.' . . . You might think of him as sort of scholarly and ex-tremely hardworking and then out of the blue he would [let out] just this enormously joyous outbreak of laughter."

Sometimes the jokes were at Jack's expense. For his senior year, Jack had decided to move to Sunset House, a small outpost of seven stu-dents in a remote corner of the campus. His dorm mate Brooks Klim-ley, captain of the Andover basketball team, used to refer to Jack as "Spermy Berman," although other than the near rhyme there was no discernible reason why. Even though they could not have been more different—according to yearbook rankings, Klimley was not only the "best dressed" senior but also the third biggest "alkie" on campus—they were pretty good friends. Jack told Brooks that chickens flirt through their eyeballs. "Of course that led to a raucous amount of entertainment," Brooks said. Another time, Brooks and Jack, who seemed to have developed an enviable level of skill on an IBM Selectric typewriter, set out to type a pornographic essay. Jack was convinced they could not pull it off; Brooks felt otherwise. He urged Jack to just start typing. "We had one of these rollicking conversations, which is totally out of character for him," he said. In the end, after about fifteen minutes, the pair erupted into hysterical laughter and the essay ended up in the wastebasket, lost forever. "Shit, I'd never seen a yarmulke before," Klimley said. "We just got to be friendly and I kind of liked him. He was very kind of dorky in many ways but he was fun."

ONE THING EVERYONE WHO LIVED with him noticed about Jack was how focused he was on the college admissions process during his senior year. Jack wanted to go to Harvard. Even though he had performed poorly in math and science at Andover, he believed he had the intellectual gifts to deserve admission to the most selective and prestigious school in the country.

Others had noticed a change in focus in Jack, too. His house counselor, Gil Sewall, wrote the Bermans in December 1974 that he had known Jack "casually" since his first year at Andover when he did "a great village history for me on Moosup" and added, "Jack is an introspective and self-contained boy who goes his own way, drinks deeply of those things which interest him, and always seems restrained and solidly grounded."

Once upon a time, in the decades before the personal computer, the internet, or the "common app," the denouement of the rigorous senior-year college admissions process arrived the old-fashioned way, in the form of either large envelopes or small envelopes, delivered courtesy of the US Postal Service. At Andover, no surprise, this annual spring ritual was a serious event. And it all came down to one day in mid-April when the seniors gathered in the basement of George Washington Hall where row after row of mundane-looking metal mailboxes took on an immense importance. Would the envelope be thick or thin? For reasons unknown, the day was known as Black Monday.

On the fateful April day, Jack did not get into Harvard. But he did get into Brown. John Barber remembered Jack being disappointed. "He was hoping for more," he said, "and was temporarily frustrated . . . and disappointed" that Harvard rejected him. Jim Horowitz, Jack's senior year roommate who had been accepted by Yale, thought part of the problem for Jack with Brown might have been that, at a forty-five-minute drive, Providence, Rhode Island, was too close to Moosup— and the past he was trying to escape—for his comfort. Part of it might have been that back in those days, Brown was not quite the revered and desirable school that many know it to be today, at least if you had been indoctrinated in the perverse logic of Phillips Academy's college counseling office, as we all were.

Jack's family attended his Andover graduation in June 1975. They could not have been happier to celebrate Jack's successful navigation through the halls of one of the nation's premier secondary schools. In the end, he had graduated with honors. "Everyone was in awe of how he looked," Norman remembered. "Just how tall he had gotten and confident. This was not the little kid that we had dropped off four years earlier. There was a huge pride."

IN HIS FIRST SEMESTER AT BROWN, Jack took four English classes. His brother, Norman, was incredulous. They had long arguments about Jack's approach to his studies. "What are you doing?" he asked Jack. "But he was hell-bent, he said, 'No, this is what I want to do, this is one of the strengths of this school.'" Slowly, Jack mentally unpacked his bags at Brown. He joined the school's radio station, WBRU Radio, and was a disc jockey for a while before he took to journalism. He reported news, did interviews, and covered the 1976 Republican National Convention in Kansas City as a stringer for National Public Radio. A few months after it began publication in August 1978, while still an undergraduate at Brown, Jack served as the production director for a fledgling Providence newspaper, *East Side/West Side*. It was clear he wasn't going to go the same route, professionally, as his fellow Brown students, at least not initially.

In 1979, Ray Rickman, a thirty-one-year-old African American man from Detroit, landed a new job in Providence as the executive director of the Providence Human Relations Commission. He had eleven employees. "They came late, they took two-hour lunches, they had part-time jobs in the post office that started early afternoon," he said. "It was hilarious, I've never seen anything like it." He would fire them and they would return a week later. "I was very isolated," he said. He needed to find a fellow traveler to work with him. He started interviewing candidates for a job that paid only the small amount of money he had cobbled together from what he was supposed to be paying interns. The fifty-year-olds he interviewed said it wasn't enough money; the twenty-two-year-olds didn't have enough experience.

Then he met Jack Berman. "I sat there and in five minutes I realized he was brilliant and in ten minutes he showed me his writing samples and I fell off the chair," Rickman said. "It was the kind of writing you'd expect from a forty-year-old with twenty years under their belt." He knew he wanted to hire Jack right away but kept up the fiction of interviewing a few others, just to make the process seem competitive. He soon hired Jack, who started at the commission soon after he graduated from Brown, in June, with a degree in sociology. For his first few months at the commission, Jack was the "civil rights director," investigating charges of employment and housing discrimination.

In January 1980, Rickman promoted Jack to be his deputy. He supervised investigations into alleged civil rights violations, organized public education programs on topics such as sexual harassment, affirmative action, and police use of deadly force. He also got it in his head that all the cases that the commission had previously received should be reviewed to make sure they were handled properly. Of course, the commission did not have staff qualified to take on that huge task, so Jack recruited a group of young, idealistic students from Brown and had them work for free. Suddenly, the commission was a hotbed of activity.

Rickman would arrange for Jack to visit every few weeks with the city solicitor so they could work on cases together. "He was educating himself," Rickman said. "He used to come a half hour early every day. . . . And he would stay an hour and a half or so extra every day. He was wonderfully zealous. . . . I've had a couple of hundred employees in my life and I'm liable to blurt out that Jack Berman was the best employee I ever had, and it's true. What he didn't know he would find out in twenty minutes." Jack seemed to have infinite intellectual curiosity. "He was brilliant and he was always at the top of his game," Rickman continued. "He would tell me, 'I don't know anything about that but I'll find out.'" Improbably, a white Jew from rural Connecticut and a black man from Detroit became very close friends. "Jack Berman was my best friend in the entire world," Rickman said. "This sounds so over-the-top but I have to say it. Have you ever met anybody and you said, *This is my friend and this is my friend for life*, and they feel the same about you? And it doesn't happen often. I believe Jack is the only time in my life that's happened."

In a testament to how close Jack was to his parents despite his years of independence, he would return to Moosup on most weekends. On Friday afternoons, Misha would drive to Providence and pick him up. Misha and Rickman would talk on the sidewalk for ten minutes or so while waiting for Jack to collect his files and belongings. "[Misha] just wanted the best for his children," Rickman recalled. "He wanted to know what he'd been doing during the week. He needed an update. He said he didn't always get it from Jack. 'Give me the details, what has he done good this week?' That's what he used to say, 'What has he done good this week?'" He marveled at how different Jack was from Misha. "Jack was this fabulous kind of upper-class person with no snobbery," Rickman said. "His diction is intelligent, his bearing, everything about him, you would think he was third generation or fourth generation. You would think his father, grandfather, and great-grandfather all went to Harvard or Yale, and of course they didn't."

After eighteen months working with Rickman, Jack decided to apply to law school. Again, he wanted to go to Harvard. Again he did not get in. He ended up at the Boston University School of Law, and he excelled there. His GPA put him in the top 25 students in his class of 449. When he graduated in May 1984, he had an offer to be an associate at the prestigious Providence firm where he had worked the previous summer. But that seemed a little parochial and way too close to Moosup for Jack's long-term comfort. "We talked a lot during that time of career stuff," Norman said. "I was already a lawyer. He was becoming a lawyer." To try to spread his wings, he interviewed for firms all over the country. In the end he accepted an offer from Bronson, Bronson & McKinnon, in San Francisco.

Before heading to California, Jack returned home to Moosup and wound up giving a brief talk at the synagogue in Danielson. He said it was an occasion for "rejoicing" because "tonight I stop spending my parents' money and start earning an honest living. For that, my parents are grateful. And I am also grateful, because it means I can come here and face my parents and their friends without shame or embarrassment." He said that if asked "thirty years from now" when he left Danielson, he would have to say he never left Danielson. "It is because this is where my life began," he continued. "It is because for many of you, this is where freedom was born, where dignity was restored. It is because this is where you relearned the joys of life and where I learned them for the first time. This is the place where many of you raised the children who used to run around in this temple. Maybe some still do. I know that after this service, I am going to go downstairs and run around a little bit for nostalgia's sake."

Ever the loyal son, though, in his first years at Bronson he would find clients of the firm who were in New York and ask to be put on their projects. He would come to New York around once a month and make sure he also saw his parents. "He needed to see them," Rickman said. "He'd come seven or eight times a year the first year and pay half the time himself and the other half the law firm would pay." He used his first paycheck from Bronson to buy Misha and Bluma a two-year-long airplane pass. He used his vacation time to take his parents on trips. "He often made me look bad," Norman said.

Jack specialized as a litigator in labor and employment law. At first, he represented big corporations, which made up the bulk of Bronson's clients, in disputes with their employees. Like many a young law firm associate in major cities across the country, Jack was working long hours. He was learning, working hard, and climbing the ladder. He lived in a bachelor apartment down by the San Francisco waterfront, in the Marina neighborhood.

One day, around Father's Day 1986, he was set up on a blind date with Carol Kingsley. She, too, was an associate at a San Francisco law firm. They met for brunch at a place near Union Square. "I remember not having any particular expectation in mind," she said. "I came from the swimming pool and threw on a sundress, and I still remember having partially wet hair." Jack was wearing a button-down Brooks Brothers shirt and a sweater-vest—one of his typical uniforms. Carol thought he was both "appropriately" and "nattily" dressed. "It certainly took me aback a little bit, thinking, *Oh gee, I should have done a little better for this guy.*" They spent the whole day together. After brunch, they walked up and down Union Street. They stopped at a toy store and played with some toys. "I could see the playful side of him, which was delightful," she said. They shared a Dove bar—she still has the stick—because they were still full from their enormous brunch. "I felt totally comfortable with him," she continued. They stopped by his apartment, which was nearby. "He had this big vase of beautiful irises on his coffee table," she said. Carol was impressed by it, even if his apartment was never again kept so neatly. "It was just a wonderful afternoon," she continued. He sent a handwritten note afterward to her office saying how much he enjoyed meeting and that he looked forward to seeing her again. It was "more of an East Coast thing," she said, "but something I truly appreciated, this very pitch-perfect note."

From that day on, Jack and Carol were virtually inseparable. They saw each other at least twice a week while they were dating and that increased over time until they moved in together, a year before they were married. "There was no gap in the relationship from the time we met each other until we got married," she explained. "We were always together."

She is not exactly sure why whoever fixed them up thought the match between a Catholic woman from the Midwest and the son of Holocaust survivors from rural Connecticut would work, but it did. Though he did not come right out and say so, it would be important to Jack for Carol to convert to Judaism, which she did about a month before they were married in 1990. By then, while he celebrated Shabbat on occasion and the High Holy Days—Passover, in particular, was a favorite holiday—he did not keep kosher. He remained devoted to Jewish culture and the faith, but in a different way.

In 1987, three years after Jack moved to San Francisco, he orchestrated his parents' move to a nearby retirement community in Walnut Creek. The Bermans sold the farmhouse and its sixty acres for around $300,000—a substantial profit above the $12,000 they had paid for it—and then wrote a check for the condo in Walnut Creek. Jack helped them get settled and navigate the new surroundings, and he and Carol visited them regularly.

Carol recalled the first time she met Jack's parents. Some six months after they had started dating, but before they were living together, Carol

invited Misha and Bluma over to her tiny apartment for Shabbat dinner. "I talked to Jewish friends of mine, including an ex-boyfriend who
is Jewish, around what I should serve," Carol said. "[I] went out and
bought cookbooks. I made two enormous challahs, one poppy and one
sesame, and made kreplach from scratch, the whole nine yards."

The first problem Carol confronted when Jack's parents arrived was
the fact that she had a Siamese cat, which came right up to Bluma and
rubbed against her. "Bluma, I could tell that she didn't care for the cat
being inside," Carol said. "Jack later explained, 'Well, they lived on a
farm.'" When Carol offered them something to eat—this was meant to
be Shabbat dinner after all—Bluma surprised her by saying, "Well,
we've already eaten. But we'll eat a little bit of the fruit." Carol was
stunned. "I'd taken off the day at work to make this meal, which had
gone into considerable planning, but they already ate," she said. "I
thought, *Oh dear, this isn't going to go very far in terms of the culinary part
of it*. Jack, of course, was Jack. He's very good-spirited and just rolling
with it, and chatting."

At one point, Bluma had to go to the bathroom, which required her
to go through the small apartment's small kitchen. "On her way," Carol
continued, "she saw the challah sitting on the table and she just shrieked.
I didn't know what the shrieking was all about and I thought she had
slipped or hit something. So I ran the few yards to get in there because she said 'Misha! Come! Come! Look at this!' Misha came in
and he broke out in a smile as she's pointing to the challah, and she
said, 'Where did you get these amazing challah?'" Carol said she'd
made them. She continued, "She looked at me just with astonishment
and she said, 'You made it?'" From that day on, Bluma made challah—
challah rolls actually—from Carol's recipe, and everything seemed to
be just fine, even though she could sense that the Bermans would have
preferred that Jack had found a nice Jewish girl. On the other hand,
Carol had agreed to convert, so there was that.

On August 5, 1990, Jack and Carol were married at the elegant

Beaulieu Vineyards in the wine country northeast of San Francisco. It was a bittersweet day. Carol's mother had died years earlier. Carol's father did not attend the ceremony because Carol had converted to Judaism, and Carol's sister and her two young daughters decided not to be in the wedding party so as not to offend their father, although they did attend the wedding itself. "This was very hurtful for me, and Jack, too," she said. Other than that, it was a joyous occasion. Allen Bennett, the first openly gay rabbi in the United States, officiated. They knew each other because Jack was on the board of the Northern Pacific regional office of the American Jewish Congress when Bennett was its newly appointed executive director. "What I think made him tick was that he was, in every sense of the term, driven," Rabbi Bennett said. "He was not I think ever content to be just as good as he could be. I think he was really driven to be the best that there was, and probably I would say more often than not he was successful in that effort."

Eventually, it was time for children. "To him getting married was the green light for starting a family," Carol said. When she shared the results of a positive pregnancy test with Jack, he was ecstatic. "His whole face turned from this tired kind of slouched-in-the-chair to literally beaming!" Carol said. "Sitting up straight, wide-eyed, huge beaming smile, eyes lighting up."

Zack Berman was born on March 31, 1992. Carol has a memory of Jack being by her side as she was giving birth, and watching him as he ate one Wheat Thin after another. "Those Wheat Thins were going in really fast and it made me laugh," she recalled. "It was just so Jack in so many ways. He was undoubtedly starving." Soon enough, both Jack and Carol were back at work and Zack was in a regular child-care program. There were the family trips together: Carol remembers when she and Jack decided to drive with his parents from San Francisco down to San Diego in Carol's small German-made BMW. The car was packed. Jack did most of the driving. A nine-month-old Zack was in his car seat in the back between his grandparents, who had barely survived the

Holocaust. It was a twelve-hour drive. They stayed for a week in an apartment on the grounds of the Hotel del Coronado. "We all had a terrific time," Carol said. "They had a barbecue area there and Jack cooked on the barbecue. His parents really loved being part of all this. They loved being with the baby."

IN 1991, JACK BECAME A PARTNER AT BRONSON. After several years of defending corporations in employment lawsuits, he began to think the time had come for Bronson to develop a practice representing the plaintiffs in these suits—the people who thought the big corporations had screwed them. The idea was in perfect keeping with Jack's desire to comfort the afflicted. But getting his relatively staid corporate law firm to agree to allow him to start a practice representing plaintiffs in employee matters was not easy.

Ilyse Levine-Kanji worked for Jack on the new endeavor. "I was nervous at first because traditionally Bronson had represented companies and did the employment defense work, and I'm politically very liberal and so I wasn't sure I was going to like that," she said. "But very soon after I joined the firm, Jack became a partner and his plan was to bring in a lot of plaintiff-side employment discrimination cases. . . . It was a huge change of mind-set for Bronson and the other people in the employment department. I know it was something that he obviously had been thinking about for a while." She said it was a testament to how deeply the firm respected Jack that it allowed him to start the plaintiff's practice, even though the payoff was not immediate. Change is always hard for people, and this was a big change for Bronson. "Jack was definitely very well respected in the law firm," she continued. "He worked very hard, worked a number of late hours, but also [was] just smart and very, very professional. Very collegial, had a good sense of humor. He was easygoing and very easy to talk to."

One case they worked on together involved Jody Jones Sposato's sexual discrimination claim against her employer, Electronic Data Systems, then owned by the flamboyant billionaire entrepreneur and presidential candidate Ross Perot. In February 1992, EDS fired Sposato from her software sales job, after months of making her professional life nearly intolerable. She hired Jack to sue EDS, alleging that the company had sexually discriminated against her.

A deposition for Sposato was set for June 30, 1993, at the law firm of Pettit & Martin, EDS's outside counsel for the case. Pettit's offices were in downtown San Francisco, at 101 California Street, a typical nondescript forty-eight-story glass-and-granite skyscraper the likes of which had started popping up in cities across the country in the late 1970s. This particular structure was built in 1982; its only distinguishing feature—although not a flattering one—was an odd entryway with a glass atrium protruding at a forty-five-degree angle. Sposato's deposition ran long; a second day was scheduled for July 1.

That morning Carol got up and went to work very early at her new law firm, Bancroft & McAlister. She was in *eat what you kill* mode there, trying to get a contract drafted. She didn't have any help at that point so she got up at 4 a.m. and quickly headed out the door to the Muni train, which took her downtown in ten minutes. Misha and Bluma happened to have stayed over at their home the night before. Before he headed downtown to 101 California, Jack had to get them to the Muni train, which would take them to the BART and then back home. He also had to drop Zack at his playdate at a nearby park, where Leona, the nanny he shared with another toddler, would watch him during the day.

The plan was for Jack to take Carol's BMW, drop off his parents and his son, then park the car downtown. After the deposition with Jody, he had to go to the airport for an afternoon flight to Los Angeles, where he had more depositions to take for a different case. At some point during the day, he needed to call Carol and tell her where he had parked her car so that she could then pick it up and pick Zack up from the park or wherever he and Leona had ended up. Carol said, "What was nice about this morning is that his parents were here. He was able to hug and kiss them goodbye. He was able to see his son that morning, hug and kiss him goodbye." In a half daze that morning, he had also kissed and hugged Carol.

At some point during the afternoon, Carol became aware that she had not heard from Jack about where he had parked her car. "I thought, *Well* . . . I was so busy, though, with this transaction that I was working, that I really didn't have time at that time," she said, and then told herself, *"He's in a deposition, so he'll call me when he's not in a deposition or not traveling. You know he'll call.* But I was just conscious that I didn't have a call or a message from him." By midafternoon, Carol had finished her work and decided to head to the Bay Club, a gym she belonged to, before picking up Zack. "I didn't know where the car was anyway and I put in a message to Jack on his voice mail saying, 'Please let me know where the car is,'" Carol recalled. "I thought that by the time I get back, I'll have a message from him telling me where the car is."

A YEAR OR SO EARLIER, Gian Luigi Ferri, a fifty-five-year-old struggling businessman, had begun to show an interest in guns and gun shows. Ferri had been living since 1992 in a one-bedroom apartment in Woodland Hills, thirty miles northwest of Los Angeles. He owned ADF Mortgage, Inc., a mortgage brokerage he founded in 1987, with offices on the second floor of a strip mall in Woodland Hills.

By all accounts, Ferri had had a difficult life, filled mostly with disappointment. At twenty, he started working as an engineer, and at twenty-seven he emigrated to the United States from Bari, Italy, settling briefly in Boston. Shortly thereafter, he moved to San Francisco. He was peripatetic, living all over the peninsula, Sonoma County, and Santa Cruz. He worked as a draftsman for Stanford Oil Co., then a counselor at Sunny Hills children's center in San Anselmo, then an instructor at Sonoma State University. In 1969, he enrolled at University of California–Santa Cruz, where he received a degree in biology and psychology. That same year, he married Donna Jean Benedetti, a mental health worker, and became a naturalized citizen. They moved to Marin County, where Ferri worked as a mental health counselor for the Marin County Department of Health and Human Services. He ran a psychodrama group, where attendees acted out various family situations. He also received a master's degree from Sonoma State.

In 1977, he and Benedetti divorced and Ferri began volunteering for the Reverend Terry Cole-Whittaker, a former Miss California turned television evangelist and proselytizer for the power of positive thinking. She coined the phrase *Prosperity, Your Divine Right*. Ferri seemed to take the aphorism to heart but didn't have much success in business. He lived between Las Vegas and the Bay Area and tried to make real estate deals in California and Las Vegas; most were unsuccessful and resulted in lawsuits. His bookkeeper in Las Vegas could not recall that he ever completed a deal.

In 1981, Ferri hired Pettit & Martin to help him arrange an $8 million deal he was trying to put together with a group of Italian investors to buy three mobile home parks in Indiana and Kentucky. He was able to borrow $6 million and used another $1.9 million, mostly from his investors, to make a down payment, which was subsequently lost when the deal fell apart due to problems that developed because the mobile home parks were on a floodplain. Ferri's investors sued him and Ferri in turn sued the seller, Marcus & Millichap, a realty firm. He claimed the seller had misrepresented the property. In 1982, Peter Russell, a Pettit & Martin attorney, flew to Indianapolis to find Ferri a local attorney to help him resolve the litigation over the soured deal. In the end, the lawyer was successful, winning Ferri a settlement of $1 million—$223,000 in cash, which he used to cover other debts, and the balance as part of the restructuring of the $6 million loan. But Ferri still lost himself and his investors $2 million in the deal.

Around this time, Pettit & Martin also advised Ferri in a land deal involving a residential development in Leadville, California. But this deal, too, ended badly: Ferri lost $300,000 when he was not allowed to build on the land. Some eighteen months before moving to Woodland Hills, he ran a real estate investment firm in Larkspur, in Marin County. One acquaintance there told the *Los Angeles Times* that Ferri was a "wheeler-dealer." He was a defendant in a lawsuit that accused him of taking $480,000 from investors but failing to return any of the profits from the investment to them. Eventually, the investors dropped the suit because they decided it would cost too much to try to unravel Ferri's complex legal and financial machinations surrounding the deal. "He didn't seem like a bad guy," explained attorney Fredrica Greene, who represented the investors, "but I definitely had a feeling that he might be of less-than-sterling character."

Once he moved to Woodland Hills in February 1992, he rented an apartment and set up his mortgage business. He demanded two months' free rent from the landlord, who described him as "an aggressive person." He quickly ran into more financial difficulties. In October 1992, he spoke with bankruptcy attorneys in Irvine about the possibility of filing for personal bankruptcy. "He was very gentle, very friendly, a chubby little guy," recalled Elias Francisco, the bankruptcy attorney Ferri consulted. "I got the feeling he had a lot of money at one time." But he no longer did, and he could not even pay the $1,100 bankruptcy-filing fee. It turned out he owed $8.7 million to investors and business creditors, and owed more than $100,000 on his personal credit cards. He was also two months behind on his $800-a-month rent and had been threatened with eviction, twice. He had a state tax lien against him, for back taxes owed, for $3,500. He was two months behind on the payments for his five-year-old white Cadillac. "We liked him and took pity on him," said Azar Torabi, an insurance broker who worked in an office near Ferri's in Woodland Hills. "He was very much a loner."

But he also possessed a vicious temper and was simply odd. He appeared to have no close friends, and his few acquaintances described him as "a loner who was given to mood swings, unprovoked fits of rage [and] long periods of seething anger." A former secretary described him as being "kind and gentle one moment" and then, without warning, "becoming very upset, sometimes fuming for several days" before recovering. She said he was very hard to work for because his mood swings were unpredictable. "He was really a strange man," said Diane Mohler, manager of the Business Center of Las Vegas, which, for $140 per month, had received calls and collected mail for Ferri's ADF Mortgage, Inc. "You couldn't get anything out of him. He was really secretive."

In June 1993, Keith Blum, a co-owner of a hair salon in Woodland Hills, remembered giving Ferri a haircut and telling one of those typical barbershop jokes. "If you were locked in a room with Saddam, the Ayatollah Khomeini, and a lawyer, and you had a gun with two bullets in it," Blum asked Ferri, "who would you shoot?" Ferri apparently had heard the joke before. He answered, "The lawyer—twice." He then reportedly erupted in laughter "so explosive he had to take off his glasses to wipe the tears from his eyes." By then, Ferri had already purchased three guns, legally, in Las Vegas, using his Nevada driver's license and his Nevada home address. On April 25, Ferri bought a TEC-9 semi-automatic pistol. A couple weeks later, on May 9, he bought another TEC-9 pistol.

On June 18, Ferri traveled to the Mojave Desert on an early-morning target shooting trip, with Michael Spivack, a recent acquaintance, and another man. Ferri practiced shooting his TEC-9. He had added a Hell-Fire trigger system to the gun, making it nearly fully automatic and capable of firing between three hundred and five hundred rounds of ammunition per minute. Ferri also added the Hell-Fire system to his second TEC-9. All perfectly legal, of course. During the Mojave outing, Ferri made an "unsolicited out-of-context" statement: "I don't like lawyers. I don't like lawyers."

A week later, on June 25, Ferri was back in the Las Vegas area. At the Pawn & Gun Shop in Henderson, Nevada, he bought a third weapon, a Norinco forty-five-caliber semi-automatic pistol, Model 1911A. He also bought five hundred rounds of forty-five-caliber Black Talon ammunition, two hundred rounds of nine-millimeter Black Talon ammunition, extra clips, a belt holster, and a black utility gun sling for the TEC-9. From Henderson, Ferri drove back to Las Vegas. The next day, June 26, he was off to Barstow, California, on the west side of the Mojave Desert. From Barstow, Ferri drove the white Cadillac DeVille up to Oakland, where he stayed at a Motel 6 on Edes Avenue. He remained in Oakland for three days. He would not allow the chambermaids to clean his room during his stay; he told them he had papers scattered around the room that he did not want disturbed. When he checked out of the Motel 6, he paid cash. He also, weirdly, left behind a seven-inch Skilsaw in an orange metal case. There was a label on it, bearing Ferri's name. The next night, June 30, Ferri spent in his Cadillac; it was filled with food wrappers, dirty clothing, empty cans and bottles, a cooler with some food in it, and some thermal blankets.

On July 1, 1993, at one thirty-three in the afternoon, Ferri parked the white Cadillac DeVille in the Embarcadero Two garage. An hour or so later, he walked the two blocks to the 101 California Street office tower—where Jody Sposato was giving her deposition in the thirty-fourth floor, with Jack at her side. Nobody stopped him. Building security was not particularly vigilant in those days, and Ferri looked like a middle-aged businessman who could easily be working in the building or visiting someone who did. At 2:45 p.m., Randall Miller, who worked as a salesman for Kodak on the thirtieth floor of 101 California, saw Ferri in the lobby by the security console as he headed to the elevator bank for floors twenty-seven through thirty-six. Miller noticed that the "quite fat" Ferri seemed to be struggling with a metal cart that some clerks at law firms use to transport legal files from one floor to another. Ferri had placed a large black canvas bag into the cart and was having great difficulty pushing it from the building lobby into the elevator.

A few minutes earlier, Ernesto Zuniga, the building superintendent, was on the thirty-fifth floor changing lightbulbs when he realized he needed to go to the supply closet, on the floor below. He took the elevator down a floor, got the supplies he needed, and returned to the thirty-fourth-floor lobby to await the elevator to go one flight up. He saw Ferri there, pacing back and forth. Ferri was dressed in a suit and tie—not unlike a lawyer at Pettit might be—but Zuniga thought he had a strange look on his face, as if he might be lost. Zuniga also noticed the luggage cart off to one side of the lobby and that it had several bags in it. He asked if Ferri needed help but instead of an answer, he got a grumble and a sense that Ferri wanted to be left alone. When the elevator came, Zuniga got on and returned to the floor above.

At about 2:55 p.m., as Randall Miller, the Kodak salesman, was returning to the lobby, Judy Robertson, who worked on the thirty-fourth floor, went to the elevator bank with the idea of going to the thirty-fifth floor to get something to eat. When she got to the elevators, there was no one there. She pressed the elevator button to call the up elevator and when the door opened, she saw Ferri, in the back of the elevator. He had a large gun in his hand. Thinking he wanted to rob her, Robertson offered Ferri her purse. He responded by flipping the elevator stop button, locking the elevator on the floor. It was 2:56 p.m. "It's okay, you just wait right there," Ferri told her. "Just wait there." He didn't want her money.

While he continued fishing around in his bags, she did not do what he ordered her to do—stay put—and instead bolted from the elevator and ran back into the Pettit office to tell her boss, Robert Burke, and her fellow employees about the fat man in the elevator with a gun. Burke was on the phone, speaking with another attorney, at a different firm. He acknowledged Robertson's warning but continued his conversation.

Seconds later, Robertson yelled into Burke's office that Ferri was firing away down the hallway and walking toward conference room 34C. Burke shouted into the phone, "Oh my God, it's gunfire. Call 911." He hung up. The attorney on the other end of the phone called for help.

It turned out that Ferri had smuggled his two TEC-9 semi-automatic pistols (now operating basically in automatic mode), the pistol, and his hundreds of rounds of ammunition into 101 California in the leather briefcase and suitcase that he was pushing around in the cart. When he got out of elevator sixteen on the thirty-fourth floor, Ferri had the two TEC-9s around his neck in a sling. The pistol was in a holster. He had earplugs in his ears and he was carrying a canvas bag filled with hundreds of rounds of ammunition. He walked out of the elevator and turned to his right, down the hallway toward conference room 34D. He passed several people in the hallway on the way toward 34D but did not stop or seem to notice them. He walked past the secretarial station also without stopping.

In 34D, Sharon O'Roke, a thirty-five-year-old in-house attorney at EDS, was trying to finish up the second day of Sposato's deposition. Jack was by Sposato's side in the conference room while O'Roke conducted the deposition. Deanna Eaves, a thirty-three-year-old court reporter from Richmond, California, was dutifully recording Sposato's words. Jack and Jody sat with their backs to the glass window, facing the interior of the office space and a glass wall that opened onto the thirty-fourth-floor corridor. A closed curtain blocked the view into the conference room. It couldn't have been a more typical, and more typically mundane, legal setting.

Whether looking inside or outside, one could only see shadows. Ferri stood a couple of feet back from the outside glass wall of the conference room and opened fire with one of his TEC-9 "automatic" weapons. The glass shattered from the impact of the rapid gunfire. Jack was shot six times. Jody was shot five times. They fell from their chairs to the ground. Then, as a protective measure, they moved under the table and lay side by side, trying to avoid further gunfire. They probably survived for around fifteen minutes, long enough to know what was happening to them. Later, when police recovered Jack's briefcase, they found his unused airline ticket for Los Angeles with bullet holes in it.

FERRI THEN LEFT CONFERENCE ROOM 34D, turned east, and lighted at the desk of Elizabeth Newark, a legal secretary. She had heard screams and smelled gunpowder and had started dialing 911 when Ferri appeared. "He looked at me, and his face was blank," she recalled. "He wasn't interested in me. I gather he was interested in the lawyers." Brian Berger, her boss and a thirty-nine-year-old litigation partner, yelled at her to run. Berger then went into the office of his partner, Allen Berk, fifty-two, who specialized in labor law, and closed the door. Ferri shot through the door, killing Berk, who was seated at his desk, and critically wounding Berger, in the chest and arm. Ferri continued moving eastward on the thirty-fourth floor, firing indiscriminately at people who were in his path.

He found the interior staircase to the thirty-third floor and another group of Pettit & Martin offices. When Ferri got to the lower floor, he encountered David Sutcliffe, a thirty-year-old intern, who had just come out of the office of attorney Charles Ross. He had just met the California attorney general at a luncheon at the firm and came away a bit starstruck. Ferri fired three times at Sutcliffe, at point-blank range, killing him nearly instantly. John and Michelle Scully, husband-and-wife attorneys at Pettit, were about fifteen feet from Sutcliffe when he was shot. Michelle Scully had been doing some legal research on the thirty-third floor when her husband told her to gather her things. They needed to leave fast because there was a gunman on the thirty-fourth floor, killing people. They grabbed their belongings and headed to the elevators. That's when they saw Sutcliffe ahead of them. From the opposite direction, she said, she saw "a fat man in a white shirt" walking rapidly. She said she thought he looked like he belonged in the law offices until he shot Sutcliffe. At that moment, she and her husband dashed into an unoccupied office and took refuge behind a file cabinet.

Within seconds, Ferri was in the doorway of the office, pointing the gun in the Scullys' direction. He walked over to where they were hiding and shot them. He then left the office, turning right. The Scullys were badly hurt. Michelle tried to call 911 but couldn't get an outside line. They lay still for a few minutes, all the while continuing to hear Ferri firing shots nearby. Suddenly Ferri reappeared in the office doorway, looked at Michelle Scully, didn't say anything, and walked on. She eventually got through to 911 and was told help was on the way. The police arrived in about fifteen minutes, she said. She tended to her husband, who was hit four times. She checked on Sutcliffe; he was dead. John Scully, twenty-eight, later died as well.

Charles Ross, who had just been speaking to David Sutcliffe moments before he was shot and killed, hadn't heard any shots, just some noise that he ignored. Suddenly the door to Ross's office swung open and Ferri was before him. Before Ross could say a word, Ferri shot him in the right upper biceps. Ross then got up and closed the door in Ferri's face. As he started back to his desk, Ferri opened his office door again and started pointing the gun at him. This time, to try to avoid being shot again, Ross pushed aside Ferri's gun, ran past him, and found some vacant office space on the thirty-third floor for ten minutes before making his way to the thirty-fourth floor after the police had arrived. "I knew I was confronting a reality I couldn't even imagine," Ross told the *New York Times* a few days later. "The gunman was cold, detached, impassive as if I could be anybody. It made me realize that I had to be as cold-blooded to him as he was to me . . . I was worried that I would die some pathetic death in the office." He broke down in tears recalling how upset he was that Sutcliffe, whom he described as "a friendly kid who had a Jimmy Stewart sincerity that was rare," had been killed moments after leaving his office. "I worked for what I got," he said. "I fought for my life. But I have survivor's guilt."

At about 3:04 p.m., Ferri headed into the fire stairwell between the thirty-third and thirty-second floors. By this time, none of the elevators in 101 California were operating. When he arrived at the thirty-second floor, he reloaded one of the TEC-9 pistols, which had been emptied of a forty-round clip. Police found the empty clip plus a full fifty-round clip in a postal mail tub next to the thirty-second-floor freight elevator. The thirty-second floor at 101 California housed the offices of the Trust Company of the West, a Wall Street investment firm, and the San Francisco office of Davis Wright Tremaine, a large national law firm. Ferri walked past the receptionist into the TCW offices and started firing through a glass window into the office of Donald "Michael" Merrill, a forty-eight-year-old father of two. He cried out, "Oh my God!" He was shot four times and was killed. Ferri then turned to his right and fired into the office of Vicky Smith, forty-one, a marketing executive who had jumped up from her desk to see what the loud noises were coming from next door. She was then hit in the back and head by "a burst of gunfire," according to police, knocking her to the floor, where she remained, pretending to be dead.

Smith heard secretary Shirley Mooser, sixty-four, take her last breath after Ferri shot her four times. Charles Stockholm, Mooser's boss, heard the shooting start around 3:03 p.m. He saw Mooser get shot and then fall into his doorway, without moving again. Ferri shot his final victim, Deborah Fogel, nine times through the glass of attorney Harry Shulman's office. Attorney Paul Smith found her there, suffering from multiple gunshot wounds. He administered CPR as best he could, but she soon died.

Ferri left the thirty-second floor of 101 California via the building's internal stairwell, which exits to the street at ground level. As he was entering the stairwell, he encountered two women who had entered the stairs on the thirty-fourth floor and were trying to escape the carnage that Ferri had created. The women thought Ferri was there to help. They called to him. He shot at them but missed. His gun jammed, giving them the opportunity to escape to the thirtieth floor. But the exit door to the floor was locked. They pounded on the door until it was opened from the inside and they escaped to safety. Ferri, too, tried to escape the stairwell by going to the thirty-first floor. But the door was locked and nobody let him in. There was blood on the door handles, evidencing his efforts to reenter the floor. Now, feeling "trapped in the stairwell," according to police, Ferri went down to the half floor between the twenty-ninth and thirtieth stories, put his head back against the stairwell wall, put the forty-five-caliber pistol in his mouth, and pulled the trigger. It was around 3:25 p.m. In addition to killing himself, Ferri had killed eight people and wounded another six in what was then one of the worst seemingly random acts of mass murder in American history. It was the worst mass killing in San Francisco history. "Nothing compared to this, and I had seen a lot of bodies in my time," explained Earl Sanders, who investigated the killings. "The (semiautomatic assault) weapons Ferri had—TEC-9s—turned a 55-year-old, pudgy out-of-shape little man into a killing machine."

POLICE FOUND A FOUR-PAGE single-spaced document—titled "LIST OF CRIMINALS, RAPISTS, RACKETEERS AND LOBBYISTS"—on Ferri's dead body when they came upon it in the 101 California stairwell. After describing his Midwest property deals in "a disconnected, hazy way," according to the *San Francisco Chronicle*, he wrote, "I spent the last 13 years trying to find legal recourse and to get back on my feet, only to find a wall of silence and corruption from the legal community." He claimed Pettit & Martin was biased against him and his foreign investors. "One possibility of the deceit of P & M is old racial and ethnic prejudice: Two of our investors are African, one Spanish. One Muslim." In another place he wrote, "What happened to me at

P & M . . . was rape"; he added that Pettit & Martin had "not attended to the details" and had given him bad advice intentionally in order to "steal the money and take over the corporation." The document also claimed that the seller falsified records and bribed people in order to achieve a "ridiculous settlement."

The *San Francisco Chronicle* described the document as a "paranoid's biography" that showed "how he thought his business deals were thwarted by evil conspiracies." Ferri had no criminal record, and there was no evidence of his drug or alcohol use at the time of the murders. Ferri wrote: "There is this condescending attitude in business that when you get emotionally and mentally raped, well 'you got screwed' and the accepted results is the victim is now supposed to go to work at 7-11 or become homeless and the rapist is admired and enveied [*sic*] as 'a winner.'"

CAROL HAD FINISHED UP HER WORKOUT at the Bay Club, was showering, and began to notice that a group of women had gathered around a television screen, with the volume turned up. She asked what was going on and they told her there had been a shooting at 101 California Street. "I was half torn," she said. She needed to go back to her office to find out whether Jack had left her a message about where he had parked the BMW, and she then had to go pick up Zack at day care. "I had this time pressure," she recalled, "but I also was concerned because then I started hearing things about 'It's at a law firm.' Mind you, nothing related to Jack came to mind because he was to be in LA. What was going through my mind was *Oh my God, who do I know that's in that building in that law firm? Who do I know at Pettit & Martin?* That's what was going through my mind." She went back to her office. There was no message from Jack about where he had parked the car. She called his secretary but the phone went to voice mail. She didn't leave a message.

Carol knew she needed to track Jack down in Los Angeles at his next deposition to find out where he had parked the car. She spoke with the receptionist, who told Carol to hold on while she got Michelle, Jack's secretary. When Michelle got on the phone, Carol could tell there was hesitancy in her voice, trying to figure out how much Carol did or did not know about what was going on. She was put on hold a few more times. "I was beginning to get a little annoyed and impatient," she said. "But at the same time something instinctively is telling me that something's amiss here and I didn't know what it was. So that was a little uneasy." Someone came on the line to tell Carol that Jack had been at 101 California and that they could not locate him. Carol was still not worried. She told his colleagues that Jack had gone to Los Angeles for another deposition, and had been on a noon flight. Actually, Michelle told Carol, the Sposato deposition had run long and she had changed Jack's reservation to Los Angeles to a later flight. But no one at Bronson seemed to know what was going on at 101 California other than that Jack had been at Pettit while Sposato was giving her deposition and that it had been delayed.

Carol turned her attention to thinking about where Jack usually parked the car. She found the street, found the car (by some miracle), and picked up Zack. She remembered being numb and not exactly sure how she'd found the car. She did take some comfort from the reassuring words of a colleague at her law firm who told her that Jack would be fine. "He seemed so assured of that, and I knew intellectually I had no reason to be assured but somehow that assurance carried me out of the building," she said of the colleague. She remembered having a premonition, a bad feeling "thinking this is it, Jack's gone." It was not only because she hadn't heard from him earlier in the day but also because "Jack was a little bit too good to be true throughout the whole relationship." She also remembered how the weekend before, when they were together at Costco, shopping for diapers, they had discussed how they wanted Zack to be raised were they both to die.

She finally made it home with Zack around 6 p.m. She turned on all the radios in the house to different stations as well as all of the televisions, to glean whatever she could about what was going on at 101 California. "They were reporting that a number of people were dead and the count would change, and they weren't sure how many were dead," she said. "They knew that the killer was dead. They knew that a number of people were taken out and taken to the hospital. They were showing that on the news. There was [a man] in fact, and I know the man now, it wasn't Jack, who was wheeled out with a resuscitator, air mask on his face. It's kind of a classic picture but I remember seeing that on TV the first time that he was rolled out." She thought at the time that the man in the wheelchair was Jack but soon enough realized it probably wasn't. She was still having trouble getting information about what was going on. The Bronson lawyers did not seem to know, either. Her instinct was to try to go down to the building and be there with Jack no matter what the outcome turned out to be but she realized she could not leave Zack and, besides, it was very unlikely she would be allowed to get close enough to the building in the first place. She called their friends the Wassermans to come over to be with her and to take care of Zack if she suddenly needed to go out.

At that point, she had not spoken with Misha and Bluma. "Bluma had a history of having what she thought were heart attacks or little heart things," Carol said. "I didn't want to upset them. They already had the news on, too, but they didn't put any of the pieces together." They just thought it was another terrible kind of American tragedy, different from the European kind they had suffered themselves. "I didn't want to trigger bad stuff in them," she said. "So I thought, *That's needless, I won't say anything until we either know he's in the hospital and we know what his condition is or whether he is just hiding someplace and unable to come out, or whether it is the worst, and if it's the worst then I need to be in Walnut Creek and tell them in person. I'm not going to tell them over the telephone.*"

After speaking with Carol, at around 9 p.m., Rick Stratton, one of the managing partners at Bronson, called someone he knew at the police department and explained that he was a law partner of Jack Berman's and wanted to know if Jack was on a casualty list. He would surely have had identification on him, Stratton explained to the police official. Had anyone with that name been killed or wounded in the attack? "She was going through a list and she said, 'No, there is no Mr. Berman there. I don't have that name.'" He called Carol and said, "Good news—not good news, of course there is no good news tonight—but it looks like Jack isn't a casualty." Of course, he did not know for sure because Jack still hadn't called Carol to check in. "That's not a good sign," he continued, "but he's not on the list."

Carol recalled she was somewhat comforted by what Stratton had told her. "I'm already expecting the worst at this point," she said, "and I'm already kind of beginning in the kind of dry shaking that your body goes through with shock or something and I'm listening to this. I'm thinking, *No, my bones are telling me otherwise*, but of course you want to be hopeful." In the middle of the conversation, the operator broke in—"like on TV," she said—"and I knew then that he was dead." She told Stratton she had to take the incoming call. "That's when I got the news that he was identified," she said. She couldn't recall exactly who told her but thought it was probably someone from the morgue, since Jack had been dead for around six hours by that point.

Sharon Wasserman came over and stayed with Zack while her husband, Steve, drove Carol to Walnut Creek to see Jack's parents. She wanted to make sure they made it out there before the late news because she was certain her in-laws always watched it and she did not want them to get the information from the news. She had made the same trip hundreds of times with Jack, but she got lost. "My brain was on freeze," she recalled. "It's like, *What exit to take?*" They eventually made it to Walnut Creek and to Jack's parents' house, through the maze of the subdivision. Understandably, she wasn't sure how to communicate the information about Jack. There was no good way. "How do I tell these people that have survived the Holocaust . . . how do I tell them that their younger son who is a lawyer working in a safe downtown building, that he was shot to death?" she said. She realized she just had to do it. "I thought there's no way other than just tell them," she continued. "You walk in there and just tell them. Don't say anything else or don't build it up or whatever. I remember being that cognizant of *I just need to walk in there*, and mind you I was not crying. I was just in a different state. I was like a zombie walking."

Her in-laws were surprised to see her. She hadn't called ahead. She had been worried that if she had told them in advance, one or both of them might have a heart attack and she needed to be there, in their presence, if that were to happen. She asked them to sit down. She told them Jack had been murdered. She remembered falling to her knees for about two minutes. She wasn't crying or anything. They were in shock. Carol recalled, "One of the things that Bluma did keep on saying [was] 'We just saw him this morning. We just hugged him. I just said goodbye to him this morning.'"

She told them to pack up some things so that they could all be together back in San Francisco. "It was better for us to be together and there would be things to talk about," she remembered. "Instinctively I knew they had to come with us. I wasn't going to leave them there. It's a small little family and it's an hour and fifteen minutes away and we needed to all cuddle and be together. We just needed to be together.

"Bluma [did] a remarkable thing," she went on. "She is really an incredible woman." Bluma decided at that moment that she wanted to bring two grapefruits with them. Would that be okay with Carol? "They loved grapefruit," Carol said, "and I remember . . . I was just dumbfounded. I didn't know what to make of the question and I don't even remember, I probably said, 'It doesn't matter, Bluma,' or something. 'It doesn't matter, just whatever you want, or forget it' or something like that, just kind of dismissed it in some way. But in my brain it wasn't dismissed at all because it was like talk about doing a survival thing.

Isn't that survival? Isn't that falling back on what you need to do to put one foot in front of the other? When you don't know what else to do and you need to keep going forward."

Norman and his family were asleep when Carol called them in Boston. It was the start of the July 4 weekend and their car was packed for an early-morning departure for a week's vacation in Nantucket. He knew about Jack's case against EDS and that Jack was doing some depositions for it. But he had not been watching the news that day. And of course, there was no internet, no Facebook, and no Twitter. "I think it was one in the morning, two in the morning our time, and it was Carol," he recalled. "I picked it up, I was in a sound, sound sleep, and she said 'Hello it's Carol.' I said 'Hi, what's going on?' and she said 'Jack's been shot.' You know, it just fully didn't register, Jack's been shot? And so I said 'What?' and she repeated it, and then I remember saying 'Well is he okay?' Because I figured, *Okay he's been wounded or something*, so she said, 'No, he's dead.'"

After Norm got off the phone with Carol, he spoke with his parents. "They were stunned, they were just stunned," he remembered. His mother was not inconsolable. Rather, she was incredulous. "It was almost like, *After all we've been through, this is what I get*," he said. "There was this almost resignation, I don't know. My sense was here's a woman who's had so much tragedy and seen it, and that I think she just saw it as like the ultimate test: *If we haven't managed to do you in, let's see if we get your son—maybe that will do it*. It was almost, it wasn't humor but there was just this sense of *Dammit, they've really done it now*. She made an immediate association with the Holocaust, an immediate association with what she had lived through and the horror and everything that had happened to her. It was like, *Fine, we're right back there and then it's just one more, just one more kick in the gut*."

Misha reacted differently. "My dad just sat down," his son recalled. "He was already a quiet and reserved man. He was very close to Jack. I identified more with my mother and I think Jack identified more with

my dad. He just shut down. . . . He was operating at 50 percent energy
and involvement but he dropped back to like 10 percent. He was often
quiet. He often seemed detached. After this he was largely checked out."

Ilyse Levine-Kanji, Jack's legal associate working with him on the
Sposato case, happened to be out of town at the start of the holiday
weekend for a family reunion, at Lake Tahoe. She recalled how on the
night of the murders, her father had watched the local news and seen
the story about the shooting and asked her if she had heard of the
Pettit & Martin law firm. She said that of course she had but didn't
give the matter much more thought before turning in for the night.
Early the next morning, her assistant, Val Evans, called her and woke
her. Evans was very upset. Levine-Kanji asked her what was wrong. At
first, Ilyse thought maybe she had somehow forgotten to get Jack the
papers he needed for the deposition he had planned to take in Los Angeles, later on the afternoon of July 1. Levine-Kanji knew she had done
the work for Jack. But perhaps there had been a snafu? "Val just started
to cry," she remembered. Then Evans let out a loud shriek. "I knew immediately that what my dad had said about Pettit & Martin, I just had
a thought that Jack must have been over at Pettit and so I realized that
was what happened," she said. Understandably, she does not like to
think about what might have happened if she had been at the deposition, instead of at Lake Tahoe. But she knows that it could easily have
been her along with Jack and Jody. "My grandfather was also murdered
when I was twelve so I have two losses from guns," she said. "It's just
awful. Obviously I'm glad I wasn't there but I just wish Jack and Jody
hadn't been there, and especially Jack."

STEVE WASSERMAN DROVE CAROL AND HER in-laws back to San
Francisco in silence. Nobody said a word. Carol put her in-laws in the
guest bedroom and stayed up all night, making phone calls. "I was trying to grapple with it myself," she said. Her instinct was to go down to

the morgue to see Jack that night. But Steve and Sharon dissuaded her. "They were saying, 'Oh you can't,' because they were hoping I'd sleep on it and that I wouldn't." The Wassermans wanted Carol to remember Jack as he was, but Carol insisted on going to see his lifeless body. One fortunate thing—if there ever could be one in such a tragic situation—was that Zack was really too young then to realize what had happened.

The next morning Carol was driven to the morgue. "I remember being escorted back [to see Jack]," she said. "And, you know, Jack didn't look so bad other than he was dead . . . His face looked peaceful. His face looked very peaceful. His eyes were covered by then so you couldn't see his eyes. The eyelids were down. But he wasn't blue or purple or anything." She then asked the coroner to pull down the sheet and yellow vinyl covering his body. His body had been washed so there was little blood on it, which surprised her. "I remember I wanted to see exactly where the bullets went in and went out," she said. "I wanted to see that. I knew that there were six at that time. I believed I was going to be looking for six. He pulled the sheet down on Jack's chest and so I only could see three bullet holes . . . if I'm remembering correctly. I could only see a few and I knew that he had taken more." She insisted that his body be turned over. "I wanted to see him completely . . . I counted and looked at the bullet holes myself and knew where they were and got a sense of that, and just could see him and that was it."

GIVEN THE LONG HOLIDAY WEEKEND and the number of people who needed to travel from the East to get to San Francisco, Carol decided that Jack would be buried on July 6, at the Oakmont Memorial Park cemetery in Lafayette, California.

It was Carol's decision. Obviously, he had died before his parents and so while it would have been nice for him to be buried alongside them, it was not clear how much longer they would stay in Walnut Creek now that Jack was gone. (In the end, they stayed another ten years before moving to Boston in 2003; Misha died in 2005 and Bluma died four years later.) Carol bought additional space at the cemetery for herself and for Zack.

At the funeral, in her remembrance of her husband, Carol referenced a card Jack had written her about a year earlier on her birthday, her first as a mother. "This year, we invented Zack, barely having completed ourselves, our own ending still to be worked out," he wrote. "We imagined Zack and did it within our schedule. He cries without provocation. He is no follower of stage directions. We can only hope he will be a gentle critic of our unfinished scripts. Happy birthday, love, Jack." Somehow she remained collected as she spoke. She wanted Zack to know that his father's influence during his sixteen-month life would nurture him forever. "Jack has left Zachary and me a wonderful legacy: his love, example, and precious memories," she concluded. "His love and memories cannot be taken away from us. Jack's love, example, and happy memories will always be with Zachary and me. Goodness in the world cannot be snuffed out."

Ray Rickman flew from Providence to San Francisco to say goodbye to Jack. He remembered that even though he was around nine years older than Jack, Jack was his teacher, his mentor, and his guide through life. "I've come across America to say goodbye to Jack," he said, "and I hoped very much to grow old with him, but it isn't going to happen. . . . Many people stand for something when they're twenty-one and when they're twenty-five. If they don't stand for it anymore when they're thirty-one, they forget they knew you. But with Jack, you knew for a lifetime that that honor and that integrity would be there. And since there's so few people like that, I hung on to that. When I flew over the mountains this morning coming into California, they reminded me of Jack, so solid, so calm, so strong, and reaching for the sky. I did so very much hope to grow old with you, but I must admit, the time that we have spent together was full of brilliance, full of life, full of intellectual back-and-forth, full of charm and wit."

THERE WAS SOME DISCUSSION ABOUT what garment Jack should wear for eternity. His parents suggested he be buried with the silk tallit he had worn at his bar mitzvah. But they deferred to Carol, who thought that one should be given to Zack, for him to use at his own bar mitzvah. She decided that Jack should be buried in a simple pine box wearing the expensive Italian silk suit that he bought soon after he and Carol were married. He adored it. "Clothing was always very important to Jack . . . he liked to dress well," she said. "So I wanted him to be buried well." She and Zack (with Jack's mother's help) also tossed roses on top of his casket.

On July 9, more than two thousand people gathered in front of 101 California to remember the victims of the shooting. By then, the calls to ban assault weapons had already started to be heard.

SOME GOOD DID COME FROM JACK'S MURDER. After an exchange of letters between Jody Sposato's widower Steve Sposato and President Clinton, Senator Dianne Feinstein arranged for Sposato, a Republican, to testify on August 3, 1993, before the Senate Judiciary Committee, then chaired by Senator Joe Biden, that was considering legislation banning the kind of semi-automatic weapons that Gian Luigi Ferri had used to kill Jack, Jody, and his other victims at 101 California. "She said there are two types of people in this world," Sposato recalled of Senator Feinstein's advice. "Those that take a tragedy like this and want to be left alone and those that want to make the world a better place, those who want to make change. So I said, 'Sign me up for the latter and tell me how I can help.'"

Sposato, tall and handsome, arrived at the hearing with his daughter Meghan in a BabyBjörn carrier on his back. His heart-wrenching testimony, which he had worked on with Jody's father, was devastating. "My wife's last words were 'I'm having trouble breathing' and then she died on the floor of a conference room, alone," he said. "The sight of our 10-month old daughter placing dirt on her mother's grave is a sight and pain I pray no other person must experience in their life. Can any of you advise me how to tell a 10-month old that Mommy is dead? Perhaps the manufacturer of the IntraTEC DC-9 assault weapon should publish this information in the instruction manual for its murderous product." Sposato was told that Senator Biden was "speechless" after his testimony and that "Joe Biden was never speechless."

After a year of political wrangling—including intense opposition from the National Rifle Association—Congress passed and President Clinton signed into law the Federal Assault Weapons Ban on September 13, 1994. Sposato was at Clinton's side for the signing in Washington; the president dedicated the law to Jody Sposato's memory. Sposato credits Dianne Feinstein with making it happen. "She is a true hero and champion," he said. The NRA managed to get into the bill a sunset provision, which ended the ban after ten years, on September 13, 2004. In 1999, California passed the most sweeping assault weapons ban in the nation, restricting their manufacture and sale. The law also prevented someone from buying more than one handgun a month, as well as mandating that guns sold meet basic safety standards and have child-safety locks on them. Since 2004, when the federal assault weapons ban lapsed, there have been any number of mass killings in America—Newtown, Connecticut, and Las Vegas, Nevada, to name but two—that might well have been prevented if there were still a ban on assault weapons. There are eighty-eight gun deaths in America each day and a total of 117,000 shootings each year.

For her part, Carol of course supported the assault weapons ban but chose not to do it in the overtly public way Sposato did. She has taken other steps to try to stop gun violence. She helped found the San Francisco–based Law Center to Prevent Gun Violence, a nonprofit dedicated to the memory of the people who died in the 101 California shooting. She is still on its board. She also served on the board of the Jack Berman Advocacy Center, at the American Jewish Congress, the mission of which was to "diminish the unacceptable levels of violence in our society through legislation, direct service, and public education." Carol explained that the advocacy center aimed to "address some of the social problems, cultural problems around guns, and starting young. The idea was to provide training in conflict resolution for young people. . . . How to use words instead of guns." She is involved with the Jack Berman Award of Achievement, awarded annually by the California State Bar to a young lawyer who has been involved in public service law.

In 2014, Carol ran for office—to be a state judge in California—and lost in the general election, after winning the primary. She served as a mayoral appointee on the San Francisco Police Commission. After more than twenty years in private law practice in San Francisco, she started her own mediation services practice to try to resolve legal disputes outside the court system.

Despite what happened to her husband, she said she felt "deep sadness" for Gian Luigi Ferri. "While my house was being filled—filled with friends, family, people that loved me, people that loved Zack, playing with him, trying to keep his life kind of on a keel even though he's sensing that there's somebody in this life that's usually holding him each day that's not—there's something amiss. . . . Ferri's body is lying unidentified by anybody in the morgue and sat there for two weeks before a distant relative in Italy could take the body. He was friendless. He was emotionally disturbed. He'd been planning this because he was angry at the law firm and the work that they had done for him some time before. It wasn't even that it was current. It wasn't that he got the information yesterday about his real estate business that went under. He went to the trouble of going to Nevada to buy firearms. He just was a man in a terrible state of mind. Nobody could do anything but pity him and feel badly for him. Don't get me wrong, I am furious that Jack died and with the loss of him, but my anger comes from our culture, our loss, the availability of the guns, and that nobody does enough about it. That's where my anger is. It happens over and over."

ZACK BERMAN FIGURED OUT at a relatively young age that his father had been killed. At his preschool program, he noticed that other kids would make Father's Day cards. He saw other kids' fathers pick them up after school. "The questions came early around what happened to his father," Carol said. Carol urged Zack to play the violin. But that was not for him. Then she suggested the piano, which she and Jack had hoped he might play. But that, too, did not fly. Ultimately, Zack focused on the saxophone, which had been Jack's favorite instrument, although Zack would have had no way of knowing that. "Zack decided on his own that his path was going to be saxophone and he picked up the saxophone, and true enough throughout high school he was always first-chair sax and he did tenor sax after a while, alto sax/tenor sax, and so on," Carol explained.

In September 1998, Zack threw out the first pitch at a San Francisco Giants baseball game, at Candlestick Park, to celebrate "Stop the Violence Day." He was a big Giants fan. Zack, then in first grade, told a reporter for the *San Francisco Examiner* that he was chosen "Because I lost my dad. By violence. By a gun. Someone shot him." He threw the pitch most of the way from the mound to home plate. His mother told the paper that Zack had a sadness that set him apart from his classmates at San Francisco Day School. "Throwing this first pitch allows him to do two things," she said in 1998. "It helps him to feel like he's doing something to stop violence. It empowers him. And it empowers all these first-graders to join with him to help stop violence."

He once used his mother's dictation device to record his thoughts about what happened to his father. "I don't know why this bad man did this to my father, period," he said. "My father is a good man, period." Carol thought, understandably, that Jack's murder made Zack "angry" and, being a smart kid, he asked a lot of questions about what had happened and why. In elementary school, Zack started "Peaceful Streets Kids Club," had T-shirts and posters made up. Local businesses put the posters in their windows. The group participated in a "gun melt" at city hall, where guns were melted down into a sculpture. "There were mixed reactions of families around us," Carol explained. "There were some families that were really enthusiastic and they wanted their kids to be participating with Zack and thought it was a really great thing, and understandably, there were other families that may have disagreed with kids that young being aware of such a serious matter and involved in it, and also a little fearful."

Throughout his life, Zack has tried to keep a positive attitude about the tragedy that befell his family. "I've definitely adapted to it in a way that I like quite a bit," Zack told me. "I've been a lot more independent than I probably would have otherwise just because had I had that sort of male role model I probably wouldn't have taken so many risks growing up or sort of thought outside the box and been as adventuresome as I was." He spent a lot of time up at Lake Tahoe, mountain biking on his own. He cycled. He skied. He felt invincible, always crashing his bike or on his skis, without consequence. One day, when he was around thirteen, he crashed his bike and punctured a tendon in his leg, which ended up making one of his legs "significantly shorter than the other one," he said. Then, two years later, while biking, he was hit by a pickup truck. He broke several vertebrae in his back and had a head injury. Suddenly, he felt less invincible. "Physiologically it changed everything and also mentally it changed everything," he said.

Instead of giving up, he focused his energy on racing road bikes and doubled down. "The commitment to racing—which involves a whole lot of crashing and a whole lot of watching your teammates crash and sometimes quit the sport because of crashes that are so potentially life changing—it really just sort of brought a new angle into the cycling," he said. "I got a lot more serious about it than I otherwise would."

He applied to Andover and visited the school with his mother. She kept telling him that if he were to go there, she would move to Andover and rent a house in town so he could be a day student. "I thought that completely defeated the purpose of going to boarding school so I basically decided she had ruined that one," he said. He can't remember if he ended up getting accepted, but he made it clear during the interview process that he wasn't all that interested in going to Andover if his mother was going to be living nearby. He ended up at the private San Francisco University High School.

Zack had a dream of becoming a professional cyclist. In 2009 and 2010, he rode for the Whole Athlete–Specialized Junior under-23 team, made up of the best young racers in the country. Specialized made him a custom bike to fit his different leg lengths. He competed in around twenty races, usually finishing in the middle or the back of the pack.

He applied to the colleges and universities with the best cycling teams. He also tossed in an application to Tulane since there was no required essay and no application fee. In the end, he had a choice between the University of Colorado–Boulder and Tulane. He chose Tulane. He made the decision on his own. "I reach most of my decisions on my own," he said. He was an English major and graduated in 2014.

For the moment, he has given up racing bikes. He still rides, though, and rides fast. He works in a cycling shop. He has taken up surfing. He heads out to Linda Mar Beach, in Pacifica, about fifteen minutes south of San Francisco, where the surf is smaller. In August 2015, he enrolled at University of California–Santa Cruz law school. He felt it was important to specialize in some professional area in order to make a more substantive contribution to society. He thinks he wants to practice law and also try something entrepreneurial. "It's probably what every lawyer says," he said. "Of course when I get all wrapped up in practicing law I'll probably just practice law like everybody else."

ON THE FIFTH ANNIVERSARY of the shooting at 101 California Street, a group of more than one hundred people gathered in front of the plaza to remember the massacre. By then, the Pettit & Martin law firm had dissolved. Jack's firm, Bronson, Bronson & McKinnon, would be dissolved the following year. The *San Francisco Chronicle* reported that there were "not many tears," just "lingering pain" and "aching sadness." Carol attended the ceremony but Zack, then six, went to a baseball game instead.

On the tenth anniversary of the killing, families lit candles, said prayers, and scattered flowers. Most of the widows and widowers had remarried, although Carol had not. "Sometimes it seems like a hundred years, and other times it seems like yesterday," she told the *San Francisco Chronicle*. "But the sadness is there." In 2007, the mass killings at Virginia Tech University dredged up the bad memories for Carol of the 101 California killings, as did the 2012 killings at Sandy Hook Elementary School. In 2013, on the twentieth anniversary of the 101 California murders, both Carol and Steve Sposato were interviewed by the local NBC affiliate in San Francisco. Sposato said that while he owned guns and understood why people would want to own guns, his view was that the ownership of semi-automatic weapons was unacceptable. "Where I draw the line is saying that anybody, regardless of [his] mental state, can circumvent the system and buy a firearm," he said. "I have a problem with that and I think most Americans do. I don't think anyone needs more than a ten-round clip." For her part, Carol said she hoped that in twenty years, the American people's philosophy about the need to own firearms would have shifted in the wake of one mass killing after another. Carol and Sposato joined together

with Senator Feinstein to hold a fund-raising event for the Law Center
to Prevent Gun Violence.

Meanwhile, the owners of 101 California have steadfastly refused
to erect any kind of memorial at or near the building. "They said that
they did not want to be the site of the biggest bloodshed in the history
of the city," Carol said. Their logic was perverse and absurd, of course.
The building *was* the site of a mass murder whether they chose to me-
morialize it or not. "They did not want that reminder," Carol continued.
"They did not want that shadow on their building. They refused, so
there's nothing."

Will

THE BIRTH BY CESAREAN SECTION of Will Daniel's older brother, Clifton, on June 5, 1957, had been front-page news in the *New York Times*. Clifton's mother was Margaret Truman, the only child of President Harry Truman and his wife, Bess. Not only was he the first grandchild of the former president, his father Clifton Daniel was then well on his way to becoming the managing editor of the *New York Times*.

The Daniels lived in New York City, in a triplex apartment at 830 Park Avenue, on the southwest corner of 76th Street, and the *Times'* article about Clifton's birth breathlessly recounted the former president's visit to the city to see him. The paper reported that President and Bess Truman had arrived at Penn Station at 11:15 a.m. on June 7 after a train trip aboard the *Spirit of St. Louis*, which had left the Trumans' home in Independence, Missouri, two days earlier.

Speaking to the waiting press corps, Truman, who was wearing a light-blue double-breasted suit, a light-blue tie, and a white Panama hat, said of his grandson that he was "an entirely healthy baby boy." From Penn Station, the Trumans were whisked off to Doctors Hospital, on East End Avenue, to see their grandson and their daughter. On June 10, the *Times* ran two photographs of the newborn Clifton Truman Daniel—both taken by his father—one of his grandparents looking into the nursery, and the other a close-up of him.

Just shy of two years later, William Wallace Daniel—or Will, as he was known—was born on May 19, 1959, to considerably less commotion than that bestowed upon his older brother. The *New York Times* made no mention of Will's birth until four months later when Gay Talese, then a cub reporter flitting between writing sports and obituaries at the *Times*, wrote about another visit his grandfather made to New York City, in part to see baby Will. The Trumans were staying at the Carlyle Hotel, on Madison Avenue, as became their wont, and the former president's visit to see Will seemed like more of an after-thought, although in a brisk, early-morning walk up Madison Avenue, he did pontificate to the pack of reporters following him on the need to stop coddling children. "The peach tree switch and the mother's slipper are the best things in the world to make a kid behave," Truman said, adding there were too many babysitters taking care of children. "It's the mother's duty to run the family and the father's duty to see that it's done," he continued. "Some parents are lazy. They want to go to too many parties."

But in a series of interviews a few months later with his biographer, Truman made clear he would not interfere in the raising of his grand-children. It was a promise he nearly kept. "These youngsters have a good father and a good mother, and I think they'll understand how to raise their children," he said. "It can't be done with undue interference from the ancestors, and I'm not going to do that." He said he doubted whether "a President ought to have any descendants" because of the pressure children and grandchildren inevitably have in living up to the family name. "Take the Roosevelt family as an example," he said. "They're al-ways watching what they do because their name is Roosevelt. That's true of Theodore Roosevelt's family; it's true of Franklin Roosevelt's family, and it makes it a very difficult situation." He said he hoped Clif-ton and Will would have teachers "who will put them in their place when they try to be smartalecks on account of the fact that they're de-scendants of a man who has been in the White House." Asked what he wished for his two young grandchildren, "I want them to be good citi-zens," he said. "I want them to forget that they had a granddad who was President of the United States and go ahead and make a name and record for themselves."

In fact, Will Daniel would spend his whole life trying to forget his grandfather was the president of the United States. It wasn't easy.

There was no presidential kinship on the Daniel side of the family but there was plenty of southern respectability. Will's grandfather Clifton Daniel Sr. was twice elected mayor of Zebulon, North Carolina, and owned the first telephone in the town. His phone number was 1. His only son, Elbert Clifton Daniel Jr., was born in 1912. The family did not have a lot of money—nobody did in rural North Carolina in those days—but managed to scrape enough together to get by. Son Clifton had no interest in farming and "displayed a premature aversion to dirt," according to a towering profile of Will's father by Gay Talese that was later part of his monumental book *The Kingdom and the Power* about the *New York Times*.

Just before the market crashed in 1929, Clifton Junior enrolled at the University of North Carolina. He was an editor of the *Daily Tar Heel*, but only after he had been fired from the paper early on for "being, or for seeming to be, a bit cocky with a senior editor," Talese wrote. After graduating in 1933, Daniel spent a year working for a small paper in Dunn, North Carolina, before moving on to one of the state's two most important newspapers, the *Raleigh News & Observer*. (Coincidentally, fifty years later, I got my start as a daily journalism reporter at the *Raleigh Times*, the *N&O*'s sister paper.) Like many an ambitious person, Daniel wanted a job at the *New York Times*. His first interview at the paper was short and not particularly fruitful, and he was not surprised he did not get the job. He turned down an offer to work for the *World-Telegram*, in New York, after it offered to pay him $35 a week, less than he made in Raleigh. Instead, in 1937, he moved to New York to work for the Associated Press, which agreed to pay him $50 per week. He buddied around town with Thomas Wolfe. Two years later, the day before the British declared war on the Germans, he moved to

Washington with the AP. He was the youngest person in the bureau and covered many military-related topics in and around Washington. In November 1940, age twenty-nine, he headed overseas, by boat, first to Bern, Switzerland, and then to London.

He stayed overseas for the next fifteen years. In February 1944, the *New York Times* finally hired Clifton Daniel to cover the Supreme Headquarters of the Allied Expeditionary Force. Daniel covered troop movements into Belgium, the Netherlands, and Germany. In 1945, he was in Paris and wrote elegantly about what he witnessed. After the war, he wanted to be the *Times'* London bureau chief but didn't get the job and instead bounced around the Middle East, London, and Germany, covering the dramatic realignment of the world. In 1954, when no one else would, he volunteered to replace the legendary Harrison Salisbury as the paper's Moscow bureau chief. Stalin had died eighteen months earlier and Khrushchev was busy remaking Soviet society. As the only permanent correspondent of a Western, non–Communist Party newspaper in the Soviet Union, he had to work his butt off to get stories. He didn't sleep enough. He pushed himself to the physical limit. He developed an ulcer and lost between thirty and forty pounds on his already thin frame. He appeared at the Big Four Conference, in Geneva in July 1955, looking so gaunt and frail that word got back to the publisher of the *New York Times*, Arthur Sulzberger, in New York. He ordered Daniel home.

He met Truman's only child, Margaret, in November 1955, at a dinner party. Years later, Daniel would tell Talese, he still remembered the smallest details about Margaret Truman from that evening: "her wonderful complexion, never suggested in photographs, and the way she wore her hair, her shoes, the dark blue Fontana dress with the plunging neckline." Daniel would tell a friend, "I looked down the neck of that dress and I haven't looked back since." By then, Margaret was a concert soprano and a bit of a TV personality. She was about to embark on her writing career.

A month later, they were sufficiently interested in each other for Daniel to be invited to the Carlyle Hotel to meet her parents. Harry Truman seemed both pleased for his daughter and a little nervous about her future husband. "He strikes me as a very nice fellow and if Margaret wants him I'll be satisfied," he wrote. But then he confided to Dean Acheson, his former secretary of state, "As every old man who had a daughter feels, I'm worried and hope things will work out all right."

They were married on April 21, 1956, at the Trinity Episcopal Church, in Independence, Missouri, the same church where the president and Bess Truman were married thirty-seven years earlier. Margaret was thirty-two; Clifton was forty-three. Ten days later, a close-up photograph of the couple was on the cover of *Life* magazine, airbrushed into 1950s perfection.

In the five years following his marriage to the president's daughter, Clifton Daniel moved swiftly up the *New York Times*' masthead. In 1957, he was named assistant to the managing editor, and two years later, the assistant managing editor. In September 1964, he was named the paper's managing editor reporting to Turner Catledge, the executive editor. Despite his success at the paper—or maybe because of it—he was not necessarily beloved by the rank and file in the newsroom. Talese attributed this, among other things, to his ambition, his appearance, and his connections. He also blamed the "highly critical" memos of the staff that Daniel authored and sent along to Catledge. Talese told the story of what happened the rare time when Margaret Truman Daniel walked into the newsroom and was introduced to a reporter, who remarked how much he admired her father. "What about my husband?" she asked.

"That," he said, "I'll have to think about."

CLIFTON DANIEL AND MARGARET TRUMAN had four sons. "Having children is like shooting craps," they once wrote. "When you roll the dice, you know what you want to come up, but often you don't get it; sometimes, it's better, sometimes worse." In his 1995 memoir about his grandfather, Clif, Will's older brother, recounted growing up in a famous family. He wrote that he did not even know his grandfather had been president of the United States until he was six, when someone at school happened to ask him about it. When he got home that afternoon he asked his mother, who was reading a book in the living room, whether Grandpa had been president. "Yes," his mother told him. "But anybody's grandfather can be president. You must remember that. You mustn't let it go to your head." He quickly put the matter out of his mind. "I had many other things to think about that year," he wrote. "That was the year I got a pair of six-guns, a cowboy hat, and boots for my birthday, taught my younger brother, Will, to read, and was sent out of class at school for picking my nose."

Of course, when your grandfather had been president of the United States and your father was managing editor of the *New York Times*, there were perks. For instance, when President John F. Kennedy was in residence at the Carlyle Hotel during his frequent stays in New York City, the idling police motorcycles outside made such a racket it rattled the neighborhood. Most New Yorkers would just complain about it to one another, but Margaret Truman called over to the Carlyle and demanded to speak with Kennedy. The president took her call, and the noise soon stopped.

CLIFTON DANIEL REMEMBERED A SEMINAL incident on a family vacation that came to symbolize his and Will's childhood. During a trip to Key West, former president Truman held a single press conference and Clif hoped to get in on the act, despite his mother insisting that he stay off to the side. He decided to climb a tree and sit down on a big limb. He succeeded in attracting a couple of reporters away from his grandfather's press conference. Will decided to climb a nearby tree and then hang upside down from a limb by his knees. This stunt succeeded in attracting the attention of the entire press corps, which wrote a story about the cute presidential grandchildren. But their behavior infuriated their mother, who lit into them. She was furious. She told them never to do anything like it again. "I thought I told you to stay out of the way," she erupted. "You're not the important one here. Your grandfather is."

"That sort of summed it up for me," Clif said. "She was always his daughter and we were sort of an adjunct. And it hurt. My parents, they provided very well for us. We lived in a nice apartment. We lived on Park Avenue. We had clothing, good food, and we went to the best schools they could find. In that regard, we were very well taken care of. And they were not physically abusive at all. And it wasn't like this all the time, but you just had the sense that we were not the center of their universe. And I don't know about Will. I know we both struggled with it. . . . For me, it's just a constant feeling that I'm not going to measure up."

Of the two older Daniel sons, Will was always the quieter, more reflective one. As a young child, his bleach-blond hair and translucently white skin gave him a mesmerizing, almost albino appearance. He was an "old soul" even at a young age, his brother said. Clif remembered a story about Will that his mother loved to tell. When the two boys were younger—around five and three, respectively—she would ask them what they wanted for lunch. Every day, Clif would do the answering for both of them: He would have a peanut butter and jelly sandwich and Will would have tuna fish. "This would go on day, after day, after day," he said, until one day Clif went off to kindergarten and Will was home without him around. "Mom came in and she found only Will sitting there. . . . And she came in and she started to ask him what he wanted for lunch, and she said, 'Oh, that's right. You don't talk.' And Will looked at her and said, 'Actually, I'd like a peanut butter and jelly sandwich, please.' It just floored her that not only could he talk, he talked better than I did. He was always a smart kid, but he was always very watchful, very quiet."

Clif picked on Will, in the fairly typical way that older brothers can torture their younger brothers. (Will, in turn, used to pick on Thomas, the youngest Daniel brother. Harrison, the third Daniel brother, was severely learning disabled.) Years later, when things hadn't exactly worked out as planned for Will, Clif and Will had a conversation about growing up together and Will put some of the blame for the way things turned out on his older brother. "He caught me off guard," Clif recalled. "So I said, 'I'm sorry. I didn't mean to do that. I didn't mean to hurt you.'"

The Daniel boys were essentially raised by their nannies, which was not terribly surprising given their social status, their mother's career as a writer of mystery novels (although it turned out she often worked with a ghostwriter), and their father's career at the *New York Times*. "They were good at what they did," Clif said. "They were public figures. But when it came to talking to children, raising children, spending time with them, they didn't have a lot of time for us. When we were on vacations together it was wonderful. Because nobody had work to distract them. Everybody was in a good mood. We loved going on trips to Florida with them because they just sort of relaxed."

Will and Clif attended the exclusive St. Bernard's School, on 98th Street, just east of Fifth Avenue. In his class pictures from those years, Will looks like a towheaded choirboy, either in shorts with knee-high socks or with a blue blazer and a repp tie. In the rarefied crowd, the Truman grandchildren didn't stick out. "We went to school with bankers' kids, lawyers' kids, doctors' kids," Clif explained. "People had bigger apartments, bigger houses, houses in the country. Walter Cronkite's son, Chip, was in my class. We were just part of the pack. In those days, our grandfather left office with the lowest approval rating of any US president. And his reputation came around about the time he died. But at the time, it wasn't a bad thing to be Harry Truman's grandson, but it also wasn't a huge thing. You weren't a Kennedy."

The Daniels made a point of renting different houses outside the city for the summer months. Clifton Daniel would commute back and forth into Manhattan, leaving his wife and their four sons to enjoy the bucolic Westchester County countryside. Once, in Tuxedo Park, New York, the two older Daniel brothers decided it would be great fun to splash their visiting grandfather, then around eighty years old, while he swam his laps in the oval pool. He used to swim the sidestroke so as to be able to keep his glasses dry while he was in the pool. Needless to say, Truman did not appreciate being splashed by his grandsons—he was not that kind of guy—and their mother told them he did not like to get his glasses wet. "Boy, he certainly did not," Clif explained. "Grandpa swam to the edge of the pool for his towel and wiped his glasses dry. Then he turned, simply glared at us, and shoved off again."

INEVITABLY, THE DANIEL BROTHERS' carefree youth gave way to a more complicated adolescence. One of the first places their instinct for rebellion began to appear was in the length of their hair. During his years in the St. Bernard's lower school in the early 1970s, the cherubic pictures of Will Daniel begin to change. In his seventh-grade class photo, circa 1972, Will has his blond locks parted in the middle, the genesis of the Gregg Allman look that became the hallmark of his high school and college years. The following year, in his eighth-grade picture, Will's hair was longer and wilder, easily the longest among the sixteen adolescent boys in the picture.

While the long-haired hippie look may have been tolerated on the Upper East Side of Manhattan, it was not particularly welcomed on

North Delaware Street in Independence, Missouri. "It was no secret what my grandfather thought of long hair," Clif wrote. Toward the end of 1971, ages fourteen and twelve, respectively, Clif and Will brought themselves and their long hair to Independence. It did not go over well with the former president. He was then eighty-seven years old, spending many hours each day in his study, reading. Upon seeing two long-haired young men gallivanting around the narrow corridors of the house, he emerged from the room and asked his daughter, "Who are those two young men with the long hair?" She wasn't sure to whom her father was referring but then it dawned on her that he meant Clif and Will. "Those are your two oldest grandsons," she said. Margaret Truman then beckoned her two adolescent sons to give their grandfather a proper greeting. "Worried about being summoned to the inner sanctum, I followed Will downstairs," Clif wrote, "through the dining room, and to the study where Grandpa was still standing, one hand on his cane, the other on the doorway. His dark gray suit seemed too big, his tie and collar loose around his neck. His face was gaunt, and his eyes looked huge behind his thick glasses. But there was something about him that made him seem anything but frail. As we approached, he didn't say anything, just looked us up and down, his mouth set."

"'Hello, Grandpa,' Clif said.

"'What was that?' Truman replied, as if he did not hear properly.

"'We just came to say hello,' Clif said, in a louder voice.

"His grandfather then assumed a presidential mien and replied, 'Well, do it then.'"

Soon enough, the boys' rebelliousness extended beyond long hair to cigarettes, alcohol, and drugs. The Park Avenue home was now the site of rambunctious adolescent partying, most likely without parental knowledge. Will's classmate at St. Bernard's and later at Andover, Richard Riker, said his older sister, who was at Brearley and then Andover, delighted in procuring marijuana for him and his St. Bernard's friends when they were in eighth grade. "My sister got us stoned a bunch of times," he said. Riker also remembered that Will lost his virginity in eighth grade, probably at his house with one of his sister's friends.

Riker recalled that one day on the Madison Avenue bus on the way to St. Bernard's for eighth-grade classes, they started teasing each other. "I definitely was sassing him because I liked to sass," he said. "I remember we were discussing it on the bus. I said, 'Just because you're the grandson of the president of the United States. Just because . . .'—I was saying this loud on the bus. He was banging me. He was really embarrassed. He's like, 'Shut up. Shut up.'" But Riker persisted. "Just because your father's the managing editor of the *New York Times*, just because your mother's Margaret Truman Daniel, that doesn't mean you can . . .'"

Will was getting increasingly upset with the teasing. "He was elbowing me and telling me to stop," Riker continued. "I could see he was uncomfortable. Of course, I was just teasing. Maybe any kid would be embarrassed, but it sticks in my mind."

Will also became irritated at the thirty-seventh president of the United States, Richard Nixon. On May 8, 1970—Harry Truman's eighty-sixth birthday—Nixon held a press conference and was asked whether he was starting to feel isolated in the White House because of increasing criticism of his Vietnam policy, in particular his decision to bomb Cambodia. "People should have the right to speak out as they do in the House, in the Senate, in the media, and in the universities," Nixon said. "The only difference is that, of all these people—and I refer particularly to some of my lively critics in the House and Senate—they have the luxury of criticism. I was once a Senator and a House Member; I thought back to this when I called Harry Truman today and wished him well on his eighty-sixth birthday, to some of the rather rugged criticisms that I directed in his direction. They have the luxury of criticism because they can criticize and if it doesn't work out then they can gloat over it, or if it does work out, the criticism will be forgotten. I don't have that luxury." For whatever reason, the two oldest Daniel brothers were aware of Nixon's reference to their grandfather. In a letter written that same day on the family's 830 Park Avenue stationery, Will and Clif wrote Nixon: "We resent the use of our grandfather's name in your television interview. If you have to lean on somebody, don't lean on us."

AFTER ST. BERNARD'S, CLIF WENT off to Milton Academy, in Milton, Massachusetts. By his own admission, he was not a very good student at St. Bernard's. His only A came in handwriting. By contrast, Will was a very good student. His raw intelligence and good grades began to change the dynamic between the two brothers. Whereas when they were younger, Clif used to torment Will physically, by the time Clif headed off to Milton, Will had started to turn the tables on him. "I had been the older brother, the older, larger, meaner brother," Clif said. "And Will just seemed to decide that he wasn't going to take that crap anymore, and he began to treat me with disdain. And I don't blame him. It really sort of flipped around. And he began to sort of take the upper hand mentally that way. I wasn't inclined at that point to punch him or chase him around. We were too old. He was really smart. And that's what he used. I wasn't as bright as he was. And it showed. He got the grades."

In September 1972, Clifton Daniel, having been relieved of his managing editor duties sometime earlier, agreed to take over the management of the paper's Washington bureau. Of course, in his new position, which did not start until the following year, the Daniels would have to move to Washington. "The *Times* had a devil of a time getting my mother to move back to Washington," Clif wrote, "and wound up having to buy her a Mercedes as a bribe."

Around the same time, Will was starting to consider where he would go to high school. Milton seemed like a logical place for Will to consider. Will, though, did not want to go to high school with his brother. He had set his sights higher: on Andover. He had the grades and the pedigree to pull it off.

On Christmas Day 1972 came word that Harry Truman was in a

coma and was not expected to live much longer. When Margaret Truman came down the stairs of the Daniels' apartment to tell her sons the news, she was crying. "This was only the third time in my life I'd seen her cry," Clif said. The first was after President Kennedy had been assassinated. The second time was a few years later, on April Fools' Day, when Clif and Will played a joke on their mother by pretending Will had broken his arm.

Truman died early the next morning, without regaining consciousness. He was eighty-eight years old. That afternoon, Clifton Daniel and his four sons flew to Kansas City, Missouri. From there, they were driven, in silence, to Independence.

In the photo that appeared on the front page of the *New York Times* of the family walking behind the president's casket at the funeral in Independence, what distinguished both Clif and Will was their long, unruly hair—Clif's was dark; Will's was blond.

An offended reader sent the two boys the picture with their hair outlined in black marker, and in the margin he had scrawled the words, "To appear at your grandfather's funeral with such God-awful hair is disrespectful, sick and sad. No wonder your grandmother stayed at home." Clif later wrote, "Will and I pinned the scrawled clipping up on the bulletin board, showed it to visiting friends, and had a lot of good laughs over it."

Whereas once upon a time, being Harry Truman's grandson was of little moment to most people, for a period of time after his death, there was no getting around it. "His popularity began to soar," Clif wrote. "Books were published. There were television specials and magazine articles. People, often people I didn't know, began to make the connection between my name and his." Eventually, Clif made his peace with being the grandson of Harry Truman. In 1995, he wrote *Growing Up with My Grandfather* and published a book of his grandmother's letters to his grandfather. He is honorary chairman of the board of trustees of the Harry S. Truman Library Institute and was the former head of public relations at Truman College, in Chicago. He has been working on a book

about his grandfather's decision to drop atomic bombs on Nagasaki and
Hiroshima.

For Will, coming to grips with his family legacy would be much,
much more difficult, and it cannot be said with certainty that he ever
really did it.

ANDOVER WAS A PLACE WHERE the working assumption—however
flawed—was that a minor celebrity (such as the grandson of a former
president of the United States) could find a modicum of anonymity.
St. Bernard's sent four boys out of a class of twenty-five to Andover in
September 1973, including Will and his friends Richard Riker and Will
Iselin. As I've mentioned, Will Daniel, Will Iselin, and I lived together for our first year in Nathan Hale West. Will's first-year written
reports, from both Reverend Pease, our housemaster, and his teachers,
hint at a multitude of mismatched priorities. In his December 1973 note
home to Will's parents, Pease observed that after his first trimester at
the school, although Will had "worn well"—a wonderful old preppy ex-
pression that one can easily imagine George H. W. Bush saying about
his National Security Advisor Brent Scowcroft—he could "sometimes
be rather easily distracted, drifting off to Bruce [MacWilliams's] or Jamie [Clark's] or Will [Iselin's] room"—no mention of what might be
going on at these gatherings but the implication was clear enough—
"or immersing himself in the full volume throb of his phonograph
when perhaps there is more work to be done." But, Pease noted, Will
was "generally sensible about his obligations."

There were some early signs, though, that Will was not necessarily
going to meet other people's expectations of him or how he should behave, either socially or academically. Jack Richards taught Will a social
science class. They could not have been more different: Richards epitomized the *hail fellow, well met* quality of Andover during the Kemper
and Sizer years; Will was a brash and gimlet-eyed New Yorker into

flaunting the rules. Will disappointed him. Richards thought he should have done better. "In short, I wish Will had committed himself to the course more," he wrote. "Perhaps he didn't like it—but I think he could have gotten a little more out of it if he had put more in. As a person: here, too, I suspect still uncommitted. He's sampling. I hope he'll join up one day." In the winter trimester of his first year at Andover, Will failed his math exam. His teacher noted that this was actually an improvement over the fall. "His manner of tackling the material was more thorough and reflected understanding and insight," he wrote, but then added, "The personal spark that was evident earlier" in the fall "wasn't as noticeable this winter."

Things didn't get much better for Will in the spring trimester. In his June 1974 letter home to the Daniels, in Washington, Pease noted the comments from his teachers and also referenced a phone call he had had with Will's father at the beginning of the term. "Several of us had the impression," he wrote, that Will "was showing signs of disenchantment with" Andover and "was testing a number of the rules of the School, and the social limitations on the campus."

Will Daniel was a regular of Upper Left, the dining haunt of the stoners. Will Zogbaum remembered meeting Will in the dining hall and discussing a philosophy text that Will was reading for one of his classes. "He was explaining about the difference between different kinds of knowledge," Zogbaum said, "and I had some response which to him indicated that I had some understanding, whether or not I actually did. And that was sort of the watershed moment where he said, 'This guy is okay and he can be my friend.' And so I started hanging out with Will." He was infatuated. "I was just a puppy dog following him," he said. "I was just so thrilled to be accepted by him at all. I think that was that ethereal quality that just sort of made him seem bigger than life for me."

After leaving Nathan Hale, Bruce MacWilliams and Will Daniel roomed together in Draper Cottage, a late-nineteenth-century house a bit removed from the main part of Andover's campus. "We bonded over music," Bruce explained. "We were also experimenting around smoking pot in that freshman year. We smoked a lot of pot together, and that bonded us, because we were kind of rebels." Unlike Bruce, Will "ended up just getting kind of lost in drugs," he said. Bruce said that he did not know anything about Will's lineage until they became roommates; in other words, he knew Will for a full year before Will let the cat out of the bag, which of course was in keeping with what his brother said was his desire: to keep himself as far away as possible from the Truman thing. "He hid all that stuff, but when we became roommates at Draper Cottage, he told me, 'Yeah, you know who my grandfather is?' . . . Can you imagine that, those shoes to step into?" Bruce said. "He was a rebel," he concluded about Will's years at Andover. "He was getting through Andover in order to kind of fulfill an obligation. But he was a loner, and he was a recluse. And he was into music and his own world, and he had his own little following, but he was not very social at all. He was social with his particular crowd, but you had to come and be let into his circle, I think."

By the end of his second year at Andover, Will was briefly on the honor roll, but the success did not carry over into the next year and Will found more solace in the "softer" coursework, like music and drawing. Christopher Zamore, Will's new house counselor at Draper Cottage, noted in a letter to the Daniels that Will was an iconoclast. "For the second year in a row, when the cottage got dressed up for the yearbook picture, Will refused to adopt the common standard of dress (this year, a coat and tie) and wore his black felt hat and cowboy boots," Zamore wrote. "Will has a strong dislike of the uniform and the standard, but his individuality and slight eccentricity are a pleasant addition to Draper. . . . I don't know exactly where Will's talents and interests lie and what plans he has in the future, so I am not sure I can give him any better advice than to choose a well-rounded course of study. Perhaps you could speak to him about his courses and advise him as to his future course of study." It is unlikely his aloof parents took Zamore's advice to heart. And in any event, Will held fast to his curricular game plan. And did well enough.

Then, in April 1976, came the inevitable "disciplinary trouble," as Jack Richards euphemistically wrote in a letter home. Given Will's ongoing flaunting of the rules at Andover, the violation he got disciplined for—"absent[ing] himself from his dormitory in the wee hours of last Saturday morning"—seemed almost comic. But rules are rules, and Richards informed the Daniels that Will's violation of them "rendered him liable to dismissal." Instead, though, he was given the "substantially more modest" punishment of "Censure," the school's official slap on the wrist, an "official statement of disapproval of Will's actions" that became a permanent part of his record.

Whether getting caught breaking the rules was the catalyst Will needed to get serious about Andover, by the end of his Upper year, he seemed to have found his stride and his performance improved, according to letters home. For his final year at Andover, Will moved to Stuart House. His house counselor was Ted Warren, who had taught him the previous year. In his December 1976 letter to Will's parents, Warren reported that Will's academic performance was again "superior," and that he failed to get an honors grade in only one class. "He is respectful, and a delight to have in the dorm."

That same spring, Will called home to his parents' house in Washington to find that they and his older brother, Clif, then finishing up his first year (of only two) at the University of North Carolina, had flown off together to Athens, Greece.

"They've gone to Greece?" Will asked the housekeeper, Eulalee, when she told him this bit of news.

"That's right," she said.

"What, you mean like Greece, New York? Greece, Indiana? Greece, where?"

"No, Greece, Greece," she said. "They went to Athens, Greece. Clifton, too." There was a long silence.

"Clifton went, too," he said. "They just all left the country and went to Greece?"

"That's right," Eulalee replied.

After another long pause, Will said, "Okay, fine. Thanks." He called her back two more times just to make sure he had understood the situation correctly.

NOT SURPRISINGLY, GIVEN HIS PEDIGREE, Will proved to be a very fine—if a little inchoate—creative writer at Andover. His writing showed up publicly in the January 1976 issue of the *Mirror*, the school's literary magazine, which he was the editor of during his senior year. In his short story "The Drowning Fly," Will tried to capture the loneliness of Norman Humphries, a sixty-seven-year-old New York City cabdriver who never quite realized his ambitions, however modest. His father had been a successful restaurateur. But that was long ago. His wife had passed away the year before. "The ensuing decades had hardly feigned to help Normy realize his glorious ambitions," he wrote in slightly overwrought prose. "The cozy brownstone on 70th Street that he had raised, floor by floor in his youthful imagination had degenerated to the reality of one mean, bare room on Ninth Avenue and 47th, with flaking walls and sagging linoleum. His Mercedes Benz sedan was an aging taxi, bearing the odors of expensive liquors and tobacco from the breath of those who had realized the fulfillment of his fantasy. He had always cursed their successes and hated passionately their disgusting flippancy which so perfectly contrasted with his despair."

There was a whole lot of despair. "Joys and tragedies were not clearly defined in Normy's mind any longer," Will wrote. "They only represented fuzzy stopping points in the torporific flow of his rapidly collapsing consciousness, for he was wearily, inevitable [*sic*] growing old." Will's protagonist took comfort in a local bar and the friends he saw there regularly. There were the occasional daydreams about his beloved wife.

When he woke from one such daydream, he saw the aforementioned fly drowning in a glass of water on the windowsill.

It is tempting to think of the short story as subtle autobiography or foreshadowing. But who knows? Maybe it was just a seventeen-year-old's odd flight of fancy.

AT THE ANDOVER GRADUATION that June—a lovely and traditional ceremony, replete with bagpipers wearing kilts, held in front of the grand Samuel Phillips Hall in the center of the campus—my parents and my grandmother Margaret Hieken, my mother's mother, sat in a row right in front of Will's parents. My mother's family was from St. Louis, where my grandfather, a watchmaker, had settled after emigrating from Eastern Europe. Harry Truman was a big deal for anyone who lived in Missouri. Upon realizing that Harry Truman's only child was sitting behind her, my grandmother, a very proud and dignified woman not prone to fits of random public adulation, turned to Margaret Truman Daniel and said that she was from St. Louis and was a great admirer of Harry Truman. Apparently, that was not what Will's mother wanted to hear. She mumbled something and turned away. The message was clear: *Bug off.* Margaret Truman Daniel's reaction to Margaret Hieken became lore in our family: The one time my grandmother did a bit of celebrity gawking, she was rebuffed with extreme prejudice.

But from Will's mother's perspective, her ungraciousness was nearly understandable: By 1977, she was probably just sick and tired of people telling her about her father and what he meant to them. We like to hope that people such as Margaret Truman Daniel and Clifton Daniel would be charming and appreciative at such moments, but often they are not. This reality is always a bit jarring.

Will Daniel grappled his entire life with how to handle the fame and adulation that came from being the grandchild of the president of the United States. Were people cozying up to him because of him or because of his grandfather or because of his parents? In truth, Will detested his family pedigree and would often go out of his way to avoid the subject, to the point where months or even years would go by without his friends and professional colleagues having any idea that he was related to a US president. That's the way Will wanted it, and the way he figured was the best to cope with his family's fame and notoriety. He could pull off this bit of alchemy in the days before social media dominated our world because his last name was Daniel, not Truman, and because he couldn't have looked less like Harry Truman if he tried.

Cha Cha Hartwell began dating Will soon after graduation. They ran in the same New York social circles, but hadn't known each other well at Andover until they both participated in the same community service program during our senior year. After graduation, they sublet an apartment together in Allston, near Cambridge, for two months. By definition, it was destined to be a short-term relationship. He was heading to Yale, in New Haven; she was going to Brown, in Providence. "I had my shitty little job and he had his shitty little job," she said. "He was working in a warehouse moving boxes." But she remembered that while she was catching up on her *People* magazine reading that summer, Will was reading *The Rise and Fall of the Third Reich*. "To me, that is a great example of who he was," she said. She added that Will "didn't do casual" or "mediocrity," or superficial. He was "one of the most brilliant people" she has known, "very demanding on himself" and "very intense." She explained that Will "was always up for a wonderful debate or conversation, philosophical or political or anything like that" but that he wasn't particularly interested in the "day-to-day" and chitchat of people's lives, the *How are you? I'm fine* conversations.

He was her first love. "That's always pretty special," she said. And then, at the end of the summer, he ended the relationship. "It got to a point where it was just too close to the bone and it was time for him to move on," she said. Her heart was broken. "I'm still getting over him," she said, joking only a little. Over the years, they did their best to stay in touch. "I'm a loyal friend," she said. She would write to Will every Christmas. "It would take him a few months to write back," she said. "There were a couple of letters that got returned because he kept on moving and so I finally just started sending my letters to his parents' address" on Park Avenue. His letter back berated her. "I'm now 35 years old," he wrote. "I do have my own place. Believe it or not I've moved out of my parents' house." But when she sent a letter to the new address he had given her, she never heard back from him. He had moved again.

WILL HAD BEEN A SHOE-IN AT YALE, probably due more to his family's stature than his academic performance at Andover. But if this bothered him, he showed no outward signs of it. He wasn't caught up in the school's elite image or the cachet it conferred when dropped into certain conversations. "Yale was important to him because he really felt it was the best education he could get," Hartwell said. "It was going to challenge him the most." Miriam Cytryn first crossed paths with Will one day at Rudy's, a New Haven bar frequented by generations of Yale students. She was the daughter of Holocaust survivors who settled in Forest Hills, Queens. Amid beers, the group they were with started talking politics, and eventually they got around to weighing the wisdom of Truman's decision to drop the two nuclear bombs on Japan. "This blond-haired guy at the other end of the table was taking a very hard stance," Cytryn recalled. He was arguing that it was "irresponsible" without better information for Truman to have dropped those bombs. He was publicly questioning the decisions of his own grandfather, and not for the last time, either. "You are the president of the United States and you have some obligation to not act until you know more," he said to the group.

Cytryn disagreed, vociferously. She broke into the debate. "I may have an unpopular view," she said, "but it's unfair to go back and think about what the president knew then with what we know now." She had been raised by her father to believe that Truman had been "good for the Jews." Eventually the conversation shifted to other topics. As she was leaving with her friend, Jim Logue, the son of the mayor of New Haven, said to her, "Do you know who you are arguing with?"

"Will something," she said.

"You have no idea who he is, do you?" he asked.

Will and Miriam clicked and became lifelong friends. She was the person Will would invite to join him at important family gatherings and ceremonies. The women who became romantically involved with Will tended to be short-term relationships or not people he felt comfortable introducing to his parents. But Miriam was special to Will. Even though their New York City backgrounds could not be more different, they got each other. They joked about how while their parents may have once upon a time paid the same amount for a Park Avenue triplex or a house in Forest Hills, over the years the value of the two diverged materially. She visited Will at 830 Park. She visited Will at the Daniel house on Fire Island. She was his date at Clif's wedding in Wilmington, North Carolina, and then at the reception at Wrightsville Beach. She was with him at the christening of a nuclear submarine named after his grandfather. He came to Passover seders at the Cytryn house in Forest Hills. She found him to be warm, intelligent, funny, and misunderstood. He could also be aloof, shy, cool, and terribly sarcastic. "There were a lot of different pieces of him and so all of those things ring true and yet I can come up with a lot of examples of how engaging he was," she said. "And I think a lot of it depended upon who he was with. I was someone I would say that over many, many, many years, he trusted, and so there was no argument or front that we couldn't get over or through. The expectation was that we were family and that was a natural part of a relationship." He dubbed her Space Station Mir.

After his freshman year at Yale, Will took a sabbatical. During his year off, Tom Hartman, our Andover classmate who was then at the University of Texas, picked up Will in New Orleans and together they began a summer road trip from Texas to the Pacific Coast of the United States. They went from New Orleans to Austin, from Austin to El Paso, and then to the Grand Canyon, where by complete coincidence they ran into another Andover graduate who was working as a park ranger that summer. From the Grand Canyon, the two friends went to Los Angeles and then drove on US 1 to San Francisco, to Portland, and to Seattle. They had one scary moment when the clutch of Tom's Saab broke as they were heading out of the Oregon hills into Portland. Will had never driven a clutch before and they ended up coasting into Portland—while constantly on the lookout for those gravel-filled truck runoffs that line treacherous highways across the country—to get a new clutch. In Washington State, they stayed on an island near Seattle with another Andover friend. They parted ways there and Will flew home. But the trip did not end well. And where once Tom would invite Will and a bunch of other Andover friends, including Will Iselin (Will Daniel's longtime childhood friend), to his family's house in Vermont, after the road trip during the summer of 1978, Tom no longer invited Will. "They were traveling together, and it ended up very badly, and Tom has really bad memories of Will," Will Iselin explained. (Hartman declined to be interviewed about Will.)

During Will's wanderlust year, his parents did not know how to reach him. Will's Yale friend Marc Wallis remembered that he and Will agreed to room together in an apartment on Elm Street, across the street from Rudy's, when Will returned to Yale from his walkabout in the fall of 1979. Marc received a letter from Will's father, dated September 11, 1979: "Dear Marc. We do not seem to have an address or telephone number for William. If you see him, please ask him to telephone. Sincerely, Clifton Daniel." "That short note speaks volumes," Wallis said.

Sharing an apartment with Will, Wallis learned about his idiosyncrasies. Will loved the Grateful Dead and the Allman Brothers. Like his grandfather he loved to drink bourbon. He loved to procrastinate.

On the other hand, when it was time to get things done, Wallis said Will knew how to buckle down. He used to sit in "this big easy chair" in the living room and place a two-by-ten board across the chair's flat arms. "And voilà," Marc said, "there was a desk and that's where he would read and where he would write." All the furniture in the apartment was secondhand, stuff they picked up at Goodwill and the Salvation Army. Will also hated overhead lighting. He only liked indirect lighting. "He hung these tapestries up over the ceiling to block the ceiling light," Wallis said. He was neat without being obsessive. And Will liked to keep himself in good shape. He had a chin-up bar in the doorway to his bedroom and no matter how much he smoked or drank, with a preference for Wild Turkey, he somehow managed to get up the next morning and go for a five-mile run.

Will loved his brother Harrison, who was four years younger and born with developmental difficulties. "He absolutely adored Harrison and so when he would come home from breaks he would arrange it or ask someone to arrange for Harrison to be home, too," said Cha Cha Hartwell. Harrison had been sent away to boarding school but not to Andover or Milton. He went to a school for learning disabled kids until he was nineteen and aged out. "It was never the same for him after that," Clif said. After a few unsatisfactory stops in between, Harrison ended up at a facility in Pennsylvania. "Will went to visit him," he explained. "Will took it upon himself to care about Harrison, to go and see him. And didn't like what he saw, didn't like the way they were taking care of Harrison. He didn't like the facility. He didn't like the people. He didn't like mainly the fact that they were giving Harrison a cocktail of drugs meant to manage people with serious psychoses."

Clif explained that Harrison did not have "serious mental issues." He did have "anger management problems," but these stemmed mostly from not fully understanding why he was being separated from his family. In the proper doses, the medicine "calms you down and evens you out," Clif continued. But Will examined the drugs, and the amounts, that the Pennsylvania facility was administering to Harrison. He was infuriated and became a forceful advocate for moving his brother to New York State, into a better program, closer to home. "Dad got his back up," Clif said. "This was *his* responsibility. He was the father. And so for several years, he and Will argued and fought over Harrison's care. And Will wound up being able to educate Dad." In the end, Will prevailed and the Daniels moved Harrison to a group home in northern Westchester, where he remains and has been much happier than he had been previously. But a tension remained between Will and his parents.

The writer Melissa Bank and Will dated for about four years in the early 1990s. She and Will always had a birthday party for Harrison, and often Will's parents would be there. She got to know them pretty well. She knew that Will was somewhat estranged from his parents but got along better with his mother than with his father. She preferred his father. "His father was really charming and elegant, smart and interesting, and I think he was, in his own way, devoted to Harrison," she said. "His mother just gave off this vibe that was *Get away from me.* That was her primary mode." Bank said Margaret Truman struck her as "kind of like a little girl in a way," and she wondered if that was because her father had been president of the United States. Fathers of all stripes are important to their children. "But what if the world corroborated your feeling about your father being the most important person in the world?" She said that might make your head spin and account for a certain amount of aloofness. "To me," she continued, "it seemed at once that she was sort of needy and also really standoffish, which is a terrible combination to be around to tell you the truth."

AFTER WILL'S YEAR AWAY FROM YALE, he returned to the apartment on Elm Street where he lived with Marc and another Yale student, Bill Parker. Will and Bill did not get along. Their dislike for each other was so intense that Will decided to move to another apartment across the street to get away. Will moved in with Mike Boschelli, who had rented an apartment next to Rudy's. He knew nothing about Will's lineage. "I had no frickin' clue and I didn't for a couple years," he said. "He was just a guy I hung out with. I never asked any questions. He never told me anything. I didn't have a clue. Finally, somebody told me. I think I was a sophomore. But he never talked about it."

One weekend that year, Will invited Boschelli to New York City. He didn't tell him where he lived. They took the train down to Penn Station, then took a cab to 830 Park Avenue. Will showed Boschelli around. He couldn't believe what he saw. "Jesus Christ," he said, "a big, huge place with a grand staircase." They had dinner with Will's parents, who were apologizing profusely that they had to order in because it was the cook's night off. "I think I'll be all right," he told the Daniels. Boschelli liked to read mystery novels, and they started talking about books they liked. He said he was then reading *Murder in the White House*, which had recently been published. Will's mother turned to Boschelli and said, "I wrote that book." He thought she was kidding. "I never put it together," he said. "I guess I didn't know too much about the history of the family. . . . The dad really was having a good time laughing at me because I was sort of surprised by some of the things that they were telling me. I was like, 'Wow. This is cool.'" He learned a lot, met Will's brothers, drank, and had a good time in New York City. "It was a surprising weekend for me," he recalled. He always admired Will. "He was truthful," he said. "He said what he meant. He meant what he said. He was forthright. I enjoy that in a person. Given my choice, those are the kind of people I hang out with. He was that guy. That's all, nothing else, nothing more spectacular than that. He had the right stuff."

WILL HAD DIFFICULTY PICKING A MAJOR at Yale. Although he ended up majoring in sociology, he took a lot of different courses—

history, philosophy, literature, cultural anthropology, and art history. Yale allowed for some curricular freedom at that time, and Will indulged himself. His bigger problem, by far, was his ongoing inability to finish his Yale thesis, then a graduation requirement. Boschelli said that Will just didn't want to do it. "It's not that he couldn't do it," he said. "He could do it in a minute, but he just didn't want to do it." Will was stubborn. "If he had something in his mind, he did it," he continued. And vice versa. "At that point I assumed he was going to go back and get it, but I didn't really follow up." Eventually, Will put something together on his thesis but not remotely in a timely way. "It was one hundred pages of great prose," Cytryn remembered, although she could not recall what it was about. Melissa Bank seemed to remember it being about homeless voters but she wasn't certain. Neither of Will's two brothers, Clif and Thomas, could remember what it was about, either. All anybody could remember about Will and his Yale thesis was that his inability to finish it meant that he could not graduate in 1981 from Yale, along with the rest of his classmates. "I think it probably was not a good moment," Cytryn said.

The unfinished thesis loomed for years. Clif remembered one hot summer day, after he left UNC, when he was living back home at 830 Park Avenue and Will came home from Yale. "He had papers spread all over our bedroom trying to get that thing squared away," he said.

In 1980, Mark Bodden was a young administrative assistant to longtime New York congressman Charles Rangel, in Washington, when he met Will. This was on another of Will's breaks from Yale. He was working for the Natural Resources Defense Council, in Washington. Bodden and his partner at the time had bought a house together on Capitol Hill and rented out the room on the top floor to Will for $200 a month. Sometimes Bodden would run with Will. But that was rare. "He ran a lot farther than I would run," he said. Bodden recalled one encounter with Will in particular from their time together in Washington. Bodden was getting ready to go to the annual White House

Correspondents' Dinner. He was getting dressed up, suit and black tie, the required uniform. Will came downstairs and asked where Bodden was going. He told Will. "You may see my mom," Will said. Bodden thought nothing of the odd-seeming remark. He had not the slightest clue about Will, or to whom he was related, because of course Will had revealed nothing. But when he thought about it, later, he couldn't quite fathom how the grandson of Harry Truman could have lived in Washington without anyone having the slightest idea.

A year or so later, both Will and Bodden were living in New York City. Bodden was working for the state of New York as the assistant commissioner of housing. Will lived in Manhattan, on East 96th Street, with some Andover friends. They played squash together and would go to Mets games. Bodden remembered Will once ran from Manhattan to Shea Stadium, near LaGuardia Airport. Bodden visited the Daniel house in Point o' Woods, even though it was not a particularly welcoming environment for a black gay man. He remembered one time at dinner, Clifton Daniel was pontificating on some subject involving the state government. Will cut his father off. "Mark is currently in government," he said. "Let him speak."

Every spring, in March, for about five years in a row, Will and Bodden would spend a week together in Florida for spring training. They would go to one or two games a day, go for a run—Bodden would have to turn around and meet Will later because Will would run for more than ninety minutes—and then they'd go to dinner, drink, smoke cigarettes, and drive around town. They each brought their cameras to Florida and took photographs of the players. Once, when they were back in New York, they went to dinner together at a Tex-Mex restaurant on Third Avenue. "I remember it vividly," Bodden said. They were sharing pictures from their most recent trip to Florida. They were talking about the friendship Bodden had with Charlie, a high school friend that Will knew.

"You two are gay, aren't you?" Will asked.

"No," Bodden replied. "Charlie and I have known each other since high school and we've done everything together but he's not gay."

"Why have you never said anything about [being gay]?" Will asked his friend. Bodden explained to Will that he was a "private person" and that there was no need to broadcast his sexual preference. At that point, Bodden remembered, Will stood up from the table and came over to him and said, "You know, if you tell people, they still love you anyway." Will's comment stayed with Bodden. "He knew," he said, "but he made a point of just letting me know that it didn't make any difference to him."

One of the people Will was in touch with when he was living on East 96th Street was his old friend Richard Riker. In the summer of 1982, Will wanted to go skydiving. Riker was living for the summer at his family's estate in Rumson, New Jersey. Rumson was near Lakehurst, where there is a small—but infamous—airport, from which people can go skydiving. (It is where the *Hindenburg* blew up in 1937.) Will took the train down to Rumson, spent the night at the Riker house, and went out drinking with Richard. Riker was understandably nervous. He had never skydived before. Will had been skydiving once. He was gung ho. Richard was not. Plus, at around $300, it was expensive. "Which probably seemed like $1,000 at the time because I wasn't working," Riker said. "I just got out of college. I had no fucking money." But Will was determined. "It's the greatest fuckin' thing," Will told him. They drove together the next morning to Lakehurst in Riker's car.

They paid and then had a three-hour training session. "I remember all the things they teach you," Riker said. "Actually the way you do it, you don't get to jump out of the plane, you actually have to stand. You have to climb out on a wing and you hold on while the fucking plane is going and then you let go. I'll never forget this. They teach you this technique." He was especially nervous about what is called ground rush, where it's very difficult to judge when you're going to hit the ground. It turns out that with an open parachute a skydiver accelerates at a constant rate, not an increasing rate. People often tense their legs too early, and lots of legs get broken as a result. Riker didn't want that to happen to him. "All of a sudden it's like the ground hits you, which is actually what it felt like," he said. He was very focused during the training session. "I don't wanna fuckin' die," he said. "Will was focused, too, 'cause you can't fuck around with this. We're gonna jump out of a plane."

They got on a little Cessna, with the seats removed. The plane itself further rattled Riker. "I'm thinking to myself, *Forget about it*," he said. "All I wanna do when I get in that plane is get out of that plane. That plane looks so dangerous. That looks like more of a death trap even than jumping out of it. I actually was happy to get out." Back then, first-timers jumped alone, without being attached to an instructor. They each had two parachutes, in case one failed to open. Up they went to four thousand feet. "It's a short ride," he said. "They don't take you super high, but it's still getting out of a fuckin' plane." He wore a headset so that the instructor could talk him through what he needed to do, from jumping out of the plane itself to trying to steer himself on the way so that he landed in the big sand pit, instead of the hard ground. The plane was shaking around. Riker jumped out. "All I remember is my mind went blank," he said. "I remember seeing the tail go by. The next thing you know is you get that huge yank. Then it's like 'Whoa, this is fuckin' great.' So afterward, of course, we probably went back and had a bunch of drinks and talked about how cool it was. I have to say it's the only time I've ever skydived, but it's thanks to Will Daniel that I went. My one and only skydiving and it was because he said, 'I wanna do this again.'"

Cocktail hour on East 96th would last for hours, often into the wee hours of the morning. Everyone was drinking wine or beer. But not Will. "Will, you really love Jack Daniel's, I notice," our friend Phil Balshi said to him once. Will replied, "In the grand tradition, my grandfather was a bourbon man, and it just so happens that this has my name on it." One drunken night at the apartment, Balshi remembered, was particularly amusing because Will had brought home a young woman and they were together in Will's small room, off the kitchen. Eben Keyes, an Andover graduate who rented out the rooms in the apartment to other Andover grads, "was in his cups," Balshi said, and at around one in the morning decided to clean up the dinner dishes that had been deposited in the sink. "He's trying to make love to this woman," Balshi continued. "And in the meantime, Eben's on the other side of the door, and he's cleaning up, banging pots all around, drunk as could be. And Will's in there, in the other room. And all of a sudden, the door opens, and Will walks out, half a wreck, and says, 'Eben, excuse me. Could you keep it down? I'm trying to, you know, make love in the other room.' And Eben turns to Will and said, 'Well, Will, I'm sorry. But to quote your grandfather, the fuck stops here.'"

IN 1985, BODDEN ASKED WILL if he wanted to help him run the political campaign of Tom Webber, who was running a long-shot campaign for a seat on the New York City Council from a district in East Harlem. Will took the job and got paid a small amount. It was his first paid job since he had left Yale without his degree. "He didn't need the money, but I wanted to pay him because that was what I felt we needed to do," Bodden said. Will worked in the office while Bodden was at Webber's side, campaigning in the district. He arranged for a group of volunteers to join Webber's team. "He worked his butt off for change," Bodden said, "but did a great job." Webber came in fourth.

In 1987, Bodden said, "continuing his pursuit of adventures that his parents would not be happy about," Will tried out for a spot on a AAA baseball team as an infielder. This ambition seemed to come out of left field, so to speak, and was further evidence of Will's contrarian nature. He had not been on the baseball team at either Andover or Yale but did love playing pickup softball. Bodden drove Will to the tryout, in Connecticut. But it didn't work out. "He wasn't happy with his performance," he said. "He was his toughest critic in terms of life, at least in my experience with him. He would always say he could be doing more. He could be doing better." Bodden thought that what Will really wanted to do was not to play baseball but rather to become a writer, or a journalist. He said Will was "a brilliant writer," who would have pursued that but for his father having been the former managing editor of the *New York Times*. "Other kids would say my father is the editor of the *New York Times* so I'm going to get a job at the *New York Times*," Bodden said. "But he didn't want to do that. He didn't want to use any of those connections. He fought that. I give him credit for that because other young people in that situation would have used that, but he pushed back." On several occasions over meals with the Daniel family in both New York City and Fire Island, Bodden listened as they discussed the subject of Will's professional future. It was clear that Clifton Daniel did not appreciate his son's intransigence. He said that Will "not only refused" to use his family connections to advance his career prospects "but held on to it and fought it." Recalled Bodden, "It was something about him, in his personality, that whatever he did he wanted to do on his own and he didn't want it to be perceived that he was becoming a writer or whatever it was by virtue of the connection to his family."

WILL WAS DETERMINED TO FOLLOW his own path in life, free of his extraordinary parental or familial connections. And of the relationships he'd made at either Andover or Yale. He did not want to be remotely beholden to anyone or anything. He could have easily worked at the *New York Times* or pursued his political connections. Or, like so many of our generation, Will could have easily gone to Wall Street and become an investment banker or a trader. He could have made a lot of money. But none of these careers, or any other typical corporate job, was for him. Even though he told Mark Bodden he wanted to be a journalist, he did not pursue journalism. Even though he had enjoyed the political campaign he worked on in East Harlem, he did not pursue politics. In contrast with Clif, who eventually embraced his DNA and worked for a time at a newspaper in Wilmington, North Carolina, which was owned by the New York Times Publishing Company, Will wanted to be as far removed from his family as could be reasonably accomplished.

There remained the unfinished Yale thesis, like some sort of Sword of Damocles. In October 1982, Will had written to Wallis, "Still haven't finished my senior essay; however, as Mao was fond of saying, 'There's great disorder under the Heavens and the situation is excellent.' And that's Will in just succinctly describing this—that he hasn't finished it, but all is well. It'll get done."

That same month, the Daniel family reunited in Independence, Missouri, for the funeral of Bess Truman, who died at ninety-seven. She had outlived her husband by ten years and had spent most of that time in isolation in the big home they had shared together. The service for Bess Truman, at the same church in Independence where Will's parents were married, was a "simple" one, Clif wrote. He and Will read passages from the Bible. Nancy Reagan, Rosalynn Carter, and Betty Ford sat in the front row of the church, near his family. Wallis wrote a note of condolence to Will and received a note back in return: "Thanks for the kind words about my grandmother. She was the balls."

But behind the impressive tableau raged a titanic family feud, instigated by Clif, who had invited to accompany him to the funeral a random-seeming couple whom he had befriended. Clif's invitation did not go over well, especially with his mother and Will. His brother's "opposition" to the idea was "violently vocal," he wrote. He recalled "an emotional scene" in the dining room at 830 Park, where Will referred to Clif's friends as "leeches," out only for "the thrill and the publicity." Clif wrote that he did not view his friends this way in the least and that he had never been aware of people who befriended him as a way of somehow sharing in the Truman limelight. Will disagreed. Clif wrote that his brother hated the "thought of having his privacy invaded by Trumanophiles." He quoted Will saying, "'I was always made to feel like being Harry Truman's grandson was the best part of me'"—a feeling he resented mightily, and so he hated "'people coming up to me and wanting to talk to me just because some son of a bitch was my grandfather.'"

Cytryn said that Will disliked Clif's "opportunistic" bent when it came to the Truman name. "He was uncomfortable with his brother's comfort level with being Truman's grandson and trading on that," she said. Will always said he did not want it to be that the first thing people thought of him was as Harry Truman's grandson. "I had an adversarial relationship with him for years," Clif said. "But that was just us. For everybody else, it was the opposite. He took care of a lot of people and he did not like being associated with our grandfather. I found that out the hard way." He had just finished writing *Growing Up with My Grandfather* and was out at dinner at an Italian restaurant in New York with Will and two of Will's friends. At one point, Will's friends asked Clif what he did for a living. Clif said he was a writer. They wanted to know what he had written lately.

"Well, I've just finished a book," Clif said.

"Well, really?" they said. "A book on what?"

"On our grandfather," Clif said. They looked at him blankly. "Who's your grandfather?"

Clif said, "And I looked at Will. Oh, he was mad. And I said, 'Harry Truman.' And they're like, 'Really?' And, God, he took me apart afterward. He said, 'Goddammit. I don't tell people that.'"

But Clif continued, "How was I supposed to know? And what was I supposed to do when they asked all the questions? . . . He didn't tell anybody. So he didn't want that to be who he was."

WILL HAD INHERITED A TRUST fund when he turned twenty-one. Cytryn noted that Clif went through his trust fund quickly but Will was far more prudent. The trust fund enabled Will to be more cavalier about his Yale diploma than most other people might have been. He did not see it a prerequisite for a corporate job or even as a way to pursue a graduate degree (although he later would). If he got around to finishing his Yale undergraduate thesis, so be it; if not, well then, he would figure out how to still do what he wanted to do in life, even if he did not get the Yale degree.

Will Iselin said that after Will came into his inheritance, he never felt the pressing need to get a summer job or pursue the kind of career path that others with less means would likely feel more compelled to do. "It wasn't like he was spoiled or extravagant or anything like that," Iselin said. But, he continued, the income from the trust fund was throwing off enough cash for him not to worry about getting a corporate job. There was also enough money "to buy plenty of recreational drugs," he said. After college, he and Will would often meet up at the Daniel apartment on Park Avenue. "We'd sit in the library and we'd talk intense politics, literature, whatever—his brain was always incredibly sharp—and do a lot of coke," he said. "Not all the time, but we'd drink a lot of bourbon, smoke a lot of cigarettes until three, four, five in the morning, and then I'd go home and go to bed and we'd get up and do it again the next night."

Will moved around a lot, mostly in and around New York City. He lived on 100th Street, between Broadway and West End Avenue. He lived on West 10th Street in Greenwich Village. He lived in Carroll Gardens, Brooklyn. He talked about leaving New York City completely, and moving to Portland, Oregon, or Portland, Maine. He never moved to either one. He lived in Hoboken for a while, in a firehouse once owned by Frank Sinatra's father. He eventually moved to a rental apartment in Englewood, New Jersey, an upscale suburb just north of New York City but an easy commute into it. He lived simply. "He didn't have a lot of furniture," remembered Clif. "You remember how you guys used to live at Andover? Cinder blocks and boards for shelves, stereo, couple of comfortable chairs, mattress. He did not spend a lot of money on furniture."

After a few years working at NRDC out of his apartment in Greenwich Village, Will decided to start a program to register the homeless to vote. He recruited both Cytryn and Bodden for the board of directors. "It was a huge idea at least at the time to support, to re-enfranchise the most disenfranchised into the system so they could represent their own interests and have a voice," Cytryn said. "There were some substantial court cases and then there were the homeless voter drives. That was the kind of thing that Will had passion for. That was rewarding."

Benjy Swett, another Andover friend, was working for a time for the New York City parks department. Swett remembered Will calling him at the parks department and asking him if he wanted to join him in Fort Tryon Park as he visited the homeless and tried to get them to register to vote. Swett agreed. Since he knew the park well, from living nearby, he knew where the homeless tended to congregate. He and Will went into the park and immediately saw a homeless man sleeping. "He had sort of a plastic thing over him," Swett recalled. "And Will just started talking to him. And the guy opened up to him. And Will had this way. He didn't say 'homeless.' He said, 'How long have you lived outside?' And he had worked out ways of talking to homeless people where it felt he was going to approach them right. He got the guy's name. And he gave the guy information about how he could register to vote. He had this long conversation."

From there, the two Andover graduates headed farther up the park, to the area north of the Cloisters. It was very woodsy, and there were many homeless people living there. "We went to all the most dangerous parts of the park," Swett said. "And Will just approached people and got them talking and somehow got them interested. People who you wouldn't know how to approach exactly. Somehow he was able to go up to them and start something. It just really impressed me."

He noted that Will "was not that social" and the only other times he would hear from him were when he was having trouble getting a permit to access the softball fields in Central Park. While many other people his age and status were busy during the summer with their rentals in the Hamptons, Will wanted nothing to do with such things. He rarely would go to visit his parents in Fire Island. Instead, he was very committed to playing softball in Central Park. Swett was the one who put Will in touch with the guy who was in charge of the softball field permits in Central Park. "After that, every year at permit time he would call me up for his softball permit," Swett said.

In 1986, while still living in Wilmington, North Carolina, and working for the newspaper there, Clif married Polly Bennett, a waitress at a local restaurant. Will spent the night of Clif's wedding in jail, in Wrightsville Beach, North Carolina, after he had been arrested for drunk driving. Miriam Cytryn had gone with Will to his brother's wedding and spent the night in jail, too. She had been a passenger in the car, but was not arrested. She just felt that she belonged next to Will that night. "When you think back about your life," she said, "buried in some of the funniest moments are some of the scariest moments. And a really high percentage of them have Will in them."

A few months before Clif's wedding, in the spring, Will's penchant for idealistic principles nearly caused a national incident, and certainly resulted in a healthy dollop of family embarrassment. In May 1986, the navy invited Margaret Truman and her family to rededicate the USS *Missouri*, a World War II–vintage battleship that had been rebuilt with nuclear power and nuclear missiles. In January 1944, when she was Senator Truman's nineteen-year-old daughter, Margaret Truman had christened the *Missouri* with a bottle of sparkling wine made from Missouri grapes. Forty-two years later, she had been asked to do it again.

For several months before the actual event, Cytryn discussed with Will whether he could behave sufficiently to attend. "Are you sure you're going to be able to do this?" she asked him. "Can you just act as your mother's son? Can you not be Will Daniel, thinking man, man with opinions?" Will gave her questions serious consideration. He decided he could do it, even though he was passionate about his opposition to nuclear weapons and nuclear power.

The navy flew the Daniel parents to San Francisco for the event, along with Clif, Polly, Harrison, and Will. Will invited Miriam to go along, too, as his date. For her, that meant getting a bunch of new clothes she could ill afford. They all flew from the Marine Air Terminal at LaGuardia Airport. "Will came along for the ride in person, if not in spirit," Clif remembered. "The day we flew out of New York, he was wearing a black NO NUKE button on his jacket lapel." According to his brother, Will objected to Ronald Reagan's remilitarization efforts, including the creation of a six-hundred-ship fleet, and how Reagan was diverting billions of dollars to the military and away from social programs that might help the less fortunate. A naval escort met the family, and they were ushered by limousines into town. Clif wrote that when the Daniel family got to their hotel in San Francisco, there were protestors behind barricades. He allowed that had the rededication been back in New York City, Will would have been out protesting it, too.

That night, there was a dinner in San Francisco in honor of Margaret Truman and the *Missouri*. Clif thought a US senator spoke, as did a navy clergyman. They both criticized the protestors. Will lost it. "Will could not sit in his seat," Miriam remembered. "He was breaking out in hives. He couldn't go through with it. And basically all I could do was say, 'Let's talk about it after dinner.' We went to the bar. We had a couple drinks and he said, 'We need to leave. I can't do this.'" She urged him to sleep on it; if he still felt he could not attend the ceremony, she would leave with him. His objection was a simple one: Nobody would give Will the assurances that the *Missouri* would never be nuclear-armed. As a result, he couldn't sanction the recommissioning. He told his mother that he was sorry but he could not attend the ceremony.

Cytryn wished it had not turned out this way. "That was not the first

time in my friendship with Will that something would be over the top,"
she said. "Moderation was not his skill set, or at least his strongest skill
set. Part of the excitement of being around him and with him were the
wonderful, wonderful highs. But there were absolutely terrible lows and
there were absolutely terrible out of bounds, too. So let me put this in
the bucket of that. I would not have expected it. We talked about it
ahead of time so there was some recognition that this could pull a string
and create a reaction. But I thought the talking-out of it meant we had
explored it and it wouldn't happen."

WHEN MELISSA BANK MET WILL, in 1990, he was running the homeless voter program out of his dingy West Village apartment. They were
introduced by two friends of her brother. There was a birthday party
out in Westhampton—where Will rarely went—and her two friends
thought she should meet Will since she had recently broken up with
her boyfriend. "Then I fell in love with Will," she said. "I was with him
on and off for about four years." She said she had an immediate physical attraction to him. "I was crazy about him," she said. "I really was."
Thanks to her friends, who had known Will at Andover, she knew about
his family background. But, she said, "in all the time that I knew him,
I never remember him telling anybody about his family. In fact, when
somebody would say something, he would turn to me and say, 'How
did she know about my grandfather?' or something like that. He wasn't
secretive exactly, but it wasn't something he told other people." She
remembered that once they were discussing the likely prospect that his
mother didn't write the mystery novels that carried her name. He
thought that his mother was "capitalizing" on the family name. For
some reason, she asked him, "Would you mind very much if when I
publish, if I publish a book, if I call myself 'Melissa Truman'? And he
said, 'Why don't you just call yourself Harry Truman?' So, yeah, I think
he did want to go his own way." (In June 1999, Bank did publish a novel,

The Girls' Guide to Hunting and Fishing, under her own name, about finding sex and love in the big city. She included a chapter about one boyfriend who bore more than a striking similarity to Will.)

Bank convinced Will to buckle down, finish his thesis, and graduate from Yale, which he did—finally—in 1991, just as Yale's ten-year statute of limitations was expiring. She told him it was "stupid" and "pointless" that he had been so foolish to let getting his college diploma hang over him. "He just decided at a certain point that he was going to do it and he did it," she said. To celebrate, she threw a small graduation party for him and a few friends. "He didn't seem really happy about it," she recalled. She conceded there were plenty of ups and downs in her relationship with Will. "He was really always wearing the white hat," she said. "I liked his politics and he just always seemed to be on the right side. . . . Will and I had a lot of fun. We just had a lot of fun." But it was also often really tumultuous. "He was somebody who was really depressed and I didn't really understand depression yet," she continued. "He'd gone through a lot of analysis and was still going through analysis, and I had very limited experience with therapy, and there are things that I sort of understand now that I really didn't then. He was a really angry guy. . . . It may have been that his upbringing made him angry or made him who he was, but anger was a feature. It was a personality trait. It wasn't that he would become furious with his parents when he got angry. He was a really tormented man."

In January 1992, Will wrote Wallis a letter. "Here in the city that never sleeps," he allowed, "we are too afraid of getting robbed. I'm working part-time with homeless people in the main bus terminal, so I don't become homeless myself. I'm looking for a real job somewhere in city government. Looking for work in this economy is like looking for sushi in George Bush's refrigerator." He then referred to Melissa Bank. "I'm also still with the woman I met 14 months ago making this the longest running relationship I've had since 1973," he continued. "Actually it's very hard to reconstruct them all with any exactness. Somehow we got at the point where she tells me she wants to make it permanent and I change the subject. And she gets really bummed out. And I feel really guilty. And we didn't split. Now what?"

"I think possibly when you're with somebody who causes you pain, they're empowered as the only person who can get you out of pain," Bank said. "So we would take breaks and be separate for a time and then come back together. We were very bonded. . . . He just was an incredibly devoted boyfriend." He loved giving her quirky gifts, including things he had made himself. He gave her a black-and-white photograph of Batman and Robin "where you could see the seams of Batman's tights," she said. He made her a menorah out of coat hangers and a pair of shoes out of duct tape. He cut out animal stories from the newspaper and sent them to her. "It was incredible," she said, "and he was really, really romantic in a way, like everything to the nth degree."

They lived in separate apartments in Manhattan. At one point, Will decided he needed to move out of the West Village to Brooklyn as a way to save money. Bank thought the prospect of moving to Brooklyn made him nervous, or scared, and so he broached the idea of moving into her apartment. She thought about it, and seriously considered it only because she thought it might lead to "a major change" for the better in their relationship. "What I realized was that it would just be more of the same, and more of the same is not good," she said. "It wouldn't have calmed him or made him happier. It wasn't going to make us a happy couple. I couldn't do anything else and be with Will. I'm not sure I could've written that book and been with Will. He was so consuming and volatile." In retrospect, she remembered a few comments he made that gave her pause. Once, when visiting her mother, Will said that he was "against marriage" because "there's a property arrangement." He also said that if he were to have children, he'd want them to try all different kinds of drugs. "That just says, 'Don't think of me as a potential father, a mate exactly,'" she said. Things got so bad that she was hoping for an "apocalypse" so that she could use it as an excuse to get out or to see that he was "so committed to this relationship" that she needed to remain in it. "At times he really tried," she said, "and I think at times he really wanted to be together." He sent her a card that said, "Your boyfriend loves you to death," which bothered her: "There was a violence to it, or something dark also," she said.

To complicate matters further, Bank was diagnosed with cancer. She was undergoing chemotherapy and radiation treatments. As she was deciding to switch her radiation oncologist to a doctor at Columbia Presbyterian from a doctor at New York University, she was "really conflicted" and "upset." This was the moment that Will announced, "I love you and I want to move in with you." His timing could not have been worse. Then, as she was riding her bicycle up to Columbia Presbyterian, a car hit her. She lost consciousness and ended up at St. Vincent's Hospital, in the Village. She had been wearing a helmet but was concussed. She had "retrograde amnesia" for a year and couldn't make any new memories or remember things from one minute to the next. She couldn't even remember for sure if Will was, or had been, her boyfriend.

Between her cancer treatments, her concussion, and Will moving to Brooklyn, that was pretty much the end of things between them. She recalled it wasn't his finest moment. "He was really pretty shitty about the concussion stuff," she said, "and he didn't really believe me about the trouble I was having. It wasn't until later that he was told or read up and found out that actually, 'post-concussion syndrome' is a real thing that does cause these problems and wasn't something I was trying to inflict on him. I think it really was pretty much over at that point. I think we still saw each other sometimes, but he was seeing other people and I was seeing other people, I guess."

She still thinks about his dark side. "Will was in a lot of pain for most of the time I knew him, through all the time I knew him," she recalled. "He drank to get out of pain, and he took a lot of chances. I remember actually getting really angry with him when I did have cancer and he was talking about dying. I remember it was so much a part of my life at that moment that I felt it was frivolous to talk to me about death when it was just symbolic [for him], seeing at that moment what I was facing. But he was not careful, and the reason that he was not careful is that part of him wanted to get out of pain in a big way." She wondered if Will had a death wish. "You live carelessly partly because the worst thing in the world would not be if you died," she said. "He was in a lot of pain, and he put himself in situations, dangerous situations, as a result of that."

In the fall of 1995, Will was living in Park Slope. One night, Will Iselin and his English then-wife invited Will to dinner at their apartment on Columbus Avenue and 71st Street. Iselin was in the business of selling beautiful antique furniture to the people who could afford it. He and his wife had two young children. In other words, even though they both lived in New York City, Will Iselin was living a very different life than was Will Daniel. "I've never been a politically active human being, it's not my thing," Iselin said. "I should be, but I'm not. And so he knew that. He would always give me a hard time. He'd say, 'When are you going to actually do something? All you do is sell used furniture to rich people, and you should be doing something better, you should be doing something more worthwhile.' He was half joking, but there was definitely an edge to it, and he could have a very moralizing tone." Will was still pursuing his efforts to register homeless voters as well as playing a lot of softball in Central Park, as part of a team called the Cats and Dogs. It was an awkward evening, at best. "It was clear he couldn't relate," Iselin said. "Here I was with a wife and two kids and sort of a company job. I think it was very hard for him." Will's way of dealing with that uncomfortable situation was to more or less shut down. Iselin said the "curtain" would "come down" and "you could talk about all this stuff but you didn't really get very far." Will wasn't one to fill the gap in a difficult conversation. "I think that must have come very much from his mother," he said. "She was not a woman of many words."

Playing softball in Central Park twice every week became an integral

part of Will's New York City life. He started pushing some of the
other, better players in the Cats and Dogs to also play in a more competitive, and more organized, all-guys game on Tuesday. Will became
the captain and the pitcher of the team, which became known alter-
natively as the Fetchers, the Bad Dogs, and then, finally, the Mad
Dogs. They recruited recent college athletes to be their teammates. Not
everyone thought Will's obsession with softball was charming. Melissa Bank remembered that on their first date, Will took her to a Cats
and Dogs party. "I played on that stupid softball team," she said.

By then, Will had decided to abandon his project to register the
homeless to vote. Instead, he enrolled in a graduate degree program—
apparently to try to get his Ph.D.—in clinical psychology at Columbia
University. In early 1996, he wrote Wallis, "I am recruiting and assessing families for another genetic study of schizophrenia. This one at Columbia. Subjects are also being collected at Wash[ington] U[niversity]
among other places. Apparently, there are crazy people out your way
too. I have taken a leave of absence from the doctoral program to do
this full-time." Then Will turned to his love life. "I am also still looking for Ms. Right, if only to make the both of us miserable," he wrote.
"I'm making progress though. I have gradually reduced the time that
elapses between the first meeting and the final scene to almost zero.
My goal is to begin breaking up with a woman before I meet her so
we won't have it hanging over us."

Will never completed his doctoral work at Columbia. Instead, he
switched over to the school of social work and earned a master's degree
from the school in 1998. After he graduated, he came to the attention
of Dr. Steven J. Donovan, a professor in the psychiatry department at
the Columbia University Medical Center. It was a bit unusual for a student with a degree in social work to end up getting a gig at the medical
school. "But I remember particularly somebody telling me there were
two extraordinarily strong social work candidates graduating and that
I should interview them and so I did," Donovan said, "and I ended up

hiring Will." Donovan had a grant to study "explosive aggression in children," he explained, and he took an immediate liking to Will. "He was a terrific guy. We became friends and he contributed a lot to the intellectual life of the project." As usual, Donovan had no idea about Will or his family. Will never talked about the Truman connection, of course. Donovan just saw a smart guy who seemed interested in the work, with whom he got along well.

The purpose of the study was to test the effects of a drug—divalproex sodium—on children who were prone to mood swings and inexplicable outbursts of aggression. Will interviewed the children and adolescents who were to take part in the study. He helped to parse the study's findings and to accumulate the data. He did the psychotherapy with the adolescents. He completed the grading forms. He interacted with the main regulatory agency—the institutional review board. "He seemed to function very well on that level," Donovan said.

But during their work together on the study about disruptive adolescents, Donovan began to notice that Will, too, was capable of similar kinds of uncontrollable outbursts. He wasn't sure what was causing Will to behave in this way—if he perhaps was reacting to how the disruptive children were behaving. But he was pretty concerned about Will's odd mood swings. "His anger was uncontrollable," Donovan explained. "His need to yell. He would have to excuse himself and go yell and then he would come back as if nothing had happened. It was a bit of a mystery as to what was torturing him. I never got to the bottom of it."

Donovan said Will's strange behavior began to appear about a year into their work together. "I started hearing stories of him staying late at work and just not going home," he said. "He would pen these little notes to me sometimes. I remember one time he had been going through some old records of mine just because he was curious as to how I'd gotten this research going. He would give me little notes just saying he liked the idea that it started out with sort of hunches and I kept pursuing this thing and it eventually developed into something that was worth researching, something to that effect. It was nice in a way, but on the other hand I mean what's he doing at three in the morning plowing through these old records? What was he searching for? What was he trying to find?"

Will had been seeing a therapist for years. He told Donovan that this process wasn't bringing him any closer in touch with his deepest feelings. He was bottled up inside, a cliché of a middle-aged WASPy guy who could not reconcile the things that were bothering him. Donovan recommended that Will go see a friend, a well-respected analyst whom Donovan thought could help Will get to the bottom of some of his deep-seated issues, mostly related to the anger he seemed to harbor against his family, particularly his father. The new approach seemed to work, up to a point. "He felt more authentic and in touch with this stuff, but he just didn't know what to do with it," Donovan said. That's when he noticed Will would have uncontrollable outbursts of rage. He said Will's explanation of his strange behavior "never made complete sense to me," but he didn't want to probe into it in too much detail. "We were friends," he continued, "but on an intellectual level. . . . I didn't want to contaminate it with things that would force me to assume a clinical role." He thought that at some point in the sessions between Will and the new analyst "something got set off" and "it wasn't contained. It wasn't resolved."

Out came Will's anger at his family for how they treated Harrison. Out came Will's own feelings that he seemed stuck socially, unable to commit to a relationship while two of his brothers had settled down, married, and started families of their own. "When he talked about his family I remember, when his father was still alive, he was very, very angry at him and would write very angry letters," Donovan said. "He felt very warm toward his mother, but I noticed that he didn't have anything particularly good to say about his father. I didn't even know that his father was the editor of the *Times*." As often was the case with Will, Harrison—and the way he was being treated—was at the center of the rage he felt toward his father. "There continued to be a squabble about whether he was being bullied by some of the people at the Westchester place," Donovan recalled. "I remember coming into his office when he was working on sending a letter to his father or to the institution trying to help his brother."

Michaeline Bresnahan, an assistant professor of epidemiology at the Mailman School of Public Health, worked with Will on a follow-up study on people who had had congenital rubella during the last rubella epidemic. Will did the interviews with the patients to see whether there was an increased occurrence of either autism or schizophrenia in the population of adults that had been exposed to rubella during their mother's pregnancy. Occasionally, she and Will would take long car rides together to visit some of the rubella patients in the study. "We talked and talked and talked," she said. "And we talked about his brother, his disabled brother." She did not know that Will had two other brothers without learning disabilities. She only knew about Harrison because he was the brother Will wanted to talk about. She shared with Will that her son, Charles, was autistic. Will began trying to figure out whether Harrison might be autistic, too. Part of Will's journey was trying to figure out what was wrong with his brother.

She said Will thought about issues of mental illness deeply. "I don't know that he carried that with him all the time," she explained. "But when we were together, that's what we talked about and that's what he seemed to understand. And he raised questions about his brother a lot. And he was concerned about his brother's care, the quality of his brother's care. I mean, how many [brothers] are doing that? This was a person of incredible character who had finally gotten his life—whatever mishaps had happened and all of his getting lost along the way—he had gotten things straightened out. He was on a path. I don't know where he was going to go, but he was on a path and he was productive and he was contributing. And he had things to contribute. And he was a decent sort of person. He was a person of high moral character. Andover looks at him as a psychiatric social worker, and I'm sure a lot of people think, 'Loser guy.' And I look at him and I think that this was a real profound human being. . . . He was a person of substance. And his brothers probably don't have any clue. They have no clue."

DONOVAN HELPED WILL GET his next gig—working with homeless AIDS patients. In February 1997, Sarah Conover was leading a new study of HIV among homeless men—to follow up her previous work—and needed a full-time field coordinator, someone to work closely with her, and others, to find and interview the men who would participate in a study designed to find ways to get the men to change their behavior—for example, by wearing a condom—to reduce the incidence of HIV among their population. Conover was looking for someone who had previously worked with mentally ill adults in a clinical setting and who could work independently. The studies were all conducted near the Columbia University Medical Center in Upper Manhattan, at the Fort Washington Armory, which was then the largest homeless shelter in New York City. Some one thousand men lived there.

In recommending Will, Donovan told Conover about Will's inexplicable bouts of rage, which he thought was probably Tourette's syndrome. "He told me that he needed to have a kind of safe place to be where the Tourette's part of his behavior would not cause him troubles," Conover explained, "because it was [a problem] over at the psychiatric institute." Will would kick the elevator door. He would swear loudly and disturb his co-workers. People were getting concerned. But Conover worked out of an apartment near the medical center—not a typical work environment. The hope was that this would make it easier for Will if his anger persisted. "In the beginning, he frightened people," Conover said, "because he would put his fist through the door. One day I came in and there's a big hole in the door. And he would swear a lot." When

Will drove around with other team members, they were struck by how he would "always" swear at other drivers. "You sort of got the feeling that there was a spontaneity to some of it that was not controllable," she said. The odd behavior was chronic: "Every day he would have little outbursts." But, Conover continued, after she explained Will's condition to the other professionals involved in the study, they realized that his outbursts were not personal. He no longer frightened them. "When I explained this and then after he charmed them, everybody got over that," she said.

Conover's husband, Ezra Susser, was the chair of epidemiology at Columbia. Although Susser never was in a position to diagnose Will, he also described his behavior as consistent with Tourette's syndrome. "That was a major, major part of his life," he said, "and one of the reasons I think that he was working here, and not in some other kind of job. It was a significant thing. He would often have outbursts, where you say something, and you can't control it. People tend to say swear words and stuff like that." He said Will had had Tourette's "for ages" and "certainly long before he came to us and so he was living with it." (If so, this was news to his brothers Clif and Thomas, as well as to people who knew him best such as Melissa Bank, Richard Riker, or Will Iselin. They were aware of his temper, yes, but none of them ever thought he had Tourette's.) Susser said having Will be a part of the study of homeless men with HIV gave him "the room" to work with other people in an environment that would be forgiving to his penchant for random outbursts. "We were working with really down-and-out people, marginalized people, there were all kinds of people both who were among our patients, and then the staff, too, so that he fit into that niche very well," he said. "Everybody was very fond of him, and he was an excellent worker, and sort of irreplaceable."

Will did not strike Conover as being any particular "type." On the one hand, he had a kind of "macho" thing going, what with his wildish hair, goatee, and athletic build. "He was a puzzle to me," she said.

"He had this way of staring. Like when I first met him I was aware of that. . . . He struck me as sort of a jock but something different was in there." She realized that he was also an intellectual. "He was reading *Exodus*, the Leon Uris book," she said, "and he would talk about the Middle East. And he thought about things very carefully. He didn't match any mold, any preconception. So that when you sort of saw him you couldn't really make it out. And over time I don't know that I got any better at it. He was very good about people themselves. He really read people well."

I LIVE ON RIVERSIDE DRIVE and regularly go out running in Riverside Park, in a loop that goes between the tennis courts just west of Riverside Church and then down to 72nd Street. One day, it must have been in the fall of 1997, I was running along and saw Will Daniel sitting by himself on a bench in the park, down the hill from Riverside Church. I probably hadn't seen him in twenty years at that point, but he was instantly recognizable to me. I stopped and spoke to him. We had a nice conversation—I can't remember about what particularly— for the next ten minutes or so, during which he told me he was doing something or other involving clinical psychology up at the Columbia medical center. Our conversation reminded me that I'd always thought Will was a bit of an ethereal guy, and somewhat enigmatic. He was not aloof, per se, because that implies a certain negative standoffishness. But his quiet affect was always noticeable. Our conversation concluded, I continued on my run. On the way back home, I thought how nice it was to literally run into an old schoolmate after so many years. I also remember thinking how odd it was that Will was sitting by himself on a secluded bench in Riverside Park. It was the middle of the afternoon, his work was much farther uptown, in Washington Heights, and it seemed kind of random that he would be there, at that time of the day.

I was left with the feeling that he was lonelier than I had remembered him to be, and I had always remembered him to be a loner.

ON FEBRUARY 21, 2000, WILL'S FATHER DIED at the family's Park Avenue apartment, as a result of complications from a stroke and heart disease. He was eighty-seven years old. His lengthy front-page obituary in the *New York Times* came with all the attendant honors of a former managing editor, not to mention son-in-law of a president of the United States. The *Times* noted his numerous accomplishments, rising from a pharmacist's son in rural North Carolina to one of the most powerful men in America. The obituary noted that Clif, Will's brother, had written of his father in his memoir, "Dad is so impeccable that even in his undershirt he looks almost formal." After their father's funeral, the family went to a restaurant up the street. "And arguments started," Clif said. "So Will was really, really angry with Dad's funeral because— I got the sense because Dad died before Will could have any kind of reckoning with him. They had not come to some kind of understanding or agreement. Will was pissed that he hadn't reconciled."

From the perspective of Will's colleagues at the Columbia University Medical Center, the only thing that really mattered about Clifton Daniel's obituary was that Will Daniel was mentioned as Clifton's son. This came as big news to them.

In the days before his father died, Will told Conover that he was thinking of leaving the homeless men project and moving to Portland, Oregon, where the cost of living was lower than it was in Manhattan. He had been making some version of this statement to other friends for years. But after his father's death, Will seemed to reverse course. He decided to stay working on the homeless men project. He also decided to buy an apartment in a modest co-op building in Englewood, New Jersey, forcing him to commute each day back and forth across the

George Washington Bridge. "It was because he got an inheritance after his father's death and was able to afford it," Conover said. Terry Gruber, a friend from softball, thought Will's spare life might have been a political statement. "It seemed like he'd sacrificed his livelihood, in a way, to devote himself to this cause," he said. "At that point in time, with moving out of the city and stripping down his life, I think he just was rebelling against whatever the Hampton society people or the Park Avenue people wanted him to do."

MIMI GABER MET WILL AT THE WEEKLY SUNDAY softball game in Central Park during the summer of 1999. A graduate of Bennington College, she was twenty-nine years old. She was more or less an acquaintance of Will's, just enough to say hello to on Sunday and to also cheer for during the more serious league game during the week. She worked for Gruber at his professional photography studio downtown. Shortly after Will's father died, he saw Mimi at a party at the apartment of one of their mutual softball friends. There they had their first real conversation, beyond just joking around or saying hello on the softball field. And then Will asked her out on a date "in that sort of old-fashioned-y kind of way," she recalled. "He was fun and smart and everyone seemed to really like him and kind of follow him. . . . He had this really nice way of making sure that everyone was included." She also thought he was handsome. "He was in great shape," she said.

But of course, being Will, his approach to their dating was pretty loose and casual. "He asked me out, but it wasn't really for a date, it was just like, 'Hey, you wanna go get beers sometime?'" she explained. "Maybe once or twice a week, we would hang out, we would get together. We'd go have dinner or go have drinks or meet up after I did something, or meet up after he did something." At some point, as summer approached, their relationship turned romantic. "I don't know," she explained, "we just started hanging out a lot more. It turned from once or twice a week to three or four or five times a week." He was also casual about the kinds of things that most forty-year-olds were no longer casual about. Will was living an itinerant's life. "If he was out too late at a bar and couldn't get the last bus back to Englewood, he would find a couch to stay on, and if he couldn't find a couch to stay on, he would just go to his mom's," she said. "He was kind of carefree. He didn't worry about things like that. Most of us sitting in a bar at one in the morning would say, 'Oh my God, I gotta go, I gotta go get the bus,' and he would just not worry about it."

Often, Will slept on the couch at Terry Gruber's apartment at 103rd and West End Avenue. He had given up his landline—perhaps one of the first people to do so—and used his cell phone as his only form of communication. At nine o'clock at night, Will would call Gruber: "Hey, can I crash at your house? I'm really not up for going back to Jersey." Claudia, Gruber's wife, always agreed, and their son, Tim, thought it was great, too. "Uncle Will's coming!" They loved Will. But having Uncle Will around was not always joyous. "That's when I saw a more sadder, troubled, or complicated side of Will," Gruber said. "Will was not the most pleasant person, a little abrasive, but there was no animosity. *He's a bit of a curmudgeon* was how I saw it. At the same time, I felt that there was this pure gold-heart person there. . . . He was almost like a literary character out of a D. H. Lawrence. I always thought of him as this mysterious guy who didn't want to talk too much about anything related to him."

In April, Marc Wallis, one of Will's Yale roommates, invited him to a St. Louis Rams football game. Will responded with an email. "On the road," read the subject line. "Wally, thanks for your mail and sorry to take so long to respond," Will wrote. "I am a psychiatric social worker doing research with both sociopathic kids and severely mentally ill adults working at Columbia Presbyterian Medical Center living just across the George Washington Bridge in Jersey. Glad to hear you and your family are doing well and thanks for the invitation.

I'd like to get out of town, but lately it seems to be only on the spur of the moment because my work schedule is so crazy. But, I would like to take you up on it."

Early that summer, Will and Mimi "hatched a crazy plan," she said, to go to Norway together for two weeks. "We didn't really know each other that well and hadn't really been seeing each other for very long," she explained. "He said that it had been a place that he had always wanted to go to as an adult, but he had been there a couple times as a kid, and I said, 'Oh, well, I have cousins there,' and that was it." In mid-August they flew to Norway, with their first stop being Stavanger, on the southwest coast of the country, where Mimi's cousins lived. They hopped in a car with one of her cousins and drove around the coast. They stayed in a country house for a day or two, then ditched her cousin and took off driving. They didn't have a plan. "We would drive for like two or three hours and decide, 'Okay, this is a cool place,' and we would find a hotel and stay there for a night, explore whatever we wanted to explore in the area, and leave for the next place before it was too late," she explained.

They split the cost of the trip. "We weren't exactly at a point where it was like everything was ours together," she said. "Everything was very separate." It was the kind of vacation, she added, that would either make or break the relationship. In their case, it broke it. "I grew to like and respect him an awful lot, but he was not going to be my husband. He and I actually talked about it on the trip. There's a religious difference, and when we were on the trip, he was like, 'You should really go find yourself a nice Jewish boy.'" She said their romantic relationship would not have lasted much longer, by mutual agreement. "He was one of the smartest, most interesting people I've ever met, and still to this day one of the smartest and most interesting people that I have ever known, but he just wasn't the guy for me." (She also disputed the idea that Will had Tourette's syndrome, and just chalked up his anger to being upset with his father, especially after he died.)

She was impressed, though, with Will's commitment to social justice. "This was the part of him that I respected and admired," she said. "Not only was his job about taking care of people who were not able to necessarily take care of themselves, but everywhere we went, if he saw a guy at a bar bothering a waitress in a way that was pretty unkind, he would take the guy to task. Even if he'd never met him before, he would say, 'You know, this person's working really hard. You might want to treat them with a little bit more respect.' That's the kind of person he was." She thought that after his father's death, he could no longer hide behind his preferred cloak of anonymity. "He built this whole environment of people that did not know where he came from and so had no pre-judgment," she said. "And now they all knew, and I think there was a little bit too much exposure."

While their relationship hadn't progressed, they returned to New York still somewhat a couple, or so people thought. On the Thursday before Labor Day weekend, Will and Mimi went to hear some jazz at Cleopatra's Needle on the Upper West Side. At the end of the night, they were talking about the upcoming long weekend. Mimi had to go to Connecticut for her grandmother's ninetieth-birthday party. Will wasn't going to that, obviously, but asked her if he could stay at her apartment—on 77th Street, between Lexington and Third Avenues—while she was away. He asked her if she wanted to join him at "some party" that his work colleagues were throwing on Friday night, in Brooklyn, before she left town. She told him no. She had to catch an early train Saturday morning for her grandmother's party. "Knowing the party was in Brooklyn, and knowing him, we wouldn't have gotten back until very early in the morning, and I just couldn't do that," she said. They talked about him going to the party alone and staying with her after. "I have a very tiny apartment, so if he'd come in, he would've totally woken me up," she said. "And he was like, 'All right, I'll just go stay at my mom's,' and I was like, 'Okay.' Well, he would call it the Old Homestead. So he said, 'I'm gonna go stay at the Old

Homestead,' and I said, 'Okay, great.'" Will called his mother and asked if it was okay for him to stay with her on Friday night. She said sure.

MARK OPLER WAS A PH.D. CANDIDATE working alongside Will on the homeless men project. "I was in my mid-twenties back then," he said. "So Will was actually, for me, kind of an aspirational figure. This was a guy who'd made his bones, who was gifted in the art of interacting with and influencing the most vulnerable." Opler was aware of Will's emotional outbursts. "There were, as memory serves, kind of minor disciplinary issues with him getting angry and swearing with such violence and such volume that people in adjacent offices would complain," he said. But unlike some of his other colleagues at Columbia, Opler did not think Will's random yelling was evidence of Tourette's. Instead, he believed it came from "a very deep and very personal sense of outrage." He was struck by how "a guy who was as human and humane as Will" played "aspects of life obviously very close to the chest. The family and their background was absolutely unknown. It never came up and Lord knows if it ever did come up he was very good at deflecting it." He noted that even in casual social settings, Will could be surprisingly abrasive. "You'd be having a casual drink with Will and folks who didn't know him well would suddenly, without warning almost, find themselves the brunt of very insightful, and perhaps even a slightly sarcastic or cutting remark that came out of left field," he said. "It wasn't intended to be cruel by any means, but it's as though this guy who you didn't really see at first was suddenly very, very present and very focused on you and something you said. You realized all of a sudden he's not only listening to you, he was hearing you, and it was a little off-putting at times. But he was an incredibly sweet guy at his core." He said Will was at his "most comfortable in his own skin" when "he was helping other people." That's when Will was able to tuck away whatever demons were plaguing him. "The times when he was able to put it aside were the times when the focus of his identity was external and magnificent," he said. "That's when he was at his best." Opler paused, then continued, "He was very, very good at what he did, and frankly one of the reasons why people put up with him—he's not an easy guy to get along with sometimes—is he's very talented and exceedingly dedicated, obviously. And he inspired, for people who got to know him, he inspired a lot of love."

It was Opler who invited Will to the party in Brooklyn that Labor Day weekend. The party was in the basement of a town house in Park Slope. Will stayed late, after the party had ended, to help clean up. He had been drinking whiskey, of course, most of the night. "Even in his inebriated state, this was a guy who, generally speaking, held his liquor well and oddly didn't become any more belligerent than he ordinarily would have been," he said. "And again, even in his more than slightly inebriated and more than slightly belligerent state, he was still a delightful guy when he remembered to be so." After the cleanup, Will tossed a Frisbee in the middle of Seventh Avenue in Park Slope for another forty-five minutes. Then, Opler said, "he kind of wandered off, still quite inebriated, into the night." It was around 2 a.m. "He waved goodbye and he just wandered off. I thought he was headed toward the subway. I don't remember if it was me or someone else asking him where he was going, but he was done and he walked away. He was headed out."

Will was headed for the Old Homestead, for 830 Park. He got on the subway in Park Slope and got out at the stop at Lexington Avenue and 77th Street. It was about 2:35 a.m. Will then walked one block south, to 76th Street, and then west toward Park Avenue. The Old Homestead was on the southwest corner of Park and 76th Street. It was a path Will had walked thousands of times before, although most forty-one-year-old men do not find themselves, at two forty in the morning, returning to their mom's tony apartment in Manhattan to sleep, after hours of partying in Brooklyn. But that's how Will had arranged his life.

Will started to cross Park Avenue on 76th. At that very moment—2:40 a.m. on September 2—a yellow taxi driven by Mohamed Dawoud was heading northbound on Park Avenue. Apparently, according to the subsequent police report, Will was crossing against the light—meaning the cars traveling up Park had not come to a stop at a red light (this fact was later disputed by Will's mother)—and Dawoud's taxi, a 1999 Ford, hit him with all the considerable force of a car driving at an unimpeded speed along an otherwise quiet Manhattan thoroughfare. It was no match. John Torres, the night doorman at 815 Park Avenue, saw the aftermath of the accident and called 911.

According to the police report filed by Constantin Tsachas, then a police sergeant, and David Zucchet, at the time he was hit by Dawoud's taxi, Will was wearing a blue button-down long-sleeved shirt and khakis—the classic preppy outfit. In their report, the cops wrote that Will "is likely to die" and that they were unable to notify "a family member."

At first, the police claimed that Dawoud had left the scene of the accident, a felony. But the police changed the classification to "motor vehicle accident" once they realized that Dawoud had not fled the scene. Dawoud had no alcohol in his blood. He had a valid driver's license. There were no warrants out for his arrest. The police report said that Will "may have been intoxicated as he appeared to be unsteady on his feet." The police concluded that "the causative factor of this accident is pedestrian error" and added, "there was an indication of alcohol usage by the victim." The police also spoke with Matthew Honigman, an employee of the Roosevelt Hotel, on 45th and Madison. Honigman was the passenger in Dawoud's cab. He told police that he did not "actually see" the accident "but he only heard the impact." He said the taxi was going around "30–35 mph before the accident." He told police that he did not see what direction Will was walking from when the cab hit him and that after he heard the collision he "looked up and noticed the pedestrian on the windshield of the cab." When Honigman got out of the cab, he saw Will "on the ground in an unconscious state." He said Will was wearing an ID badge of some sort around his neck that identified him as Will Daniel. The police concluded that there was "no criminality" involved in the accident.

The story Clif told me about what happened to his brother was a little different. He said there were actually two taxis heading north, parallel to each other, on Park Avenue, with one taxi slightly ahead of the other. Will could only clearly see the one taxi closer to him on the eastern corner of Park and did not see the other. "So he jaywalked," he said. "He jogged across. A guy in the back of the second cab—in the police report afterward—said that the first cab, it was close enough that the first cab had to kind of swerve to get around Will, and that's when the second cab and Will saw each other and it was too late. The taxi hit him, and it hit him waist-high, and his head hit the windshield and rearview mirror, causing an ultimately fatal brain hemorrhage. Will was conscious for a couple of minutes afterward. The guy in the back of the second cab, the one that hit him, was an off-duty police trainee, I think, and got out and went to Will and—and I think what the police reported—asked Will if he'd been drinking. And Will's last words were apparently, 'No.' I don't know whether he had been or not. But he lapsed into unconsciousness shortly after that and never woke up."

When he got the call from the doctors at New York Hospital, Clif had been in Indiana for the weekend with his wife and children, visiting his wife's sister, who had a house on a lake. "The doctors are funny on the phone," he said. "They're like, 'Well, he's been hurt.' Okay. How badly? 'Well, I think you need to get up here.' Okay. 'Well, it's a brain injury.' All right. All I could think about was, Will was so smart. I thought, *Shit, is this going to affect the way his thinking is? Because I don't think he could stand that.* And they said, 'No. You need to—it's not really a question of whether he—' and they wouldn't give me a straight answer.

They wouldn't say, *He's dying. Get on a plane.* So finally, after repeated questioning, they said, 'It's a question of whether he's going to wake up or not.' And I thought, *Okay.* And so I flew home. It's all a blur. Obviously, I drove myself back to Chicago and got on the plane the next morning, but I don't remember making the reservation, or flying, or anything."

Mimi had gone up to Connecticut on Saturday morning without having a clue what had happened to Will just a few hours before and a few blocks from her small apartment. "I woke up the next morning, walked over to Fifth Avenue to get a cab to go to the train station, basically right where the accident had been, but I didn't know about the accident yet," she said. She ran into an old friend on the train. She noticed there were a few voice messages on her cell phone. But she ignored them. The actual party for her grandmother was on Sunday. Her phone rang a few more times that day, with the caller leaving a voice message each time. Finally she listened to the messages and heard that Will had been in an accident. "My first thought was that Will got into some bar fight," she said. She went to see her father and then got a message to call Clif. That's when the gravity of the situation hit her. "Yeah, you might want to come down here tonight," he told her. "This is not good."

Will's younger brother Thomas came to New York from his home in the northern mountains of Vermont. Seven years younger than Will, Thomas didn't interact with Will very often. He went to boarding school in Millbrook, New York, and then to the University of Vermont for a year before transferring to Champlain College. He's a software engineer working for a health care company in Burlington. "When you see your eighty-eight-year-old father in the hospital you're definitely taken aback, you're kind of shocked, but at the same time, it's not—I don't know—it's almost expected," he said. "But to see William, I mean, hooked up to machines and lying in a hospital bed, that definitely rocked my world because he just was always so energetic, so passionate, even physically imposing because he was such an athlete even then. You know he was exercising every day, at least once a day. Yeah, it was very disturbing, concerning to see him like that. And then I think you're obviously thinking he's one of the most physically strong people in the family, he'll be fine. And then as you start to find out that you know this really isn't going to turn around, it's definitely very surreal in a situation like that."

Mimi got on the next train to New York from Hartford. She wasn't exactly sure how Clif had gotten her number. But he told her he didn't know any of Will's friends and asked her to make a few calls, which she did from the train. When she got to New York, she took a cab to New York Hospital. Will's brothers met her and took her upstairs to where Will was. His condition was poor, and not improving. "It got worse," she said. His brain was swelling, he was in a coma, and there wasn't much the doctors could do. She left that night at around two in the morning and came back six hours later. By then, there were more than thirty people in the waiting room, hoping to go in to see Will and say their goodbyes.

Miriam Cytryn and her husband were in the Hamptons for Labor Day weekend. They were closing on a new house out there. When they got back to New York City, there were a bunch of messages on her answering machine from Clif, asking her to call him. That's how she found out about Will's accident, and that he was on life support. "They were making decisions," she said. "Will was pretty clear that he wanted to be a donor and we joked often about 'Well, they are not taking your liver. There's certain things we know they're not taking. Maybe those pretty blue eyes they will take.' They wanted people to be able to say goodbye. And so we went to the hospital. And I remember thinking he looked good. There was a bandage but it was not like his head was crushed. But I remember thinking, he looked fit and a little tan. But I remember saying, 'Oh my God, this can't be true.' Yeah, wow. It still doesn't seem real after all these years."

At some point on Monday, September 4, the doctors asked Clif and

Thomas and their mother to go into a conference room to discuss Will's condition. Mimi did not think it was appropriate for her to go, but Clif and Thomas asked her to go with them and the doctors. She felt very weird doing that. "But for Clifton and Thomas," she said, "they were like, 'We don't know him as well as you do.' And at the same time, I was like, 'I don't know him as well as half the people in that waiting room.'" She was not Will's girlfriend but she was, it seemed, going to have to play that role in the moment. She said the doctors reviewed Will's medical condition and shared the fact that there was nothing more they could do for him. The only question was whether or not Will wanted to donate his organs. He had not indicated his desire to do so on his license. But Mimi knew he wanted to. "Knowing the kind of person that he is, that is probably something he would want to do," she told them. The family decided to donate Will's organs. "Okay, well, if that's the case," the doctors said, "then the process needs to start pretty soon."

The doctors told Will's friends to come and say their goodbyes, and one by one that happened. Terry Gruber from softball was there. Will's colleagues from Columbia were there, including Conover and Susser, plus many of the people who had been at the party in Brooklyn. At first, they thought Will was going to pull through somehow. "When we arrived, some of them were leaving and they said, 'Oh, he's in good shape. He's doing okay,'" Conover said. "And when we arrived the nurse said that he was, but now it doesn't look like he's going to make it. So we were shocked. So then at that point his brother Clif came in. And then the nurse whispered, 'You know who he is?' And we said no. And then his brother came over and explained more about who he was. And then we met his mother. And then we just watched him die. And it was just so sudden, and he was such a force of personality that, like, the next day I was in my car and I had just been in the car with him the day before. And when I got in the car I got this shiver because, you know, he was still there as a memory, this recent memory, but he was no more. It was just a horrible experience."

Not surprisingly, the news of Will's accident hit his mother very hard. "She'd had a double whammy," Clif said. "Dad had died that February, and there was Will gone in September." He compared his mother to her own maternal grandmother, Madge Gates Wallace. Her husband, David Wallace, was an alcoholic who committed suicide in 1904. He was very frustrated in his life. He couldn't make any money and his political aspirations went nowhere. After that, Clif said, "my great-grandmother Madge kind of folded up and became a virtual recluse, relied on my grandmother to run the household, take care of her younger brothers, and pay the bills, all of that stuff. And my mother sort of had done the same thing." In 1996, his mother had almost died from necrotizing fasciitis, a flesh-eating bacteria. After that, she was afraid to leave 830 Park. "She just became reliant on the nurses, and the care, and being at home," Clif said. "So she had sort of already made 830 Park Avenue her residence 24/7. She didn't go out. And after that, it was more of the same. She was just more alone. She didn't talk much about it. . . . My parents weren't great on sharing their feelings. But it must have been hard for her because Will got hit right outside her window. If she had been awake and she had looked out the window at two forty-five in the morning, she would have seen him. Or at least seen the ambulance. And she didn't know until the next day."

Mimi was the last one to leave Will, staying around even longer than Will's mother and his brothers. She thought that was weird, too. "When we were in Norway, we went to this Viking burial ground, and while we were there, we had a pretty intense conversation about death and dying," she said. "And one of the things that he said was that he didn't want to die alone, and so I had this incredible guilt. If I left him there by himself, that would just be contrary to this intense conversation that we had had." She left his room late that night. She asked the doctors if she should stay or go once they began the process of taking Will off life support. They said she should go. "So that was my permission to finally leave," she said. She has often wondered what might have been different if she had agreed to let Will stay with her that Friday night, or if she had insisted that he come with her to her grandmother's birthday party. "Even still to this day I think about that," she said. "But there's nothing that I can do about it. There are like a million scenarios."

The next morning, Mimi joined Clif and Thomas at the Frank Campbell funeral home. The family had just convened there seven months before for Clifton Daniel's funeral. Now they were back again. There were decisions to be made: What kind of funeral would Will have? Would he be buried, or not? Who would identify his body at the medical examiner's office? Who would handle the calls from the press?

The day after Will died, the *New York Times* ran a story about the accident and his death, which the paper explained was still "under investigation." The paper quoted both Clif and Mimi. "He was just coming to spend the night, to sleep in his old bed," Clif said. "We have no clue what happened. We don't know how fast the cabby was driving or whether he was even speeding." Added Mimi, whom the paper described as Will's girlfriend, "He was always the captain of everyone else's good time. He was always arranging something or doing something spontaneous; the kind of guy who would hang glide across the Grand Canyon if someone challenged him." The paper also spoke with Susser, who said Will's co-workers at Columbia had no idea of his family lineage: "He never told anyone. I guess he wanted to be known for his work, not his family background." *People* also ran a piece about Will's death under the headline "Private Citizen" and the subtitle, "Before his untimely death, Harry Truman's grandson William Daniel lived quietly and touched many lives." There was a picture of Will, as a towheaded young boy, walking a few paces behind his grandfather, the former president of the United States, and a picture that Mimi snapped of Will in the canoe they had shared a few weeks earlier on a lake in Norway. Will's softball friends placed a paid notice about his death in the *Times*, as well: "With profound heartfelt sadness we mourn Will: Great Friend,

Wild Friend, Sweet Friend, El Jefe, Captain, Wolfman, our Ace. 20 year member of the Cats & Dogs Softball League. Founding member of The Fetchers, Bad DogsMad Dogs. Sundays and league play will never be as enjoyable without you. You will be sorely missed both on and off the field."

Will's longtime friend Mark Bodden read about Will's death in the *Daily News*. He had gone out for a run with a friend, and when they were finished, his friend noticed the obituary. Nobody had called Mark. He was surprised, obviously, but not shocked. "Will was the type of personality that this type of death was something that we both thought would happen," he said. "Because that's the way he lived his life. He did everything with passion—the things he wanted to pursue. And reading the account of how he died is consistent, as far as I know, with how he acted. This was two o'clock in the early morning. And he was crossing Park Avenue at two o'clock in the morning. Why are you going to visit your parents at that hour?" And then there was the fact that he had been drinking, and might still have been inebriated. "Having witnessed him and participated with him, I know what that does to him or what it did to him when he pursued it with abandon," he continued. "So that's my point about it in terms of not being surprised with the tragedy of his death and the way it occurred."

Will Iselin also did not get a call about the accident. He heard the news from another Andover classmate. Iselin's first thought was "what a terrible waste. . . . the profound sensation was, *Well, oh my God, I can't believe I just lost my oldest friend, run over by a taxi.* You never think it's gonna happen that way." He continued. "It was a real tragedy. Here's a guy who, God, had so much, and underneath it all, what he ended up with, he didn't want that. He wanted something more. People end up like that because they don't care, but he actually, underneath it all, he really cared. That's why, bit by bit, he saw less and less of a lot of his old friends. Because it was too difficult for him. Everybody was kind of moving on. He was still battling. I'm sure he was thrilled when he found the whole softball crowd, who didn't know him."

MIMI WENT TO THE MEDICAL EXAMINER'S office and answered the questions about Will. She also shared her insights about him with the staff at Frank Campbell, including the fact that Will had told her he thought his father's funeral was "very lonely." (For some reason, seven months later, Clifton Daniel's ashes were still at the Campbell funeral home. "When we sat there," Mimi said, "They were like, 'Can you take these, too?'") To try to avoid that feeling of loneliness that Will so disliked about his father's funeral, Mimi and Will's brothers decided to have his funeral in a small room upstairs at the funeral home, rather than the large one downstairs where his father's had been. But when on Friday, September 8, at four o'clock in the afternoon, more than three hundred people showed up for Will's funeral, they ended up moving his service to the larger room downstairs. There was a make-shift program that featured color pictures of Will and a request that donations be made in his honor to United Neighborhood Houses.

After the service, everyone was invited to walk to the Heckscher Ballfields in Central Park (at around 65th Street). That was where Will's ashes would be spread. It was technically against the law but nobody seemed to be worried, and of course it was exactly what Will would have wanted, given the importance softball ended up having in his life. About half of the people who were at the service showed up, sitting in the bleachers around the ball field and telling stories about Will. According to Cytryn, about eight "beautiful women" stood up and spoke about Will, causing some guy in the group to remark that Will "got more action dead than I got alive."

Then they spread his ashes on the mound. "There was a cop car right there, and the cop didn't do anything about it," Mimi said. Clif remembered it being a pretty funny scene. "It was hilarious coming into Central Park and seeing seventy-five or a hundred people all dressed in black, all trying to look nonchalant," he said. "They were just all standing around sort of whistling. It was ridiculous because there were so many of us. But that was his funeral." After Will's ashes were spread, the group then went off to the Saloon Grill, on 64th Street and Broadway, to celebrate Will's life.

As the tragic events unfolded that Labor Day weekend, Clif came to the realization that he did not know his brother very well, and had not known much about him for years. "When Will died, he was a surprise to me," he said. "I did not know my brother at all. I met his friends for the first time. I found out what he had really been like to them for the first time. It was a very different person than the guy I grew up with; because of the family relationship, because of our relationship, he shut me out of a lot of it. I don't know how intentional it was on his part, but I didn't know what his life was like. And he didn't tell me and I, to be fair to him, I didn't ask. It wasn't my life. We had a standoffish relationship. So when he died and all of these people started telling stories about him, this was somebody I had never known, somebody who worked hard to make sure that everybody else was okay. If they were down, he would try to lift them up. If they needed help, he would help them. . . . I learned all sorts of things about him that I did not know. I learned that he was kind and thoughtful to all these people. I had an adversarial relationship with him for years. But that was just us. For everybody else, it was the opposite. He took care of a lot of people and he did not like being associated with our grandfather. I found that out the hard way. . . . He led a completely different life from the one that he led around me."

IN MARCH 2001, SIX MONTHS AFTER Will died, Margaret Truman Daniel sued Mohamed Dawoud and Kinky Cab Corp., the cab company that owned Dawoud's taxi, for $4 million. The suit accused

Dawoud of being "negligent, careless and reckless." The suit said that Will had been a "lawful pedestrian" when he was crossing Park Avenue at 2:40 a.m. on September 2 when Dawoud "suddenly and without warning violently struck and knocked down [Will] causing him to sustain severe and serious injuries resulting in his death [two days later], following conscious pain and suffering." The suit further argued that Will "in no way contributed to said occurrence and [Will's] injuries were due solely to the negligence and carelessness" of Kinky and Dawoud. The *Times* dutifully—and briefly—reported the filing of the lawsuit and also contacted Dawoud for a comment. He denied the allegations against him and told the paper, "I drive carefully." Dawoud continued to deny having any responsibility for Will's death in his legal filings. He claimed Will, and Will alone, was responsible for the accident that led to his tragic death. For the next seven months or so, the case proceeded through the typical legal paces in state court, and looked to be heading to a trial. But then, on November 13, 2001, the case was suddenly settled "without costs to either party against the other."

Clif Daniel told me the cab company ended up paying Will's medical bills—of about $50,000—as part of the settlement. In the end, Will's brother felt it wasn't Dawoud's fault. "He wasn't grossly negligent," Clif said. "He wasn't speeding. He was going about thirty miles an hour. It was just a horrible accident."

Margaret Truman Daniel died on January 29, 2008, in Chicago, where she was in the process of relocating to be near her oldest son, Clif. Her ashes, and those of her husband, are interred in her parents' burial plot at the Truman Library, in Independence, Missouri.

Harry

H ARRY CALVIN BULL WAS BORN in La Grange, Illinois, in
1960. He was named after his step-grandfather, Harry Calvin. Calvin was a lifelong army guy. He was referred to in
the Bull family as The Colonel. "He had a collection of shotguns in the
house and he'd put on John Philip Sousa music and we'd march around
in my grandmother's house having a great time," Karna Bull, Harry's
oldest sister, remembered.

Harry's father, Richard Bull Jr., was a 1944 graduate of Andover,
two years after George H. W. Bush. He had finished Andover a semester early, at seventeen, and like Bush he joined the navy. But Richard
Bull detested the navy. "Oh God, he hated it," Karna said. He didn't
like being bossed around. He didn't like the rainy, dreary weather in
Seattle, where the navy sent him. And he had pretty much decided
that war never accomplished much good. "Even back to the Revolutionary War," she remembered her father used to say, "were we any
better off than the Canadians?" He made it through the war unscathed
and graduated from Yale and then Yale Law School. His first job was
back in his hometown of Chicago, in the legal department of Swift &
Co., the meat processing company made infamous by Upton Sinclair's
1906 novel, *The Jungle*. He didn't join the family business, Bradner
Smith & Co., until 1960, but within a few years he was chairman and
CEO. Bradner Smith, founded in 1852, was one of the biggest paper
manufacturers west of the Mississippi and a big deal in and around
Chicago for generations. John Bradner Smith, a founder, was Harry
Bull's great-great-grandfather. The Bulls of Illinois were, of course,

not the Kennedys of Massachusetts or the Trumans of Missouri, but, in their way, they were a shining example of midwestern American rectitude and values, and Bradner Smith, for a long time, was one of Chicago's most important companies. It once had the largest paper warehouse in the world.

Harry's father would serve as CEO until he retired in 1991. He was an old-school Republican, steeped in conservative views, family values, charity, and modesty. He loved his clubs—he was a member of sixteen at one point, including the fictitious Khyble Bay Yacht Club, which was a family joke but also a testament to the Bulls' longtime love of sailing—and he loved serving on boards, lots of boards. He was not prone to ostentatious displays of wealth, despite the family's status in the Chicago area. The Bulls, and their children, moved to Hinsdale, where Harry grew up, a well-to-do suburb west of Chicago. The Bulls eventually had five children, of which Harry was the second youngest. Their father would give them a minimal allowance each week. "My father was pretty careful to keep us, at least the older ones—and I'm not sure about Harry—humble and regular and here's your allowance and don't ask for more," said Karna. Added Rick Bull, Harry's brother, "We all started getting allowance as soon as we learned arithmetic. I can remember I was given a nickel a week. One penny went to savings, one penny went to charity, and I was given three cents to operate with as I saw fit."

Thanks to Richard Bull's firebrand Republicanism, the children had been raised to "kill and steal from the next village," Rick said. "Fierce individualism if you will. . . . It doesn't take a village, get your ass out of bed and go to work." The kids would get GOP lapel pins during elections.

It was an interesting time in wealthy enclaves such as Hinsdale, as the gauzy Ozzie and Harriet childhood gave way to the cultural revolution of 1960s. Rick remembered how around 1970 during his counterculture period he told his father he was going to add his

father's name to "the death list" when the revolution happened because of his status as a CEO oppressor. "He chuckled politely," Rick
remembered, "and said 'Do what you like. Would you like another
hamburger?'"

RICK WAS FIVE YEARS OLDER than Harry and remembers him well as
an extremely precocious toddler. When he and his friends weren't beat-
ing up on Harry—in typical sibling fashion—they would often find
him "in a soggy diaper" visiting a neighbor and talking about "the finer
points of washing an automobile" or "mowing a lawn." Harry, his brother
said, was "just extremely curious about the world around him and was
never one to hold back." By around second or third grade at the Elm
Elementary School, it was increasingly clear that Harry had a special
intellect and an IQ, at 146, that was in the genius range. Traditional
schools could barely contain him. One of the toughest moments of
Harry's life, he later recalled, was when the teachers at Elm told him
to take his books and move out of the second-grade classroom, into
the third-grade classroom. Then they asked him to move again to the
fourth-grade classroom.

That's when the Bulls decided to move Harry to a private school with
a more rigorous program. There, he completed fourth-grade work in one
semester. By the time he was in eighth grade, and twelve years old,
Harry wanted to go to his father's high school, Andover, as a ninth-
grader, but Andover decided he would have been too young. And so
Harry instead spent his ninth grade year at the private Williston
Northampton School, also in Massachusetts.

He was a faithful correspondent, and it is clear in his letters that
Williston was only a temporary stop. "I have reviewed the Andover
magazine," he wrote his father in October 1973, a month or so into his
year at Williston. "I am gung ho and looking forward to going to Andover next year."

In January 1974, Harry applied to Andover. In answer to an admittedly odd application question, he selected *The Exorcist* as the movie that had "strongly impressed" him in recent years. "After see [*sic*] this movie I was, and still am, wondering about the possibilities and consequences of being possessed," he wrote. "This feeling was left in me not only by an excellent plot, but also by a number of special effects." In a longer essay, Harry tackled the question about what his generation could do to overcome the problems in society. He was concerned about the problem of "corrupt politics" and the "infamous Watergate incident" that had left "many Americans dumbfounded." He urged his contemporaries to take fewer vacations, engage in fewer "recreational activities," to buy fewer plastics and nylon, and to reduce the use of televisions and stereos.

While not exactly *Profiles in Courage*, Harry's application, and his impressive academic accomplishments, not to mention his legacy status, ensured him admittance to Andover. He began as a Lower in September 1974. Like so many others, Harry had a rough start academically. He also did not pass the so-called Competence exam—few did—that attempted to determine who could avoid taking a course in the rudimentary skills of clear and concise writing. "The reason he did not pass was that his style became awkward and priggish when he tried to comment upon the waste problem in the U.S.," wrote his English teacher Frank Bellizia. "His analysis of structural problems in the short paragraphs was also too thin."

Outside the classroom there was trouble, too, about "parietals," the euphemism used for Andover's odd set of rules about when members of the opposite sex could visit your dorm room. Harry wasted little time in breaking these rules. On October 11, at 8:45 p.m., he invited two female classmates to his room, where they stayed for an hour, along with two other boys. "This, of course, was in violation of the room visiting rule," Clem Morell, the cluster dean, wrote Harry's parents, "even though it was a social gathering and they were listening to records." At the disciplinary meeting, three days later, "Harry had no real excuse for his action," Morell continued. Harry got probation, plus a restriction on "room visiting," until the end of December.

By the time he returned home for Thanksgiving, his older brother could tell Harry had changed, and that he had settled in to life at Andover. "He immediately came back smarter then everyone," Rick Bull said. "He had turned into Socrates. He was in the saddle when he came home. He'd learned more in seven weeks than the combined knowledge of everyone at the Thanksgiving table. . . . Then of course by Christmas, he had realized that perhaps he wasn't Aristotle after all. We had knocked him down to Einstein."

Peter Begley lived across the hall from Harry during his first year at Andover. Begley, a class ahead, and Harry became fast friends. "He was wildly precocious in most things," Begley said. "He looked like a little choirboy, sort of very baby-faced. But at the same time, he knew all sorts of stuff and was well ahead of himself." He remembered that Harry loved the blues and was always playing jazz guitar. He also recalled that Harry had an older girlfriend who would come to visit him, without, apparently, the knowledge of the Andover authorities. "A lady would show up from time to time," he said. Harry would tell him, "'Oh, yeah. That's my woman.' It was crazy. It was well beyond parietals." Harry was fourteen and the youngest member of the Class of 1977. (I was the second youngest.)

Begley invited Harry to New York City to stay at the apartment of his father, the writer Louis Begley. "There's a distinct memory of Harry with a snifter of brandy and a big fat cigar," he said. "It was absurd. But he pulled it off effortlessly. And in retrospect, you had a feeling that Harry was heading toward the wall somehow or other, and that he couldn't keep up that rhythm."

The rest of Harry's first year at Andover continued academically in much the same vein that it had begun—some of his teachers found him captivating, others couldn't figure him out. "Harry is full of it," English teacher Paul Kalkstein wrote about him in March 1975. "But what a man! What a pen!" But Vincent Pascucci, a legendary Latin teacher, wasn't buying Harry's shtick. He complained of his absences from class, and how he started off the course well—but then, with considerable understatement, he wrote, "the regularity of his application gave way while the material gained in sophistication and difficulty." He then added, "Seems like a nice boy. Should demand more of himself." Hale Sturges, his house counselor, was of two minds about him. "Harry is intellectually alive," he wrote, "socially poised and thus a seemingly mature man with unlimited potential. To date, however, this potential rests largely unrealized." For the first time in his life, it was becoming clear, Harry was faced with an academic challenge he was not meeting with ease, and he seemed not sure exactly how to proceed. The problem for him was that the numbers don't lie, and they indicated his brilliance, which he was not achieving.

Harry was precocious to say the least. At around this same time, he wanted to hitchhike to California, as his older cousins had done. His parents said no. But what they did allow him to do was to take a Greyhound bus to Mackinac Island, in northern Michigan, and get a job washing dishes. He then joined a sailboat crew, sailing the 330 miles or so from Mackinac to Chicago. Given the distance and the fact that Lake Michigan is not dissimilar to an ocean, the event can be dangerous. People have died. "The weather can turn very quickly, and it's a long way to go," a family friend recalled. "If he was sailing down, that's not an insignificant sail."

When Harry returned to Andover for his Upper year, he roomed with Peter Begley, against the counsel of Sturges, who worried, correctly, that they would not be good influences on each other. Will Zogbaum, who had also become imprinted on Will Daniel, lived near Harry and Peter, in Fuess. They became close. He remembered the odd configuration they had in their room, which reminded him of a harem. "They had their room all done up like a seraglio with those Indian prints," he said. The walls had been covered with hanging tapestries. There were tapestries hanging at weird angles. It was, Zogbaum said, as if a tent had been created inside their dorm room. "It was like walking into a different world," he said. There was an armchair in the corner of the room, where Harry held court. "He was like the prince at his feast in there," Zogbaum remembered. "It was a really happy role for him because he was a good entertainer and he was good at drawing people out and telling stories and getting a conversation going." And there was a bong kept behind the armchair. When you walked into the room, it was impossible not to experience the sweet smell of marijuana. "Those things definitely were absorbent," he said of the Indian prints. "You couldn't help mask the activities that were going on there. But it gave a great atmosphere." They all had radio shows at WPAA, the campus radio station. Harry had a big record collection and they were just "spinning records" at WPAA. He said they tried to be "mavericks" at Andover by not conforming to the traditional norms of the place. "For someone who was partying as much as he was, it was kind of sometimes a little surprising that he was so lucid," Zogbaum said.

Harry was a gleeful participant in pranks, including one involving an obnoxious jock who enjoyed tormenting his fellow dorm mates. They figured out a way to lock him out of his room while he was in the shower. The timing of the prank was such that Sturges, the dorm master, was not home. Harry's friend Giles McNamee said: "So he had to go to Mrs. Sturges, who was basically always in the bag by about 11 a.m., wearing nothing but his towel, dripping wet, and having Mrs. Sturges, who I think definitely wanted to jump his bones, unlock his door." Only Harry and Giles were even cleverer than that. They had devised an ingenious system whereby they could control whether the door could actually be unlocked, key or no key, by drilling a hole in the top of a beer can, running a string through it, and tossing the string out the window, where they could grab it and pull the can top away from the lock at a time of their own choosing. The consequence of the prank was that when Mrs. Sturges went to open the guy's room door, she couldn't do it with the master key. "After Mrs. Sturges failed to get the door open, there's this guy sitting in his towel in her living room waiting for Mr. Sturges to come home. Of course, by then we had pulled the can top off and Hale said it looked like he had been trying to pick up Mrs. Sturges."

Harry's studies suffered amid the fun. He wrote his parents in January 1976 that his History 35 teacher, Gil Sewall, "was shocked that I went from being an Honors (5) student to a (3)." Sewall told him he would have done just fine on the final had he had a good night's sleep. "He is probably correct," Harry told his parents. Despite his academic struggles, Harry's letters home were alive with details of the books he was reading and thoughts he was having about subjects as diverse as the Civil War—"I find the whole war pathetic, an atrocity," he wrote, and yet "It is amazing to realize that many of my previous conceptions of the war are utterly wrong"—and the poet Emily Dickinson. His favorite course was photography. "I really love it," he wrote his parents in February, "and I hope I can pursue photography as a hobby forever."

Despite failing the History 35 exam, Sewall rightly saw considerable potential in Harry and recommended him for the school's prestigious Washington Intern Program, in which a group of Uppers spend the third trimester of the year working for a congressman in Washington. Harry was accepted into the program—an honor—and Sturges wanted to make sure Harry knew that since he would not have any grades during his springtime in DC, the upcoming winter term was one that "colleges look at carefully." But unlike almost everyone else, Harry seemed to have few worries about where he would end up after Andover.

In Washington, Harry worked for Illinois congressman Philip M. Crane, one of the leading conservative Republicans in the House of Representatives. Crane, who represented a district in the wealthy northwest suburbs of Chicago, had won a special election, in 1969, for the seat vacated by Donald Rumsfeld, who was joining the Nixon administration. Harry and Representative Crane got along famously. Another Andover classmate, Benjy Swett, shared a room with Harry in Washington. It was in a decrepit hotel, the Bellevue, where one window faced Union Station and the other window faced the Capitol. Swett was working for Congressman Mo Udall. "It was just unbelievable to think that we got to do this," Swett said. "We just were sent off junior year to cavort in the Capitol basically unsupervised." Harry, like his father, was a Republican. "And the rest of us were Democrats," Swett said. "Harry just seemed to be very amused and not at all afraid in defending his Republican positions against us and telling us we were full of hogwash and here's why."

The days in Washington were fairly structured but there was also lots of unsupervised freedom. Each week of the program, which also included students from Exeter, featured seminars with various Washington insider briefings at the State Department and a "law enforcement day" at the drug enforcement division at the Justice Department. Richard Riker, who shared a suite with Harry and Swett, remembered the visit to the drug agency particularly. One of the agents was passing around a sample of crack cocaine. As the rock was being passed around, another Andover classmate in the Washington Intern Program broke off a piece and shoved it into his pocket. "These guys went back to where we were staying and they smoked it, which they got from the DEA," Riker said. "Isn't that fucking amazing? . . . He actually broke that thing off . . . They didn't realize what kind of little fucking animals that we were."

FOR HARRY'S SENIOR YEAR AT ANDOVER, he moved to Sunset House, a tiny dorm on the other side of campus from Fuess, run by Gil Sewall. By then, Harry and Sewall had become quite close. That fall, Harry took Sewall's History of Art survey course (as did I) and excelled in it. "Harry was one of the outstanding students in Art History this fall,"

Sewall wrote about him at the end of the first trimester. "He is a splen-did young man in every respect." Harry did well in math, too. "He is serious about his own learning," George Best wrote, "self-motivated and very competent." There was more. "It should come to you as no surprise that I consider Harry one of the real standouts in the Senior class at Andover," Sewall wrote the Bulls, in a letter home. "I have had him as a student now for two years, have been wholly impressed with his per-formance and invigorating, quick mind, recommended him for the Washington Intern Program last spring, and currently find him the pre-mier resident in Sunset House. Our conversations have been frequent, fascinating and sincere. I have found on several occasions his reactions and fine judgment a good litmus test for my History of Art section. I am even more heartened by Harry's ability to move in many different groups inside Andover, maintaining cordial relations with all but never becoming absorbed in a clique or particular social viewpoint. Harry is highly independent. He thinks for himself with a brilliant head on his shoulders and his feet ever more firmly implanted in hard ground. It is all this that makes Harry a widely respected character by both students and faculty—a young man with a sensational future indeed."

But Harry was also still getting high a lot. Marty Koffman remem-bered going to Harry's room in Sunset House with Will Iselin and get-ting stoned. He said Iselin kept spilling the bong water. "Harry was the first Republican teenager I ever met who was seriously Republican," Koffman said. "Harry was the only guy I knew on campus who wanted Ford to win, which was kind of funny."

In the spring of 1977, though, something happened to Harry that is still mysterious and difficult to explain. Swett remembered a telling in-cident in the urban history course he took with Harry in the winter and spring of senior year. The conceit of the class was to study Ameri-can history by studying the history of her cities. The teacher Ed Quat-tlebaum took the small class to Lawrence, Massachusetts, to study the old, abandoned textile mills. Lawrence was the next city over from

Andover but of course it was a world away from the manicured charm of an old New England town. One day the class was meeting in the Underwood Room, where there was a large projection screen at the front of the room that could be used for slide shows. After Quattlebaum finished his slide presentation, he went around the room asking questions. "There were only about five or six of us in this course," Swett remembered. "And he called out our names and asked us various very pointed questions. And I just remember he went to Harry and asked Harry a question. And Harry just looked back at him, and his mouth sort of opened a couple of times. And he just stared back at Dr. Quattlebaum and didn't answer. And eventually Quattlebaum went on to someone else. And it was the most startling thing for Harry, who would be the kind of person who would immediately come back with a very strong response and an interesting response and have something to say." Concluded Swett, "I guess he had kind of a nervous breakdown."

Peter Begley remembered driving through Andover the following spring on a road trip from the University of Virginia, where he was a freshman, and seeing Harry. "He was not in good shape," he said. "He looked strung out." Said Koffman, "Through senior year, Harry disappeared for a while. Harry never talked about it with me or if he did I've forgotten exactly what he said. . . . Somebody said he had some sort of breakdown. . . . He was down in Gil's cottage. I remember once going down and Harry just wasn't around so I didn't think anything about it. I said, 'Where's Harry?' Nobody knew and then he was back."

Of course, this was not the kind of thing that got talked about much at Andover in those days. He ended up taking a leave of absence but returned to school in time for graduation. There was no mention of his temporary withdrawal from the school on his record and there was no letter home from Sewall discussing it with his parents or explaining what had happened. Ironically, the winter trimester of Harry's senior year turned out to be his best academically, with a 6 and three 5s in his four courses. The only sign that something was not quite right was the

2 he received in Quattlebaum's history class that trimester, after receiving a 5 the trimester before. But there were no comments from Quattlebaum, or any other teachers. His younger sister, Mary Ellen, remembered that Harry took a leave from Andover but couldn't recall the details. His older siblings Rick and Karna remembered his return home, too, but again without details. "There was not a horrific uproar in the family that Harry's gone crazy, what are we going to do?" Rick Bull said. "Back in those days everybody had a kid that went bonkers."

Harry's troubles continued at Yale, where he matriculated the following year. It probably wasn't the right school for him, but he seemed to feel an obligation to carry on the Bull family tradition. "Going to Yale was an incredibly important thing to him," Giles McNamee said. But he hadn't really done much academically at Andover to distinguish himself. Harry's admittance to Yale was not atypical of the era: He was a Yale legacy and it was a time when fully half of the Andover senior class of 300—150 people—were accepted to Harvard, Yale, or Princeton. "Everybody was going in herds to Harvard and Yale and Princeton," said Marty Koffman. It's just the way it was at that time and Harry, along with many others, was a beneficiary of having the right DNA at the right time.

That didn't make him happy to be there, though. In fact, whatever had been bothering him in his senior year at Andover pretty much continued during his time at Yale, abetted by copious amounts of drugs and alcohol. Peter Begley recalled another road trip that took him and a friend up to Harvard to visit his brother, Adam. He picked up various friends along the way, including Harry. "He was smoking, drinking, and snorting enough for three guys," Peter said. "I mean completely out of control." Harry then just passed out in the car. "Harry seemed fairly whacked out," he continued. "You had the feeling like Harry was burning the candle at both ends. But he was extraordinarily game. He could put away booze. He could put away drugs."

Harry's time in New Haven was short: one semester, and then he took a leave of absence. He was allowed to return to Yale, but he never did. "I think at the time they called it a nervous breakdown," McNamee said. "I don't know what you'd call it now, but essentially this was a guy who was too young for everything he did. He punched above his weight every step of his life and it just got to him." McNamee said the catalyst for Harry's problem was a "romantic entanglement" gone wrong. It seemed he caught a girlfriend cheating on him with another student.

It can be assumed the failure at Yale stung, given the expectations of Harry being the keeper of the Bull legacy both there and at Andover. "He idolized his father and really wanted to be successful," McNamee said. Harry's parents were "absolute sweethearts," making the pressure on him to succeed something altogether subtler. "He was always sort of chasing some shadows," he continued. "He was chasing his own personal demons that he brought with him. This was a kid who needed a few hours on the couch."

Harry returned to Chicago. He was living at home. He spent some time at his grandmother's house in Winnetka. He worked in some menial jobs for a few months until he resolved to get back to the task of doing what he needed to do to succeed in an academic setting. The family took Harry's departure from Yale in stride, although they insisted he get a new start somewhere else. Rick thought his brother's problems at Yale were more or less just a continuation of the problems he'd had in his senior year at Andover. "The same self-doubt, bonkers, call it what you will," he said.

Harry eventually buckled down. He took summer classes at Elmhurst College, in Elmhurst, Illinois. He also worked as a clerk on the Chicago Board Options Exchange. After a semester and summer spent regrouping, he was ready to go back to school. The question was where. He and his father got in the car and started driving east on the Stevenson Expressway toward downtown Chicago. When they got toward Lake Shore Drive, his father asked him if he wanted to go north or south. Should he drive toward Northwestern, in Evanston, or toward

the University of Chicago, on South Ellis Avenue? Harry said, "North."
They drove up to Evanston, walked into the Northwestern admissions
office, and enrolled Harry into the class of 1982. Those were the days
when such things could happen, especially if you were from a prominent Chicago-area family and you were transferring from Yale. And if
you were as inherently brilliant as was Harry.

At Northwestern, Harry was a star. He graduated Phi Beta Kappa.
He was no longer the immature reckless party boy he had been at Andover and during his brief stint at Yale. He was finally coming into his
own, and achieving the academic success that so many had expected of
him for so long. "By comparison to Andover and Yale, Northwestern
was a cakewalk for him," McNamee said. "He went from being just another guy at school to being the smartest guy in his class."

Of course, Harry still managed to have fun. He hung out often with
his older brother Rick, who was then a bond trader in downtown Chicago. Harry started off living in Evanston but then moved down to
Wrigleyville to live with Rick; he commuted back and forth to Northwestern. They shared a case of Budweiser every day. "I know he had a
twelve-pack every day because I was having another half a case every
day," Rick said.

From Northwestern, Harry enrolled at the University of Chicago
Law School. He wanted to be an attorney. Becoming a lawyer would
be one way for him to express his admiration for his father. Harry
quickly fell in with a group of law students who remained friends
throughout their time together at the University of Chicago and beyond. They were smart. They were serious. But they weren't overly serious. "Harry was fun," said Kathy Roach, one member of the group.
"Harry enjoyed life to the fullest and he was a super smart guy." Harry
was interested in the arcane aspects of tax law, which only a few
students—out of a class of around two hundred—found compelling.
Even for someone interested in tax law, Harry "had a heart full of

gold, too, and was a smart guy who obviously did well for himself with pretty much everything that he did," Roach continued. The summer after his first year, Harry worked at Tenney & Bentley, an old-line Chicago law firm founded in 1847 that did legal work for the Bulls' paper company. He did research and drafted memoranda on the law of gifts, unfair competition, indemnification of corporate officers, and environmental protection.

Ken Cera transferred to the University of Chicago Law School after one year at the Boston College Law School. "I didn't know anybody or anything," he said. "I just kind of showed up." He had missed the first, intense year of law school, where covalent bonds are forged among the law students. "I was an outsider," he said. He lived in an apartment by himself. One day, early on, he went to a law school party. He met Harry. They chatted. No big deal. The next day, the doorbell rang at his apartment. It was Harry. Cera thought it was a bit odd that this guy he barely knew was at his apartment door. But Harry just sensed that Cera needed a friend and someone to show him the ropes. "It was very generous," he said. "I think it was motivated by nothing other than kindness." They remained friends from that day onward: a liberal from San Francisco and the neo-conservative, establishment figure from the suburbs of Chicago.

Harry invited Cera out to Hinsdale to meet his family. Harry offered him invitations on holidays and during vacations, when it made little sense for Cera to go back to California. He recalled the family's "beautiful suburban" house and heard all about Bradner, "the third oldest company in Illinois," and its history. Although the Bulls and Cera could not have been more diametrically opposed politically, their conversations were always cordial. Harry could hold his own in their debates, too. "He expressed his opinions but he was always polite," Cera said. Reagan was a particular point of contention. Harry was a huge Reagan fan; Cera not so much. Harry was "very pro-business," with typically conservative views: "We need less regulation. We need lower taxes. Get the government out." But he was also utterly tolerant on social issues, including abortion.

Not surprisingly, the academics were intense. It was a highly pressured environment with very motivated people. "It was a tough place," Cera said. "It was very competitive. People are calculating grade point averages to the hundredths of a point." He and Harry took tax-law classes. "Tax law is a very esoteric thing that most people in law school try to avoid like the plague," he explained. After his second year, Harry worked as a summer associate at Jenner & Block, one of the city's premier law firms and one of the best in the country. His focus was on corporate law and tax law.

During that summer, Harry proposed that he and Cera share an apartment together for their third year of law school. Through a family connection, Harry had found a beautiful apartment on Burling Street, at the edge of Lincoln Park, one of the nicest neighborhoods in the city. Harry furnished the place and had a car they could use to commute the thirty minutes to the law school every day. All Cera had to do was show up, and delight in his good fortune to be Harry's friend. "Still, to this day, I don't know why me," he said. "I mean, we were friends, but there were lots of other friends, but just like when we first met, for some reason he reached out to me and I guess we connected despite our many differences." The apartment had a balcony, where they kept a barbecue. "We would sit out on the balcony and barbecue chicken or whatever it was, and drink beer and smoke joints," he said. "We would just have a great time. That's what I remember from those days. It's a really great memory, and it was all made available by him." Harry was the kind of guy who was as happy drinking a scotch, neat, as he was eating a sausage at Wrigley Field. "Give me two tube steaks, all the way," would be a typical Harry Bull request. For his part, Cera wasn't sure what Harry was referring to until he realized it was two hot dogs in one bun with all sorts of toppings and sauces. "I remember at the time eating three of them and enjoying it," he said. They also went sailing together a few times on Lake Michigan in the Bull family sailboat, a twenty-six-foot Grampian named *Semper Spero* ("Forever Hope" in Latin). Cera didn't know much about sailing, but it was clear to him that Harry did.

In his third year at Chicago Law, Harry met Pam Kyros. She grew up on Chicago's South Shore, a predominantly black neighborhood along Lake Michigan. Her grandparents were Greek immigrants who settled in Chicago and had done well in the restaurant business. After graduating Hope College, she worked at the I. Magnin store in Chicago, selling clothes while looking for a better job in the advertising business. She was working at I. Magnin when she met Harry at a brunch hosted by mutual friends. "When I arrived at the brunch, there were people mingling around in the house but mostly the crowd was spilling out onto the wooden back porch and the small backyard," Pam recalled. She remembered being "squished" into a corner and meeting Harry. But she was in a long-distance relationship with another guy and left abruptly. "I left Harry standing there with a disappointed look on his face," she said. "The whole way home I regretted my stupid awkward exit!" She had not given Harry her phone number. A few days later, Harry called Pam's friend and asked her for Pam's number. But she told Harry that Pam was dating someone else. She also called up Pam right away. "You don't want to go out with him, do you?" she asked Pam.

"Call him back and give him my number," she instructed. Harry called her the next day. They had dinner. They started dating and were pretty much a couple from then on. "You [could] tell right away he was smart and funny and very engaging," she said. "I knew he was very interested at that party because every time I turned around, he was right next to me." At the time, Harry was about to graduate from law school, take the bar exam, and start a full-time job at Jenner & Block. Pam wasn't quite sure what that was, though. "I kept telling people I was dating this guy who worked at H&R Block," she said. "Harry was never pompous about it. He'd be like, 'Pam, I don't work at H&R Block.' And so then, it became like kind of a joke."

Early on in their relationship, Harry needed to prepare for the bar exam. He and Ken Cera had been studying like crazy for weeks. "They had set up card tables in the living room and had all their law books and study guides spread out everywhere," Pam said. As exam day got closer, Harry told Pam he was holing up in a hotel room to study for three days straight. He did not tell her where he was. He asked her not to call him. Right away, though, he kept calling her when he was supposed to be studying for the bar. "He was cute," she said. On the night before the exam, she called him and suggested they go see a movie "so he could relax and stop worrying," she said. He agreed right away.

After the exam, Pam recalled, Harry and Ken had a "scrum," their word for a barbecue party. Pam remembered that the law students at the scrum were comparing notes about the exam; they were all convinced they had failed. Of course, they all passed.

PAM AND HARRY WERE MARRIED on September 28, 1986. He was twenty-six; she was a year younger. Lots of their friends were getting married so it just seemed like the natural thing to do. "We were going to weddings all the time," Pam said, "and then one day, Harry just said to me, 'Well, I guess we should get married,' and I didn't like the way he asked me and I'm like, 'What?' So then he had to ask me better." But she said yes.

Harry's parents threw a shower for her at the Union League Club. "It wasn't like stuffy or anything, but they did everything really nicely," she said. The wedding, for around two hundred guests, was at the Saints Constantine and Helen Greek Orthodox Church in Palos Hills. The church is large, with a lot of white and gold. The reception afterward was at the Drake Hotel in Oak Brook. It was a traditional Greek wedding, with the usual boisterousness and dancing. Harry loved it.

"He was somebody you could put anywhere and he'd have a good time and everybody would love him," Pam said. They honeymooned in Hawaii, at the Hotel Hana Maui.

Harry and Pam quickly settled into married life. They lived in the shadow of Wrigley Field, in a rented apartment on West Eddy Street. Harry was an associate at Jenner & Block; Pam was a graphic designer for a menswear manufacturer. They were typical young urban professionals, and seemed to be enjoying every minute of it. After a few years, Jenner & Block asked Harry to open a new office for the firm in Lake Forest, a wealthy suburb north of Chicago. They were in their mid-twenties and didn't want to move out of Chicago, and Harry didn't want to commute from Chicago to Lake Forest. He told Jenner & Block he wouldn't do it.

Instead, Harry moved to Jenner's Chicago rival, Winston & Strawn, where he continued his legal practice focused on tax and tax-related issues on behalf of corporations, municipalities, and individuals. He was becoming a tax expert, and a well-regarded one. On schedule, he and Pam moved out of their Wrigleyville rental and bought a fourth-floor, six-room walk-up condominium in a prewar building on Lake Shore Drive, overlooking Lake Michigan, off Waveland Avenue. It had a sun-room in the front and windows on three sides. They could see both the lake and park from the apartment. "When I looked at the pictures [from back then]," Pam said, "we looked like we were fifty when we were thirty." On September 4, 1991, Harry and Pam had their first child, Madeline Francis Bull, known as Maddie. Pam decided to leave her job to be both a full-time mother and a part-time freelancer.

Harry did well at Winston & Strawn, and advanced quickly. "His reputation here was very good, as a very smart guy, a very careful guy, and a very analytical guy," explained George Lombardi, a Winston partner who knew Harry well. "Just a top-flight tax lawyer. What made him a little unusual . . . Harry always had a mischievous sense of humor. He wasn't the stereotypical guy you would find in a tax department."

He was doing a bunch of complicated airplane leasing deals, which had a complex tax component, making Harry nearly indispensable.

In 1993, Winston asked Harry to move to New York City to be part of its burgeoning office there. The implied promise was that if he moved to Winston in New York, and continued to perform as well as he had in Chicago, he would be on the two-year fast track to partner. "Harry would not have been asked to go out there had it not been in the works that he would become a partner," Lombardi said. "I don't know the specifics of that conversation but they wouldn't take somebody who wasn't [a] highly-thought-of attorney and ask him to go out to New York." Harry took the deal. They moved to Rye, New York, a Westchester County suburb, and rented a house. Harry commuted each day to Winston's downtown Manhattan office. "He went from the frying pan into the fire," Pam said. "It was big-time deals and it was hard." As they were thinking about the move to New York, Harry conceded he wanted to make partner but that he been practicing law long enough and maybe was ready for a change. Pam said that longer-term, Harry wanted to teach English or history at a place like Andover: "That was really what he wanted to do."

Pam joined the Newcomers Club in Rye, and she and Maddie joined a playgroup. "We made friends right away with little kids," Pam said. "A lot of our life was kid stuff." Harry joined a sailing club in Rye, on Long Island Sound, and he would go sailing there nearly every weekend. They also took trips into the Hudson Valley. Each Wednesday, Pam took an art class at the Metropolitan Museum of Art on Fifth Avenue. She and Harry would then have dinner in the city. "It was actually kind of fun," she said. Within months of moving to Rye, in October 1993, the Bulls' second daughter—Alexandra Lois Bull, known as Lexi—was born.

But it was not exactly home. The commute was hard on Harry, as was the daily grind. Pam had friends but not like the ones she had in Chicago. Will Iselin and his (then) wife and daughters used to visit

Harry and Pam in Rye. Iselin recalled that Harry "was not all that happy" working at Winston & Strawn. He didn't love going back and forth from Rye to Manhattan each day. Pam didn't want to live in the city, and they probably couldn't have afforded to live there in any event. Iselin thought, in the end, neither Harry nor Pam loved living in Rye, but for different reasons. Pam, he believed, was homesick and wanted to return to Chicago, while Harry felt "suffocated" living in the suburbs.

On September 1, 1994, Harry made partner at Winston & Strawn, some nine years after graduating from law school. That day, Dick Bull called Pam to see whether Harry had made it. When she said that, yes, he had been promoted, he called his son. "How 'bout you come back and work at Bradner?" he asked. His father offered him the job of general counsel, working for Terence Shea, the chairman and CEO. Pam said it was a "tough decision" because they were increasingly comfortable in New York. "But I think his dad really wanted him to come home and run this company," she said. It seemed it was what Harry wanted to do, too. He had achieved his goal of making partner in a major law firm. But he was tired of practicing tax law, tired of the daily commute. He was eager to return to Chicago (as was Pam) and to raise his family in a more traditional, and familiar, environment. On some level, he recognized that working at Bradner, with the understanding that he would one day run the business (once he had learned what it was all about), was his birthright, and what his father needed (and wanted) him to do. "When I look back at the pictures, he wasn't looking healthy," Pam said. "You know? I mean, it was a stressful job. He had gained weight. It probably was, looking back at it, a relief. I'm sure his dad meant to give him an easier lifestyle." Giles McNamee said there was little doubt that he would return home to run Bradner. "He respected his father more than anybody else on the face of the earth," he said, "and so if his father asked him to do something, he would do it. No questions asked." It may have seemed odd that Harry quit Winston &

Strawn on the day he made partner—very few people would do such a thing. But for Harry, the chance to return home and raise his growing family, to know that he would one day take over the family business and that he could more easily enjoy the good life—sailing on Lake Michigan, hanging out at the family's cabin on the Upper Peninsula of Michigan—proved irresistible.

The Bulls moved back into their condo on Lake Shore Drive. Maddie went to preschool in Chicago. Harry moved up quickly at Bradner. In short order he was named the company's secretary and vice chairman, and then, in 1998, he was named chairman and CEO. His brother, who also worked at the company, said Harry was "an unbelievable administrator" and had the ability to make "logical leaps." The company did well in those years, although it was clear the demand for paper and paper products was beginning to decrease as the internet era unfolded. After a few years, when it came time for Maddie to go to school, the Bulls decided to sell the condo downtown and move back to Hinsdale, on Briargate Terrace. They lived five miles from Harry's parents. On September 14, 1998—the same year Harry became Bradner's CEO—his son, George Harry Calvin Bull, was born in Northwestern's hospital.

Things were good. Harry enjoyed being a father. He impressed his kids' friends by spelling *Mississippi* backward, or by playing guitar and singing with Maddie and Lexi. As for his new role at Bradner, Lombardi remembered that although the job of CEO was very different from that of corporate lawyer, Harry seemed to enjoy it. There was a lot more socializing to do than when Harry was a lawyer but the hours were much more genial, and he could control his own schedule in a way he couldn't in New York as a partner in a major law firm. "At Bradner, the job was more taking clients to baseball games," Pam said, half joking. "I mean it was a business. He was a smart man and he ran a company, but it wasn't like people forcing him [to do things]. It wasn't the hours that he had. It was a nicer lifestyle."

Whether in Long Island Sound, or in Lake Michigan, or at the family's small cabin in Hayward, Wisconsin, Harry enjoyed sailing. "Wherever wind and water came together, you'd find Harry in a sailboat," his brother said. Whenever they went on vacation to a warm-weather place, sailing was always a big part of how Harry, Rick, and their father spent their time. They saw it as fun, relaxing, and an escape. "Get away from the things of man," Rick said. He called Harry "a fine sailor" and "a tough sailor," noting that they had sailed together through a snowstorm. When Harry was at Northwestern, he had a little twelve-foot Butterfly that he would use to go sailing on Lake Michigan, in addition to the larger boat the family shared.

Pam said the whole "sailing thing" was a bit of a "thorn in our side." She was not a particularly enthusiastic sailor—she would get seasick—and of course Harry could not get enough of it. Bottom line, Pam knew that sailing was an important part of Harry's life. Harry had been sailing since he was two years old. "I knew he was sailing from way back," she said. "His dad liked sailing. He liked sailing." The Bull men would rent a sailboat in the Caribbean and go sailing for a week. "It was great," said Karna Bull, Harry's older sister. "It was fun to be out sailing with them, really." Harry had enjoyed being part of the yacht club in Rye, allowing him to easily go sailing in the Long Island Sound. And of course, there was the sailing up on Round Lake, in Hayward. When Harry and Pam lived on Waveland Avenue, downtown, they were near Lake Michigan, and Harry would go sailing regularly. "For him it really was a passion," Harry's younger sister, Mary Ellen, said. "He loved it. . . . If you were golfer, you would try to golf if it was appropriate. Well, if there was an opportunity to sail he wanted to try to do that. So they would go out on that stupid boat."

Harry's love of sailing was something he wanted to share with his two daughters, Maddie and Lexi. He could always count on them wanting to join him on a sail on Lake Michigan, even though it was a bit of a trek—twenty-three miles—to get from Hinsdale to Monroe Harbor, on Lake Michigan. In August 1999, Harry wanted to take his two daughters on an overnight sailing trip on Lake Michigan. "It wasn't unusual," Pam said. "He had taken the girls sailing before." He had even taken them on an overnight sailing trip. So far that summer, in fact, they had gone sailing together three times. But this was to be their first overnighter of the season. He liked to be with them and preferred having them with him alone rather than with other friends or relatives. It wasn't for Pam. She had not sailed with Harry for two years. "I never liked it," she said. Pam was not a big sailor and, in any event, George was less than a year old and a sailboat was no place for an infant. She would generally vote to stay with him at home, in Hinsdale, while Harry, Maddie, and Lexi headed to the sailboat.

That was the plan for Saturday, August 14, 1999. Harry packed up the family's Lincoln and set off with Maddie and Lexi for Monroe Harbor. The idea was to sail overnight in the *Semper Spero* to Waukegan, Illinois—forty-seven miles up the coast—and sail back to Monroe Harbor on Sunday. Then the family was going to head up together to the cabin in Hayward for a week's vacation. Harry had let his management team know he was going to be out of the office for two weeks. "I was to stay home with George, who was a baby, and I was going to pack," Pam said.

Harry drove with his daughters to the harbor. When he got there on Saturday at around noon, Ilse Krause and her boyfriend, George Petkovic, were at the marina, too. They were hoping the regatta that day, the Verve Cup, would be taking place, although the wind was particularly strong. Krause spotted Maddie and Alexandra. She noticed Maddie was carrying her backpack, a life vest, a bag of gear, and a sleeping bag. Harry asked her if she could carry it all. Maddie said that she could, which made Krause smile. "It was such an endearing moment," she recalled. Harry and his daughters took the launch out to the sailboat.

But Harry decided the water in Lake Michigan was too rough for a sail that day. The Verve Cup race was also postponed because of the inclement weather. "Harry is a very safe sailor," Cele Bull, Rick's wife, said later. So Harry turned around and drove back to the house in Hinsdale. They all stayed at home that night. But Harry was determined to go the next morning. "I really want to do this," he told Pam. "I really want to go. I want to do this sail." A cousin, in his late teens or early twenties, was supposed to join Harry and the girls on the trip. "At the last minute," Pam said, "he didn't go and Harry went anyway."

The next morning, Harry and his daughters set off again in the Lincoln for Monroe Harbor. Harry had brought along three Playmate coolers filled with food and drinks, including some beer. As before, they were planning to be out on the lake for the next two days. At twenty-six feet long, the *Semper Spero* was nothing fancy, in keeping with the Bull family ethos: It was a 1973 Grampian with a mainsail, a jib, a small cabin, two small benches facing each other, with cushions, for people to sit on, the tiller, and a small, 9.9-horsepower outboard motor, designed to get the boat into a harbor and to a mooring after a day of sailing. The Bulls had bought the boat about ten years earlier, and the three Bull men shared in its ownership and its use. At around nine Sunday morning, Harry called his brother and told him that he and the girls would be either sailing northeast, to St. Joe's or Benton Harbor across the lake in Michigan, or sailing north along the Illinois side of the lake to North Point Marina, right on the border between Illinois and Wisconsin, in Winthrop Harbor.

Krause and Petkovic were back at the marina, too. Again, Krause noticed the two girls. They rode together on the tender. "I was quite taken with how pretty and sweet the girls were," she recalled. "I think it was the little one, 'Lexi' that had her hair in pigtails that morning. Her hair was goldish brown, a gold color that comes from sun and water. Mattie [sic] was more blonde, and may have had a cap on. I remember one of them had incredibly long eyelashes. . . . I thought of how perfect and unfreckled their arms and legs were. The older girl's blond hair on her legs reminded me of mine when I was a little girl. Both girls were wearing matching birkenstockish sandals with a print that had a lot of green and yellow. They were wearing their blue life vests. They were so good on the tender—looking around, looking at me, absorbing everything that was going on." She remembered Harry commenting to Maddie that the weather was much better on Sunday than it had been the day before. "He got a big nod out of her," Krause continued. "The father seemed so connected with the girls. I was impressed with the casual, comfortable way he spoke. I thought to myself, what lucky parents." The temperature was in the upper seventies to low eighties, and the wind was light. The sun was shining. "We could clearly see Indiana," Krause remembered. "The water was a lovely, light greenish translucent color. It was warm and wonderful."

At about noon, Colleen D'Agostion, at Monroe Harbor, took Harry and the girls to mooring 31. She dropped Krause and Petkovic at their boat first. Krause recalled she had observed "a unique harmony between the girls and their father, and that was beautiful." On the way out in the tender boat, Harry told D'Agostion they were going to have "a sleepover," either at St. Joe's or North Point Marina or possibly Michigan City, Indiana (southeast of Chicago), or New Buffalo, Michigan (due east of Chicago). "The girls just [want] to swim at a nice beach," he told her. He also said they would be returning sometime on Monday "after the journey." She reported they appeared to be in "good health and good spirits."

Although the wind that day was blowing predominantly from the north toward the southeast, Harry decided to sail in that direction, which would have made the sail a bit of a slog, given that it would be a close haul just off the wind and with the sails tightly trimmed. Pam thought they were headed to Lake Forest, Illinois, some thirty-five miles north of Chicago. At around seven thirty Sunday night—an hour or so before sunset—Sara Pederson, from Kenosha, Wisconsin, was "powering back" from Chicago to Racine, Wisconsin, when she saw a "white and blue sailboat" about seven miles east of Waukegan, Illinois, with "two young girls sitting on the bow," heading "in an easterly direction." She remembered that the temperature was in the low sixties—she was wearing a jacket—and the wind was blowing at about fifteen knots, in a southeasterly direction. She said she saw Harry in the stern of the boat. She seemed to think it was a bit odd that the Bulls were heading east at that time of the day, when most people around then are heading west into a harbor for the night. She didn't think much of it at the time, though. As the two boats passed, she waved. "The girls waved back," she recalled.

USUALLY, HARRY WOULD CALL PAM "a lot," she said, when he and the girls were out sailing. He had his cell phone with him but he didn't call her that Sunday. Even though he was not supposed to be back in Chicago until the next day, she was worried enough about not hearing from him that she called Rick. "Don't worry," he told her. The battery in his cell phone had probably died. "I'm sure when he docks, you'll hear from him," she recalled him telling her. "But I thought, *Isn't it weird?* He would've called me from somewhere, at the marina or something." They both agreed not to worry about the fact that Harry had not called Pam on Sunday night. Harry's mother came over to stay with Pam. "I did think something was wrong," she said. "I was very worried." Harry's father tried to comfort her. "Look," he told her, "I've had a lot of situations in my life like this and they've all turned out okay."

But on Monday, when Pam still had not heard from Harry, she got increasingly concerned. She called her brother, Tom, himself an ardent sailor who had sailed with Harry. "Monday morning when they hadn't checked in was when she really panicked," he remembered. "When she called me it was almost one of those calls where we were not wanting to believe the gravity of the situation. She didn't really communicate a huge level of concern. It was more [like] something weird is happening: 'Harry and the girls aren't home and I haven't heard from them. What do you think?' And it was a beautiful sunny day and I remember probably saying something like, 'Well, maybe they're just in the doldrums out there and the batteries are dead, everything will be fine. Call me as soon as you know something,' and that was that, and I hung up." Tom went to a meeting at his law firm but couldn't concentrate as he began to process in his mind what may have happened. After about twenty minutes, he left the meeting, got in his car, and drove the three hours from his home in Grand Rapids, Michigan, to Chicago. "I remember driving ninety miles an hour the whole way there," he said.

Rick tried several times on Monday to try to reach Harry on his cell phone without luck. He and Pam decided to go to the media with the news that Harry and the girls were missing. Rick called the local radio and television stations, shared the news, and asked them to put the word out. "Rick pulled the pin out of the grenade on this press thing and then left, and so I became the family spokesman and that got more intense," Tom Kyros said. "I never once thought anything other than *This is all going to get resolved, but somebody has got to help Pam from going crazy until this all gets figured out, because everything's fine*," he continued. "We talked about that and I told her everything was going to be fine, I was positive. She wasn't hysterical freaking out. She wasn't crying and wailing. She was worried. But she's pretty tough." They decided that Tom had better call their parents, who were then in Arizona, before WGN-TV, a local superstation, started reporting the news nationally. Tom told his parents they might be hearing something in the media about Harry and the girls but not to worry. "My father was worried but he said, 'All right, well, keep us up to date. I'm sure it will be fine.'" However, half an hour later they called back and said they were leaving Arizona and flying to Chicago.

On Monday evening, Rick called the North Point Marina, to see if the *Semper Spero* had been there on Sunday night. But the marina could not confirm whether Harry had been there or not. Rick also called the Waukegan Port District to see if it could confirm that Harry had been "at a transient dock" on either Sunday or Monday. He had no luck there, either. Of course, Rick explained, on overnight sailing trips, it was not the least bit unusual for his brother to pull into harbors during the evening hours "for the purpose of avoiding paying transient slip fees."

Rick said his brother had some idiosyncratic "boating habits." He liked to leave the 9.9-horsepower motor in gear when the motor was off. He also liked to drop the jib onto the forward deck, in an unsecured fashion, when swimming off the boat. He and the girls liked to swim off the stern, most often without wearing life preservers. Rick said the girls were "reasonably proficient" in swimming. Sometimes, for "safety purposes," Harry would attach a "flotation device" to a mooring line and throw it off the stern so that if the girls "became tired" while swimming, they could grab onto something. Harry's father said that when Harry and the girls would swim off the sailboat, the ladder would be down, the main sail would be stowed, the jib would be down on the deck, the motor would be in the water, life jackets would be tossed into the water but not worn, and the fifteen-foot mooring line would be tied to a flotation device. He had been swimming with Harry and the girls in Lake Michigan a month earlier. Rick's wife, Cele, also said she had been swimming with Harry and his girls on numerous occasions from the boat. "Harry knew how quickly the boat could drift away even when the sail was down," she recalled. "Harry would never be far away from the boat if he was also in the water with the girls." She said both girls were very good swimmers and belonged to Salt Creek Club, a private swim club in Hinsdale, near the Bulls' home. "During the summer, the girls would swim almost every day."

Rick said that over the years his younger brother had reformed the somewhat reckless behavior of his youth and had become the "most prudent of men" as an adult, except in two ways. One was his daredevil approach to downhill skiing. He was like "greased lightning on skis," he said. "Fearless. Harry would just come screaming by me." Rick could not recall an instance when another skier passed him—except for his brother, Harry. The other "imprudent" thing Harry did was to swim off the back of the little sailboat even if someone had not remained behind on the boat. "He'd just dive over the side," Rick said, "and many was the time. It's hot around here in the summer and you've got wonderful fresh water all around, so frequently we would just swim over the side into the sacred swimming grounds. The 'sacred swimming grounds' were right below wherever we were at that instant." There was no anchoring a boat in Lake Michigan, of course, where the depth of the water can reach 925 feet. "This started early on between me, Harry, and Dad," he continued. "Dad and I would be in the water and Harry would cannonball over the side."

On those occasions, Rick recalled reminding his brother, "There's no one on the boat, you moron."

"Oh, don't worry about it," Harry said.

But Rick worried about it. "Well, I'd immediately zip over and up the ladder," he said. "This just went on for a decade. I'd go, 'Harry what are you doing?' He didn't get it. He didn't see the danger."

Rick figured that since it was a hot, summer day in August, "I'll bet you one John Lennon guitar" that Harry said to his girls, "Hey, let's go swimming, let's take a dip." He's sure this is what happened because that's "what he did every time, 'Everybody in the sacred swimming grounds.'"

On Monday night, around nine o'clock, Rick called the Coast Guard at Calumet Harbor in Chicago to report that the *Semper Spero* was twelve hours overdue and had not returned home as expected. The next day, at 10:29 a.m., the Coast Guard asked the Lake County, Illinois, Sheriff's Office Marine Unit to help it with the investigation. Their mission was to find the boat and to find Harry, Maddie, and Lexi. To Pam, the search seemed like an eternity. "It was crazy," she said. "It was horrible." Planes were searching. Boats were searching. Friends in their boats were searching in the area off the coast of Lake Forest. Several boats from the Lake County Sheriff's Office were dispatched; one searched north, between Waukegan and Winthrop Harbor, another south between Waukegan and Highland Park. Each boat moved farther and farther offshore as the search widened.

The Bulls gave a picture of Harry and the girls to the media. "The idea was to make it a news story so people are talking about it, so people are out there looking, and it really did become a news story," Tom Kyros said. "It was the CEO of this old-line Chicago company and his two little girls are lost. Then there were TV trucks parked out in front of Pam's house, and there were people with microphones in their hands surrounding me out on her front lawn." The TV reporters did live stand-ups from the Bulls' front lawn for the ten o'clock news. "It was crazy," he said. "It was really, really a different world."

The news media camped out on Pam's front lawn. There were cops at the house and reporters everywhere. Pam didn't even dare to look outside the front door of her house. "I do remember one night I went out the back door and cut through the neighbor's yard and went for a walk," Pam said. "I never even went out the front door ever. And coming back and seeing the lights were on, it was nighttime, all these people, I was thinking, *Whose life is this?*" A month before, on July 16, the world had just witnessed the media firestorm that resulted from the disappearance of JFK Jr.'s plane off the coast of Martha's Vineyard. Pam remembered that she and Harry had been at the family's cabin that weekend in Brown County, Indiana, to celebrate his parents' forty-ninth wedding anniversary. CNN was in a continuous loop over the missing plane. "He's like, 'Oh, he's toast,'" Pam remembered. "And his mother said, 'Harry, that's horrible to say.'" Of course, the Bulls all knew that Harry had known John at Andover.

Mary Ellen Bull remembered being at her parents' house and sick with worry. "There was this sense of concern and horror before we really knew what was going on," she remembered. "Just initially Harry hadn't checked in and it was twelve hours later and nobody was really sure where they were. I remember being on the phone because I couldn't sit still, I had to do something, I had to take control in some way, and being on the phone with like private boating people trying to hire other people to help go out and search, because I thought at the time that was the right thing to do, to get more people out there on their boats trying to find them."

At 7:09 p.m. on Tuesday, the Coast Guard located the *Semper Spero* about twenty-seven miles off the coast of the North Point Marina, in Lake Michigan. Nobody was on it. Pam and Tom were on the phone with the Coast Guard. They could hear the report coming through on the Coast Guard radio. Tom was convinced Harry and the girls were sleeping down in the cabin. "We had this tortured twenty minutes," he said.

Two Coast Guard officials boarded the boat and quickly "determined that the boat was unoccupied and abandoned." They took photographs of the boat before they boarded as well as while they were on it. Nothing unusual had obviously happened on the boat and there was no indication of "force, trauma or wrongdoing." When the boat was found, the mainsail was stowed and the jib was down but not secured. The engine was in the water and the throttle was engaged. The gas tank near the engine was empty. The swimming ladder was down. Six adult life jackets and two child life jackets were found stowed away on the deck of the boat. Whereas often when Harry and the girls would swim off the stern, he would throw the fifteen-foot line out the back, tied to a flotation device, this time the line was found inside the boat.

The next day at 10:55 a.m., four members of the Lake County Sheriff's Office boarded a Marine Unit boat and headed out to Harry's boat. The idea was to tow it back to Waukegan Harbor. At 12:43 p.m., while the deputies were on their way to where the *Acacia*, a Coast Guard cutter ship, was holding the *Semper Spero*, another Coast Guard boat reported that it had found Harry's body floating on the surface of the

water about seven miles east of Lake Forest, Illinois. The deputies decided to go to where Harry's body was found, and another Marine
Unit vessel was sent to tow the *Semper Spero* back to the harbor. He was
wearing his bathing suit, but no life jacket. He had left his shirt on the
boat; his brother said he would only take it off to go swimming, because
of his sensitivity to the sun. While the deputies were en route to ren-
dezvous with the Coast Guard boat that had found Harry's body, a
Coast Guard helicopter had located what seemed, at first, to be seven-
year-old Maddie's body floating four feet below the surface of the water,
also about eight miles east of Lake Forest. She was not wearing a life
jacket, either. One report stated that Maddie's body was a mile and a
half away from her father's, but the sheriff's report put their distance
apart at two hundred yards. She was found at 12:59 p.m. on August 18.
Their bodies were loaded onto the Coast Guard ship and brought
back to the Waukegan Harbor south fuel dock, where the Lake County
Coroner's Office took possession. Meanwhile, the search for Lexi
continued. Tom Kyros remembered that "every time something would
happen, I was the one that would go and report it to Pam."

The bodies of Harry and his daughter arrived back at Waukegan
Harbor around 2 p.m. "Unfortunately the image that sticks with me
the most is when the Coast Guard had retrieved Harry's body and him
in a body bag with them taking him off a boat onto a dock, and that
was on the news and that was so horrible," Mary Ellen Bull said. "You
don't realize, until that happens to you personally, the horrific things
that we see on the television all the time that impact people. It doesn't
occur to you how those loved ones are going to have to see that over
and over again. So that was pretty horrific."

Prior to performing autopsies, the coroner's office met with Harry's
father. After viewing Polaroid photographs of the two bodies, he identified them as his son Harry and granddaughter Maddie. Autopsies
were ordered. At 3:45 p.m., a pathologist in the Lake County Coroner's
Office performed an autopsy on Maddie. She was wearing a one-piece

pink, yellow, and orange bathing suit. Just prior to the autopsy, one sheriff's deputy saw no signs of trauma on her body, either before or after her bathing suit was removed. Harry's autopsy began at 4:40 p.m. He had been wearing only a purple, green, black, and maroon swimsuit. There were no signs of trauma to his body, either before or after his bathing suit was removed; the sheriff's deputy noted he had a large bruise inside his right biceps, but it appeared to be from an older injury. Dr. Witeck observed that, in his opinion, both Harry and Maddie had died of asphyxia due to drowning from an unspecified "boating/ swimming mishap." A subsequent toxicology report found no drugs or alcohol in Harry's body.

The next day, the two bodies were brought to the funeral home. There, it turned out, Harry's father had misidentified his granddaughter's body. The found body was not that of Maddie, age seven, but rather that of Lexi, age five.

Mary Ellen Bull had asked to view the bodies at the funeral home. "I actually had a dream that it was wrong, that it wasn't Maddie," she said. "I don't know why, and even now I don't know if it matters or why I did it, but the next day I went to the funeral home and made the guy show me her body, and it wasn't Maddie. It was Lexi." She told Pam, who had been sleeping in Lexi's bed, hoping that by doing so Lexi's body would be found. "All that Pam did was switch beds," Mary Ellen said. "For me personally those early days, and even weeks, were hoping against hope that somehow Maddie was still out there. That, who knows, that somehow she'd be returned to us." But Maddie's body was never found. "It's just a huge, deep lake," Pam was told. "It's like how hard it was to find the boat, think of finding one little body." She thinks Maddie's body "sank" and now she's in "heaven somewhere."

There are many theories about what may have happened aboard the *Semper Spero*. Rick Bull thought that everyone went swimming on a hot day—at his brother's urging—and then the unanchored boat drifted away. "It was pretty darned hard to swim over a mile an hour, even in a panic situation, for any distance," he said, "and the boat just got away from them." He said Harry was "pretty buoyant at this time in his life"—he weighed 250 pounds—and probably could have somehow swum to shore. "But as Pam said, 'He wasn't coming home without those girls.' And so this prudent, thoughtful, caring guy, who thought through almost every mundane decision in a methodical fashion, had a fatal error in judgment. It changed my religion. Prior to that day I was more concerned with staying out of hell. Now I'm more concerned with getting to heaven so I can kick his ass.'"

Mary Ellen Bull posited that a gust of wind might have blown the boat beyond their reach. "The girls had been on a swim team that summer, and so they were—even though they were young and little—they were pretty strong swimmers," she said. "I sort of imagine that either they were all in the water swimming and a gust of wind kind of pushed the boat farther away from them, or [it] drifted away from them. And Harry couldn't get back to the boat. Or that maybe one of them fell in and Harry jumped after that one and the second one got scared and jumped in the water, too. . . . The boat was getting farther away so she jumped in, too. I don't know. Every family has losses and illnesses. But people are supposed to die when they're old and sickly and not when they're young and healthy, and certainly not when they're children. I mean as horrible as that is, I just remember my mom, of all people, saying we just have to remember how lucky we are that we had known them at all. How blessed our lives are that we had them even for that short period. Because that was the only thing that could give me any sort of peace at all."

Karna Bull's theory of what happened was slightly more nuanced. "Lexi, the younger daughter, was sort of a defiant kid," she said. "And I think Harry was saying, 'Yes we're going to go swimming, wait, wait, wait,' and she decided to jump off the boat. Now, they could swim, but normally what would have happened is he would have put the anchor out, he would have thrown the life preservers out, and that kind of thing because they were out in the middle of the water. She jumped the gun. He went in because she probably didn't seem safe and I think what happened was that he swallowed a lot of water. This is my picture: that Maddie was on the boat watching this and that's why her body wasn't found, she was separate from them, and she went in to save them. After all, she knew how to swim. She could save them. They had planned to go swimming and she got ahead of the game. But there are no witnesses and we really don't know what happened."

Pam said her intuition is that they all died together. "I know whatever happened, Harry died trying to save them," she said. "There's no doubt in my mind about that. It was a calm day. I think they—I hate to think about it, truthfully—but I think maybe they went swimming without their life jackets, just like a dip, and something happened and one of them was in trouble and then they all . . ."

There had been some speculation in the media about foul play or something "untoward" happening, but she rejected those suggestions. "There was nothing suspicious about him or creepy or anything," she said. He would pack at most one or two beers in the cooler to drink once the boat had docked for the night, she said, so he hadn't been drinking. "I don't know how to solve the mystery," she said. She can't explain why none of them were wearing life jackets or why one "flotation device"—a *U*-shaped yellow buoy—belonging to the boat was later found by Paul Wanamaker, of Waukegan, around noon on Tuesday, August 17, straight east of Waukegan. She said when she was on the boat in prior years, she would make sure everyone was wearing life jackets. But she acknowledged that lots of people would swim in the lake without wearing them.

Harry was not reckless, Pam said. "Everybody who knew him knew he wasn't," she said. "The funny thing was, at the lake house in Hayward, we would be up there with the kids and friends sometimes with kids or cousins with kids and Harry was the one who always wanted them to wear their life jackets even just running around on the docks and stuff, so that we didn't have to be so worried. He would make them wear the life jackets to play on the beach so we could have a glass of wine and not be like, 'Where are the kids?' Not that we weren't watching them."

To this day, it is understandably a very difficult subject for Pam to discuss. "I don't think I can," she said. "I spent seven years in therapy over it and I still can't. You're like you lost ten years of your life or something. I couldn't open my day planner because nothing was relevant anymore. I had been planning a birthday party for Maddie. Nothing that was in the book was my life anymore."

Tom Kyros did not want to think about what exactly might have happened. He recalled how on Wednesday night—the "most terrible night of them all"—his wife, Sally, was staying with Pam, and they were woken by three thunderbolts. "These were the only three thunderclaps that were heard that night," he said. The recollection of the thunderstorm was the best answer he could muster about what happened. "I will not talk about it with anybody, and don't think about what really happened," he said. "I don't want to know. I don't want to speculate. It's too painful and scary, and so anytime I ever get close to it, it's *change the subject* time. So don't plan on asking me that question."

ON AUGUST 19, SHERIFF'S DEPUTIES returned to the *Semper Spero*, which by then had been towed to Larsen Marine, a company in Waukegan. The deputies collected a few more items from the boat, including a *Chicago Tribune* from August 15, a blue Squaw Creek Resort sweatshirt, a bag of Crayola crayons, a Bic lighter, and a current Saks Fifth Avenue catalog. There was also a green-and-black duffel bag with the words SEMPER SPERO HARRY on the side, which held Harry's wallet, containing $192 in cash, and his Nokia cell phone. The deputies concluded that there was "no evidence which would be consistent with foul play." Larsen Marine also inspected the boat and concluded that all mechanical and electrical systems were operating properly. On Harry's car, the deputies found two notes: one from his father telling him to call the Coast Guard—"They are looking for you. Call Pam and mom too"—and one from Andrew Lewis, a longtime Bradner employee, giving Harry the coordinates for where to meet him at the PGA golf tournament that was held at Medinah Country Club, in Medina, Illinois. The deputies had a few meetings with Rick Bull. Rick had the awful task of sailing the *Semper Spero* from Larsen Marine back to Monroe Harbor, and told the deputies that the boat was functioning properly, other than that the jib cleats were out of alignment.

The deputies gave Rick a nautical chart that showed where the bodies of Harry and Lexi had been found. He told them that, given the autopilot setting of 135 degrees southwest and where the bodies were found, he believed Harry was heading toward Wilmette, where a Bull family member lived along the shoreline. Apparently what the Bulls liked to do when sailing along the coast north of Chicago was to contact the relative and, once he'd sighted them through his telescope, go to visit with him.

GILES MCNAMEE, HARRY'S FRIEND from both Andover and (briefly) Yale, is skeptical that Harry's death was accidental. He conceded there is little evidence of foul play—in our conversations, he referred to what he thought was Harry's missing wallet as one potential piece of evidence of foul play, although his wallet was found with cash in it—but he said he can't reconcile the meticulous, law-abiding, responsible Harry Bull that he knew so well with his senseless death and that of his two daughters. He hadn't been drinking. The weather was calm. There is no logical explanation for what happened. "From the facts, it struck me that there might have been foul play of some sort," he said. "The facts didn't add up to the outcome." He said the Harry he knew would play by the rules, meaning that young children would wear life jackets on the sailboat and when going swimming. "Harry would have had a life preserver on and the girls would have had [life preservers] on," he said. "It doesn't make sense, and even if it was a circumstance where say he got hit in the head with the boom and got knocked out, the girls were little and they wouldn't have been without life preservers. It just was, that's not him, so it didn't make any sense to me. . . . You can't have little kids on a boat without having life preservers on little kids. That's the law and Harry would have obeyed the law. If they jumped in after life preservers, they would have been wearing life preservers." Of course, all the life preservers on the boat were stowed away. And Harry and his two girls still ended up in the water.

But McNamee is ultimately right to be puzzled and confused. The events of those August days remain nearly inexplicable.

HOW PAM WAS ABLE TO RECOVER from this inconceivable tragedy is itself unfathomable. But she did. "I feel very lucky that Harry came into my life," she said. "I feel lucky for the years I had with the girls and Harry. It's because of the foundation they left me with that I was able to go on." Baby George helped, of course. He was eleven months old at the time of the tragedy. "George was at a very cute age," she said. "He took his first three steps the day of the funeral. And George is a bright little star, too, so he's a good guy and he's a handful, so that kept me busy." She got involved with the Boys and Girls Club. She said her girlfriends helped her get through the extraordinary pain of the loss of her husband and two of her three children. Before George was in school, she would spend the winters with him in Arizona at her parents' home. Her parents and their friends would eat dinner at 5 p.m. She would go and order a glass of wine. With her braces, she looked so young she got carded. "I felt like I lost a lot of time in my life," she said. "I felt like I lost ten years."

She put George in the Hinsdale public schools. She stayed in the house in Hinsdale, even though the memories were painful. "Maybe it was too hard to move because I had all those boxes of things I would've had to go through. . . ."

When George was still a baby, she quit the nearby Salt Creek Club. There were bad memories there, and she wasn't using it anymore. But when George was three years old, she decided to rejoin. That's where she met Paul Garvin. He was the director of racquet sports at Salt Creek. Paul was always nice to Pam, who was thirty-nine years old when Harry died. "I couldn't always tell if he was being especially nice," she said. But he never asked her out or anything, and Pam never got the hint that perhaps he was interested in her. Paul would always give George a Tootsie Roll when he saw him at the club.

It turned out that one of Paul's favorite restaurants was Bob Chinn's Crab House, in Chicago. "They have great key lime pie," he told Pam. But she didn't take the hint. Her friends told her that Paul was probably sitting by himself at Bob Chinn's waiting for her to show up. During the winter, Paul was a ski bum in Banff. So he was only around Hinsdale during the summer months. The following summer, Pam was in downtown Chicago one day and noticed a sign declaring that another Bob Chinn's was opening up downtown. That night she went to Salt Creek for a "ladies drill," where Paul instructed a group of women on their tennis games. "The way Paul would tell the story," Pam said, "is like in front of twenty ladies, I pinned him against the fence and said, 'I was in the city today. Bob Chinn's is opening,' and he said, 'Oh, I've got to check that out,' and I said, 'When you do, I want to go with you.' And right away, he didn't drop the ball. He said, 'How about Friday?' So that was our first date, so we went all the way downtown to dinner and then there was a family from Salt Creek with little kids sitting at the table next to us going, 'Hi, Coach Paul.'" He took her ice climbing in Banff. He took her to Paris to go to the French Open, one of her dream vacations. They got married in 2005. People usually assume that Paul is George's father.

ON AUGUST 23, 1999, THE REVEREND Christine Chakoian led a funeral service for Harry and his daughters at the Community Presbyterian Church, in Clarendon Hills. It was the congregation that Harry had been part of for most of his life. Pam's brother Tom said what everyone was thinking: "These people left us far too early. There is an overwhelming sense in all of us that they were robbed of the incredible future that was promised by their amazing potential." He remembered what Maddie had once told him: that people are like flowers and balloons. "They don't last forever."

In her homily, Reverend Chakoian spoke for everyone else. "A week ago today, Harry, Maddie, and Lexi were having a wonderful time—sharing a ride on their sailboat, enjoying the wind and the sun, and most of all reveling in each other's company," she said. "Then suddenly, tragically, it was over, in the blink of an eye. Three vibrant lives cut short. Till our days' end, we may never know what happened; till our last breath, we will not know why it had to turn out this way."

She urged the grieving to learn from the tragic deaths. "Our days are never certain," she said. "None of us can ever know what time we have left to spend with those we love. None of us can ever know how many days are ours to make a difference in the world. Life is so precious, and the loved ones that people our lives are only ours to borrow briefly. It is so easy to be careless with our time, to imagine that we have forever to be kind, to accomplish our dreams, to give back to the world. Today is always the only day you may have: Seize the day. It is so easy to be thoughtless with our loved ones, to take them for granted. Treasure them with your whole heart. In life and in death, Harry and the girls have taught us this: In the end, the largest paycheck or the fanciest house or the most coveted title doesn't matter. The meaning of our lives is gained from the joy that we share and the good that we do and the people whom we love. There is much that we will never know about how or why this tragedy occurred. In many ways, it really doesn't matter. It is what we know that matters more: that Harry and Maddie and Lexi's lives have meant the world to us; and that even their deaths have the capacity to ennoble us, inspiring us to pledge ourselves to what ultimately matters."

Harry and Lexi are buried next to each other in the small cemetery down the road from the house they lived in together with Pam and George. There is also a grave marker there for Maddie. Harry's parents have both since passed away as well. After Harry's mother died in 2016, Pam replaced the three separate grave markers for Harry, Maddie, and Lexi with one headstone for the three of them, flanked by headstones for Harry's father and mother. They are all buried near one another, allowing Pam and George to visit them whenever they want. Each passing season, Pam replaces the besotted flowers on the headstones of Harry and their two young daughters.

John

FOR WHAT IT'S WORTH, NEITHER he nor his mother liked the name *John-John*. His mother told Paul Fay, one of her husband's navy buddies, that she "took issue" when he referred to "John-John."

"The president never called him John-John," she told him.

"Jackie, you've got to be kidding," he said. "He called him John-John all the time."

"He did not call him John-John," she replied. "He called him John."

Concluded Fay: "Well now, how do you argue with something like that? I mean, you could take any number of people around the president who knew that he called him John-John."

John F. Kennedy Jr. was the first—and so far only—child in history born to a president-elect of the United States. The coverage of his birth in the heightened period of a presidential transition was especially dramatic. His birth was scheduled for cesarean section on December 1 at the Georgetown University Hospital. The precautions were a medical necessity given that his mother, Jacqueline Kennedy, had suffered a miscarriage in 1955 and, a year later, a stillborn.

Despite the careful planning, John's arrival twenty-two minutes after midnight on November 25, 1960, took everyone by surprise. With his wife on doctor-ordered bed rest at the couple's Georgetown home on N Street, the president-elect had headed down—at eight o'clock the previous evening, in the family's two-engine Convair private plane—to his father's house in Palm Beach, Florida, for a post-election vacation. "There was not the slightest indication," the *Times* reported, "... that the birth of the child was imminent." Two hours later, though, as Kennedy was approaching Palm Beach, his wife called Dr. John Walsh, her physician. Walsh ordered an ambulance to take Mrs. Kennedy to the Georgetown University Hospital. Word of her emergency was conveyed to the president-elect a few minutes before his plane landed in Palm Beach.

On the ground, Kennedy walked "briskly" through a crowd of "a few hundred," the *Times* reported, to an office inside the Palm Beach International Airport. He spoke to a nurse at the Georgetown hospital by phone. She told him that his wife was in surgery, having entered the operating room at 11:30 p.m. He promptly turned around and informed the Secret Service that he was returning to Washington. The family Convair was abandoned in favor of a chartered American Airlines DC-6 that had ferried the press corps to Palm Beach. Accompanied by his aides Kenneth O'Donnell and Pierre Salinger, Kennedy commandeered the front of the jet, along with the Secret Service, for the return flight to Washington.

He was told of his son's birth at 1:15 a.m., by radio, as he cruised at thirteen thousand feet above the eastern coastline of Florida. The news was relayed to the press in the back of the plane by the captain, resulting in a spontaneous burst of applause. Dressed in his shirtsleeves, Kennedy then visited with the press. Seven minutes later, at 1:22 a.m., Kennedy went into the cockpit of the plane, donned earphones, and heard directly from the hospital that both mother and son were "doing well."

At 2:50 a.m., as Jackie was being wheeled out of the delivery room, Thomas Freeman, an Associated Press photographer who had hidden away in an empty hospital room, took her picture with a flash camera. "Oh, no, not that," she said. The Secret Service agents nearby seized Freeman's camera and took out the film. The president-elect arrived at the Georgetown hospital at 4:18 a.m. He caught a quick glimpse of his six-pound, three-ounce son, in an incubator in the nursery before heading to see his wife in her room. Dr. Walsh told the press that John

Jr. was "good looking and healthy." Asked if he resembled more his mother or his father, the doctor said, "Frankly, new babies look mostly like new babies."

On December 8, John's baptism in a chapel at the Georgetown Hospital made the front page of the *New York Times*. Dressed in his father's white "christening gown" that he had worn in 1917 and a white lace bonnet that belonged to his mother, John was asked by the Reverend Martin Casey, the pastor at the Holy Trinity Church, "Wilt thou be baptized?" Mrs. Charles Bartlett, the baby's godmother, delivered John's response: "I will." For his part, John "gave one subdued cry during the eleven-minute ritual and opened his eyes when a news photographer took his picture," the paper reported. "Otherwise the baby appeared relaxed and drowsy." After the ceremony, the twenty or so guests—chiefly family members and close advisers to the president-elect—returned to Jackie's third-floor room for sandwiches and champagne. At one point, Jackie held John in her arms and asked her husband: "Isn't he sweet Jack? Look at those pretty eyes."

The media could not seem to get enough of John or his sister, three-year-old Caroline. They had been left behind in Palm Beach for their father's inauguration, but their February 4 move into the White House was also front-page news. Two bedrooms in the White House had been newly renovated prior to their arrival: John's was white, with light-blue trim on the moldings and doors; Caroline's was pale pink, with white woodwork and lots of chintz curtains. As an infant, John slept in the same white wicker bassinet that Caroline, and before that their mother, had used. Their White House code names were Lark, for John, and Lyric, for Caroline.

John's ability to stand up in his own crib—at ten months—also made the news, along with the fact that he had seven teeth, four on top and three on the bottom. "He's a very healthy baby," Jackie's press secretary said. "He stands in his crib and he crawls on the floor." As his first birthday approached, the White House released several "official" photographs of John, two of which, of course, made it to the front page of the *New York Times*: one of him being held by his mother and smiling, the other of him playing with one of the toys given to him by President and Madame de Gaulle.

JOHN F. KENNEDY JR. (unlike Will Daniel, for instance) never even had the option of hiding, of being decidedly invisible or, as a grown man, of ratcheting down his extraordinary star power. He had the lost president's name and was even more handsome. But even before his father's death, the hopes and dreams of an entire nation seemed to be fully invested in the life of John F. Kennedy Jr., and there did not seem to be a whole lot he could do about it.

Two pictures on the front page of the *New York Times*, in May 1962, captured John's first steps and his first appearance in the Oval Office. The pictures, under the headline "The President's son displays new and old skills," showed John in his overalls taking a few steps and also crawling on the floor of the office. On October 5 of that year, the White House announced that a twenty-two-month-old John would start nursery school in the next week in the solarium in the White House, along with Caroline who was to start kindergarten there. The idea, at least at first, was for the children to be homeschooled in the White House. Even John's haircuts and change of haircut styles became news. (Indeed, his hairstyle became a point of contention between the president—who wanted John's hair short—and the First Lady—who wanted it longer and in the European "fringe style" that she preferred.)

In a 1961 letter to her grandmother, Caroline described John as "a bad squeaky boy who tries to spit in his mother's Coca-Cola and who has a very bad temper."

From an early age, John seemed particularly drawn to airplanes. Accompanying his father by helicopter to Andrews Air Force Base, he

decided he wanted to go with him on Air Force One for a speech at the
Air Force Academy in Colorado Springs. Photographers captured pictures of the nearly three-year-old John crying when he discovered the
news that he would not be able to join his father on the trip to Colorado and instead had to return to the White House. In September, at
Otis Air Force Base in Massachusetts, John again tried to accompany his
father on Air Force One and again was brought back to the reality that
he could not go along—this time by his cousin Robert Kennedy Jr. In
October 1963, the *Times* ran a photograph of John crying yet again,
this time as his father left Andrews Air Force Base to deliver a speech
in the Midwest. To make it up to him, his father would take John to
the hangar where the helicopters were kept. John would put on the
pilot's helmet and push around the control stick and press a bunch of
buttons. John's uncle Teddy later recalled, "A famous photograph
showed John racing across the lawn as his father landed in the White
House helicopter and swept up John in his arms. When my brother saw
that photo, he exclaimed: 'Every mother in the United States is saying,
"Isn't it wonderful to see that love between a son and his father, the way
that John races to be with his father." Little do they know, that son
would have raced right by his father to get to that helicopter.'"

Maud Shaw, his nanny, thought that John "suffered a great handi-
cap by being brought up in the White House, surrounded by all the
restrictions that have to be placed on a President's children." By contrast, she thought Caroline had benefited by spending her first three
years growing up in Georgetown, away from the spotlight, where
she could go with Shaw for walks and to get ice cream—"things that
John could never do without Secret Service men trailing behind him
and, unwittingly, causing a sensation." One of the benefits of John's security detail, though, was that he developed a close bond with them—
Lynn Meredith, Bob Foster, and Tom Wells—and it was Foster who
taught John how to ride a bike after hours of trial and error. "At times,"

Shaw wrote, "their devotion to the children was a bit frustrating, for whenever John wanted anything, he knew he had only to ask one of the Secret Service men for it," and a pattern was set.

Once, when President Tito of Yugoslavia visited the White House in October 1963, John wanted to go out on the Truman Balcony to have a look at the preparations that had commenced on the lawn below. Maud Shaw let him out. "He loved that," she wrote, "staring at the men putting the platforms and microphones in place and watching the television and film cameras being lined up." He had dressed up like a gunslinger, with a couple of toy six-shooters on his belt. Unbeknownst to Shaw, one of his plastic guns slipped from the belt and fell to the ground below. Soon thereafter, she and John were off to Dumbarton Oaks, a public estate in Georgetown, for a walk around the gardens there. By that evening, the press was reporting that John had dropped one of his toy guns on Tito's head. The next morning, John's father asked Shaw to come to the Oval Office.

"Miss Shaw," he said, "I thought I asked you to keep John-John out of sight yesterday."

"Yes you did, Mr. President," she replied. "And I did take him away from the White House during the ceremony. I assure you we were at Dumbarton Oaks when he was supposed to be dropping his gun on President Tito's head."

"Is that right?" he responded.

"Yes, Mr. President," she said. "You can check with the Secret Service detail."

"All right, then," the president said. "Thank you."

Jackie strictly limited photographers' access to the children, but in October 1963, she set sail for a two-week vacation aboard the yacht owned by Greek shipping magnate Aristotle Onassis. (The trip followed the tragic death of her second son, Patrick, two days after his birth.) With Jackie away, the president allowed *Look* magazine to take candid photographs of the children. The *Look* issue contained the most famous photograph ever taken of the president and his son—the one where Kennedy was seated at the Resolute desk while his son peeked out of a secret hideaway at his feet, which the magazine claimed he called his "secret house." Years later, John sent a note to President Clinton about the famous picture of him. According to Paul Begala, one of Clinton's senior advisers, "I was working at the White House and I was on the impeachment team. And there was a moment. I'm sitting in my office. I had a private fax, and the thing starts whirring and it spits out a one-page note, handwritten. It says, 'Dear Mr. President, I've been under that desk. There's barely room for a three-year-old, much less a 22-year-old intern. Cheers, JK.' I have to say I took that thing into the Oval Office, and Bill Clinton laughed so hard—tears. It was a great release. It was a great moment."

On November 4, a day after a coup in Saigon toppled the South Vietnamese president, John walked into the Oval Office while his father was taping some of his thoughts about the coup and the other events of the day. Suddenly, a big "hello!" could be heard on the tape—John—followed by his father asking him some questions: Why do the leaves fall? Why do leaves turn green? Why does the snow cover the ground? Where do we go on the Cape? John's responses were muffled. There seemed to be lots of giggling.

NOVEMBER 22, 1963, "BEGAN PERFECTLY NORMALLY, of course," Shaw wrote, with both Caroline and John coming into her room to say good morning. Caroline went off to school in the solarium in the White House converted for that purpose. Shaw and John went for a walk. At lunch, along with two of their cousins—Senator Ted Kennedy's children Teddy and Kara—they talked about the upcoming birthdays of John and Caroline. Shaw was about to put the children down for their naps when she got the call from Nancy Tuckerman, Jackie's secretary, that the president had been shot.

On the plane back from Dallas, a call went out to Jackie's mother that Caroline and John should be brought from the White House to the ten-thousand-square-foot Auchincloss mansion at 3044 O Street, in Georgetown. Jackie's mother spoke with Shaw, who told her, "I will bring enough things so that they can stay as long as Mrs. Kennedy wants them there." John's grandmother brought a crib down from her attic— it was tied together with string—and asked her cook to make them supper. She wasn't sure what time exactly the children arrived at her house. "It was so dark, as it is November afternoons," she recalled. When Jackie's mother met up with Jackie at the Bethesda Naval Hospital, in Maryland, where the president's body had been brought after Air Force One had landed at Andrews Air Force Base, they eventually got to speaking about how Caroline and John were at the Auchinclosses' O Street mansion. It turned out that Jackie hadn't given that directive at all, and wanted the children returned to the White House. "Fortunately they hadn't gone to bed yet," Shaw continued, "and they were taken right back to the White House. So they thought they had just simply come to have supper with their grandmother, which they had done before. And I never have known exactly who that message came from. I think it must have been somebody who thought that Jackie wouldn't want them at the White House and had taken it into their own hands and decided that this is what she would have wanted to happen. Whoever it was, was wrong. I think that Jackie's reaction was exactly right, as it certainly was through all of the ensuing days."

On his third birthday, John bid his father goodbye in front of a nation overcome with grief. "A little boy at his grieving mother's side saluted the passing coffin," according to an account in the *New York Times*. "And in that moment, he seemed the brave soldier his father wanted him to be on this day." He was dressed identically to his older sister: red shoes, white socks, shorts, and a powder blue double-breasted overcoat. Odd attire to be sure, but one guaranteed to stand out against the black funereal garb worn by his mother—along with a nearly opaque black veil—and by his two uncles, Bobby and Teddy. That historic photograph, taken by *Daily News* photographer Dan Farrell, seared into our collective conscious the image of an adorable little boy, dressed like Little Lord Fauntleroy, saying goodbye to a father he had barely known. "That salute of John Jr. is the first extraordinary celebrity moment in John Jr.'s life," explained Laurence Leamer, who has written extensively about the Kennedys. "From that moment on, his life was different."

Although understandably in a state of shock and despair—a condition that would drive her to the brink of suicide at times during the years after her husband's assassination—Jackie tried desperately to re-establish some semblance of normalcy for her children. After a few days in Hyannis Port, the family had returned to the White House on December 2, with the expectation that they would move out three days later. Even though she would later say of this period that she was "not in any condition to make much sense of anything," on the evening of December 4, she secretly arranged for the caskets of her two deceased children, Arabella and Patrick—which had been removed previously from a family cemetery in Massachusetts—to be placed into a grave beside their father in Arlington National Cemetery. While Caroline and John remained at the White House, Jackie, her sister, her mother, and Bobby Kennedy headed to Arlington for the reburial. "Seeing the three—father, daughter, son—back together again, albeit in death was a stark reminder of the Herculean effort made by their parents to bring these babies to term," wrote Philip Hannan, the pastor who presided over the ceremony.

Jackie bought an eighteenth-century brick house at 3017 N Street, in Georgetown, and asked the decorator to re-create in the new home the kids' rooms exactly as they had been in the White House. By the time she and the kids were ready to move in, in February 1964, N Street, where they had already been staying at the borrowed home of W. Averell Harriman, had become "one of the tourist sights of Washington," Shaw wrote. "There was never a time when there were not crowds of sightseers

gathered outside, waiting to see her and the children, taking photographs and trying to peep into the windows."

Much to his delight, John discovered that their new house had an
elevator. He and Caroline lived with Shaw on the top floor of the house,
along with a large room filled with toys that had been packed away at
the White House but were once again ripe for playtime. "John found
an old machine gun and went round the room firing the thing off," Shaw
wrote. He had a life-sized tiger on wheels and a huge tile construction
kit. John especially liked to go up to the top of the house and look out
of the skylight.

As the first anniversary of her husband's assassination loomed,
Jackie decided to move to New York. "It was obvious that the contin-
ual stares of the people who gather day after day outside No. 3017
upset her," Shaw wrote. "What was hard for John to accept was that he
no longer lived in the 'big white house' in Washington. Whenever he
saw a photograph of it, he would frown and ask me: 'That's where we
live isn't it, Miss Shaw?'" She had to remind him that he no longer
lived there.

In New York, the family spent six weeks at the Carlyle Hotel while
the renovations of their penthouse apartment at 1040 Fifth Avenue were
completed. By this time, Shaw had made many observations about John.
She found him to be intelligent but not as "studious" as his sister. "He
always much preferred horsing about to studying," she wrote in 1965.
"While Caroline tends to be a little shy and reserved, John is outgoing
and full of self-confidence. He is the clown of the two and a natural
comic." She recalled how John's imitation of the Beatles, with his hips
swaying and singing, "She loves you, yeah-yeah-yeah," cracked up her
and his mother. She found John to be "as sharp as a tack" and not easily fooled. She also thought he had "his father's gift" of being able to
ask "just the right questions" and being able to continue to ask them
until he received satisfactory answers. "John was one hundred percent
boy," she wrote. "He was much more interested in cowboys and Indi-

ans, guns, swords, soldiers, airplanes and space rockets than anything else. And he was just as bloodthirsty as any other boy."

At least high above Fifth Avenue, there were not people peering in their windows or lining up outside their doors, hoping to catch a glimpse of one of them or another. The doormen at 1040 Fifth Avenue made sure of that. But despite New York's more blasé attitude toward celebrities, Jackie and her two children—and John especially—remained the object of fascination for both the media and the paparazzi, which could never seem to get enough of them, or him. Jackie had an office on Park Avenue, which she used to answer thousands of letters sent to her and to begin to frame what the Kennedy Library would be. For Caroline and John, one of the best things about New York City was that their new home was situated directly across from Central Park. The Secret Service would bring their bicycles into Central Park, for John and Caroline to ride. They went to the Central Park Zoo and visited the two deer that had been at the White House with them and had been donated to the zoo near their apartment. (John still considered them *his* deer.) They went to the Bronx Zoo and rode camels and watched the lions being fed. Another benefit of living in New York City was that any number of their cousins lived nearby. The only negative about New York from John's perspective was that he could no longer play on the presidential helicopters and jets.

In July 1966, the front-page news in the *New York Times* was that John, while on vacation with his family in Hawaii, had accidentally fallen into the remains of a charcoal fire and suffered first- and second-degree burns on his right hand, forearm, and butt. He was at a private resort owned by Laurance Rockefeller when the incident occurred and was flown back to Honolulu for further treatment. A month later, while in Hyannis Port, John had his tonsils removed at the Cape Cod Hospital. He also broke his wrist when he fell off the pony he was riding in New Jersey.

In August 1968—two months after the assassination of his uncle

Bobby—the papers reported that John would be leaving St. David's and moving across town to the Collegiate School, the oldest school in Manhattan. John's mother decided to make the switch because the teachers at St. David's believed John should repeat second grade until he "becomes mature." One father of a student in John's class described him as "restless" and "inattentive" and often "disruptive." Another theory for the change was that Leonard Bernstein, the famous conductor, had urged Jackie to make the switch and that his son was an eighth-grader at the school. But Carl Andrews Jr., the school's headmaster, told the *Boston Globe* that John was "no more rambunctious than any other second grader. He applied, was tested and accepted. It's that simple." It was a difficult time for the Kennedys. After watching Bobby Kennedy be buried in Arlington National Cemetery next to his brother, her husband, Jackie famously said, "If they're killing Kennedys, then my children are targets . . . I want to get out of this country." But of course, that did not happen. She instead sought the security she thought a billionaire shipping magnate might provide.

Jackie married Aristotle Onassis on October 20, 1968, on Skorpios, Onassis's private Greek island. John went to the wedding, of course. (He skipped a few days of school to attend.) And there were plenty of stories about his return to New York City, without his mother, three days later. According to the *Boston Globe*, the Kennedy party was the last to leave the TWA flight from Athens to New York. John was the first Kennedy to emerge from the jet, wearing "a tan topcoat, short pants, gray knee socks and brown shoes." He "gave a quick smile and skipped down the steps" into a waiting limousine.

Eric Pooley at *Time* described John at Collegiate as being "a distinctly average student, restless in class, jiggling his leg nervously, rarely speaking." Pooley's description made sense to Peter Blauner, John's classmate. "My personal impression of him was lots of brown hair," he said. "I believe the de rigueur light-brown corduroy jacket of the day, and I seem to remember red turtlenecks. When he would sit in class, he often sat with his legs pretty far apart and then, again, in the manner of adolescent boys, was able to wiggle them back and forth with amazing speed, almost like a hummingbird." Another classmate claimed John "ate erasers."

He was given permission to miss a week of school to commemorate the fifth anniversary of his father's death—which was, of course, front-page news—and to celebrate his eighth birthday, which he did with school friends at the country home his mother had rented in the horse country of Peapack, New Jersey. John spent much of the summer of 1969 in Greece aboard the *Christina*, his stepfather's luxurious 325-foot yacht. In an August 7 letter to McGeorge Bundy, who had been her husband's national security adviser, Jackie thanked him for the "extraordinary" letter he had written to John in the weeks after the July 20 moon landing, which his father had once envisioned. "If you could have seen his little face when he opened it," she wrote on the yacht's stationery. John read Bundy's letter to himself and then he asked his mother to read it aloud. There was silence as Jackie read it; her small audience was moved nearly to tears. "All the thoughts at those days of going to the moon," Jackie wrote to Bundy, "and Jack not there to see it and John who must find his father through long years of searching."

On February 3, 1971, President Nixon invited Jackie and her children to the White House for a private dinner with him and his family. It was their first visit back since the days after the assassination. They were together for a bit more than two hours, including a visit to the Oval Office. At one point during dinner, John spilled a glass of milk into Nixon's lap, who reportedly "reacted graciously." In his thank-you note to the president the next day, John thanked him and the First Lady for showing him the White House again. "I don't think I could remember much about the White House," he wrote. "When I sat on Lincoln's bed and wished for something my wish really came true. I wished that I [would] have good luck at school." He told Nixon he "really loved" his dogs and noticed that when he got home to New York, his dogs were sniffing him. "Maybe they remember the White House," he concluded. John obviously had a much higher opinion of Nixon than did the Daniel brothers.

John spent most of the summer of 1972 with his mother, sister, and stepfather on Skorpios, in the Greek islands, although on June 4, before heading there, he and a friend went to the Mets game and sat in the dugout with Willie Mays. At one point, while they were all cruising around on the *Christina*, the military-backed government of Greece announced on July 15 that it had foiled a plot by eight Greeks, "mostly laborers," to kidnap John, among others. Their targets, the government alleged, were the Greek minister of labor; the chief of the armed forces; Thomas Pappas, a wealthy Greek American businessman; and John. The alleged kidnappers were arrested, indicted, and put on trial. One of the alleged kidnappers denied that John was a target of their plot.

His school friend Peter Blauner recalled John inviting him to dinner at 1040 Fifth. "I remember [Jackie] playing the cast album from *1776* over and over and over again . . . It wasn't *Camelot*," he said. "It was that record. I remember them playing it. I remember thinking, *This is what the world would be like if there were no blacks or Jewish people around*." He remembered seeing John's mother in her sunglasses and thinking, "The face would strike you as being mask-like, but then she would smile at you and she would speak to you in a way that seemed genuinely warm and interested." He also recalled another time when John was put in an awkward position at a father-son event in the Collegiate gymnasium. Instead of his father, John brought as a surrogate father Roosevelt "Rosey" Grier, the former NFL football player who had tackled Sirhan Sirhan, Bobby Kennedy's killer, on the night of his assassination at a Los Angeles hotel.

"At one point," Blauner recalled, "the exercises involved the fathers and sons standing in a circle and throwing a medicine ball back and forth to each other. Roosevelt Grier actually was throwing the medicine ball back and forth with the other parents and the kids. There's probably a few people that still have EVERLAST backward on their chest."

As John moved into adolescence, he developed a taste for experimentation. In the summer of 1971, he spent two weeks on an island off the coast of Wales sailing, canoeing, camping, and rock climbing. After Aristotle Onassis died outside Paris, in March 1975, John spent the following summer on Skorpios with his mother. He palled around with Christos Kartanos, a local resident whom John had befriended years earlier. They took speedboats around the island. Kartanos said that John loved his scotch. "Whenever I went to see him," he said, "I carried the scotch in a cloth shoulder bag. We used to swig it straight from the bottle. John said it made him feel good. But we never got drunk. I think that all the things that John did—like drinking wine and whiskey and smoking Greek cigarettes—were his way of showing off. It's as if he were saying, *Look, I'm not a kid anymore.*"

In the late afternoon of May 14, 1974, around 5 p.m., while John was riding his bike into Central Park for a tennis lesson, Robert Lopez, then twenty, mugged John, who was then thirteen. "Get off that bike or I will kill you," Lopez told John. Lopez took John's tennis racket and his bike and rode off with them both into Central Park. Lopez, who later told police he sold John's bike in order to buy two bags of cocaine, approached John with a tree branch in his hand and told him to "get out of here." He said John was "an easy hit." John reported the theft to the police who then took him in a patrol car around Central Park, looking for the assailant and his bike. But he did not find them. Two months later, the police arrested Lopez, who was unemployed and lived with his wife and two-month-old child on Second Avenue, after he surrendered to a police precinct on

East 102nd Street. Lopez helped the police recover John's tennis racket, but the $145 ten-speed bike was not recovered. Lopez pleaded not guilty to the crime but was later convicted of it and sentenced to two years in prison.

BACK AT COLLEGIATE, JOHN HAD BECOME close friends with Wilson McCray, whom he dubbed his "partner in crime." Said McCray, "We were bad little boys." As fourteen-year-olds, they would evade the Secret Service and head into Central Park to play Frisbee. They also got high together. "At school we were always getting caught for getting stoned," he said.

It is not exactly clear to anybody why after he returned from a three-week service trip to Guatemala, John left Collegiate at the end of tenth grade to go to Andover as an Upper. Some thought he left Collegiate because he was getting into too much trouble. Some thought he wasn't distinguishing himself enough academically and needed a fresh start at a new school. Some thought he wanted to follow McCray to Andover. At any rate, John's arrival at Andover necessitated a healthy combination of drama and nonchalance. On the one hand, he was JFK Jr., the only son of the glamorous assassinated former president of the United States. He was a favorite son of the commonwealth of Massachusetts, Andover's home state, and given Andover's illustrious history, it certainly seemed appropriate that John would want to come to Andover and that Andover could handle the hoopla and attention that his arrival would merit. On the other hand, Andover is known for its discretion generally and especially so when accommodating the children of the rich and famous. After all, there was barely a ripple when Will Daniel entered three years earlier. In John's case, the campus was abuzz with the news that he would be enrolling, but it was also clear that there would be a minimal amount of special treatment for him and that he would have to (mostly) play by the rules. He would also have to (mostly) meet the same academic requirements as the other twelve hundred students on campus.

What added to my excitement when I first heard the news was that John would be living down the hall from me in Stearns House West. The Secret Service had insisted that John be placed in the dormitory that was closest to the Andover Inn, where they were holed up and at his beck and call. One week before school started in September 1976, the Secret Service met with the dorm master, Meredith Price, and his wife, Nancy. "They all, of course, had hats on and suits and they came over and they gave me what I guess would be called an alarm," Price recalled. "And they said 'See this, well, we'll run this right through walls and windows if you press this and you think that John is in some kind of danger.'" Of course, the alarm went off by mistake six times the first day that John was in the dorm. "They gave up and then they just came over and washed their cars with our hose," he said.

The day we returned to school for Upper year, I remember being in my friend Mike Somers's room, across the hall from mine, and looking out his windows as Jackie and John came down the path to the front door of the dorm. It was surreal, and it was really happening. What were these two incredibly famous people doing at our school, in my dorm? All I could think of was how excited my mother would have been to see Jackie O entering our dorm. And of course she was an amazing sight, although I noticed then and later that she never looked quite as beautiful and glamorous as she did in pictures. She was that rare human being who looked better in photographs than she did in person, where her wide face and deeply separated eyes made her look more striking than stunning.

When Jackie and John arrived, they knocked on Meredith Price's door. His daughter, Amy, was in awe. Price was just slightly rattled with the arrival of the famous guests, and as he went to open the door to the apartment, he hit his head on one of the metal posts that was holding up the roof. "I opened the door and there's a bump forming on my fore-head," he said, "and there's Jackie O, and honest to God, she sounds just the way she sounded like, 'Oh, I'm so happy to see you . . .'" She and John sat down on the couch in his study. They made small talk. "When she left Amy went over and patted the sofa on which Jackie O had sat," her father said.

One of Price's responsibilities was to do occasional room checks. "And make sure kids' rooms were not hovels and shouldn't be immedi-ately fumigated," he said. When he went to John's room, which he shared with Robert Van Cleve, an Upper (and a legacy) from St. Louis, Missouri, Price would have been confronted by a life-sized, carved-wood, bare-breasted mermaid, the kind of sculpture that might be seen on the prow of a ship, not in a prep school dorm room. There were plenty of fake reports about how John was living at Andover. One ac-count included the fiction that he had in his dorm room a signed silkscreen print of Chairman Mao from Andy Warhol—to "John F. Kennedy Jr."—as well as a silk boxing robe with MUHAMMAD ALI sewn in stitching on the back. (For what it's worth, I was in John's room hun-dreds of times and never saw either of these items.) There was a framed photograph of his father hanging above his desk. "It could take you aback," Price said when he saw the photograph.

Like John, Sasha Chermayeff was from New York City and went to Andover as an Upper, making them a bit of an anomaly in the Ando-ver firmament—coming to the school one or two years after everyone else. They became best friends. Chermayeff, the daughter of the famous graphic designer Ivan Chermayeff (Andover Class of 1950), first met John briefly at a party in New York City the previous year. Her first reaction to him was "Oh, so what. Big deal." She didn't find him par-ticularly handsome, either. "He wasn't like this dream," she said. At Andover, though, they became fast—and lifelong—friends. They had three classes together that first year. They talked about their families. They clicked. She recalled how they were once dancing around in the dorm and he started talking about how uninformed women seemed to be about their sexual power over men. "He said, 'God, women have no clue that you're driving men completely crazy, being like super sexual and stuff like that,'" she said. She remembered that John was getting "pissed" at her for being so naïve about how her innocent-seeming flirting was affecting the teenage boys at Andover. He was being protective the way an older brother would be to a younger sister. "I remember being so shocked that he was saying, 'You don't see what you're doing?'" she said. "'Why don't you see what you're doing?' And I'd be like, 'Because I'm sixteen!'" Sasha laughed. "But he was like, 'No, it's not right, you can't do that. This is what's happening. This is what the guy is thinking.' And I was like 'Really?'"

She and John were never a couple. There was one moment, during the fall of their first semester at Andover, when it might have happened. They were in the old part of the stately Oliver Wendell Holmes Library in an area where books had been removed from the shelves. They decided to climb onto the shelving and lie down. They started making out a little bit. The next day, Sasha remembered, they got into "kind of an argument" about what had happened "and then we were both like, 'Okay fine, we would just go back to where we were before, it's okay,' and we were and we just stayed there."

John "was the shit," said Ed Hill, one of John's closest friends from Andover. Hill, a legacy, came to Andover from Yonkers, where his mother was the headmaster of a Catholic school in the Bronx that Hill attended. They met playing Frisbee inside the dining hall. Hill's overriding impression of John at Andover was of a kid who "was all wound up with nowhere to go." He never discussed with John whether he suffered from dyslexia or ADHD, or was taking Ritalin, as rumor had it. "But it had filtered through to me over time that his eggs were scrambled in some way," he said. "He certainly behaved in a manner consistent with ADD/ADHD." John had a lot of nervous energy. "He had as much energy as anyone I've ever known," Hill said. "He was a bit klutzy. He looked like the most athletic individual you'd ever know and he had the stamina of a great athlete, but he didn't have the coordination." Ed was the captain of the cross-country team and the captain of the spring track team. He was also for a period of time—before he was kicked out of Andover over the summer before his senior year—the school president. "One of my impressions of John was that he was drawn to people who he perceived were better than him in various categories," he said. "John in a million years would not have been the captain of any team." Hill also remembered John's curiosity. "I used to joke that you had to be very careful if you were pontificating in front of John, because the two most common words in his vocabulary were *Really?* and *Why?* He'd fuck you because you'd run off on some rant. He'd hear you out and then say, 'Why?' and you'd realize that the only answer was, 'Well, actually because I'm ill-tempered and full of shit.'"

Ed, Sasha, and John all ended up in remedial Math 30 class. "One of the things we always tried to do together is study math, and we were both so hopeless," Sasha said. "It was just so not going to happen."

I remember once John asked me to teach him how to divide. I was enough of a diligent math student that I consistently got 6s—As—in just about every math class I took at Andover. I am not sure how John discovered that or why he felt comfortable asking me for help in teaching him how to divide. Maybe he just intuited that the son of an accountant would have an aptitude for math. Anyway, by the time I got done with him on that particular day, I felt certain he knew how to divide. But it didn't take.

I'm not exactly sure why John and I became friends. Ned Andrews—my roommate during senior year—and I were asked to help John navigate Andover in his first few months at the school, and the friendship just developed. We lived down the hall from each other. I was a senior and he was an Upper, trying to figure out what Andover was all about. We both liked to have fun, although I suspect John had far more fun than I did.

I remember the time John was hungry at ten o'clock at night and decided to enlist the Secret Service to take us to Bishop's, an eastern Mediterranean restaurant in Lawrence, Massachusetts, about a ten-minute drive away. "That's where all the fat people in the area went," explained Meredith Price, our dorm counselor. Of course, this was completely against the rules, which required us all to be signed in to the dorm by ten o'clock at night, not driving around northern Massachusetts in search of food courtesy of the US Secret Service. But the Secret Service obliged, no questions asked, and we enjoyed a late-night snack of homemade pita and hummus.

Another time, John got a call from his sister, who had been driving up to Andover in her car from Harvard to visit John. It seemed that Caroline's car had suffered a flat tire about a mile or so from the Andover campus. Could John come help her fix the tire? John asked me to go along with him to help, as the two Kennedy children had aged out of Secret Service protection by that time. In any event, off John and I went, heading south on Route 28, which bifurcated the campus, in the direction of Boston. After a walk of twenty minutes or so, we found Caroline and her wounded car. It quickly became apparent that neither Caroline nor John knew the first thing about changing a flat tire. I didn't know much about it, either, but the job fell to me, and John and Caroline were only too happy to cede responsibility for the whole operation. Soon enough, the tire was fixed and we were all on our way back to campus.

One of the more curious facts about John at Andover was that he never seemed to have any money in his wallet (assuming he could even find his wallet, which eventually he had to chain to his pants so as not to lose it). There weren't many things to buy at Andover, since food, shelter, and tuition were paid up in advance. There was a small store on campus with candy and sundries. There was also the small pub in the Andover Inn, where eighteen-year-olds could drink alcohol legally as well as within the parameters of the Andover rule book. (But neither

John nor I was eighteen.) For John, the chief reason he seemed to want, or need, money was to buy extracurricular substances, such as marijuana or cocaine. He seemed always to have these items in stock. How he got them I have no idea, but he did seem to have his ways. Occasionally, he would ask me—the accountant's son from Worcester—if he could borrow some money without making clear what he needed it for. I was always pretty sure he was using it to augment his drug inventory.

Frankly, it didn't matter to me what he was using the money for; all I cared about was that he pay me back. But over time, that increasingly began to seem like a very tall order indeed. I don't think John was trying to stiff me. It just seemed that he was operating a kind of Ponzi scheme, borrowing from one person to pay another, not out of any particular maliciousness but rather because he never seemed to have any money of his own. He did this with lots of people, not just me. It did always strike me as a bit ironic.

One day, during the spring of 1977, John invited me down to 1040 Fifth Avenue, in New York City, for a visit. By that point in my life, I had been to New York a few times, but I had never been to an apartment on Fifth Avenue before, let alone the penthouse apartment of one of the most famous families in the world. Needless to say, my visit was big news around my house, at 11 Old English Road in Worcester.

After the extremely discreet doorman at 1040 Fifth ushered me into the lobby of the building and then up into the family's fifteenth-floor penthouse apartment, I remember being overwhelmed by the splendor of the place. Of course, I had never seen anything like this apartment before. There was a marble foyer dotted with Greek and Roman statues and busts. There was a small den, off the foyer, crammed full of books around a coffee table. I remember desperately wanting to look at one of the books, a large leather-bound tome with a gigantic embossed seal of the president of the United States on it, but of course doing so would have been totally uncool. At one point, John and I went into his bedroom. I recall that John took a few hits off his bong and then poured the used bong water out of his bathroom window onto Fifth Avenue, fifteen stories below. For some reason, I figured this would be as good a chance as any to get John to repay me the money he owed, which at that point totaled $40, a not-insignificant sum for a high school student in the mid-1970s. I asked John for the money. Without protest, he left his room and went to find his mother. I'm still not sure whether he felt emboldened to ask her in the wake of his bong hits. In any event, just outside the door to his room, I overheard him explaining to his mother how he owed this guy—me—$40 and that it was a long-over-due debt. Without missing a beat, she gave John two $20 bills and then said to him, in her best Jackie O voice, "John, tomorrow we talk about money."

There were more intimate moments as well. In a February 1977 letter, Jackie sent John some newspaper clippings. In the letter, she worried a bit that she had become his "current events editor" but knew the articles could not be found in the Boston papers. She wrote that the "one nice thing" about having him grow older was that he would under-stand better what people he and his family knew were writing about in the newspaper. And then she was back to reminiscing about her baby boy. She wrote that she had been going through Caroline's scrapbooks and found a picture of John's first time on skis, on Easter 1964, when he was three years old. "In case the cold weather is getting you down, look how you went through it like a little chirping red bird 13 years ago," she wrote. "Those huge instructors and that pained small creature—is that how you feel now, when your Math, Spanish teachers and Mr. Price loom over you[?]"

I REMEMBER ONCE GOING FOR A WALK with John around Rabbit Pond, behind our dorm, and out of the blue he asked me if I thought his father was a "good president." We had never before broached the subject of his father—his mother and sister, yes—and needless to say I

was quite surprised to hear him ask me about him. At seventeen, I was
hardly in a position to answer the question with anything remotely akin
to insight, and of course he must have known that. I think he just felt
like talking about his father—the man he barely knew—if only for a
moment. It was at once flattering—that he thought I might have something meaningful to say—and also shocking.

When I shared this story with Ed Hill many years later, he could
barely contain himself. "Oh my God," he said. "There you go. There
you go. That's pure John. What he was feeling, what he was asking, who
he was asking, and why he was asking that guy, it's all there. That's what
he was. You were senior to him in some perception that he had. You
were more intellectually reliable than him, in his perception. You were
better informed, in his perception. So just the whole nature of the in-
quiry and the vulnerability that it exposed, that was him. . . . That was
it. That was him. That was the whole thing right there." Had John, he
said, then asked me to race him around Rabbit Pond to see who could
get back to the dorm refrigerator first, the whole episode would have
been a "crystalline" example of John's personality.

Hill continued, "His father was murdered when he was three years
old, and that was a subject that he never touched—never. That was the
third rail of John's existence. He did not touch the fucking assassination, which I learned for the first time at Andover, sitting on the steps
on Samuel Phillips Hall, leafing through the pages of *The Best of Life*
with John and Sasha and we hit the inevitable assassination chapter.
And he almost tore the pages out of the book he flipped through them
so—just quick. Then suddenly we're on, like, the moon landing. He
didn't even look at those pictures."

Hill said he always believed that John's closest friends "all seem to
have come from the Land of Misfit Toys"; this was the "interesting
dichotomy" in John's personality. "I think John understood and believed, as I did, that he would and should be the president of the United
States, that he was born to it," he said. "Everything about his personality

and his life made it appropriate, and his commitment to do the right thing. It was all there. So you had that part of him that recognized his own ways in which he was extraordinary and competent, but I think there was a part that was horrible, too."

It seems doubtful that John had figured out at Andover what was going to be expected of him—in terms of a political career, if any—but there was little question that his mother wanted him to have a variety of different physical and intellectual challenges, many of which were available only to him. It was as if Jackie was curating for John a series of experiences that together would force him to mature and to come to grips with his unique position in the world, while also giving him the chance to be a goofball, if that's what he wanted to do.

After John's first year at Andover, Jackie signed him up for an Outward Bound sailing trip in and around Hurricane Island, Maine. The monthlong trip, twelve miles off the Maine coast in Penobscot Bay, was a difficult seafaring adventure, featuring rowing and sailing small boats in weather that alternated between monsoonlike rains and pristine, warm sunny days. The crescendo of every Outward Bound trip is the "solo," three days and nights alone, without any food, in the middle of nowhere. On his three-day solo, John was by himself on an uninhabited island in Machias Bay. He had a gallon of water and a tarp. His family insisted that the media keep its distance from him while he was on the solo. For his protection, Outward Bound stationed a small boat near the island in case its "famous charge" needed anything, the *Boston Globe* reported.

Of John's many bespoke experiences, nothing he did ever inspired me personally as did that Outward Bound trip to Hurricane Island. I can't say exactly how or why this happened, but there was something about John's trip and his unique combination of privilege and a certain common touch that made me feel that if he could survive such an ordeal, so could I. Moreover, I felt that the time had come for me—at age eighteen—to overcome my fears and give it a try. So I went on an

Outward Bound trip to the Gila Wilderness in New Mexico, a decision that changed my life. The monthlong experience was beyond exhilarating, and gave me a sense of well-being and confidence—akin to
what I imagine a huge shot of adrenaline might do—that I have rarely
experienced since. John also inspired Ed Hill to go on Outward
Bound—to Hurricane Island, during the summer of 1979. "Whether
he was inspiring me to do that or whether he was holding me accountable
for a poorly founded opinion or statement, that was a big part of who he
was," Hill said. "It was a great thing about him." But, he added, "Sadly,
he would cross a line repeatedly in his own life, where he would move
beyond invaluable inspiration to outright recklessness."

DURING HIS SENIOR YEAR AT ANDOVER, John roomed with John Pucillo,
a middle-class kid from Boston. His mother had died when he was
three years old, which gave him and John something in common. That
year at school Pucillo and John also had girlfriends—John had started
dating Lydia Hatton, a classmate from Grand Haven, Michigan—and
they both had parental permission to smoke cigarettes in their dorm
room. "We had people coming in and out of the room," Pucillo remembered, "smoking up a storm, playing Bruce Springsteen's *Born to
Run*—we probably played that thing a hundred times a month, simu-
lating the guitar." The roommates signaled to each other when one's
girlfriend was over so they knew to keep out of the room. "There was a
little bit of negotiating," Pucillo said. According to Chermayeff, Hatton "loved partying and really loved New York City partying" especially at Studio 54. "She loved that, and John had so much access to
that." Chermayeff remembered partying in New York City with John
while they were all at Andover as "insane—we would be ushered into
the Studio when there was like a thousand people outside, ushered in
to do coke with Steve Rubell." (Hatton declined to be interviewed
about her relationship with John.)

Pucillo found himself in a bit of a difficult position, rooming with
John. He had resolved at the start of his Upper year that he was going
to buckle down, study hard, and avoid breaking any rules—at least while
on the Andover campus. He also was elected the cluster president of
Rabbit Pond, which put him squarely in between his classmates and
the Andover disciplinary system. In the nicest way, John Kennedy, of
course, had pretty much figured out that these rules did not apply to
him, or if they did, there always seemed to be an intervention at the
highest levels to make sure that any rule he happened to violate—should
he be caught—would be dealt with through compromise. While it was
fine for others to be dismissed from Andover for breaking the rules—
and several of John's best friends were, such as Wilson McCray, his former Collegiate classmate, and Ed Hill—it was an unwritten rule that
John F. Kennedy Jr. would not be tossed out of Andover for smoking
pot or for drinking or for being with a girl after hours. As Bruce Mac-
Williams discovered—when he was the Rabbit Pond cluster president
before Pucillo—John's infractions could be dealt with quietly and ef-
ficiently, giving everyone a way to save face and to avoid the unwanted
publicity of John leaving the school. During John's senior year, the rule
breaking continued, of course, but his roommate, Pucillo, was now the
cluster president and in a position to make sure the unwritten rules
about John were followed to everyone's benefit. "We had the perfect
cover for everybody to come smoke pot because we got that smoking
permission," Pucillo remembered. "You would light up a cigarette.
They'd light up a bong, put the bong smoke through a wet towel to
decrease the smoke, get a couple of cigarettes going and no smell of pot,
and put the bong away."

Pucillo wasn't abstemious, just careful not to break any of the rules
while he was on Andover's campus. He and John would go drinking in
New York or in Cambridge. "On a lot of weekends, we would take a bus
into the Sevens [Ale House] on Charles Street," he said. "At that point,
if you were sixteen and you had a fake ID and [looked] reasonably

official, they'd let you in." He also took John around Boston's notori-
ous Combat Zone. Going out with John in Boston could be riotous.
Once, I remember, he and I went to The Black Rose, a classic Irish bar
on State Street. Pictures of John's father were everywhere, of course,
and John, immediately recognized, was treated, appropriately, as royalty.
There was no question of whether he was old enough to drink—he
wasn't—or whether I was—I wasn't—but we were served plentifully.
I don't think we had to pay.

The fact was, nobody wanted to read a newspaper story about John
leaving Andover before graduating. According to C. David Heymann,
in his book *American Legacy*, an Andover security guard once caught
John smoking pot in the men's room of the Oliver Wendell Holmes Library but did not report him. Another time he was caught getting
high, at night, on a ball field. He got off with only a warning. "I was in
a number of situations where I had to exercise, I would say, the best
political skills I could have, I guess, considering that it was my roommate," Pucillo said. "So trying to present it in somewhat of a nonbi-
ased way or objective way. . . . But also truthful. The kid, he was a
good guy. . . . I protected him a lot. I was always vouching for him
and positioning him in a positive way."

Sometimes, his friends called John out for his bad behavior. Once,
one recalled, he and John were met at Andover by a couple of John's
friends from Boston and they all drove together to a party about an hour
away. They were drinking beers and getting stoned in the car when at
one point John finished a beer and then threw the empty beer bottle
out the window onto the street. "No one else in that car would have
possibly done that even if they were really stoned," recalled one of
the people in the car that night. "Why did he do it? He almost didn't
realize that that was a big deal. [Was he too] sheltered? I don't know.
He was isolated." His friends in the car got really pissed at him. And he
was contrite. "He got it," this person recalled. "He actually really apologized at some point, but it was interesting."

There were plenty more innocent high school shenanigans. For some reason, John had more than his share of adolescent body odors, and one time in particular he had a medical problem with his feet that made them stink more than usual. Pucillo remembered he was getting some treatment for the problem. "It was like fucking disgusting," he said. "So we're all just saying, 'John, that's fucking disgusting.' He decided to have fun with it." Pucillo got back to the dorm one night, got into bed, and noticed a funny smell emanating from his pillow. "He put two of his fucking socks in my pillow," he said. "I had to throw the fucking pillow out and get a new pillow."

On another occasion, when Pucillo was visiting John in Hyannis Port, John suggested they take the family's fifteen-foot Chris-Craft motorboat over to Martha's Vineyard for a visit. It was the same boat the two Johns used to drive to take Jackie waterskiing. "She loved to water-ski," Pucillo said. The trip was to take about ninety minutes, each way. They went to Martha's Vineyard and then headed back to Hyannis Port. When they were about halfway home, the boat ran out of gas. "We're fucking stranded in the middle of the fucking ocean," Pucillo said. John called the Coast Guard on the boat's radio. From the call letters, the Coast Guard knew immediately that it was a Kennedy boat. They waited about twenty minutes, bobbing up and down, in the Atlantic Ocean between Hyannis Port and Martha's Vineyard for the Coast Guard to bring John enough gas to get back to the dock. "I knew him enough that that wasn't a big shock to me and it was just part of the adventure, I guess," he said.

AT SOME POINT EARLY IN HIS SENIOR YEAR, it was obvious to the Andover administration and to Jackie that John's ongoing struggles with math were not going to be resolved easily. He also had a problem in English—there had been "a question" about a paper he wrote, Pucillo said. Andover made the decision that John should not graduate in June 1978 with his class but rather stay at Andover for another year, a postgraduate year of sorts, to see if he could his act together. "In a way it's nice not having to think about colleges this year," John wrote a former girlfriend, Meg Azzoni, that fall, "but in the long run next year here will probably suck. They're cracking down even more. How long can I last?" In truth, John was upset with the decision. "We had been seniors together, right?" Pucillo said. It also wasn't a private embarrassment. The news made the *National Enquirer*. The newspaper reported that John was "such a poor student" that he had to repeat his senior year "at the posh prep school that he attends." The paper somehow tracked him down at Andover by telephone and asked him if he were a "poor student," prompting him to answer, "Well I don't know. It depends what you call a poor student."

John started dating Jenny Christian, an Andover senior from Englewood, New Jersey. Her father was a doctor. Jenny and her older sister, Vicky, were legendary at Andover for their combination of beauty and intelligence. They attended the premiere of *Saturday Night Fever* together over Christmas 1977 and managed to upstage John Travolta, the star of the film, leaving him alone on the red carpet as photographers and fans rushed to John's side. As with many of his other Andover relationships, things with Jenny eventually ran their course.

Jackie curated another series of special experiences for her son, this time out west. She was very focused on him having a male influence aside from Secret Service agents. After a stint at the Youth Conservation Corps program at Yellowstone National Park went awry due to too much press attention, Jackie hatched another plan. She contacted Teno Roncalio, a longtime US congressman from Wyoming. Roncalio told Jackie about John Perry Barlow, a Grateful Dead lyricist who had inherited his father's cattle ranch near Pinedale, Wyoming. Jackie decided that John should spend the rest of the summer working for Barlow.

Jackie called Barlow on the phone. Barlow remembered: "It was fairly late in the evening. I was sitting at the galactic headquarters of the Bar

Cross Land and Livestock Company in Cora, Wyoming. I get this breathy voice on the phone that says, 'Hi, this is Jacqueline Onassis.' And I said, 'Well, in the highly unlikely event that this isn't some kind of a joke, what can I do for you?' Two days later, [John] was on the ranch. . . . My job was to transform him into a ranch hand for about a month. He dug holes for fence posts and looked after some of the animals. . . . He was rambunctious and at that point a bit directionless," he said. "But he was full of good juice and amiability and that wonderful alert curiosity he had about everything all of the time. Everything was interesting to him. He wasn't afraid to ask questions."

Barlow used to fly his plane around his ranch, and John took a keen interest in it. "He always wanted to go along on that," Barlow remembered, "and I eventually said, 'Obviously, you want to know how to drive one of these things. It's not that hard. Let me teach you.'" They just clicked. "It was one of those moments you have in your life every now and again when you meet someone and you know you're going to be friends for life," he said. And they were.

John returned to Andover for his unwanted third year without the group of friends he had surrounded himself with during his first two years. Even his mother abandoned her usual practice of staying a day or two at the Andover Inn when she dropped John off. He returned determined to settle down for the rest of the school year, and to make it to graduation. He made the varsity soccer team—even though he wasn't much of a team sports athlete—and scored a goal in the game against rival Exeter. He got more involved in the drama department at Andover, acting in Shakespeare's *The Comedy of Errors*; he also played the lead in Ken Kesey's *One Flew Over the Cuckoo's Nest* and Neil Simon's *Come Blow Your Horn*, and directed Edward Albee's *The Zoo Story*. John's interest in acting was genuine and passionate. But while his mother encouraged him in it for a while by attending his performances, she was dead set against John getting too caught up in the pursuit of it. She thought it was too trivial for him.

There was no doubt John was still struggling academically at Andover. To try to help him, his mother enlisted Ted Becker, a noted New York City child psychiatrist who specialized in helping troubled teens. For several months during his senior year at Andover, John went to New York once a week to see Becker. Jackie was upset about his poor grades, his interest in acting, and his pot habit; she feared the negative influence of other members of the Kennedy clan. By all accounts, it was a bit of a peripatetic extra year for John. He was at Andover during the week and then would head to Boston on the weekends. He would stay at Harvard with Jenny Christian or with Pucillo, who recalled how when John attended the dedication ceremony for the Kennedy School of Government, in October 1978, with his mother and his sister, he didn't have a suit to wear. So he borrowed from Pucillo a rather unstylish and pedestrian tan three-piece suit and an ugly tie. "His mother was horrified because it didn't quite fit," Pucillo said.

On January 5, 1979, John applied to Brown. (He dated the application 1978, seeming to have forgotten the calendar year had changed.) He matter-of-factly listed his father as deceased, with a former occupation listed simply as "government." He indicated on the form that he was interested chiefly in studying political science, international relations, and American civilization, and also that he had an interest in studying the dramatic arts. Without guile or irony, he wrote that his "academic interest" had always leaned toward "conceptual studies" and that science and math "have never been particularly interesting." He wrote that his primary extracurricular activity at Andover was the theater.

With his Brown application in, John seemed unfocused in his final months at Andover. He even lived a few months during the winter and spring at his father's apartment at 122 Bowdoin Street in Beacon Hill. The family had been renting it since John's father started living there as a freshman congressman in 1947. What's not the slightest bit clear is how Andover allowed John to live at his father's apartment while also being an enrolled student at the school. Permission to do so would have been hard to come by for a mere mortal.

He also spent time living at the Andover home of his friend James Spader, who was a day student and had left the school before graduation to pursue what turned out to be a very successful Hollywood acting career. Spader and John would also hang out together at 1040 Fifth when John was in New York City. (Jackie had offered Spader the use of the guest room at the apartment on the weekend, when she headed out to the horse country of New Jersey.) One day, Spader recalled, he and John had had a "rather festive afternoon" together and "we found ourselves in the library in the apartment"—the same room where, during my own visit to 1040 Fifth, I had once wanted to look at a scrapbook with a huge presidential seal embossed on it. It was late afternoon and John turned on the television to a sporting event of some sort. "He was on the floor on pillows," Spader recalled, "and I was sitting on the couch just sort of spaced out, and they always had this big bowl of pistachios on the coffee table in front of the couch. Well, things being festive and all, I started eating the pistachios and sort of thumbing through books and things, and magazines that were on the coffee table, and I was just sort of sitting there eating the pistachios. Well, I finished the entire bowl of pistachios," which may very well have been in that bowl for more than a decade. He found himself surrounded by three hundred or so empty pistachio shells.

Soon enough, it was dinnertime and he and John joined Jackie, Caroline, and their cousin Anthony Radziwill at the dining room table. They were chatting away. Out came the first course from the kitchen. "We're sitting there and eating away and chatting about this and that," Spader continued. "And I started to feel really hot all of a sudden. But I figured it was winter and their heat registers just sort of converged right in that corner, and so I figured it was just sort of that I need a little air in here. Jackie was very slim so she kept the apartment warm. But I started getting hotter and hotter and eventually sort of a cold sweat, and really started to get that feeling that *Wow, this isn't right. Something's not right*, and really like a flop sweat. But you know the conversation is going well and it's a great dinner, and I'm still continuing on with the eating. So I sort of slow down a little bit and all of a sudden I start to feel like *Wow, I think I'm feeling a little nauseous. This isn't great.* I'm just about to get up to say *You know, excuse me, I think I'm going to go to the bathroom for a second*, and I threw up on my plate. At which point, Jackie without missing a beat said, 'Good shot, Jim!' And of course John is across the table from me now hysterical. He thinks it's just the funniest thing in the world. And I said, 'Excuse me.' I put my napkin over my plate, and I went down to John's room and I sort of washed up. I came out and by the time I came out they'd moved on to dessert. They said, 'Are you all right?' and I said, 'No, no, I'm fine. Really. I think I ate something'—clearly probably a dozen of the pistachios were rotten or something—I said, 'No I'm fine,' and John was hysterical still across the table from me, and he kept leaning back in his chair. And Jackie turned around and said, 'John, stop leaning back in your chair, these are nice chairs and please stop leaning back in them.' And he just kept laughing and looking at me, and he leaned back again and the chair crumbled underneath him. He completely collapsed, *he completely collapsed* and he disappeared from view behind the table, and all you could hear was this sort of giggling below the table, okay? And at this point Jackie turns and says, 'Dammit, John, if I've told you once I've told you a dozen times, do not lean back in those chairs and now see what's happened! Look what you've done, it's just so rude,' and he bounced up above the table with this huge grin on his face and says, 'Jimmy just threw up at the table!'"

JOHN WAS ADMITTED TO BROWN and to Harvard, and chose Brown. He became one of the few members of the Kennedy family to explicitly reject Harvard. This was national news. Some members of the Kennedy clan were upset by John's decision, but his mother thought it was

great. "He went to Brown because he wouldn't go to Harvard," Ed Hill
said. "He wasn't going to do that. He knew he was going to probably
do crappy. I mean he was not a good student. Brown was a conscious
choice, to not insult everyone else's intelligence by going to Harvard."

On June 7, 1979, John graduated from Andover. Celebrating with
him on campus were his mother, his sister, and his uncle Teddy. That
summer, in keeping with his mother's insistence that he get the best
experiences, John was off to a seventy-day National Outdoor Leadership
School course in Kenya. NOLS was Outward Bound on steroids—and
the expedition through the Masai Mara game park nearly ended in
disaster. The story was of course reported in the *National Enquirer*.

Toward the end of each NOLS trip, the students, supposedly fully
battle-tested, are given a topographic map, a compass, and some food
and told to get from point A to point B using only the tools provided.
The leaders leave the students to fend for themselves, making the assumption that the survival skills imparted in the previous weeks of the
trip would serve them well during the final test. Usually, that works out
perfectly well. But not always. (I went on a NOLS trip to Glacier Peak
in the Pacific Northwest that worked out just fine.) For their final NOLS
expedition, the seven teenagers of John's group were sent on a sixty-two-
mile, eight-day hike through the dense Kenyan jungle. They had dehy-
drated food, some flour and cheese. "But they only had a sketchy map of
their route," the paper reported, "and after seven days found themselves
lost in the forbidding jungle, which is crawling with deadly cobras and
mambas and is almost impenetrable in places." The trees were 120 feet
high and the undergrowth was said to be more than six feet high. "The
group pushed forward," the *Enquirer* continued, "desperately hoping to
find their way out." John later told friends in Nairobi, "We just followed
the instructions we'd been given, set our course by the sun and our com-
passes and kept as calm as possible." But they were lost in the jungle.
They didn't eat for a couple of days. At one point, John was leading the
group when he saw a rhino, weighing several tons, fifteen feet ahead of

them on the path. He was getting ready to do what he'd been told to do under such circumstances—drop his pack and climb up the nearest tree—when the animal lumbered away into the bush. (A few months before, a charging rhino had trampled another NOLS student.) When John and his six colleagues didn't show up at the appointed spot after eight days, the NOLS team grew concerned. They dispatched an airplane, locals, and a group of volunteers to try to find the missing teens. A Masai tracker finally found them.

THE CONSENSUS AMONG THE PEOPLE WHO KNEW JOHN best was that he was by now a fully formed, thrill-seeking adrenaline addict. Barlow said he talked to John about his close call on the NOLS trip but that it didn't affect him that much. "His desire to do things a little edgy was never slaked in the slightest," he said. Ed Hill recalled how he and John jumped off eighty-foot-high cliffs, how they went skydiving in New Jersey. "I did it twice," Hill said, "and after the second time I just said 'No more.' The first time I was so nervous about it and he gave me so much shit that I felt I needed to vindicate myself by doing it a second time, but after the second time I said, 'I was right in the first place, fucking stupid.'" He remembered driving back from Conway, New Hampshire, with John after a day of ice climbing. They had rented a Cadillac. John was driving. "It was the dead of winter and the roads were terribly icy, and at one point we passed a horrific automobile accident, but he didn't convince himself, nor did I convince him, to drive more carefully," he said. He told the story of a little-known incident when John went kayaking by himself to Great Island, off the coast of Hyannis. "He set out in terrible weather," he said. "It was a miracle that he made it. He capsized, I think. But anyway, he made it to Great Island and then he had to break into someone's house. He was so hypothermic that he had to break into someone's house and get in the bathtub. He did that alone. That was typically the sort of thing that you'd ex-

pect him to do with someone else." John left a note for the homeown-
ers and signed it. "They got back to him," Hill said. "They were very
nice about it: 'Glad to be of assistance, John.'"

Chermayeff said John's compulsive desire for physical risk-taking was
an essential part of his being. "He was always looking for that," she said.
"He really was looking for some kind of depth so that he could really
feel like a human being on the planet, in this life. He wasn't religious.
I don't think he believed in God or heaven or hell, or an afterlife. He
might have had his background, but he felt everything had to be realized
in this life and the ante was always up. I don't know, that's a guy, male
explorer thing. Look at all the people, they all end up dead."

MARK THREE STARS'S FAMILY was from Pine Ridge Reservation in
South Dakota. He grew up in Phoenix, Arizona. When he showed up
at freshman year at Brown, he had never been east of the Rio Grande
before. Move-in day "was just a madhouse of cars and parents," he said.
He was hot and sweaty. "There's people coming and going, and I saw
this woman," he said. "She was carrying this box of albums, you know,
vinyl. She had a box of vinyl in her hands, in her arms. I'm coming up
the stairs and she was next to the railing and I kind of went past her
very quickly so I could open the door at the top of the stairs. So I got
in front of her and opened the door. It was one of those heavy fire doors,
and she looks up and she goes, 'Oh my God, thank you so much,' and
it was his mom, Jackie. My mouth kind of flopped open a little bit and
I was like, 'Ah, you're welcome.' She was having the whole *moving my
son into college* experience. Then I quickly realized there was this whole
group of guys in suits who were also there."

At first, he wasn't sure how to process the fact that John F. Kennedy
Jr. was living across the hall from him. Like John, Mark was raised by a
single mother. Beyond that connection, though, it was clear that John
existed in a rarefied "other world" that would be nearly impossible for

Mark—or nearly anyone, really—to penetrate. "He was a very hand-some guy and he was also very charming and affable," Mark said. He wasn't sure if John just wanted to be left alone. "I'm not going to be one of those crazy people that's fawning all over him," he thought to him-self. "How annoying would that be?" By the end of the year, he ended up being somewhere between a friend and an acquaintance of John's. "He wanted to be one of the regular guys," Mark said, "but he wanted to be one of the regular guys who went to a very prestigious prep school who was really wealthy. He didn't want to be one of the regular guys like I knew regular guys." He said that a cadre of "prep school friends" sur-rounded John, making it difficult for him to get to know John well. "I never felt like I was going to break into that sort of circle of friends." He remembered playing Frisbee with John for a long time at a freshman-class party. "Really just having a great time," he said. "It was a very physical kind of experience, you know, chasing and running around and stuff like that. We had this funny physical bonding, no words were really spoken or *great catch* or whatever, and then we leave."

John's prep school friends "formed this, like, phalanx around him," Mark said, "and I kind of saw his demeanor change, and I thought a lot about it afterward and then it was sort of like this banter that was inaccessible to me. And then I realized: He has to take on this demeanor whenever he's out in public. He's kind of steeling himself. He walked differently. He just looked different. . . . It was interesting to see him change. Then we got up to the dorm and it was like we're in the room and it was all very relaxed."

His same personality quirks once again manifested themselves at Brown. Among these, of course, were John's bad habits of borrowing money and of losing his wallet, which occasionally had some bor-rowed money in it. Mark remembered that when John came back from Christmas vacation he had a new "biker" wallet, one of those wallets with a thick chain attached to it that could be clipped onto your pants, making it theoretically difficult to lose. "His mother was so angry with him because he'd lost his wallet like four or five times in the first semester," he said. A few weeks later, he said, John came into Mark's room, dressed only in his boxers. "He goes, 'Have you seen my khaki pants?' And I'm like, 'Jesus man, it's like put some clothes on. Why would your khaki pants be in here?' And he was like, 'Oh God, I lost my khaki pants,' and I'm like, 'Don't you have other pants to wear?' and he goes, 'Oh, my wallet's attached to my khaki pants.' So he lost his pants and his wallet. He was like, 'Oh God, my mom is going to be so pissed.'"

Gary Ginsberg met John in their intellectual history class at Brown. They sat together in the back of the room. Ginsberg remembered being struck by how Mary Gluck, the professor, "doted" on John. He gave John grief about it for the next twenty years. "He could say things that were utterly incomprehensible and the professor would walk toward him as he spoke," Ginsberg said. "She didn't walk toward anybody else when they spoke but she would walk close to him, nod her head vigorously, and opine about how insightful and brilliant his observations were. And I was just looking at him, shaking my head, and say[ing], 'That was really nonsensical.' I guess there was a certain irreverence in our relationship from the get-go." John did receive an academic wake-up call early on at Brown. Ed Beiser, a political science professor, gave him a failing grade on a paper. "He was really shaken," Beiser remembered. "He said, 'What am I going to tell my mother?' 'You don't have to tell her anything,' I said. 'You just have to write another paper for me.'"

John's first-year academic struggles at Brown were real, and he was placed on academic probation. Once again, his mother had to deal with the situation. On July 2, 1980, Jackie replied to a letter she had received from Brown academic dean Karen Romer about John's failure to complete two courses. "Living up to academic responsibilities has always been of first importance in our house, so neither John nor I will fail to be galvanized by your message," she wrote. "I have never asked for special consideration for my children because I feel that is harmful to them but there is an extra burden that John carried this year that other students did not—and I would like to mention it. He was asked to campaign almost every weekend for his uncle." Jackie wrote to Romer that she would try to get in touch with John, who was again in Africa, and get him to come home earlier than expected in order to complete the classes by September 15 that he had failed to complete the previous academic year.

John and Rob Littell, a Lawrenceville graduate from New Jersey, met at the beach in Newport, Rhode Island, during Brown's freshman orientation week. Littell played lacrosse at Lawrenceville and was recruited to play lacrosse at Brown. He and John hit it off quickly, and ended up rooming together their sophomore year, in the Phi Psi house.

Much of their social life during their first two years at Brown together centered on Phi Psi, which was once a fraternity but had become a fun, raucous dorm without the official fraternal affiliation. There was plenty of alcohol and drugs, especially cocaine. Sasha Chermayeff said that Littell and John "snorted coke all the way through college." (As for her own use of cocaine, she said, "I always prided myself in saying the only time I snorted coke was when I was with John Kennedy.") Sasha recalled how when John was younger and he had to fulfill a family obligation by giving a speech or making some comments, he would reward himself with a cup of ginger ale, "which he really wanted." As he got older, the rewards changed. "He worked hard all day," she recalled, "and he'd smoke this pot and then he's going to maybe have a glass of wine, or maybe I'll do a line [of cocaine], maybe he'll smoke a cigarette. He was like, 'This is my cup of ginger ale.'"

There were other rewards for John, too. One night a group of freshmen, including John and Rob, were hanging out together in the Phi Psi television room when along came Billy Way, who had gone to Andover, too, followed by a group of six "attractive and evidently inebriated" co-eds from Providence College, according to Littell. With yellow eyes and a mane of flowing hair, Way, from Bermuda, was on both the

Andover and Brown tennis teams, and supposedly was a legendary Lothario. "He had made love to more girls by his eighteenth birthday than most guys fantasize about in their whole lifetime," Littell explained. Way brought the "cutest girl" over to meet John. At first, there was no "spark" between them, he continued, but then Way told the woman she was talking to John, the president's son. "She lit up like a Christmas tree," Littell wrote, "as if this news changed everything." She asked John to "prove it," causing him to show her his New York State driver's license. "The girl, all business at that point, reviewed the license for a moment and then, with a Cheshire kitten's grin, stuffed her right hand down the front of John's pants and led him out of the room."

Unlike at Andover, where everyone was younger and less experienced sexually, Brown seemed more like a sexual free-for-all, and no one benefited from that more thoroughly in his way than John. Women were literally throwing themselves at him. Mark Three Stars recalled how on "more than one occasion," he would open the door of his room to find a young woman standing in front of John's door in her underwear. When the question was posed what exactly she was doing at John's door in her underwear, she said, "I'm supposed to meet John here." Remembered Mark: "It was such bullshit, and I said, 'Well, you know he's out for a while but you can come wait in here.' So she went in our room for I don't know, maybe about ten minutes, and then took off." The dorm resident advisers quickly got wind of the practice and put an end to it by more closely monitoring who was going to John's room. "I never have seen anyone get reactions the way he did," said Chris Cuomo, the CNN anchor and a friend of John's. "Not the biggest rock star, not the biggest movie star, because he wasn't an entertainer. He was the real deal. He was the living legacy of the closest thing to greatness a big slice of this country thought that we had ever experienced in a leader. That's what Kennedy was." Added Cuomo's CNN colleague, Christiane "Kissy" Amanpour, who shared a house with John during his junior year at Brown (she went to the University of Rhode Island), "I remember watching in sort of a combination of horror and awe, the way men and women threw themselves at him, of all ages. Even if they physically weren't throwing themselves at him, they were emotionally throwing themselves at him." John Perry Barlow had noticed the phenomenon, too. "People would come up to him and you could see them just shedding IQ points as they approached," he recalled. "I mean the closer they got, the dumber they were. You knew that they'd been pretty bright over here someplace, but by the time they got there they were just dumb as bait."

The summer after his freshman year at Brown—while his mother was handling his academic problems—John spent part of July in Johannesburg, South Africa, visiting the diamond company run by Maurice Tempelsman, his mother's new boyfriend, and part of the month in Zimbabwe visiting with student and government leaders. John seemed quite moved by what he witnessed in South Africa, and seemed determined to do something about it. After his sophomore year, John spent the summer in Washington, working at the Center for Democratic Policy, a liberal think tank. While he was in Washington, he lived with his aunt and uncle, the Shrivers, and their son Tim (his good friend). He spent time on the weekends exploring—"I wanted to come to Washington because I've never been here before," he told the *New York Times*, in a piece arranged by his uncle Ted, without irony. "I wanted to see what it was like"—and he spent evenings "teaching himself to play the guitar . . . I don't really go out a lot." Ted Van Dyk, John's boss at the think tank, told *Time* that John "had never really been to Washington. He didn't even know where the White House was." (It's not clear why the myth of John's unfamiliarity with Washington was being pushed.) John accompanied Van Dyk on a fund-raising trip to Hollywood. The Hollywood stars couldn't get enough of him. "He began to realize he was a celebrity," Van Dyk continued. "He had his first contact with clutchers and grabbers. He handled it."

At the start of his junior year at Brown, John made the papers because he failed to pay $108 in parking fines. John shared a five-bedroom Victorian town house at 115 Benefit Street, in the tony section of Providence. John had the smallest room in the house. It only had room for a desk and a bed. One Saturday morning, though, the phone rang and briefly upset the delicate balance that existed in the house. The anonymous caller announced to Christina Haag—John's friend and roommate, who had answered the phone—that he hated the Kennedys and knew where John lived. He threatened to kill John. What to do? Tell John? (He was not in his room, having spent the night elsewhere.) Call the campus police? Call the Providence police? Call Senator Kennedy's office? When John eventually returned home, Chris Oberbeck, another housemate and close friend (John was the best man at his first wedding), summoned the courage to tell him about the phone call. But John could not have cared less. This was not the first time he had been threatened. He quickly decided it was a prank. He wasn't the slightest bit worried. "I felt more protective of him than I ever had," Haag recalled, "and, in a strange way, more in awe of his fearlessness."

That same year, John got named to *People* magazine's "best dressed" list, although it was not exactly clear why, except for the fact of who he was. "He is the preppy's preppy, sporting the Ivy League costume of chinos and shirt (often with tails out), Shetland sweaters, loafers—and no polyester," the magazine observed.

In the second semester of his junior year, John got the lead role of Christy the playboy in J. M. Synge's *The Playboy of the Western World* about a meek underdog who gets transformed. "He had a way about him that was grace personified," remembered James Barnhill, one of John's theater professors. "He took direction well and he improvised well." But the *Brown Daily Herald* panned the production and especially John's performance in it, essentially because John was too good-looking to portray an Irish peasant who evolves. John also appeared as the character Longshore, a tough, hip Irishman in his mid-thirties, in

Miguel Piñero's play *Short Eyes*, a drama about men in prison directed by Santina Goodman. John's character murders a child molester. The reviewer for the *Brown Daily Herald* praised the "frightening realism" of Goodman's production and said of John that he played the role of Longshore with "perfection" and that he "[threw] his bulk around the set with infinite self-assurance and an air of stubborn defiance." (Best-selling author Jeffrey Eugenides, a classmate of John's, "skillfully" played a "cynical" prison investigator.)

BY THE TIME JOHN WAS A SENIOR at Brown, where he majored in American history, he had finally shaken off the yoke of academic ineptitude and become something of a decent student. Mary Gluck, for one, had noticed the improvement from the first class he took with her to the last. His final college paper, which he hand-delivered to her wearing cutoff shorts, was about Wordsworth. "He said, 'Just hot off the press,'" Gluck recalled. "I'll never forget the enormous pleasure." She gave him a B-plus on the paper.

On June 6, 1983, John graduated from Brown. It followed an all-night party, and no sleep for John and his friends. His classmates did their best to surround him to try to prevent the swarm of photographers from taking his picture (which of course failed). The day after graduation, John had a party for about fifty classmates at the family compound in Hyannis Port. "I don't remember much more than people sleeping in the emptied pool and in the screening room beneath the grand matriarch Rose's big house," Rob Littell said. From there, a smaller group of John's friends accompanied him to his mother's new 150-acre spread, Red Gate Farm, in Martha's Vineyard. "We stayed for days, reluctant to let the party end," Littell remembered.

For about a month after graduating from Brown, John returned to Providence to study for the LSAT. He had decided to go to law school, no doubt with the support and approval of his mother. The LSAT completed—his score was just average—he spent much of the follow-ing year in India. With the help of the Indian and American govern-ments, John traveled through India largely unnoticed. In Delhi, he stayed at a variety of places, including the embassies of foreign nations and in fleabag hotels in the center of the city.

At a cocktail party one night at the Irish embassy, Narendra Taneja, a local journalist, met John, who was staying in a sleeping bag on the second floor. (He didn't know it was John initially.) "We just got talk-ing," Taneja recalled, "and I asked him where he was staying for his trip to Delhi, and he, with a smirk, pointed toward a corner of the room's floor." At the time, Taneja had the use of a large four-bedroom home belonging to a professor at the Indian Institute of Technology and so he offered John one of the empty bedrooms, figuring he would prefer it to sleeping on the floor. "He took up the offer," Taneja continued, "and after some time we took a tuk-tuk and left for my place. As we talked sitting in the living room and having instant noodles for dinner later that night, he brought out his diary and started to flip pages, showing his written musings about travels, family and so on. As he flipped through the pages, there were photos of him and his family. After quick glances, I started to realize that most of his pictures were with John F. Kennedy and his wife, Jackie Kennedy. I inquired about the photo-graphs, and he replied, 'Well, they are my parents,' and that is when I realized I had John F. Kennedy Jr. living in my house." The next morn-ing, the American embassy called to check on John and to make sure his whereabouts were kept secret from the press and other institutions.

That wish was a short-lived one. Word quickly got around that John F. Kennedy Jr. was staying on campus. One professor called Taneja and invited the two of them to tea, hoping to score a visit with John. "I hesitated but agreed, telling him no one else should know about him staying here," Taneja said. But when they arrived at the professor's home, they discovered that he had invited about twenty others to join, appar-ently in order to show off that he knew the son of the former president of the United States. "We decided to stay even though I had asked him specifically not to let anyone know," Taneja continued. "After a while, the professor decided to ask John a question, and he asked, 'So do you remember when your father was assassinated?' John, aghast, looked at me, and I stared at the professor in disbelief that this question was actually tabled to him. We left his house within minutes, and I apologized to him. 'It's O.K., it's just that no one ever asks me that,'" he said.

The next day, Taneja told John he was heading to Tundla, a small town near Agra. John asked to join him on the trip, despite the fact that the accommodations and transportation were decidedly third-class, at best. In Tundla, John met a bunch of the locals. A palm reader, or *jyotishee*, wanted to read John's palm. He agreed. After a few minutes, the palm reader declared, "This man is the son of a king." John was a bit startled by the pronouncement, understandably, but said nothing, given his desire to travel incognito. Later that day, however, he returned to visit with the palm reader, and spent two more hours with him.

John spent another week with Taneja in Tundla before heading to the spiritual city of Varanasi, also in Uttar Pradesh, on the banks of the Ganges. From there he spent another week in Calcutta. With the help of the Indian government, John stayed for a week with another journalist, M. J. Akbar. "It was great fun having him," Akbar recalled. "I remember that women used to line up around the staircase of the building as he ran up and down, bare bodied, for eight floors whenever there was no electricity and the lift would not work." (Akbar later served as the Indian minister of state for external affairs.) In Calcutta, John also visited with Mother Teresa and, at the behest of her charity, helped to teach English to children in the slums of the city. John ended his time in India in the resort state of Goa, where his mother met him. They traveled together for two weeks.

After India, John returned to live and to work in New York City. For the first two years back in town, John and Rob Littell rented a two-bedroom, two-bath apartment together at 309 West 86th Street, on the Upper West Side. While Littell worked at a small brokerage firm, John spent much of the next two years first working at the city's Office of Economic Development and then as the deputy director of the 42nd Street Development Corporation, which was formed to revamp the area from a seedy, drug-and-porn-infested corridor into a major tourist attraction, along the lines of Piccadilly Circus, in London. Shaaz Ali, who worked with John at the Office of Economic Development, remembered he used to go into the stairwell between the floors of the office and scream, just so he could hear the echo. He also used to chew the tops of the pens, and people would hide their pens from him as a result. Ali gave John his first paycheck. "But he lost it," Ali remembered. "It was sent to the cleaners in his pants, so we had to send him another one."

According to Littell, their work was not really the point. They just wanted to have fun in New York, which "at that particular moment in history," he wrote, was one of the most "exhilarating" places to live. "The city was edgy, raw, more dangerous and less civil than it is now, but also coursing with energy," he observed. "Cocaine and pot were the drugs of choice in the city then, available anywhere anytime. You could have your cocaine delivered, or you could stop by the dry cleaner and pick it up on your way home." He said they worked hard to moderate their intake of such substances, in part because of their own vanity and in part because, as Littell commented, "We both had friends who lost control, some who battled back to a healthy life and others, sadly, who were swept away."

Ed Hill remembered just soaking it all in as one of John's sidekicks. Things would happen that Hill found hard to fathom. "I would find my eyes rolling on a regular basis." He remembered being out with John somewhere in New York City when he reached into his pocket and pulled out a scrap of paper. "I looked at it and there written in cursive was this woman's name and her phone number," Hill said. "I recognized the name right away"—it was that of Julianne Phillips, an actress who was then married to Bruce Springsteen—"and said, 'What the fuck is this?' Of course he just laughed, because here he's got Springsteen's wife's phone number in her handwriting."

There was always time for the requisite weekend touch football game in Central Park. John and Gary Ginsberg probably played touch football in the park every weekend for the next fifteen years. "It was an ungodly amount of time," Ginsberg recalled. "I mean hundreds and hundreds of hours. What was interesting is how much time we would spend organizing these games, and it would start at phone calls. There was no internet back then. There was no email. He would do it all by phone, and the phone calls would start early on Saturdays."

Along with working on the redevelopment of 42nd Street, John continued to dabble in theater. At the end of January 1985, he and his old friend and housemate from Brown, Christina Haag, who was studying acting at Juilliard, began reading through *Lovers*, by the Irish playwright Brian Friel. It was a way for Haag to escape what she called "the rigidity" of Juilliard and a way for John to rekindle his love of the theater. Robin Saex, a director and mutual friend of theirs from Brown, had been looking for a play that would work for her two friends and that might actually get produced off-Broadway. After months of read-throughs, in June Saex informed John and Christina that the play would be staged at the Irish Arts Center in Hell's Kitchen. There would be six invitation-only performances. At John's insistence, there would be no publicity (of course, this proved impossible to prevent). Although they both were in relationships, they started falling for each other. "No matter how many times you fall in love," Haag later reflected in her book, *Come to the Edge*, "it always comes at you sideways. It always catches you by surprise."

It was a relationship with many fits and starts, and over the years that followed, it had its own unique challenges. For example, there was the time, in January 1986, when they were set to go to Pennsylvania together for the weekend. A day or so before they were to leave,

John called to cancel. She was confused. The *Challenger* shuttle had exploded, killing its crew, he explained to her, and he had to go to the Johnson Space Center, in Houston, for the memorial service with President Reagan and other government dignitaries. It had to be either him or Caroline, he said. It was his turn.

JOHN HAD APPLIED TO MANY of the top law schools, not because he wanted to practice law—he most certainly didn't—but as a way to buy time. It would be three years where he could hang out and where no one could criticize him for being a slacker. Plus his mother wanted him to go and figured law school would divert him permanently from his continuing interest in acting. (She had once nixed him from guest-hosting *Saturday Night Live*.)

Of course, his LSAT scores were not particularly good—he gave Littell the thumbs-down once when asked about them. Heretofore this had not been a problem. He had moved from St. David's to Collegiate, despite academic concerns. He had moved to Andover from Collegiate, despite academic concerns. He had moved from Andover to Brown, despite academic concerns, rejecting Harvard (and other top schools) in the process. But law school for some reason was different. Maybe it was the LSAT scores. Maybe it was his choppy academic record at Brown. Maybe it was that the schools intuited that he wasn't devoted to the law. In any event, he was rejected from Harvard Law, despite his family's lineage at the school. Eventually, after other rejections, John got into the New York University School of Law. He decided to go there, beginning in the fall of 1986, once again a full-time student.

John's relationship with Haag was in full swing. The summer before John matriculated at New York University law school, they went together to Red Gate Farm, in the southwestern end of Martha's Vineyard. It was an extraordinary—and very valuable—property, with a

mile of ocean frontage, that Jackie had purchased from the Horn-
blower estate in August 1978. Jackie had built a series of shingle-
style saltbox homes on a small portion of the property in 1981. There
was a garage, a caretaker's home, tennis courts, and a vegetable garden. There was a guest cottage, known as the Barn. Next to the Barn
was the Tower, an attached "faux" silo with a bedroom at the top.
This was John's lair.

In June 1986, *People* named John America's "most eligible bachelor."
The magazine touted John's "self-effacing charm" and that he liked to
"hang out" at the Palladium disco, in Manhattan, where he would introduce himself to women with "Hi, I'm John." But the magazine
incorrectly reported he would be attending Columbia Law School—
where Caroline was entering her second year—in the fall, and repeated
the error in another short piece on John the day before his sister's July
wedding. The second piece on John noted that he was making $20,000
a year as an assistant to the commissioner of the Economic Development Agency of New York and that the "only blemish" on his record
was that he had been caught speeding, three years earlier, on the Connecticut Turnpike going eighty-one miles per hour in a fifty-five zone
and then, incredibly, had his driver's license suspended because he
failed to show up for the court appearance.

Departing from the apartment he shared (and trashed) with Littell,
John decided to stay on the Upper West Side, moving—per his mother's
recommendation—to the top floor of a brownstone on West 91st, between Central Park West and Columbus Avenue. Haag moved from
Brooklyn into the same neighborhood, a studio apartment on the
ground floor of a shabby building on West 83rd Street. They settled into
a boyfriend-and-girlfriend routine—John focused more or less on his
law school studies, Christina on her burgeoning career as an actress.
Most days, after breakfast at a health food restaurant on Columbus
Avenue, he cycled the four miles down to Washington Square to go
to class.

Like many people, John found the first year of law school difficult. The summer after, he and Christina lived together outside of Washington. He was working at the Civil Rights Division in the Reagan Justice Department; she had an acting gig in town. Often during the summer, she urged him to visit for the first time his father's gravesite in Arlington National Cemetery. Haag knew that John would occasionally recall memories of his father: His father would sometimes take a buttercup and put it under his chin and tell him he liked butter; John would do that to Christina, too. He remembered that his father sometimes called him Sam, which he found somehow upsetting. He remembered playing under his father's desk in the Oval Office. He remembered one of the last times he and his father were together, nine days before he went to Dallas, on the balcony overlooking the South Lawn of the White House when the Black Watch bagpipers were performing. But despite Haag's urging, John always seemed reluctant to go to Arlington, until the last day, as they were heading back to New York together, when he decided to visit the grave.

BEFORE STARTING HIS SECOND YEAR of law school, John planned a fabulous trip for him and Christina to Venice at his mother's recommendation. But it was not to be. Haag got an offer to play Ophelia in Baltimore. When she called John to tell him, he said he was excited for her and urged her to come over to 91st Street so they could celebrate together. When she got there, though, his mood had darkened considerably. She found him sitting in a metal chair on the small deck off his bedroom. He was smoking a cigarette and staring blankly into the middle distance. "You will always be leaving me," he said. She tried to console him, to break his funk. The next morning, he was better. He had moved on. "I'll get used to it," he told her.

He saw Haag perform twice in Baltimore that fall. While visiting, John asked her if she would spend the summer with him in Los Angeles, where he had been offered a job as a summer associate at a prestigious law firm founded by Charles Manatt, former head of the Democratic National Committee. Haag got to pick where they lived, and she chose a clapboard cottage on Thornton Court, by the beach in Venice. John bought her an old powder-blue Buick Skylark Custom with a black interior to drive. As they were living near Santa Monica Airport, John took up flying lessons. Nearly every Saturday, he went up with an instructor "and always came back happy," Haag reported. His skills improved throughout the summer, and one day he decided he wanted to fly—with the instructor seated next to him—to Catalina Island, off the coast of Los Angeles. He invited Haag to join in the fun. "Don't worry, Puppy," he told her. "The instructor will be there." One cloudless morning, with John at the controls, the three of them headed out over the western Los Angeles neighborhoods and then over the Pacific Ocean. With the Catalina runway in view, atop a sixteen-hundred-foot mesa, the plane began to shake, and John was afraid of stalling. Fortunately, the instructor perked up, mentioned something to John that perhaps he had forgotten, and the plane relaxed, the wings leveled. John landed the plane smoothly. They celebrated with buffalo burgers at the Airport in the Sky café inside the small Catalina terminal.

On July 11 that summer, John went to Atlanta for the 1988 Democratic convention to introduce Teddy, the senior senator from Massachusetts. The Speaker of the House, Jim Wright, introduced John by reminding everyone how beloved he was, is, and would be again. Then twenty-seven, John was dressed in a navy-blue suit, white spread-collar shirt, and dark tie. He looked radiant and as handsome as ever. The crowd gave him a standing ovation for two minutes.

Gary Ginsberg and John went together to a party that Al Gore, then a senator from Tennessee, threw for his staff. There, Gore had had a lot to drink, Ginsberg remembered, and said to John that he needed to come visit him in his Senate office. "We've got to talk," Gore told John, "because we're both American royalty and I think I've got some lessons that I can teach you about how to cope with it." For years afterward, John and Ginsberg would laugh about what Gore said to John. "Not even close," Ginsberg said.

It was no surprise, after his star performance, that many wondered whether John was considering a political career. It was so obvious, given his good looks, his pedigree, his intelligence, his theatrical skills, and his natural sense of empathy. "Stars are born at conventions," one Democratic official told *New York* magazine. "He certainly came out as a Democrat everyone will be watching for a long time."

That September, just as he was starting his third, and final, year at law school, *People* magazine, not content with previously bestowed honors, named John the "Sexiest Man Alive." The magazine's writers commented on his abs, his thighs—"legend has it that if he lived in Tahiti, instead of Manhattan, he could crack coconuts with them," the magazine fawned—and his butt, and wondered what he would look like naked. His relationship with Haag was mentioned, as was the fact that they had shared a house together in Los Angeles. But there were also passing references made to other women with whom John had been seen: There was a Madonna look-alike (but not Madonna) that showed up with him at Zanzibar and Grill, on East 36th Street, and model Audra Avizienis, who told *People* that they had been out together on a few dates but that they were not "dating" because he had a girlfriend.

Some said he loved the attention. After *People* awarded him the hollow honor, he "used to sprawl at an outdoor table at the Jackson Hole hamburger joint, shirt off," according to the journalist Michael Gross. "One neighborhood woman says Kennedy would stop her to ask for the time. 'My sense was that he was dying for attention, dying for people to look at him,' she says." But there was also a sense, among his friends, that being named the "Sexiest Man Alive" was a bit of a dividing line in his life. While there were times when he could walk around New

York City, or Providence, or Andover unnoticed and undetected, after the *People* magazine cover story, that possibility decreased materially.

Sasha Chermayeff thought that after the *People* story, it became harder and harder for John to make new friends. He could no longer trust people's motives quite as easily as he had before. "He used to make fun of it and complain to us, like 'You guys get to meet new people, you get to make new, really close friends. I can't.' He couldn't really go out in the world that way. It was too overwhelming. It was too much. John was too much for everybody. Everybody was just so blown away by him, that side of him. He was kind of stuck with people he'd known for a very, very long time, at a certain point."

And the old friends loved giving him a hard time after the story came out. John Perry Barlow said, "It turned out to be a really great way to take the piss out of him, 'Oh, do I have the sexiest man in the galaxy on the phone?'"

TOWARD THE END OF HIS LAST YEAR in law school, John won a coveted spot as an assistant district attorney in the office of Robert Morgenthau, the Manhattan DA. It was a very difficult job to get, and John was not the first son of the rich and powerful whom Morgenthau had hired. John agreed to stay in the office for at least three years. At his May 1989 graduation from NYU School of Law, the paparazzi bombarded him with questions. To answer the query of what he would do next, he answered, "Pass the bar."

Ah, the bar exam, the bane of the existence of many recent law school graduates. It's a grueling twelve-hour, two-day ordeal, filled with rote questions best answered through brute memorization. He set about studying for it soon after graduation. His plan for the summer was to take some vacation time—Hyannis Port and Martha's Vineyard—and to study for the bar, which was in July. None of this played to John's strengths, considering his abundant nervous energy and his inability to focus on his studies for an extended period of time. "What really struck me was his restlessness," someone who took a bar review class with John told *People*. "He couldn't sit still for more than 10 minutes at a time. The classroom had a door that opened onto a little deck, and every day he'd get up and open the door three or four times for really no reason."

His job in Morgenthau's office started on August 21. The deal with Morgenthau was that you could keep your job as an assistant district attorney if you failed the bar twice. There was a $3,000 raise when you passed and another $1,000 when you formally joined the bar. If you failed three times, though, you were fired. By June, John could tell it was going to be a tough slog for him. He told Haag that studying for it was "a mother beyond belief" and that his day-to-day existence was monklike. Haag had her doubts about that. By then, their relationship had become more episodic, periods of distance followed by periods of great intensity, followed again by periods of distance.

The previous December, John said he wanted to see other people "for a time," with the implication being, at least from Haag's perspective, that the separation would be brief, more of a last sowing of oats before the ultimate get-together rather than a parting of the ways. He told her he loved her. But by then he had already met the movie actress Daryl Hannah and supposedly had been on a date with another model of some sort, or maybe even Madonna after all. But he denied those encounters. In any event, their separation was just six weeks, and then they went to Jamaica together (where they barely survived an ill-advised and harrowing kayaking expedition). But Haag was still a bit concerned. She had found among his stuff a wayward earring, a Filofax that did not belong to either of them, and a bent pair of cat-eye glasses.

That March, Michael Gross wrote a long piece about John, "Favorite Son," in *New York* magazine. It was a cover story. Despite his denials to Haag of his rumored dalliances with other women, Gross's piece made them harder to believe. He wrote that Madonna had "set her cap" for John and that she was "obviously the aggressor." She invited him to one of her concerts in Madison Square Garden. They worked out at the same gym. There was also a rumor that John had proposed to Daryl Hannah, and one about John dating Molly Ringwald, the actress, but "Ringwald" turned out to be Haag, whom Gross described as his "steady girlfriend of four years." Haag described herself as John's "law widow." But according to Gross, "there were the models."

Gross also revealed that the year before John had paid an astounding $2,300 in parking fines. The only reason he paid them, Gross reported, was because he had to clear his name before applying for the job in Morgenthau's office. "I don't think he enjoyed writing the check," the administrative law judge who presided over John's appearance told Gross. "He said in view of all the tickets, perhaps he ought to get free parking in the future." Instead, the judge gave John "a gratuitous little lecture. I told him he's going places. He should take care how he's perceived."

John wrote Gross a letter after the cover story appeared. (It was not a model of articulateness.) "Now that I can stop glaring at myself glaring back at me," he wrote in longhand, "I wanted to write you what was not quite a thank you letter—yet since I've never written one of these before—defies a better label." He conceded that while he could not be "a dispassionate critic" of Gross's article, he did find it fair and largely accurate. He wrote that he had heard through the grapevine that Gross had conducted himself professionally in the reporting of the article and joked, in a concluding nod to how thorough Gross had been, "Incidentally, I've lost a few phone numbers over the years—perhaps I could borrow your file and renew some old ties. Anyway, as my English nanny used to say after force-feeding me lima beans (but surely you must know this already): 'It wasn't as bad as you thought it was going to be was it?' That was. This wasn't."

After he graduated in May, John again asked Haag for some space. They still saw each other but Haag had her own "distractions." Around the same time, she was offered a part in a new production of

Molière's *The Misanthrope*, in La Jolla, California, and in Chicago. They had a last night together in June. John was deep into his studying for the bar exam; Christina was leaving for Los Angeles the next day. They were going to go to the tony Café des Artistes but instead ended up at the All State Café, a basement pub on West 72nd Street. "I took that night with me," she reflected, "one he later called pure pleasure. I took it with me that summer, through phone calls of back-and-forth, and misunderstanding and possibility. Through distance, through humor. I took it with me, until frayed and worn, it no longer was enough."

In November, John found out he had flunked the bar exam.

ON THE WAY TO HIS FIRST DAY of work in Morgenthau's office, the press followed him from 91st Street into the subway and then rode with him downtown. Their burning question for John seemed to be if this was the start of his political career. Gracious as ever, he replied, "Hey, this is just my first day at work." The swearing-in ceremony was private. Still, hoping to catch a glimpse of John, some one hundred reporters congregated outside the office building. A paralegal, making $15,000 a year, was offered $10,000 for a picture of John at his desk. The next day, there was an article in the paper that John had mu-shu pork for lunch. As an assistant district attorney, John worked in a special prosecutions unit focused on cracking down on white-collar crime, low-level political corruption, and other felonies. He was not permitted to actually try a case—he could only do research—until he passed the bar exam. When people would come to the office with a complaint, he would interview them. "It was funny to see the way they'd react," his boss, Michael Cherkasky, said. "Having this legend sit down and scribble down your complaint has got to be a little strange."

Jill Konviser and John started at the district attorney's office on the same day. They had adjoining offices and were experiencing similar feelings of being fish out of water. Every two weeks or so they would be assigned to the "complaint room," yet another specialized section of the strange world they found themselves inhabiting. It was where people who'd been arrested first met with prosecutors. "This place was the great equalizer, a dungeon where you would be working through the night," Konviser recalled. "It's three o'clock in the morning and you haven't eaten and you are exhausted. You are getting paid $35,000. It doesn't matter if you're John Kennedy or Jill Konviser or anybody else. You're wrecked. And I think John appreciated that. Everywhere else he was the son of a president. Here it was disgusting, it was filthy. You had to steal a chair if you wanted to sit down. You are sitting there interviewing a defendant who is handcuffed to a chair. And it stinks, and people scream at you. We *all* complained; he never did." (She is now a New York State judge.)

When John failed the bar exam the first time, it caused barely a ripple in the media. Of the sixty-five new staff members in Morgenthau's office who took the bar for the first time, seven failed. John resolved to work harder at studying for his second attempt at the exam, in February 1990. The test was graded on a 1,000-point scale; passing was 660. In May, John discovered he had flunked the bar exam again. This time, the media went berserk. Three New York newspapers trumpeted the news with some variation of the one that appeared famously on the cover of the *Daily News*: "THE HUNK FLUNKS . . . AGAIN." Photographers who caught up with John on the street "made him look like a startled mobster fleeing a grand jury room," according to Bob Greene, the syndicated columnist. John told the media, with his usual charm and humility, "I am very disappointed, again. God willing, I will be back [to take the test again] in July. I am clearly not a legal genius. Next time you guys are here, I hope it will be a happy day." He vowed to keep trying to pass the exam "until I'm 95 if necessary."

John's private humiliation was now public, and there wasn't anything he could do about it, other than to suffer in silence. More than half of the other twenty-five hundred people who had taken the New York bar exam had also failed, but no one heard a peep about them. Ed Koch, the New York City mayor, wrote John, "Don't feel badly, I failed my bar exam, too, and it didn't stop me from becoming mayor." John wrote back, "It was very kind what you wrote, but I'm going to have a lousy summer."

There wasn't much time to stew. The next bar exam was in July, a couple of months away. He got himself a serious tutor—who promptly advertised that John was a client—and took four weeks off to study. John somehow arranged to take the bar exam alone, by himself, and with looser time restrictions. This time he passed. This was big news, too. "The Hunk Finally Does It" blared the headline of the *New York Post* on November 4 after he passed. "We never doubted that he would pass," Morgenthau told the *New York Times*. His salary was increased to $34,000 and he remained in the special prosecutions bureau, and was now able to try cases.

John won the first case he prosecuted in the Manhattan DA's office. It was known as the case of the "Sleeping Burglar" and, if the *New York Times* was to be believed, it was the easiest case to win ever. Apparently, the defendant, David Ramos, thirty-three, fell asleep in the apartment of the woman he robbed on East 29th Street, with her jewelry in his pocket. He was arrested on November 1, 1990. The trial, in August 1991, lasted a week and the jury reached its verdict in less than a day.

Ed Hill remembered how John really enjoyed meeting the genuine, salt-of-the-earth-type New Yorkers who inhabited the offices of the Manhattan district attorney. "In fact, he affected kind of a New York accent," he said. "I would talk to him on the phone and he would say things like, 'Ah, fuhgeddaboudit.' You'd never heard him speak like this before." They would go out drinking with the cops and the other assistant district attorneys. He asked Hill to take him around to parts of the city he had never seen before. "I remember taking him up through Inwood and taking him around all over the Bronx," Hill continued.

"He'd never been to these places before. So here he was suddenly liberated from 1040 and actually learning something about the city, and he loved it." After two and a half years investigating and prosecuting white-collar crimes, he moved to the trial bureau.

Brian Steel met John soon after he started in Morgenthau's office in 1991. They found themselves together in the Early Complaint Assessment Bureau. It was the late shift one night. They were prosecuting misdemeanors. The attorneys prosecuting felonies had their own offices. They talked throughout most of the shift. They clicked. The next day, John called Steel and asked him if he wanted to play Frisbee with him in Central Park. They became friends.

They used to go kayaking together a lot, especially after John moved to Tribeca. There was a rental place at the west end of North Moore Street, on the Hudson River, where John stored the two kayaks he owned. He and Steel would use them regularly, usually during the day. They would kayak to New Jersey. They kayaked around the Statue of Liberty. One night at around ten o'clock, Steel remembered, John suggested they go kayaking from North Moore Street to the George Washington Bridge, a distance of nearly fourteen miles. It was a ridiculous suggestion, of course. But out they went anyway, into the middle of the Hudson River at night. At the time, the New York Fire Department used to keep a boat docked along the Hudson River, and as they were kayaking along, John spotted it and decided they should stop and check it out. "He was always curious," Steel said. As they got closer to the fireboat, they saw there were firemen on board. He wanted to go say hello. They invited John and Steel on board. John was wearing some sort of goofy hat but when he took the hat off, the young firefighters, many of whom were Irish Catholics, recognized him. They stayed on the boat for about thirty minutes.

Another time they set off across the Hudson to the New Jersey side of the river. As they approached the marina, they heard someone bellowing out, "John, John." John said he thought it sounded like his uncle

Teddy, and sure enough it was. Senator Kennedy had been invited as a guest onto the massive sailing yacht of Wayne Huizenga, the founder of Waste Management, parked at the marina. John insisted to Steel that they go "hang out with Teddy." They docked their kayaks and headed to the yacht. "There are ten deckhands all dressed in red jackets," Steel recalled. "They've got shrimp this big and bottles of Dom. We have like four or five shrimp, a glass of Dom, a tour of the boat, and kayak back. That was John's life: We were kayaking to Jersey and you run into Teddy."

John loved his kayak, and he loved kayaking adventures. "The more dangerous the more exciting for him," Gary Ginsberg said. In July 1991, John and three of his friends decided to go on a ten-day kayaking trip to the Baltic. "Four desk jockeys in search of manageable danger," he wrote a year later in the *New York Times* about the trip. It was classic John: an off-the-grid adventure that defied logic and sense but promised a once-in-a-lifetime experience. Their destination was the Åland archipelago, a collection of sixty-five hundred islands equidistant between the coasts of Finland and Sweden, in the Baltic Sea. John's idea was to fly to Stockholm and then take the overnight ferry to Turku, Finland, and paddle their one-man kayaks west to the islands, hopping from one to the next and camping along the way. The final destination was Åland, the largest of the islands, and its capital Mariehamn, from which they would take a ferry back to Stockholm.

The trip was not for the faint of heart, even for someone as skilled and experienced in the wilderness as John. The plan was to kayak for 135 miles from the Finnish coastline to Åland, packing their food and supplies in the seventeen-foot-long hull of each kayak. It was important to make good progress in the early days of the voyage, where they could hug the coastline through calmer passages. Once they got into the open ocean, the four paddlers were at the mercy of the weather, the winds, and the waves. It turned out the winds were calm at night. "We slept by day and paddled at night through still water, marveling at the extravagance of a sky where sunrise, sunset, and moonrise occur almost simultaneously," John continued. For readers wondering why the hell anyone would undertake such a challenging expedition without a guide, let alone rope three friends into it, John provided an answer: "The sea kayak, derived from the Eskimo word 'qajaq,' is well suited to the archipelago's coastline. Longer and more stable than the river kayak, the sea kayak offers an easy way to observe the ocean environs more intimately than would be possible in any other craft. Despite the occasional discomforts of tired shoulders and dampness, the rewards are immediate."

As expected, the trip became more challenging when the group hit the open water of the Baltic, away from the Finnish coastline. The wind in their faces was punishing, but John found a "certain sustaining smugness" that each wave was overcome "aided by our own weary arms." There were others rewards, too—a school of perch here, a flock of black swans there, as well as long-tailed ducks and otters. John's plan was to zigzag for eight miles to get to the island of Ahvensaari, which they chose because they liked its name. Some three-quarters of the way across the channel, with the waves getting more formidable, they heard a yelp and discovered that a group member's kayak had capsized. They hightailed it back to him, knowing he "was no great swimmer and that in the 50-degree water, hypothermia was possible." He climbed up onto the back of John's kayak, his feet dangling in the water. He was starting to "shiver fiercely," an early sign that his body was trying to fight off hypothermia. None of the four of them were doctors, of course, and there was no way to request a rescue if needed. But John obviously knew a thing or two about what to do for him, given his experiences on Outward Bound and NOLS.

They made their way to a nearby island. By the time they got there, his legs were so numb that he could not walk. They carried him and put him inside a sleeping bag and set up camp to wait out the wind. That's all John wrote about that; the reader could only assume that his friend warmed up and continued on the journey with the three others.

They stopped on one small island and convinced the owner of a pine cottage to give them some water from his well. They resumed the voyage, through narrow waterways by small, rocky islands, and traveling at night. They sunned themselves on the rocks in the morning. They kept moving forward, taking into account a request for a less treacherous passage to Mariehamn, and the ferry back to Stockholm. They got to a large lake within ten miles of the Mariehamn ferry when a ferocious summer storm hit. The four men took refuge in a two-man tent they had set up under a stand of birch trees to wait out the storm. "At dawn it was raining and blowing even harder," John wrote. "The entire coastline of the lake was eclipsed by rain and fog, and huge slate gray rollers with whitecaps beat against the rocks below us."

It was certainly not a day for kayaking. But they had no choice. They had to go out into the storm anyway. That was a poor decision. "At my first stroke beyond the shelter of the island, the wind lifted my paddle and threw it over my head, nearly capsizing me," John wrote. "I righted myself just in time to see [his friends' kayaks] capsize after being slammed by a huge wall of water. The trip was over. We washed back up on shore in pieces." They towed their "yaks" back to the island. That's when they caught a break. A Finnish couple had watched the fiasco from their bedroom window and offered to drive them the final ten miles in the back of their van to the ferry. They had paddled 125 miles in eight days and had made it within 10 miles of their destination.

This love of treacherous kayaking had taken him into the Hudson River and into New York Harbor (despite the looming presence of ocean liners and reckless motorboaters), into dangerous Jamaican waters, and into the frigid Baltic somewhere between Finland and Sweden. He also, apparently, took a ten-day kayaking trip—alone—to the Arctic. "He was dropped off in the middle of fucking nowhere," Sasha Chermayeff remembered. He told her that if he capsized at any time, he would have died nearly immediately in those waters. "You would freeze to death no matter what," she said. He told her how scary it was to get on and off floating pieces of ice, where he'd go when he wanted to rest. She was at a loss to explain why he would do such things, by himself, in the middle of nowhere, when certain death was merely one bad move away. "It's a thrill-seeking thing these guys need to just be able to survive," she said. "I'm a nesty-type woman so there's no way I can explain to you why a man needed to go and be, like, dropped off alone in the Arctic to kayak."

John's kayaking trip to the Arctic remains a bit of a mystery—he supposedly did it alone after all—and it almost seems apocryphal. Who would possibly do such a thing solo, with the risk of an unmitigated disaster being so high? But Sasha said that not only did John do it but also, while he was there, he found a perfectly preserved skeleton of a baby whale on the shore of an island, and brought most of it back to New York with him. He asked her to make, if she could, two Calder-like mobiles out of the perfectly bleached whalebones. It was not a completely crazy request. She had made some jewelry. And she read a Calder book that explained the intricate twists and turns of his sculptures. She decided to give it a try, for him. He was living with Daryl Hannah at the time. Using the small rib and vertebra bones, John took a stab at making the mobiles and then handed them over to Sasha for her to "fine-tune" and to fashion into balanced Calder-like mobiles. "Fine-tuning," she laughed, "was like undoing what he had just done." John gave the whalebone mobiles to his mother, who loved them, and then hung them above the dining room table at her home in Martha's Vineyard.

John's love of kayaks and kayaking extended to the point of trying to buy a handmade kayak company in the Adirondacks. He teamed up with Michael Berman, a New York City friend, and formed Random Ventures, a mini buyout firm. Using Berman's name, they went together to upstate New York to visit the crusty old guy who owned the kayak company. He had no idea who John was and was not that interested in selling his company in any event. John's next idea—also quickly abandoned—was to start a business that rented dogs, so that people could have a dog when they wanted one but not all the time. That one was not for Berman.

After working at several major ad agencies and public relations firms, Berman started his own public relations and marketing firm—PR, NY—representing Fortune 500 companies. After meeting on the New York social scene, John asked Berman to handle his press inquiries. "The press became an issue," one of John's friends told *Esquire*. At first, the requests for John were a few every week, but after he failed the bar the first time and then the second time, the press inquiries became nearly overwhelming.

John stayed a fourth year at the district attorney's office before quitting in July 1993. Soon thereafter, Jackie asked Joe Armstrong, a magazine publisher, to meet with him and chat about what he might like to do next. "Jackie admired the fact that he was so open to things, so curious, that he loved adventures," he remembered. "She identified with John—he was full of life and good humor, a constant spark—but she worried about him, too. She knew he had leadership potential, but he was so charmingly casual all the time. He needed to go out and do things on his own, but she was always working behind the scenes, totally vigilant, trying to subtly make things happen, come up with options and ideas."

John made visits to both the Labor and Justice Departments, in Washington, fueling speculation that he was about to get a job in the Clinton administration. There was speculation he might enroll at the Kennedy School of Government, at Harvard, or that he might run for Congress. He was encouraged to run for the congressional seat in Manhattan that became available in September 1992 after the death of Democrat Ted Weiss. John turned down the chance. By this time, his on-and-off relationship with Daryl Hannah was decidedly on again. Although they had first met in the early 1980s on St. Maarten, a Caribbean island, when they were both vacationing with their families, and saw each other again in 1988 at a wedding, it wasn't until her longtime, tumultuous relationship with the singer Jackson Browne ended in

September that they finally got together as a couple, confirming the rumors of their dalliances when he was still dating Haag. After that, they were nearly inseparable. According to *People*, "It has been John and Daryl biking in Central Park; John and Daryl eating apple pancakes at their favorite Chicago breakfast spot, the Original Pancake House; John and Daryl cooing at Manhattan's China Grill; John and Daryl nuzzling and teasing each other on an Amtrak train headed for Providence, site of his 10th reunion at Brown University (where they played touch football with other alumni); John visiting Daryl on the L.A. set of her latest movie, HBO's *Attack of the 50-Foot Woman*." John moved out of his Tribeca rental, back to the Upper West Side, and into Hannah's "sprawling" apartment on Central Park West. The paparazzi captured them making out in Central Park, on the stoop of a West Side brownstone, leaning against a parked car. They vacationed together in Switzerland, England, Vietnam, Hong Kong, the Philippines, and the remote beaches of Palau, in Micronesia. "He really liked dating Daryl because she was as famous as he was," Ed Hill said, "and he saw the possibility there of getting some attention off himself. But that, again, is reflective of that period in his life where the attention that was being paid to him was just frippery. The press loved him and the American people loved him, but you know darn well that the tabloid press had their fingers crossed every day wishing for a great scandal. So it made perfect sense that during that period of his life he enjoyed the possibility that his girlfriend might actually provide a distraction to the press."

But they also drew attention to themselves for their very public spats, on Manhattan's streets, in movie theaters, and in Central Park.

One summer evening, it must have been in 1994, I was walking home from my job at Lazard, in Rockefeller Center, to my apartment on the Upper West Side when I ran into John at Columbus Circle. He was just getting off his mountain bike outside what was then the Paramount Communications building on Columbus Circle—it's now a

Trump-branded hotel. He was dressed in shorts and a T-shirt. His fly was open. We hadn't seen each other in a few years, probably since the last time I had bumped into him around town, but we picked right up where we left off and had a nice thirty-minute conversation. After a while, as he was locking his bike to some scaffolding (I was thinking that it would make an inviting target for an ambitious thief, who might take apart a piece of the scaffolding to get to it as had once happened to me when I locked my bike to the scaffolding surrounding the Columbia University School of Journalism), I asked John what he was doing there. He said he was seeing a movie with Daryl. "Then why have you spent the last half hour talking to me?" I wondered. The question triggered his realization that he had left her waiting downstairs in the theater, and off he went. By then, tabloid readers knew that John and Daryl had their problems, but that was when I knew for sure the relationship was unlikely to last, what with all their passive aggressive behavior toward each other.

But there were other issues with Hannah, too, namely the fact that neither Jackie nor Caroline much cared for her. What especially upset Jackie was that John and Hannah made a mess during a party at Jackie's farm on Martha's Vineyard, over Memorial Day weekend in 1993.

After John left his job at the district attorney's office, he spent the rest of the summer with Hannah, in Massachusetts, New York, and California. With the two of them living together in New York, and Browne left far behind, Hannah was focused on getting John to marry her. "She was *desperate* to marry him," Hannah's friend Sugar Rautbord told Christopher Andersen in his book *The Good Son*, about John. In July 1993, it almost happened. While in Santa Monica, they got a marriage license and Hannah bought a vintage wedding dress at a flea market at the Rose Bowl in Pasadena. But according to Andersen, "another round of petty quarreling" put those plans on ice. In September, when John and Daryl visited Jackie for dinner at 1040 Fifth, her disdain for Hannah was so palpable that she wouldn't even eat with them, preferring to have her dinner on a tray in her bedroom. Jackie and Caroline were set to attend Ted Kennedy Jr.'s wedding in October, but when they discovered that John was bringing Hannah, they decided not to go at the last minute, leaving John and Daryl to fend off the paparazzi on their own. Soon thereafter, John told some of his friends that he and Hannah were going to get married in a "top secret" ceremony in Martha's Vineyard. But three hours later, he called them back and said the wedding was off.

November 22, 1993, marked the thirtieth anniversary of his father's assassination. Jackie decided to eschew the plethora of events commemorating her husband's death, and instead went horseback riding at the Piedmont Hunt Club in the Virginia countryside. At one point her mount, a gelding named Clown, stumbled and fell on some rocks that had been loosened along a wall by a previous rider. Jackie was thrown to the ground and knocked out. She was rushed to the hospital amid fears she may have been paralyzed from the fall. She remained unconscious for thirty minutes. When she came to, the doctors noted a swelling in her right groin and diagnosed a swollen lymph node. She was prescribed antibiotics, and the swelling went down but did not completely disappear. A month or so after her fall in Virginia, Jackie and Maurice Tempelsman, her wealthy boyfriend, were cruising on his yacht around the Caribbean for the holidays when she became ill, complaining of a cough, swollen lymph nodes in her neck, and a pain in her abdomen. She called her doctor in New York City. He recommended she return home for an examination at New York Hospital.

Back in Manhattan, her doctor discovered enlarged lymph nodes in her neck and armpit. A CAT scan revealed swollen lymph nodes in her chest and deep in her abdomen. A biopsy of one the lymph nodes in her neck showed that she had non-Hodgkin's lymphoma. In early January, she began a standard course of four treatments for the disease that led to an "apparent remission," the *Times* reported. In February, she signed a living will, making clear she did not want to receive aggressive medical treatment for a "grave illness." In March, Jackie developed "weakness," according to the *Times*, "became confused," and had pain in her legs. An MRI showed that the lymphoma had disappeared from her neck, chest, and abdomen but had spread to the membranes surrounding her brain and spinal cord. For the next month, at 1040 Fifth, she received radiation therapy in her brain as well as in her lower spinal cord. She gained strength but still had trouble walking except for short spurts and still had pain in her neck, for which she received painkillers. On April 14, she was admitted to New York Hospital after she developed a perforated ulcer in her stomach, a normal consequence of the steroid treatment she had been prescribed. The doctors sewed up the hole in her stomach that day. But the cancer in her brain and spinal cord was nearly relentless and responded poorly to treatment. Needless to say, John was deeply upset by his mother's life-threatening illness.

IN THE FALL OF 1993, John and his friend Michael Berman decided to revive Random Ventures in order to start what they were soon describing as a "post-partisan" political magazine. Its slogan was "Not just politics as usual." In coming up with the idea for the magazine, they were inspired by the hipness of the recently inaugurated president, Bill Clinton, who seemed to attract a new generation of Americans to his young, cool affect. Anyone who saw Clinton play saxophone on *The Arsenio Hall Show* appreciated John's desire to try to make politics as entertaining as Hollywood and celebrity. Over time, John and Berman discussed the idea for the magazine and how they might capture the excitement that Clinton's election had seemed to generate. (It was difficult not to make the obvious comparison to the enthusiasm his father's election had ignited thirty-two years earlier.)

They quickly landed on the idea of starting a flashy political magazine. Early on, Berman explained to the *Los Angeles Times* their vision for *George*: "People talk about politics the same way they talk about film or fashion or business. And if you can make those industries exciting, you can certainly make the political world exciting. You stand at a movie theater these days and hear 16-year-old kids talk about last week's gross and who the original director was supposed to be—that was trade information before the advent of *Entertainment Weekly* and *Premiere*. Now, all of a sudden, it's consumer information. And that's what this is, too." For John, it was also a way to enter politics, to honor the family legacy and to effect change but to do it his way.

John and Berman were an odd match. John had the killer looks, political connections, and extraordinary access; Berman, with little interest in wonky politics, was a marketing and advertising whiz. Neither man, though, had much of a publishing background, let alone an MBA. What they lacked in publishing acumen, they made up for in energy and enthusiasm. At the start, they were intent on blurring the lines between what it meant to be a magazine editor and what it meant to be a magazine publisher. For a while, they each did a little bit of everything. Being John's business partner, though, Berman once said, was "like being Dolly Parton's feet. I am sure they are nice, but they are overshadowed by other features."

After Jackie had arranged for John to meet Joe Armstrong, he, John, and Berman met regularly to discuss what the concept for *George* should be. "When they began, they didn't know anything about publishing," Armstrong said. "They didn't have any idea they were doing the absolutely hardest thing in publishing, to start a magazine from scratch. But John wasn't intimidated by what he didn't know." Armstrong worked with John and Berman on the basics—editorial structure, design, circulation, direct mail, advertising, creating a business plan. John "read other magazines and looked for the kinds of stories he wanted in *George*, the kinds of writers," Armstrong said.

John had stayed in touch with Gary Ginsberg. By then, Ginsberg had graduated from Columbia Law School and spent a few years at Simpson Thacher, the big New York law firm; then—at John's urging—he took a leave of absence to go down to Little Rock, Arkansas, and join the Clinton presidential campaign. After Clinton was elected, Ginsberg worked in the White House as a lawyer and then in the Justice Department. John was fascinated by how the drama of the 1992 election had transformed politics in a fundamental way. George Stephanopoulos interested John particularly, and the way he transcended the role of a typical presidential adviser to become a national celebrity. "He was witnessing something that he hadn't seen before and it really interested him and it gave him kind of the kernels for what later became *George*," Ginsberg said. "Because he saw the intersection of popular culture and politics through the 1992 campaign." Ginsberg, among others, started working with John and Berman on a business plan for *George*. They would get together on the weekends and scope it out.

On May 17, 1994, Jackie developed "shaking chills" and became "disoriented," according to the *New York Times*. Maurice Tempelsman and a nurse took her back to New York Hospital. She was diagnosed with pneumonia and administered antibiotics by injection. At first, she "rallied," according to the paper, but the next day took another turn for the worse. On Wednesday, a CAT scan showed that the cancer had invaded her liver "in huge amounts." The doctors told her there was nothing medicine could do for her at that point. She asked to go home to her apartment, on Fifth Avenue. Christiane Amanpour, John's old Providence housemate, had stayed close to him during her career as CNN's chief international correspondent. "John called me," Amanpour remembered, "and said, 'Mommy's coming home. She wants to be at home, and there's nothing more to be done.' I said, 'Okay, I'm coming. I'm coming.' So I got on a plane and I came to New York." She continued, "On a human level, there's nothing else to say. It was a very big tragedy, a personal tragedy. Somebody's mom was dying." She declined to speak about what it was like being by Jackie's side as she lay dying. "It's private," she said, "but just to say that she was surrounded by her family, her friends, and a huge amount of love."

At 10:15 p.m. on May 19, Jacqueline Kennedy Onassis died. John, Caroline, and Maurice Tempelsman were with her. She was sixty-four years old. The next morning, it was John who came out to speak with the throngs of reporters. He was dressed impeccably in a navy-blue suit. "She was surrounded by her friends and family and the books and the people and the things that she loved," he said. "She did it in her own way, on her terms and we all feel lucky for that. And now she's in God's hands. There's been an enormous outpouring of good wishes from everyone both in New York and beyond. I speak for all of our family when I say we are extremely grateful. Everyone's been very generous and I hope now we can just have these next couple of days in relative peace. Thank you very much." Chris Cuomo, for one, found John to be incredibly brave at this particular moment. "Losing his mother was intensely personal for him, but, again, with everything else in his life, there were these added layers of significance to it," he said. "Jackie O was sick and that meant something in American culture. He had to process all that."

On May 23, Jackie was buried next to her husband in Arlington National Cemetery. Some one hundred family and friends attended her burial, each of whom kissed her mahogany casket to say their goodbyes. John also leaned down to touch his father's gravestone. At the funeral mass, John read passages from his mother's favorite poem, "Memory of Cape Cod," by Edna St. Vincent Millay. John said the reading was chosen in order to evoke his mother's "essence" and her "love of words, the bonds of home and family and her spirit of adventure." In her thirty-six-page will, signed March 22, she left the bulk of her estate—estimated to be between $100 million and $200 million—to John and to Caroline. They would also share equally in the ownership of her 1040 Fifth Avenue apartment and her estate on Martha's Vineyard.

"That was rough," Sasha Chermayeff said. "His mother's death was very, very painful for him. . . . [He said] things like 'Until both of your parents are dead, you don't really know how alone you are.'" Amanpour said, "I remember one day going with him, to the house. You know, knock, knock, knock, on the door. His mom answered the door and I remember her saying, 'Oh, angel.' She called him 'angel' sometimes, and it was just so from the heart. She loved him to bits." Added Chris Cuomo, John "was one of the few adult males who was still very much attentive to his mother's expectations. It mattered to him to make his mother proud."

Ginsberg said he thought John handled death better than anyone he knew. "He lost cousins, he lost parents, and he was incredibly unemotional," he said. "Not that he didn't feel it, but externally was able to hold it together better than anybody I knew. I remember saying, 'John, how the hell do you do it?' And he said, 'You know, I just learned from my family. You just don't wallow in death. You move on. You hold it inside.'" A few days before Jackie died she wrote a letter to John, to be opened only after her death. Many interpreted her message as urging him to grab hold of the Camelot legacy and fulfill his destiny in politics. "I understand the pressure you'll forever have to endure as a Kennedy, even though we brought you into this world as an innocent," she wrote. "You, especially, have a place in history. No matter what course in life you choose, all I can ask is that you and Caroline continue to make me, the Kennedy family and yourself proud." Doug Wead, a historian who has written about the Kennedys, interpreted Jackie's deathbed letter to John as permission to enter the family business. "This was a real departure for her, putting any kind of pressure on him at all, which she avoided—she studiously avoided," he said. "She knew in her heart that someday the stars are going to line up and he's going

to be president. The money will be there. The mood of the nation will
be there. The polls will be there. The country will be ready for it, and
he will be president." Chermayeff said Jackie's death and the deathbed
letter further ratcheted up the pressure on John. "It's a complex thing,
right?" she said. "You have this legacy. It's clear. You can't ignore it. It
has great privileges that come along with it. It has very difficult things
that come along with it. There's a lot of pressure. And yet he had enough
confidence to sort of want to live out his own life, but he didn't want to
let anybody down. It was a complicated thing just to be that son of that
fallen idol."

IF JOHN WAS FEELING any new pressure after his mother's untimely
death, it was likely immediately only to somehow figure out what he
and Michael Berman wanted *George* to be and to get someone to back
it financially. On the morning after his mother's burial, John was back
at his desk. "He did exactly what Jackie would have done," a friend told
Esquire. "He went back to work." But finding investors for *George* was
proving to be more difficult than either he or Berman expected, despite
John's unparalleled access to nearly everyone. Susanna Howe, a recent
graduate of Barnard College, was *George*'s first hire that summer. They
spent five months in a conference room "trying to figure out the magazine," she recalled. "John and I had lunches with the most amazing ar-
ray of media people. He brought me along because he didn't want to go
alone. We would just go and have all these 'advice lunches,' where people
would pontificate on their luminous career in publishing and tell John
how hard they worked." Thanks to John's celebrity, they met with everyone from David Koch to Ron Perelman. By the fall of 1994, they
had commitments for something like $7 million from around fifteen
different people, but it wasn't enough. No one individual had enough
skin in the game to help them achieve their ambitions. Berman later

told the *Los Angeles Times* he found fund-raising to be "demoralizing, humiliating and, after a while, boring."

They changed tacks. Berman leaked the previously confidential news of the magazine to Page Six. They heard from hundreds of people. Out of their own pockets—costing hundreds of thousands of dollars—they paid for a direct-mail survey to a list of 150,000 other magazine subscribers asking them, without a commitment, if they would consider subscribing to *George*, which they described by comparing it to other established magazines. "*George* is to politics what *Rolling Stone* is to music. *Forbes* is to business. *Allure* is to beauty. *Premiere* is to films," the mailing said. And added that the magazine would answer the questions: "Who's under the covers. Who's under indictment. Who's running the country. And who's running them." By direct-mail standards, the response encouraged the two men, with around 5 percent of the people who received the mailing saying they would subscribe to such a magazine. They kept fighting to find a financial backer who would give John and Berman a meaningful share of the equity while putting up most, if not all, of the money. It was not an easy task. "Sensing, finally, that something might happen with their project, Kennedy and Berman also began changing," Michael Gross wrote. "The high-mindedness with which they'd originally approached the venture began slowly giving way to a desire to succeed, whatever changes in tone, look, or content that required."

Their luck began to change when they decided finally to meet with the now infamous David Pecker, then the CEO of Hachette Filipacchi Media, the US magazine division of Hachette, a big French conglomerate. They had decided they needed a deep-pocketed partner who could provide *George* with distribution and printing, with a keen focus on the bottom line. They met over lunch in December 1994 at an Italian restaurant on East 60th Street. John arrived by bike, with his briefcase slung over his shoulder. John told Pecker he wanted *George* to "combine

politics and pop culture" and to be "prime time for public life." Pecker
said he was "skeptical" and magazines "about politics and religion
don't sell." He asked John why Hachette should invest the money in
George. "He said he'd put celebrities on the cover—commercialize the
covers," Pecker said. John shared with Pecker the encouraging results
of his direct-mail campaign. "It was reassuring to me that he was willing to put his own money at risk," Pecker said, referring to the hundreds of thousands of dollars John and Berman spent from their own
pockets getting the advice of consultants and magazine professionals
to guide them. John also reassured Pecker about the central contradic-
tion of *George*: that the magnetic scion of the same family that did its
best to keep the media at bay as an understandable matter of course was
now wanting to publish a splashy, gossipy glossy magazine about the
celebrity of politics. It seemed like an irreconcilable conflict. But if it
was, John had made his peace. He told Pecker that after his father got
out of the White House, "he had planned to be a reporter or an editor
for a newspaper, and his mother worked for Doubleday, so publishing
was in his blood. He could make a career for himself." Added Amanpour, "*George* was John's soft entrée into politics, in his own way, where
he fused celebrity, politics, and real issues, which is what we're all doing
today, right. I mean that's what's happened. It's all sort of fusion."

Pecker was sold. He dug into the business plan. He asked the car
advertisers in Detroit if they would be interested in supporting the magazine. There were lunches with the Hachette editorial director and
with Daniel Filipacchi at Le Bernardin. In February 1995, John and
Michael signed a deal with Pecker that would give Hachette a 50 percent stake in *George* and Random Ventures a 50 percent stake, with
John and Michael each having a 25 percent stake in the magazine. John
and Michael would have editorial control over the publication, but
since Hachette had put up the money, at the end of the day it would
have the final say over the magazine. They celebrated the signing of the
deal over dinner at Rao's, the famous Italian restaurant on 114th Street

in East Harlem. "After dinner," Pecker recalled about John, "he just walked over to his bicycle and put his cap on. As he was going down 114th Street in the middle of the night, the photographers were all chasing him."

Berman became *George*'s executive publisher; John became editor in chief. Neither man had much of a clue about how to do either job but they were motivated, ambitious, and excited to succeed. They moved into a conference room at Hachette, on the same floor with *Elle* magazine, *Elle Decor*, *Family Life*, and *Metropolitan Home*. John asked Roger Black to design a prototype of the magazine. Black admired the way John went about his work. "He wasn't acting the part," he said. "He admitted that he was a complete amateur and said that he didn't know anything—but let's go from there. Of course, he got everyone to work for him for nothing. The fact that it leaked to Page Six that he was hanging around my offices was payment enough for me." Maryjane Fahey was Black's art director. She remembered what would happen when John came into the office. "Every woman and gay guy would immediately have to show me the layouts for *Esquire Gentleman* or some other project," she said. "One time John asked to see some of our other work, so I tried to find a copy of *Out*, which we had designed. I couldn't find it, so I said, 'Well, you can certainly get a copy on the newsstand.' And he laughed and said, 'Can you imagine what would happen if I bought a copy of *Out* on the newsstand?'"

The editorial battles began almost immediately. Pecker and Hachette, which at first agreed to produce two issues of *George* and committed to the magazine as much as $20 million if things went well, were not fooling around. Pecker wanted a return on his investment. "Suddenly, the struggle over the direction of the magazine is very serious," a *George* insider told Gross, at *Esquire*. "There are different conceptions. John is smart, but he lacks an edge. He's one of the least assertive people you'll ever meet; he's never had to assert himself—he's John Kennedy! Now, suddenly, he's in a huge corporation. He wants a magazine of ideas with a sugar coating. They want a political *People*." One Hachette executive suggested changing the name to *Criss-Cross*, from *George*, to better capture the idea that the magazine wanted to position itself at the nexus of power, celebrity, and money. They also considered the name *GW*. "Maybe we'll change it to *John* someday," Berman joked to *People*.

Jackie's death occasioned other changes in John's life, too. Ironically, given Jackie never liked Daryl Hannah, her death was a catalyst for John to move on from her. Soon after his mother's death, he moved out of Hannah's apartment on the Upper West Side back down into a newly renovated loft apartment in an industrial-looking building on North Moore Street, in Tribeca. But John being John, he was not alone for long. By then, he had met Carolyn Bessette.

JOHN WENT TO THE VIP SHOWROOM AT Calvin Klein and saw her there. A mutual friend thought they would hit it off. The head of public relations at Calvin Klein, Bessette was a bombshell with an exotic look. He was gobsmacked immediately. "John was attracted to women who were not intimidated by him," his friend Richard Wiese said. "He liked women with a point of view." Bessette grew up in a big white clapboard house on Lake Avenue in Greenwich, Connecticut, where she and her older twin sisters, Lauren and Lisa, moved with their mother after her parents divorced and she had remarried an orthopedic surgeon. Carolyn graduated from St. Mary's High School, in Greenwich, in 1983, where she was voted the "Ultimate Beautiful Person." At Boston University, she majored in elementary education and appeared on the cover of a calendar, "The Girls of B.U." After college, she did publicity for a few nightclubs in Boston before being spotted by Calvin Klein and being lured to New York to work at his headquarters on West 39th Street.

John first told John Perry Barlow about Bessette in early 1994. He was still living with Hannah but he told Barlow that he had met Bessette and that she was "having a heavy effect on him." He added that he wasn't going to "pursue her" because he was loyal to Hannah. "But it was hard for him," Barlow said, "because he couldn't get his mind off her." Barlow asked John about her and who she was. "Well, she's not really anybody," he said. "She's some functionary of Calvin Klein's. She's an ordinary person." Barlow met Bessette in the fall of 1994, after John and Hannah had split. "Carolyn was as charismatic as John was," he said. "*Charisma*, you know, was once a theological term meaning 'grace.' And she had that. I was also impressed with the fact that she was a bit eccentric. She was not conventional in any sense." She reminded him of Jackie "in her quirkiness" and in "her unbelievable capacity to engage one's attention." He thought also, "eccentric, artistic [and] Bohemian." Carolyn, he said, had Jackie's ability to "be talking to six people at one time and make everyone feel like the only one in the room. . . . It was based on genuine interest. Having a beautiful woman want to know all about you is not such a bad thing." Sasha Chermayeff was also struck by Bessette's physical beauty, among other things. "Carolyn was hilarious," she said. "She was sarcastic without being mean. She was funny. She was engaging. You cannot tell in photographs how beautiful she was in real life. I never saw a picture of her that did her justice."

Some two months after John's friends had been summoned to Martha's Vineyard for his supposed wedding to Daryl Hannah, he was spotted kissing Carolyn Bessette at the finish line of the New York City Marathon. They were just there watching the race but the picture of them together was on the cover of the *New York Post*, much to the irritation of Michael Bergin, a Calvin Klein underwear model and Bessette's on-and-off lover. "Yes," she told Bergin when he called her about the picture. "It's nothing."

"Nothing!" he yelled at her incredulously, knowing that even he could not compete with John.

Ed Hill said he thought the reason behind John's attraction to Carolyn was similar to what attracted him to Hannah: that she seemed to be able to handle *his* fame while at the same time using her own wiles to attract her own attention, thereby taking some of it away from him.

In January 1995, *People* once again put John on its cover, under the headline "JFK Jr. on His Own." The point seemed to be that he was "alone as never before." He was working on pulling *George* together. He had campaigned for his uncle Ted the previous fall. He went skiing in Colorado over New Year's. He celebrated his thirty-fourth birthday with some friends, family members, his German shepherd, Sam, and his 104-year-old grandmother in Hyannis Port.

Since he did not speak with *People*, the magazine was left to interview two political operatives about what John's political future might be. The political consultant Robert Shrum told the magazine, "I don't think there are a lot of people who'd want to run against him," while William Schneider, at the American Enterprise Institute, added, recalling John's appearance at the 1988 Democratic convention, "It was a success the minute he showed up onstage. There was an audible gasp. I'm not sure anyone remembers one word of what he said."

Regardless of the never-ending speculation about his political aspirations, John was fully devoted to getting *George* up and running. He had Berman, his operating partner, and Hachette, his financial partner. What *George* needed more than anything was advertising. And to get that, John was dispatched to Detroit to meet with the money men at the Big Three automobile companies. "We knew that if we could get Detroit, we'd be OK because they're cautious advertisers in terms of content and newness," Berman told *Esquire*. In April 1995, John agreed to give a luncheon speech at the Adcraft Club, a ninety-one-year-old organization that was the largest association of advertisers in the country. His presence nearly caused a riot. The car companies' executives went wild for John and the prospect of advertising in *George*. One magazine publisher told the *Los Angeles Times*: "It was bizarre. I can't think of anyone else in this country who could have drawn the range of interest that he did. Everyone wanted to see the guy. Everyone. I've seen GM and Ford keep the likes of Ted Turner and Si Newhouse waiting. But the people there were waiting on [Kennedy] like he was visiting royalty." GM committed to becoming *George*'s largest advertiser. Chrysler followed quickly thereafter. The first two issues of *George* had 175 ad pages each, at a time when *Vanity Fair* averaged around 115 ad pages. In terms of ad pages sold, it would be the most successful magazine launch ever.

Editorially, Hachette's executives wanted John to be "as public as Tina Brown." He certainly was using his fame to get interviews, including with George Wallace and Colin Powell. John commissioned pieces about Newt Gingrich's lesbian half sister and one by Roseanne Barr imagining what her life would be like if she were president. (That piece did not work out.) He hired Herb Ritts to photograph the model Cindy Crawford to pose as George Washington for the premiere issue and had Anthony Hopkins lined up for the second cover, dressed up as Richard Nixon, whom he played in the Oliver Stone movie about the thirty-seventh president of the United States. John asked Robert De Niro to contribute, and he did. He asked Ann Coulter to write, and she did. "My family was not a Kennedy-fanatic family, so I never really distinguished one Kennedy from the rest," she said. "I knew he was at least the good-looking one of this motley crew. He was certainly fair to Republicans and no other magazine was."

The *George* pre-publication hype was in overdrive. Hachette's original commitment to publish two issues of *George* had already been increased to eight following the unexpected ad-page blowout. It was to go bi-monthly at the start of 1996 and then monthly starting in September 1996, in time for the 1996 presidential election. The dream was for *George* to sell somewhere between three and four hundred thousand copies a month on the newsstand, in line with what *Vanity Fair* was selling. A senior editor John hired, Richard Blow, recalled what a complicated position John found himself in at the magazine—on the one hand being pushed to use his Rolodex to get prominent writers to contribute to the magazine but on the other not feeling particularly comfortable doing it. "He'd usually make the call, but not happily," he wrote. "He seemed to feel he was exploiting himself, asking a personal favor, rather than making a business proposition—and he wasn't entirely wrong. If the writer said no, John felt he'd cheapened himself for naught." He'd failed repeatedly to convince Doris Kearns Goodwin, the presidential historian and wife of one of his father's closest advisers, to write for *George*. He had dinner with Henry Louis Gates Jr., the Harvard professor, to see, unsuccessfully, if he would be willing to write for the magazine. "He's not going to write for us," John told Blow. "He just wanted to have dinner with me." Nora Ephron turned John down, too. "I must be losing my juice," he told Blow.

John started suffering from Graves' disease, a thyroid disorder that "sapped his energy" and made him "cranky," according to Blow. "By midafternoon on many days, he would be slumping in his chair, looking mystified by his body's betrayal. To treat the condition, he drank an iodine concoction washed down with seltzer, grimacing as he did. John admitted that he was waking up at five in the morning, so taut with anxiety he could not fall back asleep."

Not missing a beat, though, he flew out to Los Angeles and filmed a minute-long segment on *Murphy Brown*, which was to air after the first issue hit the newsstands on September 26, 1995. In it, John, dressed in a business suit, was playing Murphy Brown's new assistant—the exact role that *Seinfeld*'s Kramer had played three years earlier. In fact, Murphy Brown said the same thing to John that she had said to Kramer when they first met: "Hi, I'm Murphy Brown, you must be my new secretary." When she realized quickly enough that her new secretary was John Kennedy Jr., she said, "Oh, John, hi. I guess that whole lawyer thing didn't work out. That's a tough break." It was a brilliant stroke of publicity, and product placement that got the magazine—for free—fifty thousand new subscribers after the show aired, saving him, Berman, and Hachette around $1 million. (When he appeared on *Larry King Live*, on CNN, on September 28, *George* received a hundred thousand new subscriptions, another expense-saving coup.)

Berman intentionally created a bit of media circus for the launch of *George* at Federal Hall, on Wall Street. He knew John could sit for maybe one interview, as he did with the *Washington Post*, but he would have little interest or patience in doing one interview after another. Why not get permission to use Federal Hall for the announcement and hold a big press conference there to announce the magazine? As many as three hundred reporters and camerapeople packed into the room. John took the stage, to the strains of "Movin' on Up," the theme song to the *Jeffersons* TV show. Paul Begala, a former Clinton adviser, had helped John with his speech. "I don't remember seeing this many of you in one room since the results of my last bar exam," he said at the start, before ending with, "Ladies and gentlemen, meet *George*." He then flipped over a mock-up of the first cover, featuring Cindy Crawford posing as George Washington, dressed in a powdered wig and a colonial uniform, with plenty of her taut midriff showing. It was a big hit. Joe Armstrong, the magazine consultant and friend of Jackie's, was in the front row. He thought John spoke with "authority" and "conviction" about the magazine and what it could become. "I thought of Jackie, who had died the year before," he said. "John had tried very hard to convince her that this was a smart magazine idea, and though she hadn't been quite persuaded, I know she would have been very proud that he got this done."

The actual publication date of the first issue was still two weeks away. But the transformation of *George* from an intimate, wonky version of the inside-the-Beltway *New Republic*—minimal advertising, 125,000 circulation—to a major, overhyped national publication about politics as entertainment with John Kennedy as its editor in chief—350 pages of advertising, 500,000 copies printed—was nearly complete.

The first issue of *George* was a remarkable piece of work. It looked like a mature adult, even though it was a newborn. It was chock-full of ads—for Clinique, for Calvin Klein (of course), for Ralph Lauren, for Giorgio Armani, for Cadillac, for Valentino . . . you name it. There was even an ad for Tommy Hilfiger featuring preppy-looking guys who could easily have gone to Andover with John and me. John's buddy John Perry Barlow wrote a piece about Newt Gingrich. Paul Begala wrote a piece about the media and whether it was biased. In his editor's note, John recounted *George*'s difficult two-year slog getting off the ground. He praised Hachette Filipacchi for recognizing the "viability" of the idea of a nonpartisan political magazine focused on personalities "after 14 months of dubiously successful fundraising." The driving force behind *George*, he wrote, was a belief that "if we can make politics accessible by covering it in an entertaining and compelling way, popular interest and involvement in the process will follow."

Gary Ginsberg joined *George* as both its internal attorney and a senior editor. He believes the magazine was ahead of its time, something for which John and Michael Berman deserved much credit. "They saw politics as more than just black and white," he said. "They thought that politics was inculcated in everything with American life and culture—that there was politics in sports, there's politics in fashion, there's politics in entertainment, there's politics in business, and he wanted to explore those intersections. They wanted politics to become much more accessible to women, to people who were younger, to people who weren't members of a political party, to independents, to people who had never bought a political magazine. They wanted to broaden it, make it more appealing, make it more accessible, make it more colorful literally and figuratively, because they wanted to excite people about the political process. So they defined it as broadly as they could. They added color to what until then were magazines that were only in black and white—that only came at politics from an ideological perspective." Ginsberg said their approach offended some members of the "guardian class of political journalists," such as Maureen Dowd,

Charles Krauthammer, and Leon Wieseltier, who saw *George* as "heresy" and who "didn't want John to succeed." Jealousy was part of it, he said, but so was their view that *George* was frivolous. "They couldn't define it, they didn't understand it," he said.

The first reviews of *George* from the "traditional" journalistic community were decidedly mixed: The *Philadelphia Inquirer* called it "revolutionary fun. Not to mention zippy." The *Wall Street Journal* said its editorial content was "an afterthought." The *Boston Globe* called it "disappointingly vapid," while the *Detroit News* claimed it was "a political gem." Clay Felker, the founding editor of *New York* magazine, was merciless. "Of course it's not going to work," he told the *Los Angeles Times*. "It's a magazine without a function, with no point of view. Magazines are interpretive vehicles." Of John, he said, "He's clearly no editor."

ONCE THEY HAD FINALLY GOTTEN together, John and Carolyn were nearly inseparable. Sometime in the spring of 1995, she moved into John's loft on North Moore Street. RoseMarie Terenzio, John's assistant at *George*, could tell they were getting increasingly serious about their relationship because he always took her call when she phoned the office. His sister was the only other person whose calls he always answered. Once *George* moved into the forty-first floor of Hachette's offices, at 1633 Broadway just north of Times Square, Carolyn would come by regularly, sit in John's office chair, and make phone calls. She also spent time with Matt Berman, the magazine's art director (no relation to Michael), hashing out ideas for the covers, or photo shoots or stories. She was not a *George* employee but, given her sense of style, her relationship with John, and that she had decided to leave her post at Calvin Klein, she had a big influence on it—over time perhaps too big an influence.

When some of John's close friends had taken her measure and decided, for one reason or another, that she was not in John's league, John

wouldn't hear of it. He was totally smitten. "John was ecstatic in Carolyn's company," Richard Blow explained. "When she visited the office,
he would gaze upon her as if he couldn't completely believe what his eyes
were taking in. He could not stop touching her, running his fingers
through her hair, stroking her arms. Carolyn accepted his attentions
but rarely reciprocated. At least in public, John was the more openly
affectionate of the two." If his friends questioned him about Carolyn,
John did something a little unexpected: He told Carolyn that a particular friend—naming him—had his doubts about her. Instead of getting
overtly angry at said person, she'd go out of her way to win him over by
lavishing attention on him, flirting, touching his arm or shoulder—
figuring correctly that a charm offensive was the way to go, at least at
first. "He was completely besotted by her when she was at her best,"
Brian Steel said. "She had him wrapped around her finger. . . . Could
come up behind you, touch you on the back of your neck. You knew it
was her and then she would look you in the eye like you were the only
person in the room. She was mesmerizing."

Over the Fourth of July weekend in 1995, Carolyn and John
headed to Martha's Vineyard. At one point, John asked Carolyn to
go fishing. While they were out on the water, John asked her to
marry him. "Fishing is so much better with a partner," he said to her.
He added that many things in life are better with a partner. He gave
her a platinum ring surrounded by diamonds and sapphires, courtesy
of Maurice Tempelsman. Carolyn did not respond to John affirma-
tively for three weeks. (The press made it out to be because there
were problems in their relationship, but Terenzio said that was not
true; it was more a matter of making sure she wanted to become the
wife of John F. Kennedy Jr. and what that meant about surrendering
her privacy.)

In any event, the news had to be handled very carefully. It could not
be announced before its time, obviously. Still, there was a segment on
A Current Affair, a television gossip show, about John and Carolyn to-

gether in Martha's Vineyard. Calvin Klein model Michael Bergin, the other man, happened to see the segment and was furious. "With Carolyn," he wrote later. "*My* Carolyn. I was in total shock. Carolyn was wearing a T-shirt and something that looked suspiciously like underwear, and John Jr. seemed to be helping her into her pants." Bergin confronted Bessette again about John, and again she said John was "just a friend" who was "going through a difficult time." And she kept on lying to Bergin about the depth of her relationship with John despite the fact that they were all living in New York City—Bessette kept her own apartment, even though she was basically living with John. She would still, on occasion, be with Bergin.

Somehow, though, John and Carolyn managed to keep the explosive news of their engagement under wraps until the Friday before Labor Day. That's when the *New York Post* reported their engagement, according to a "good friend" of the couple's, and for good measure showed a close-up of Carolyn's diamond-and-sapphire engagement ring.

During Thanksgiving 1995, the writer Peter Alson went with a group of twelve people, including John and Carolyn, to a secluded resort in Guanaja, Honduras. They were all together for ten days. One morning, Alson found himself alone at breakfast with John. "So if you weren't spending Thanksgiving here, where would you be right now?" he asked John. He quickly realized he hadn't thought through the question carefully enough. "For a moment he stared at me without saying anything," Alson recalled. "Then he looked down, and I saw tears in his eyes. I hadn't been thinking. The date was November 22, the anniversary of his father's assassination, and a year and a half since Jackie had died. He was turning 35 in a couple of days, and it would be one of the first Thanksgivings he would spend without her. The fact that I, an almost-stranger, knew all these things about him, made me understand his need for the self-protective force field he always seemed to have. I felt bad that my thoughtless question had upset him, but moved, too, that he could, even for a moment, be so vulnerable."

The following February 25, on an unseasonably warm day, the full range of John's and Carolyn's emotions would be on public display, and unfortunately for them both were captured by a video photographer for all to eventually see (when still pictures were sold to the *National Enquirer* and the video made it on to *Hard Copy*). What started out as an innocent enough walk to Washington Square Park on a gorgeous day, with his new dog Friday in tow, turned into a shouting and shoving match, ending in tears. At one point, it seemed, John succeeded in ripping the engagement ring he gave Carolyn off her finger.

The incident was a cause for much concern back in the *George* office. "We circled the topic like airport guards around an abandoned suitcase," Richard Blow wrote later. "I knew that John had a temper and that Carolyn was no shrinking violet, but the violence of their rage presented a harsh contrast to the tenderness I'd seen between them." John said nothing about the fight to his colleagues. "Even though the video suggested that Carolyn was more the aggressor than John, the fight was bad for *George*."

Berman, for one, was furious at John—not only because he lost his temper but also because he had not told Berman about the whole incident before it hit the media. He was worried that advertisers would not like the look of John and Carolyn fighting. "Michael had attempted to stake his claim as John's closest adviser, and failed," Blow wrote. "Carolyn lost, too, in a way I don't think she fully understood. The fight helped create an impression of her as high-maintenance and melodramatic." A few weeks later, in connection with Howard Stern's appearance on the April/May 1996 cover of *George*, John went on his radio show. The whole incident seemed to have blown over, more or less. It was a hilarious segment that touched on many subjects, including how buff John was, how he could get any woman he wanted, when he lost his virginity—it turned out that happened at Andover—and the fact that gay men had come on to him. They also spoke about his fight with Carolyn in Washington Square Park. "There was some silly argument,"

John told Stern. "We've been going out for a long time. We're in love."
Stern asked him if he had seen the tape of the incident. "No I haven't
seen the tape," he said. "Why do I need to see the tape? I was in it."

Carolyn and John's engagement was news to Michael Bergin, whom
Carolyn was still seeing on occasion. In March 1996, she called him
up out of the blue. "She seemed to have reached a breaking point," he
remembered. "She could only go a few months without seeing me:
She needed her fix." She came by his apartment and gave him a pet
bird, which he soon thereafter returned to the pet store. A few weeks
later, she came by his apartment again and then insisted they go for a
walk. They got as far as the nearby pizza parlor, and ordered two slices.
She did not touch her pizza and then abruptly got up and left. A week
later, in April, she called Bergin again and said she needed to talk, and
invited him to her new one-bedroom Washington Square apartment,
even though she was spending most of her days and nights with John
on North Moore Street.

They sat on her bed together for a long minute, holding hands and
not saying anything. "The reason I came to see you last week is that I
was pregnant," she told him. "I needed someone to talk to."

"You're having a baby?" he asked, no doubt recalling that when
she had previously become pregnant by him, she decided to have an
abortion.

"No," she told him. "I lost the baby. I had a miscarriage."

Bergin spent the night with her. "I knew it was wrong and she knew
it was wrong but we both found ways to justify our behavior," he remembered. He still thought he might have a chance of winning her
back. "The way I saw it," he continued, "she probably didn't even tell
John Jr. about the pregnancy. She had come to me. What did that say
about their relationship?" The next morning at seven o'clock, they woke
to the sound of one of their mutual friends banging "crazily" on Carolyn's
apartment door. "Get the fuck out of here," he told Bergin. "He's on
his way over." John had been trying to reach her but she had taken her

phone off the hook and so when she continued not to answer, he decided to go to her apartment and see if she was there, having called their mutual friend first to see if he knew where she was. Carolyn was "freaking," he recalled, and he got "the hell out of there," carrying his shoes, since he didn't have enough time to put them on. The next time he saw Carolyn, she was a married woman.

In early July 1996, Billy Way, John's friend from Andover and Brown, was killed by a taxicab as he crossed Madison Avenue after leaving Nello, an Upper East Side restaurant and bar where he felt at home. Way, a professional tennis player, had drug and alcohol addiction problems. It turned out that Way had no close relatives around New York and was nearly destitute—*New York* magazine later reported that he had stopped paying rent on the apartment he lived in nearby and the electricity had been turned off—so John was the one who had to go to the morgue and identify his body. John was visibly shaken by the experience, Chermayeff remembered. "It was one of those accidents where he said, like, literally half of Billy's head was like Billy and the other half was just, like, split kind of right down the middle," she said. "The other half was like mush, like hamburger. He said it was so intense. I saw him afterward and he was just, like, sitting in this chair and he just looked like he was old." Way was thirty-five. John and Carolyn went to the memorial service together. John was devastated. A few years later, John was having breakfast with a friend down in Tribeca and brought up the memory of Billy Way. "I still get choked up when I think of how he died," John said. "He was a party guy, too, just like Carolyn. And look at what happened to him. Dead at 35. What a waste! I often wish I could pick up the phone and just call him."

AFTER LABOR DAY 1996, John's fellow *George* colleagues noticed he was having trouble focusing. He was in a good mood but he was skipping editorial meetings, signing off quickly on story ideas, and leaving the office early. "He was practically whistling through the corridors," Blow recalled. "It could mean only one thing: after about a year and a half of dating, John and Carolyn were getting married. Everyone at *George*, I think, guessed John's secret. But no one said a word to him, and even among ourselves we barely alluded to the possibility."

In the end, John used every piece of wisdom he had gained through a lifetime of deft media manipulation—both avoidance and charm— to keep his wedding plans secret. He and Carolyn decided to get married at the tiny, whitewashed First African Baptist Church on the northern end of Cumberland Island, Georgia. (He had visited the same church years earlier on a trip with Christina Haag.) The wedding ceremony occurred at 4 p.m. on Saturday, September 21, 1996. John's sister was the matron of honor, and her two daughters, Rose, eight years old, and Tatiana, six years old, were flower girls; her son, Jack, three years old, was the ring bearer. Anthony Radziwill, his cousin, was John's best man. Ted Kennedy toasted them. The couple danced to Prince's "Forever in My Life." The biggest coup of the event, though, was that it had been pulled off without the press knowing. "It was the paparazzi fake-out of the decade," one magazine concluded.

Those few friends fortunate enough to be invited to the secret wedding said it was special. "The wedding was really, really nice," remembered Sasha Chermayeff. "It was beautiful. It was a beautiful little church." Added Amanpour, "His family was there, and nobody knew till the end. And how fabulous is that? What a great sense of freedom, so uncomplicated, so un-grand, so simple—so simple. They released one picture, and that was that."

There was some (misguided) thinking that with John married, and settled down, perhaps the media focus on him and Carolyn would abate. After all, as a newlywed, he was now unavailable, so to speak. But in fact, the media attention on the couple seemed only to intensify, and in a way that began to cause problems both for them and for those around them. Fresh from his two-week honeymoon in Turkey, on

Sunday morning, October 6, dressed elegantly in a navy-blue suit and red tie, John came downstairs from his North Moore Street loft to the stoop at the front of the building. There was no doorman, and barely a lobby. When he got there, he was met as usual by a swarm of photographers who always seemed to be charting his every move and those of his new bride. His thought was to charm the photographers by asking for their indulgence when it came to Carolyn. It was a risky ask—after all, the appetite for pictures of them was nearly insatiable. *National Enquirer* had reportedly paid $250,000 for the photos of John and Carolyn fighting in Washington Square Park, and regular photos of John or Carolyn walking around or of John tossing his personal trash into a city garbage can or of him in-line skating without a shirt on went for hundreds of dollars. He knew that what he was asking the press to do was far outside the norm. But, he must have figured, it was worth a shot, especially since he had the ability to be extremely charming and persuasive when he wanted to be.

He stood on the metal stoop and in his best *aw shucks* voice asked for forbearance. "This is a big change for anyone," he said to the assembled gaggle. "For a private citizen, even more so. I just ask [for] any privacy or room you could give her as she makes that adjustment. It would be greatly appreciated." Then he turned around, went back inside, and a few minutes later emerged with Carolyn holding his hand tightly. "She looked terrified," *Town & Country* reported. As they started to drive off in his Saab, the photographers circled the car, boom microphones looming ominously.

John's plea failed. In December, John nearly "came to blows" with one photographer who trailed after him on the streets of Tribeca. In Hyannis Port, one summer, he took a bucket of water and dumped it on a paparazzo's head. Before Christmas, another time, he confronted the two photographers who had taken the pictures of his fight with Carolyn in Washington Square Park. First he talked to them, then he jumped on the hood of their car—staked out near his apartment—and reached through the roll-down window to try to grab the car keys. That's when one of the photographers rolled the window up, squeezing John's arm in the process. Carolyn, meanwhile, tried to pull his arm away. In the end, the incident won John and Carolyn a cover story in the *National Enquirer* under the headline, "JFK Goes Berserk." There were the rumors that accompanied the photos. There was one about how Carolyn ran off to Europe to be with her sister after a particularly nasty fight. There were rumors about her infertility, and about how they were consulting with medical specialists to help them conceive. There was a rumor about Carolyn consulting with her lawyer to figure out how to increase the $1.36 million she would be paid if their marriage lasted fewer than three years. She supposedly disliked John's Brown friends; he supposedly disliked her expensive shopping sprees. "The punishing attention began to wear Bessette down," *Town & Country* reported. "Carolyn got dumped into the deep end of the celebrity thing pretty unceremoniously," said John Perry Barlow. According to Chris Cuomo, "She could have never anticipated the intensity that would then be transferred onto her, because now it's not just 'Well, you're hanging out with this guy that we all care about,' it's 'Wow, you're the one? You're the one.' So it became this combination of everything you would have to deal with if you were dating a rock star, when that rock star also happens to be royalty."

Complicating matters—whether John knew or not—was the fact that Carolyn had not gotten over Michael Bergin. By April 1997, he had moved to Los Angeles to join the cast of *Baywatch*, the long-running television series about Los Angeles lifeguards. Shortly after his move, Carolyn had called him and asked him when she could see him again. According to Bergin, they began an affair in July 1997 while John was kayaking in Iceland. He claimed the affair continued off and on through the fall of 1997 and spring of 1998, in Los Angeles, in a motel in rural Connecticut, and during a funeral for a mutual friend's mother in Seattle. According to Bergin, Carolyn seemed desperate and

begged Bergin to "save" her from her marriage to John. When they
were in Seattle together, "She began to bawl uncontrollably, huge, gasp-
ing sobs, so powerful she could hardly catch her breath," he wrote. "I
was getting scared. I was watching her come apart at the seams and I
didn't know what to do." He believed that she was asking him "to give
her strength" to leave John. In the end, he could not do what she wanted
him to do. He loved her, yes, but he did not want to be the one responsible for breaking up her marriage. That would be a scandal for the ages,
and he did not want any part of it. It was too late for them. He told her
no, and eventually left the motel in a cab and returned to his Los Angeles apartment, ultimately refusing her pleas. He never saw her again.

There are those who dispute Bergin's account of the affair he had
with Carolyn after her marriage to John. In *American Legacy*, C. David
Heymann quoted any number of Carolyn's friends who said it wasn't
true that Carolyn and Bergin had rekindled their affair and that John
was the love of Carolyn's life. He also poked holes in Bergin's time line.
It's hard to figure out the truth. Heymann's book about John is itself
riddled with mistakes. But John's closest friends knew it was true,
whether John could bring himself to believe it or not.

One trip John did take solo during the summer of 1997 was to Oshkosh, Wisconsin, to attend the annual Experimental Aircraft Association fly-in. He told people he met there that he had been interested in
flying since he was a little boy. After his visit to Oshkosh, he wrote a
letter to the association's president: "Best of luck with your work at the
EAA. The next time I see you at the air show, I intend to fly there . . .
myself." In fact, on July 6, 1996, John had purchased a Buckeye Powered Parachute, from Buckeye Industries in Argos, Indiana. It was a
one-seat flying machine that resembled an Everglades boat with a large
parachute attached to it. The powered parachute was able to take off
and land in an open field. On October 13, John took his first trip in his
parachute in Saratoga Falls, New York, about twenty miles north of Al-
bany. He flew around for thirty minutes. He asked the flight instructor

on the ground below if he could stay up longer. "The sunset is so beautiful up here," he said. When he finally landed, he was of course smitten. "That was incredible," he said. "I can't believe it. I have never done anything that compares to this."

While at the Oshkosh air show, John made arrangements to buy a new, two-seat Buckeye Dream Machine, a larger version of the parachute that would enable him and Carolyn to fly together. He had arranged to pick up the new Dream Machine from Buckeye, in Argos, Indiana, on November 22, 1997—on the thirty-fourth anniversary of his father's death, in keeping with his practice of having a diversion on that day.

JOHN'S CLOSEST FRIENDS seemed to know that something was not right with John's marriage. Ed Hill said Carolyn was complicated; she fit perfectly what John thought he wanted in a wife but she was also often more than he could handle. "John inhabited the world of [Calvin's wife] Kelly Klein's beach house in Southampton," he said. "That wasn't the only world he inhabited, but it was a big part of his world, and it was a part that he couldn't avoid because he was the Prince of America. So he needed someone by his side who was, in his words, 'a player,' who could navigate that world with him. She was beautiful. She was truly beautiful. She had all the looks and all the moves and all the wiles. She was also completely full of shit and was a nightmare. The things that he liked about her were real. Whether or not that's what he needed, that's anyone's question. But in terms of what he thought he needed and what he thought he wanted, he found it all in her. She could move fluidly among the movers and shakers. You could not intimidate her. She could pull rank. She could turn a cold shoulder. She had all the skills. At the end of the day she was selfish and manipulative and damaged in her own way."

Hill said he could "see it in her" that she might be having an affair

with Bergin. "I could see how she took advantage of John," he continued. "It was that whole thing that she was a girl who played by 'The
Rules'"—a reference to the 1995 bestselling book about dating. "The
legend was that she was sort of the ultimate product of 'The Rules.'
She executed all 'The Rules' in the best possible manner and nailed
herself John Fitzgerald Kennedy Jr. I think that there is probably substance to that." Hill was making these observations as someone who
got along fine with Carolyn but whose ultimate loyalties were unquestionably with John. "If you listen to the way I'm talking about her now,
you can see that if push had come to shove in a given situation, I would
have thrown her under the bus in a heartbeat," he continued. "Because you're so fucked up and you do and don't love the guy. You see
him more as a conquest than a person. But even in your heart of hearts,
if you love him and it's what you wanted, and you've managed to get
beyond the game that led you to him in the first place, you're still so
fucked up you can't stop. You're like an addict."

Sasha Chermayeff said that after the wedding "everything changed"
between John and Carolyn. "She got nervous as hell," she said. Carolyn was "nervous" before the wedding, to be sure, but afterward, she
said, "it sort of went down and down and by the last year they were not
able to communicate, like not at all." She said Carolyn was "obsessed"
with Bergin "being her salvation" and hoped that she could "go back
and kind of pretend" with him that her life wasn't what it was with John.
"She was just having some crazy sexual thing with the other guy," she
said. "I never understood it." At first, like Hill, Chermayeff thought that
Carolyn could handle life with John. "She's smart enough, she's strong
enough, she's kind of like almost ruthless," she said. "She can do it."
But the reality of the intense spotlight was more than she could handle,
even though she thought she could. "It just broke her down to the point
of real fear and paranoia, like she wouldn't go out of the apartment,"
she continued. "She got agoraphobia."

She also stopped having sex with John. "I never quite understood what happened, why that was the way it was, and I felt really sad about it because I wanted so much to see him really, really fulfilled and he wasn't," Chermayeff continued. "She wanted to be with John, but she wanted to have sex with the other guy because that is where she felt more at home. John, she was just going to deny. In fact, she just wasn't going to fuck him. Sorry to be crude." John couldn't live like that. "And a lot of people can't," she said. "Her excuse—that she was really shut down sexually—wasn't really true. But she was shut down from him. It is mind blowing, but it happened. People are so strange, and love and chemistry, and who people want to be with, and intimacy. God knows there's no making any sense of any of it."

Chermayeff said she spoke with John about the fact that his wife wouldn't sleep with him anymore. He was upset about it. He was in therapy. He may have, eventually, had casual sexual interludes with Julie Baker, a former girlfriend, but he was, Chermayeff said, "very serious, and very seriously committed to the fact that he had fallen madly in love with Carolyn. They had this really passionate beginning, which Herb Ritts photographed incredibly . . . I mean when they were madly, madly, madly sexually in love. He took these incredibly super sexy pictures of John and Carolyn where they were like on fire. She even said to me, 'We were like on fire during this session,' and you can tell." (The photographs have never been made public.) But she was fickle, Chermayeff continued. Carolyn was married to John but had fallen back in love with Bergin. "She wanted it all. It was fucking her up and then she couldn't sleep with John. They were really hot and heavy, I remember it, and then there's a lot of stress. They had fun. They got married. They had a great wedding. It was a great party. We all loved it, it was like a love fest, and then shit started stressing her out. There was more stuff going on with her than I clearly knew about. There were more serious issues that I wasn't really privy to." Carolyn was in pain. "It came from real dysfunction and was dysfunction," Sasha said. "She was good at seeming really together but she actually wasn't. Maybe she was a coke addict and sort of a sex addict, who knows?"

She said John remained generally hopeful he and Carolyn could work through their issues. But then he realized, according to Chermayeff, that Carolyn's "issues were much more serious than he had expected or thought them to be, and that the sexual shutdown was like—I don't think anybody had ever done that to him before—and this was during that period where she didn't want to go out and was really paranoid." John asked Chermayeff to spend some time with Carolyn. "She was talking about 'How do I keep passion in my relationship?' Questions of course where in hindsight it was like 'Oh yes, you are talking about yourself' and 'Why aren't I picking up on all the cues, that you're telling me that you don't have passion for John anymore, and you're desperately messed up about it and you're really stressed out about the paparazzi and you rush off to LA whenever you can to go with your old boyfriend.'"

JOHN WAS ALSO HAVING HIS headaches at *George*. The euphoria of the first two issues faded rapidly. Gary Ginsberg said that pretty much by the third issue of the magazine—after the 350-page ad buy of the first two issues had ended—he feared *George* could soon be in financial trouble. "The big advertisers couldn't quite categorize it," he said. "They didn't know: Is it a fashion magazine? Is it a political magazine? Is it a general interest magazine? So it required buyers to think more broadly and to think more creatively about how they would use it in their media buys. At a certain point they just kind of gave up."

Around April 1997, John had a falling-out with Michael Berman, his longtime business partner. There would have been no *George* without the combination of the skills that both John and Michael brought to it, but it's probably fair to say that each of them was having trouble sharing that credit. As one person who knew them both said, "A political magazine with Michael Berman had no value. But apparently a political magazine with only John Kennedy didn't have a lot of value, either."

And then there was the influence of Carolyn on John's decision-making at *George*. The editors would come up with story ideas and Carolyn would change them. A decision would be made about whom John would interview for the magazine or what meeting he should attend and then two days later John would announce that he had changed his mind. She would go into the *George* offices and opine on the colors that should be used in the magazine—she was the master purveyor of style after all—despite the color scheme having already been determined. John was unreliable and would triple-book lunches or meetings. He would surround himself with people who were in his thrall and were afraid to tell him when things weren't going right. Carolyn would call up Michael Berman and complain about John. She complained about Michael Berman to John. John and Michael were fighting every day about something or other. There was the time that John inadvertently tore the cuff of Michael's shirt in the midst of a heated argument about the direction of the magazine. After that, John locked himself in his office and then Michael tried to pick the lock with a pair of scissors. (He later apologized to Berman and bought him a new shirt.) "It was a shit show," said one former *George* employee. "The last year of that business while I was there was a complete shit show."

Carolyn seemed to be encouraging the chaos. She also believed John could run *George* without Berman. "He just seemed to think he could do it by himself," the *George* employee continued. In this telling, it all seemed rather sad: "I think John was always alone. He seemed like he had a big, full life but he was just kind of always alone, and maybe he just thought he could do it by himself. In this case I think it was his wife who said, 'You can do this better on your own.' . . . I think there are two Johns and I think one was before her and one was after her. I honestly believe his life turned into a free fall. Personally and professionally. Who else did he have? All he had was his sister and his wife."

In any event, as the *Daily News* reported, by June 1997 the divorce between John and Berman had been finalized. "Ending months of tense negotiations," the paper reported, Berman ended up as the head of a new division at Hachette that would produce films and TV shows. "I'm looking forward to another new challenge," he said. He also denied the rumors that John's marriage to Carolyn had in any way hastened his split with John. "That's just silliness," Berman told the paper. "It was always professional. It wasn't a dispute so much as a maturing of differences. For me, *George* was an entrepreneurial idea and a challenge, but it wasn't anything I expected to stay with throughout my career." Terms of Berman's settlement with John were not disclosed—he used what he received in the settlement as the grubstake for the private-equity business he now runs—but high-powered attorneys were employed to reach it. The two men never spoke again. John didn't replace Berman. He was now unequivocally free to do whatever he wanted to do with *George*, with little meaningful interference.

It was July 16 when Richard Blow first saw the photo of John. It was to accompany John's editor's letter for the September issue, which was just about to be sent to the printer. It was the first issue that John produced after he had split with Berman and was an idea Berman had long opposed. The color picture, taken after office hours by Mario Sorrenti, featured John sitting in a dark room with no shirt on and what looked like nothing else on, either. (His private parts were a hazy blur.) His muscled arms were wrapped around his knees. He was supposedly gazing at an apple dangling from an imaginary ceiling, although the apple had been added later. "But John only looked naked," Blow remembered. "He had left his boxers on." He had also been very careful to insist that Sorrenti use a Polaroid camera to take the picture, and in the process made sure there was no film negative floating around that could make its way into the gossip rags. "It occurred to me that John had lost his mind," Blow continued, "and that was before I read the editor's letter that accompanied the picture."

John's editor's note—written at the last minute without consulting anyone—would garner more attention, and controversy, for *George* than anything he had done before it. The piece was ostensibly about the twenty "most fascinating" women in politics that *George* had profiled for the issue. But the actual writing was more than a little opaque about exactly what he was trying to say and to whom. Surrounded by a respectable number of full-page ads for the likes of Saks, Armani, Burberry, Polo, and Clinique, John wrote without any context, "I've learned a lot about temptation recently." Whatever he was referring to, though, he did not elaborate. Instead he wrote about how interesting it was to consider those people who give in to temptation, instead of wrestling with it. He then referred to some article he had read—without citing it specifically—in which the author reflected upon the virtue of living a "respectable life." The unknown writer, according to John, argued that leading the straight, narrow, and predictable life in many ways is a departure from true human nature—"one that's ruled by passion and instinct." He then lamented: "Conform utterly and endure a potentially dispiriting, suffocating life." He wrote that he had witnessed this "cycle up close" in the past year. And then swatted at a hornet's nest. "Two members of my family chased an idealized alternative to their life," he wrote, without mentioning any names but clearly referring to his first cousins Michael and Joseph Kennedy, two of Robert Kennedy's sons. "One left behind an embittered wife, and another, in what looked to be a hedge against mortality, fell in love with youth and surrendered his judgment in the process. Both became poster boys for bad behavior. Perhaps they deserved it. Perhaps they should have known better. To whom much is given, much is expected, right?" Joe had divorced his wife after twelve years of marriage; Michael allegedly had a five-year affair with his children's teenage babysitter. Joe was contemplating running for governor of Massachusetts with Michael as his campaign manager. (Michael died a little more than a year later in a ski accident in Aspen.) It was not precisely clear what John was trying to say in his editor's note about his cousins. But the combination of it and the half-naked picture caused a media sensation.

At around the same time he and Carolyn had another public spat—this time on a twelve-passenger Continental Express flight from Newark to Martha's Vineyard. According to *Boston* magazine, John and Carolyn were bickering pretty much the whole time. But their argument reached its nadir when John said, according to someone seated two rows away, "Maybe we should get divorced. We fucking talk about it enough!" To which Carolyn replied, "Oh, no. We waited for your mother to die to get married. We're waiting for my mother to die to get a divorce." Their dispute intensified after the flight landed and they headed together to Red Gate Farm. According to the *Star*, Carolyn soon thereafter left the island by private charter and "John spent the entire next day frantically bicycling around the island. He just wouldn't stop."

In September 1997, they celebrated their one-year anniversary at a spa resort in Big Sur, California. They "emerged looking refreshed and in love," one writer for *Cosmopolitan* observed. And a few weeks later they were photographed together lovey-dovey in Tribeca. On October 9, Carolyn and Caroline accompanied John into Lenox Hill Hospital, where he underwent surgery on his hand as a result of an injury from playing touch football. Everyone looked happy. "Bessette-Kennedy seems to be finding her footing as both Kennedy spouse and media darling, even smiling for the camera," *Cosmo* reported.

There were rumors that Pecker and Hachette were going to pull the plug on the magazine. In an interview with the *Los Angeles Times*, Pecker denied the rumors and said that *George* was actually doing better than he and Hachette had expected. He added that John had a multiyear contract with the magazine, wasn't going anywhere, and was a hard worker. "I've never seen a community so negative about a person and wanting him to fail," Pecker said. "People are very surprised that he's successful. He works 12 hours a day, he travels all over the place, he does the interviews."

Despite Pecker's public assurances about *George*'s future, behind the scenes he was turning up the pressure on John to improve the magazine's financial performance. In November 1997, John organized a retreat at the Beaverkill Valley Inn, in the Catskills, for editorial employees. The idea was not only to get the staff revved up again about the magazine and its mission but also to acknowledge the pressure coming from Pecker. There were hikes, friendly games of soccer, and family-style meals interspersed with some serious tension inside the inn's conference rooms. At one point, John lost his temper when, after he explained how *George* intended to sell more copies of the magazine on the newsstand than did *Men's Journal* or *Esquire*, Terenzio pointed out that those magazines had a staff twice as large as *George*'s. "It's never going to happen unless Hachette steps up and gives us what we need to be competitive," she said. But John didn't appreciate her insight and told her so, in front of everyone. "That's enough," he told her.

"But—" she started to say.

John cut her off. "I said that's *enough*," he said. "We don't need to hear that anymore."

Terenzio had been publicly humiliated. "I turned beet red," she recalled in her book, "humiliated in front of the editors, who quickly averted their gazes." Afterward, everyone was still in shock, as was Terenzio. "They were visibly uncomfortable after witnessing John lash out at me," she continued. "It had shocked them as much as it had embarrassed me. They weren't used to it. But I was." It was one thing for John's assistant to see a side of him in daily interactions where he was less than charming and politic; it was quite another for the whole staff to witness such a display.

He later more or less apologized, and Terenzio understood his position. "Look, I'm sorry about today's meeting," he told her. "But when you say stuff like that, people assume it's coming from me. I can't go around being negative all the time about Hachette. It's bad for morale and bad for business."

Terenzio recalled how Maggie Haberman, the daughter of Nancy Haberman, the magazine's press spokesperson, was working as an intern at *George* one summer and spent an afternoon answering Terenzio's phone. After the phone rang at one point, Haberman yelled to John that someone was on the line for him. "What are you saying?" he said nastily. "I can't even hear you." Terenzio, returning to her desk, told John that he was yelling at an intern. "Oops," he said. "Sorry, Maggie." Maggie later told her mother, "I can't believe how he talks to [Terenzio] sometimes." (Haberman would go on to become a White House correspondent for the *New York Times*.)

On November 22, 1997, John and Carolyn went for three days to Argos, Indiana, of all places, to the headquarters of Buckeye Industries, the manufacturer of his Buckeye flying parachute. He asked the Buckeye executives not to alert the press. A Buckeye executive was dispatched to Chicago and flew Carolyn and John back to the Argos area on a private jet. John had two purposes for the trip: to get his basic flight instructor rating for the Buckeye and to trade in his single-seat Falcon 582 for the new Buckeye Dream Machine that he had previously ordered. Carolyn took her first flight in the solo Buckeye when they were in Argos and she seemed to love the experience as much as John did on his first flight. She turned out to be almost as big a daredevil as he was. "Now you know why we are here," he told her after she had landed, "to get a two-seater so we can fly together." They ordered pizzas and went out to breakfast with the Buckeye executives, who completely fell for John and Carolyn. They especially found Carolyn to be warm and funny—and very pleased to be out of the Manhattan spotlight.

After Christmas that year and following the *George* second-anniversary celebration, John headed to the FlightSafety Academy, in Vero Beach, Florida, to resume his study for his pilot's license. "All

John's life, he wanted to be free," remembered Laurence Leamer, a family biographer. "He wanted to fly above celebrity. He wanted to fly above this attention and be his own person, and the ultimate way to do that was to fly, and from the time he was a boy he wanted to do that." By then, John had been working on his pilot's license off and on for some fifteen years. After getting a small dose of flying while on John Perry Barlow's ranch, John had started his training in 1982; six years later he had logged forty-seven hours in a plane, with six different instructors. In only one of the forty-seven hours was he alone as the pilot; the rest of the time, he flew alongside an instructor. For the next nine years, John suspended his training, and when he resumed, in Vero Beach, he went at it with passion. "I worry about John flying," Maurice Tempelsman told a friend. "He's so distractible." Between December 1997 and April 1998, he flew another fifty-three hours, forty-three of which were with an instructor. According to the National Transportation Safety Board, the instructor at FlightSafety who prepared John for his "private checkride" said he had "very good" skills for someone with his level of experience. He earned his private pilot certificate in April 1998. (A few years later, FlightSafety would also train the terrorists who committed the September 11 attacks.) When he graduated he gave the FlightSafety instructors a picture of himself, inscribed to "The bravest people in aviation because people will only care where I got my training if I crash. Best, John Kennedy."

Gary Ginsberg said that for John, flying was a total and necessary release from the unending pressure on him. "He literally wanted an escape from being on the ground where the pressures on him were so immense," he said. "The physical pressures on him in New York City, the constant attention—and the lack of any way to avoid it. Going up in the clouds in the sky was a really important physical escape for him. He talked about that. He talked about the solitude of being in the air. It gave him great comfort, which I think is as much a reason why he wanted to fly as wanting a way to get to the Vineyard. It was a psychological escape for him." But Ginsberg worried about his friend flying and whether his mind was sufficiently logical to be a pilot. "He was the most non-linear thinker I knew," he continued, "and to fly required an ability to think very logically and very linearly. You've got to go down a checklist essentially and that's a physical checklist, and that was so not the way John approached problem solving. When he started flying I thought it was not the smartest thing he'd ever done because it was the last thing he should have been doing given his intellectual bent."

A close friend also worried about what he called John's "death wish." He remembered having dinner one night with John and Carolyn during the summer of 1998. John had been out kayaking the night before in New York Harbor by the Statue of Liberty, and a huge boat had come bearing down on him. He barely escaped from being run over. "You definitely have a death wish," he told John. "Carolyn said, 'You definitely have a death wish, John,' and he was like 'Are you guys fucking mad? Stop! Stop!' But we both agreed that he did because he just took too many crazy chances."

JOHN SEEMED QUITE STYMIED by Carolyn and how poorly they were getting along. There was her drug use—cocaine mostly—as well as his gnawing suspicion that she was cheating on him—a suspicion that turned out to be true. He confided many of his concerns about his marriage to the private journals that his mother encouraged him to keep and that he seemed to write in frequently, and to his close friends. During the summer of 1998, John was having coffee at an outdoor café in Greenwich Village with one of his friends from Brown. John was writing furiously in his journal while his friend was reading the newspaper. When John got up to go to the bathroom, his friend couldn't resist the temptation to see what he had written. "What happened to us, C?" he wrote. "What happened to our love?" He stopped reading when he sensed John coming back from the bathroom but asked him how he was doing. "Carolyn and I are fighting," he said. "We're not close any-more. We haven't had sex in months. We're not even sleeping in the same bed! One minute she's up and happy and the next she's mean and angry. Carolyn and her gay friends are snorting more and more co-caine, staying locked away in her room for hours at a time. . . . Some nights I stand by her bedside and stare at her as she sleeps. All I keep thinking is how much I want to lie beside her." A few months later, when the same friend stopped by his North Moore Street apartment, he happened again on one of John's journals on the coffee table. In it, John had written that he suspected Carolyn of having an affair with a friend who was a married antiques dealer. "I can't believe she is doing this to me," read the journal entry. John saw his friend reading the journal entry but didn't seem upset. "My life is a mess and it's all because of Carolyn," he told his friend. "The only question is how do I get myself out of it."

IN NOVEMBER 1998, on his annual out-of-town trip to avoid the news of his father's assassination, John convinced Brian Steel to join him on a camping trip to Maine. Obviously camping in Maine in November is not exactly expected to be pleasant, given the cold temperatures. But Steel was game. With his new pilot's license in hand, John convinced Steel to fly with him from Teterboro Airport, in New Jersey, to north of Bar Harbor, Maine. "Carolyn would call me up and she'd be like, 'He's dying to have you go in the plane,'" Steel said. "And I would say to Carolyn, 'I'm not going to be the biggest footnote in aviation history.' And then it became a joke between the three of us." They spent the first two nights of the three-day weekend camping out. "It was twenty degrees and we're in a tent freezing our asses off," Steel recalled.

After two days of that, they decided to fly to Bar Harbor Airport, rent a car, drive to Acadia National Park, and hike around there. They arrived at Bar Harbor Airport at around nine forty-five at night.

The rent-a-car agency was open until ten, and John urged Steel to run over to it and keep it open long enough for him to tie down the plane and join him at the rental counter. Steel got to the counter, and the clerk told him there were no cars for him to rent. But he kept delaying her long enough for John to arrive, after securing the plane. "John comes walking up," he said. "She melted. We got a car. We got like the nicest car they had—'Oh, do you want an upgrade?' He knew he could pull that off. Unquestionably." They got a motel room somewhere and the next morning got up early, had a big breakfast, and spent the next eight hours hiking around Acadia. "Keeping up with him was not easy," he said. "I was in good shape for a whatever-year-old but John was like a panther, like he's hopping all over the place." They flew back together that night to Teterboro. "I like adventure," Steel said, "but I don't have any death wish: I would never have gotten in the plane if I thought I was at risk of dying. I just wouldn't have. I'm essentially one of those guys that believes you've got maybe eighty years and you should try and make the best of it."

IN APRIL, JOHN MADE THE FATEFUL decision to upgrade the single-engine Cessna 182 Skylane, which he had been flying in the two years since he obtained his provisional pilot's license—a license that allowed him to fly by sight only, since he had not been sufficiently trained in instrument flying—for a more powerful 1996 Piper Saratoga II HP, a three-hundred-horsepower, single-engine six-seater. It cost John $300,000. Pilots compared the power of the Piper Saratoga to that of a sport utility vehicle—in other words, much more powerful than his Cessna. The Saratoga had state-of-the-art equipment, including automatic pilot, plus two fuel tanks that required the pilot to switch from one to the other as needed. There was a lot to do as the Saratoga's pilot, and John was learning how to fly the plane thanks to a flight instructor who would accompany him and his passengers. By then, John had around two hundred hours of flight experience, "not a rookie, but not deeply experienced," a pilot later told the *Boston Globe*.

Over Memorial Day weekend 1999, John and Carolyn went to Red Gate Farm in Martha's Vineyard. They were joined by a number of John's old friends, such as Rob Littell and Sasha Chermayeff, her husband, and their son, Phinny. Littell and his wife flew up with John and Carolyn in the new Saratoga, along with John's flight instructor. John was in control the whole flight. "His landings were barely noticeable," Littell recalled, "something he took pride in. None of us felt nervous about flying with John. He was the opposite of reckless, with the attitude of a cautious and serious pilot."

At one point, as sunset was approaching on Saturday, John decided to go up in his Buckeye Dream Machine, the two-seater version of the flying parachute. John liked to fly the Dream Machine when he was up in Martha's Vineyard. Some of his friends liked to join him, including Littell and Sasha's husband; others, such as Brian Steel, refused. "I thought it was a death trap," Steel said. John took off in the Dream Machine from the lawn of Red Gate Farm. "We were all watching," Sasha said. They then were going to go to the beach and would meet John after he finished his flight. "He went up and we saw him have problems and then we saw him crash," Sasha recalled. "When he crashed he went up and down and we all went running to him." The Buckeye had hit a tree that John had tried to avoid, and crumpled to the ground. His foot had been bent backward, and the ligaments in his ankle shredded.

John was in considerable pain. "He put his arms around us and literally it was like 'I think I hurt my leg,'" Sasha continued. "Yeah, I think I hurt my leg but I'm okay. But I've got to go to the doctor.'" Sasha and her husband wrapped their arms around John, walking him up back to the house, dragging his leg behind him. "Then he went off to the hospital and came back with his cast on," she said. Rob Littell had helped get John ready for the flight that day and remembered how things were fine until an unexpected gust of wind blew the Buckeye off course.

Two days later, back in New York City, John had surgery to put a metal plate in his leg. Littell urged John to "slow down"—to take the crash as a sign to cut back on his grueling work schedule and on the tough job of being him. John's thyroid condition left him "lethargic, cranky, and frighteningly thin," according to Gary Ginsberg. The winter before he had also hurt his hand on a broken champagne glass. Perhaps, Littell suggested, he was pushing himself too hard. "No shit," John replied. His friend John Perry Barlow also told him the crash was "a sign" that he should chill. "I was afraid to fly that thing and I'm not afraid to fly much of anything, but that was a very treacherous aircraft," said Barlow. "He was flying around up there by himself and Carolyn said, 'He's all alone up there. He couldn't be happier.'"

John had decided to spend many of the following summer weekends in Martha's Vineyard to be with his cousin—and best friend—Anthony Radziwill, who had been diagnosed with cancer and knew he was dying. John "wanted to help Anthony just relax that summer," Sasha said. After John broke his ankle, which obviously put a serious damper on his mobility, he waxed philosophical about why he thought it had happened. "He was upset with himself," Sasha said. "But he said he thinks it happened because he's just meant to sit down in a rocking chair with Anthony and they could just spend the summer, the two of them, just sitting there and not being able to do anything while Anthony died. He kind of immediately saw the good side of that accident."

John had also become increasingly protective of Ed Hill. Hill had a rough few years and John urged him to grow up, settle down, and mature. He approved of Hill's decision to go to law school and then to practice law. When he met the woman whom Hill would eventually marry, John encouraged him to do so. "He never stopped trying to push me to straighten up and fly right," Hill said. At one point during the spring of 1999, John asked Hill why he had not yet become engaged to

Holly, his future wife. "I told him it was because I didn't feel that I could afford an adequate wedding ring, which was true, because of course I wanted to go platinum and I wanted to go big because that's the world I live in," Hill said. "He looked at me. He was speechless. He was incredulous when I told him that. He almost stutters. He's like, 'Eddie, Eddie, your best friend's mother's boyfriend is the most powerful diamond merchant in the world, and you are worried about affording an adequate wedding ring?' That was part of John. As silly and reckless as he liked to be, there was always the point where it was time for him to become the adult in the room, and by [this] time we had reached that point in life where that obligation arose on a daily basis and he wasn't taking things as lightly anymore." Hill, humbled, apologized to John for forgetting how helpful his friend could be. John talked to Tempelsman, who put John in touch with David Schwartz in his office, who agreed to help Hill. He ended up with a 50 percent discount on a $20,000 engagement ring. "That was all [John]," he said. "He might not have been able to clear that up when he was seventeen. He might have been too distracted at that time." But by the time John was thirty-eight years old, he was able to deliver for Hill and not give it a second thought.

Hill also got another unexpected gift from John, who had decided to get custom-made suits through a service that arranged to have a tailor come to the office and take measurements, supposedly making the process easier for busy executives. "He was measured for four suits, a silly sort of pleated-pants, three-button-jacket style that was pure late 1990s," Hill said. "They set him back $400 or $500 apiece." But somehow the measurements for the suit jackets were wrong. "They didn't fit right," Hill said. "So what did he do? What does this prince of a guy do? Rather than rat out [the sales rep] and get her in trouble with the company, he paid the bill, put them in a garment bag, and gave them to me with a note that he had scribbled in an orange highlighter that simply says, 'Cosmo, the clothes make the man.'" He reveled in the memory. "There's so many things that are indicated by every aspect of

that story, the ring and the suits, of what he was capable of at that stage of his life, the generosity, the kindness, the sense of propriety, the need to get the fucking shit together because there are no rehearsals anymore," Hill said. "We're in our late thirties."

JOHN'S LEG INJURY IRRITATED him to no end. He was a guy who hated to miss a single workout. With a cast on his leg, he was sidelined for much of the summer. "It's an emotional thing," Chermayeff said. "You break your leg. It's the beginning of the summer. It's sort of like a symbolic, just, everything's broken down." He was not happy. "When he returned to the office, hobbling on crutches with his lower left leg encased in a cast, John was in a foul mood," recalled Richard Blow. "His ankle sent shooting pains up his leg, and the painkillers he took were making him woozy. To keep his leg elevated, John had to recline in a long black lounge chair, only inches off the floor, his head about knee-high. He was embarrassed by the accident and quickly tired of people asking what had happened. He even gave different versions, telling some people that he had hit a stone wall while landing and others that he had hurt himself Rollerblading."

John was also struggling with the realities of running *George* with a financial partner—Hachette—that understandably demanded a return on its investment. Frustration was building on both sides. "He had been told that Hachette was going to basically pull back on its funding," recalled Gary Ginsberg. "It was up to him now to keep it alive." Audited circulation for *George* for the last six months of 1998 had fallen to around 403,000, slightly above the guaranteed circulation of 400,000 that *George* had promised advertisers. The plan had been to get to a circulation of half a million by 2000, a goal that looked increasingly elusive but was key to the magazine breaking even. Ad pages for the first half of 1999 had fallen 30 percent. *George* was expected to lose $10 million for the year. "We were still successful in the sense that we could keep

the lights on," Ginsberg said, "but we had fallen from those early highs and fallen so dramatically that it felt deflating, and I think Hachette at a certain point just wasn't willing to invest the dollars because they didn't see any big return."

In May, John had fired *George*'s publisher and associate publisher—both of whom had been appointed by Pecker—and was looking to replace them with a publisher of his own choosing who might be more amenable to leaving the Hachette fold if it came to that. On June 1, Jack Kliger replaced David Pecker as Hachette Filipacchi's CEO. Kliger gave permission for John to explore finding new investors who could inject fresh capital into *George*. He told John that Hachette wanted to retain its 50 percent stake in *George*; any new capital, which was much needed, would have to come from third parties. (Although initially John and Michael Berman had put their own money into developing the magazine, John had still not invested any equity capital into *George* in exchange for his ownership stake and had no intention of doing so. That meant that a new investor would be diluting John's ownership.) John made some discreet inquiries. He had lunch at San Domenico with Steve Florio, then the president and CEO of Condé Nast. On July 11, John and his flight instructor flew the Saratoga to Toronto to talk to the executives of Magna International, a Canadian auto-parts company, and also reportedly spoke with Paul Tudor Jones, the hedge-fund manager and driving force behind the Robin Hood Foundation, where John was on the board.

John still had a hankering for politics, beyond just editing a magazine about it. In November 1998, Senator Daniel Patrick Moynihan announced that he would retire from the Senate at the end of his term, meaning that a US Senate seat from New York was up for grabs. Many people urged John to run for it. "John immediately started exploring his viability," Ginsberg said. He and Ginsberg spoke sporadically about the possibility of John running for the Senate and studying the numbers to see if it might work. Ginsberg, who had recently left *George* to be the head of public relations at News Corporation, introduced John to Roger Ailes, the onetime political operative who had created Fox News. "He and I spent a long time with Roger discussing whether he would be viable and how he would put together a candidacy or campaign," Ginsberg said. "And Roger was very supportive."

One person who was not particularly supportive of this idea was John's wife, Carolyn. She continued to shun the spotlight. "John knew that his wife had not fully adjusted to her new role," Richard Blow wrote in *Vanity Fair*. "She was neither entirely comfortable nor entirely happy, and she certainly wasn't sure what she wanted to do with herself beyond being John's wife."

But it was quickly a moot point. Hillary Clinton effectively thwarted John's plan to run for Moynihan's Senate seat by announcing that she was moving to New York and running for it. "John felt like he could not go against her because it would be too disruptive to the state Democratic Party," Ginsberg said. "He would look disloyal and he felt like she just outranked him in the pecking order, and for his first campaign he did not want to go after a sitting First Lady. He thought that it would be too bruising, so he decided to drop it." But he still had not abandoned the idea of entering politics. Instead, he just reoriented his thinking. Rather than running for the Senate, he decided he would challenge New York governor George Pataki in the 2002 gubernatorial election, an idea he discussed with his friends. "John recognized that he was a much more natural executive than he was a legislator," Ginsberg said. "He talked about how boring the Senate was and how he wasn't cut out to sit on a committee and listen to endless hours of testimony. He viewed himself much more as a chief executive and thought that his skill set was just much more suited to being a governor than it would being a senator."

By then, Brian Steel, John's friend from the Manhattan district attorney's office, had moved to Washington to work in the White House. John had invited Steel to the White House Correspondents' Dinner in

April 1999, and the next day they worked out together, had lunch, and discussed his future. Steel drove John to the airport—he had flown down in the Saratoga—and on the way they discussed what he was planning to do about *George* and about a potential political career. "He was very concerned about all the people that worked at *George*," Steel said. "He didn't want to leave because he knew when he left that was it. He had that in the back of his mind." He said he knew that Hillary Clinton had called up John and reiterated, "'I'm going to run for Moynihan's seat unless you want to run. If you want to run I'm not going to run.' And John said, 'I'm not going to run.' John is telling me this story but then he said, 'You know what? If I had to run for anything I want to run for governor. Listen, a lot of people from my family have run for office—I think that's great—but no one's been a governor. I like being the boss. I like being a CEO. I think I'm better suited to be governor." The big unknown was what would happen with Carolyn. "She had to stabilize herself because she was pretty unstable at that point," a close friend said.

During one of their many arguments, Carolyn had shared with John that she was still sleeping with Bergin. "She threw Michael Bergin in John's face," the Hollywood producer Clifford Streit told *Vanity Fair*. "I think she used Michael Bergin in any way she could to get whatever she wanted out of John. The only one in the world who thought Carolyn would choose Michael over John was John." John wasn't sure whether to believe her or not, but what with her mood swings, her drug use, and her extreme reticence, he wanted her to see a psychiatrist. She agreed. In March 1999, he agreed to join her at marriage counseling.

On July 12, Carolyn moved out of their bedroom into a spare room in their loft that John used to store his exercise equipment. John checked into the Stanhope Hotel, on Fifth Avenue. It was just down the street from where he grew up. His room overlooked the Met, where he used to play Frisbee and hang out as a kid. There were page proofs and cover mock-ups of the upcoming issue of *George* strewn around his hotel room. John spent a lot of time on the phone, contemplating with friends how things had spun so badly out of control. "It's all falling apart," he told one friend. "Everything is falling apart." That afternoon, with his ankle still in a cast, he flew in his Saratoga with a copilot to Toronto to meet a second time with the Magna executives.

On July 14, Richard Blow was sitting in his office at *George*, which was near John's, and he could hear John screaming through the closed doors. "In startling, staccato bursts of rage, John was yelling," he recalled. "His yells would be followed by silences, then John's fury would resume. At first I could not make out the words. Then, after a particularly long pause, I heard John shout, 'Well, goddammit, Carolyn, you're the reason I was up at three o'clock last night!' The shouting lasted maybe five minutes, but John's office door stayed shut for some time." For lunch that day, John met Carolyn and her older sister, Lauren, an investment banker for Morgan Stanley, at the Stanhope Hotel. Carolyn's sister thought the get-together would be a good idea to try to clear the air and get the marriage back on track.

At the lunch, Lauren also convinced her sister to fly with John that Friday night up to Hyannis Port for the long-scheduled wedding of his cousin Rory Kennedy. In her fit of pique, Carolyn had decided she would not go to the wedding. But of course, her absence would be noticed and remarked upon. Even though their marriage was troubled, John wanted to avoid that at all costs and was desperate for Carolyn to agree to attend the wedding with him. In that regard, Lauren played a crucial role, convincing her sister not only to attend the wedding but also to fly up to Hyannis Port with John in the Saratoga. Lauren agreed to go with John and her sister, even though she was spending the weekend on Martha's Vineyard, not in Hyannis Port. She convinced John to fly to Martha's Vineyard, drop her off, then continue on to the wedding. "Come on," she told them, "it'll be fun." John and Carolyn agreed to the proposal. "Great," Lauren said. "Then I'll see you guys at the airport."

But John was still very unhappy. That night, from his room in the Stanhope, he was on the phone with a friend, unleashing on Carolyn. "I want to have kids, but whenever I raise the subject with Carolyn, she turns away and refuses to have sex with me," he told his friend. "It's not just about sex. It's impossible to talk to Carolyn about *anything*. We've become like total strangers. . . . I've *had* it with her! It's got to stop. Otherwise we're headed for divorce." He told the same friend he had even picked out a name for his son—Flynn.

The next morning, the *New York Post* ran a piece suggesting that Kliger and Hachette would "probably" pull the plug on *George* when the agreement was up with John at the end of 1999. "Though neither of us was at liberty to say so," Richard Blow recalled, "Kliger and I both knew that the situation had progressed beyond 'probably.'" Kliger had invited the staff of *George* to lunch at the Palm, on West 50th, that day as a way for him to get to know people better and vice versa. But John blew the lunch off. "His absence was a poorly hidden sign that John had other priorities," Blow continued. After lunch, John called the *George* editorial staff together. First, he apologized for being a bit cranky and withdrawn of late. He said he'd been preoccupied by a "family problem" that "will be resolved soon." He also wanted to assure people that *George* was in better shape than the tabloids would have everyone believe. *George* would carry on, either with Hachette or with a new partner. "Don't worry," he said. "We will all have our jobs at Christmas." Later that afternoon, John conducted a similar meeting for the business side of the magazine. "As long as I'm alive," John said, "this magazine will continue to publish." He also made a stop that day to Lenox Hill Hospital to see his orthopedic surgeon, who removed the cast on his leg and told him to keep using crutches until his foot returned to full strength; it was still too weak to support his six-foot-one frame. The doctor also told him not to fly the Saratoga for at least ten more days, until the foot improved, since he needed his feet to fly the plane. But Ginsberg remembered how important it was for John to get back to flying after a six-week layoff. He had invited John to his son's bris that morning, but John declined. It was either the bris or getting his cast removed. "If I don't get my cast off then I can't fly my plane and I really want to fly the plane," John told him. "He hadn't flown in a couple of months, and he was really itching to get back up there."

That night, after John had gotten his cast removed, John and Gary went together to the Yankees game. Ginsberg had also invited to the game James and Lachlan Murdoch, Rupert's two sons. They all sat together in the box of George Steinbrenner, the Yankees' owner. Part of the idea was to have John meet the Murdoch sons to see if there might be some interest in News Corporation replacing Hachette as John's partner for *George*. Murdoch already owned one political magazine, the conservative (now defunct) *Weekly Standard*, and the more liberal *George* might be a way to balance out his holdings. Plus, unlike Hachette apparently, Murdoch was able to understand what it might mean to have John F. Kennedy Jr. as a publishing partner. They spent around eight hours together that night, talking about John's future at *George* or in politics. "We had a full conversation about 2002 and there's no doubt in my mind that he was going to run against Pataki," Ginsberg said. After the game, Gary dropped John off at the Stanhope. A cover story was concocted for his friends about how John had lost his keys to the North Moore Street apartment and that he was working in the hotel on editorial spreads for the magazine—but the truth was obviously quite different.

Some of John's closest friends were convinced the breach with Carolyn was irreparable. Chermayeff recalled, "He said to me one time, 'Sasha, I think I'm finally ready for a real woman. I finally think

I can handle a woman.' I was like 'Ah.' That last year with Carolyn had been a disastrous year and he was really in pain about it. He was really in a tough way about it and really felt like it was over. . . . Anybody who knew them well knew how serious the problems were that last year. But he was always barking up the wrong tree when it came to women. He didn't quite ever find a woman who was a whole [person], especially in his thirties with Daryl and Carolyn. He was ready finally at the end. He had chosen women who didn't make him happy. He wasn't happy with Daryl and then he wasn't happy with Carolyn. Why? The different reasons that he was attracted to them to begin with then became the thing that he couldn't be with. You know when you're young the thing that makes you fall in love with a person, and then the thing that makes you fall out of love kind of thing. I think he was finally starting to feel that he was whole enough to find a really whole woman. I think he wanted to have children. He really did."

There are others, including Rob Littell, who remained determined to perpetuate the notion that John and Carolyn were getting along just fine. It wouldn't fit the gauzy narrative of America's favorite son for their marriage to be failing. They were "two very passionate beings, and when their flames crossed, there were sparks," Littell told *People*. If a breakup were even a possibility, "they would have made plans to go to a marriage counselor, to a priest at the church his mother went to. It wasn't on the radar. John was very keen on the long term. He felt that Carolyn was his best shot at a successful marriage." (Either Littell did not know that John and Carolyn had already sought the advice of a marriage counselor, or he was covering for them.) According to Littell, Carolyn's ongoing affair with Bergin, her drug use, her maniacal fear of the press, and her refusal to have sex with John were just the adjustments she was making to being a newlywed, along the lines of "This is where my toothbrush goes," he said. "Yeah, there was tension. But they were also just as passionate as the months before—and I'm talking right up to July of 1999."

John also was having a difficult time getting along with his sister. He was never particularly close to Ed Schlossberg, Caroline's husband, who he thought was arrogant, condescending, "and such a prick," as a friend put it. "It would be hard if your one sibling after your mother died was married to someone that you just thought was an asshole. That would suck. And that's what happened." Occasionally, he would see Caroline and Ed in New York City, but he did not want to be in Martha's Vineyard at the same time his sister and Ed were there— which was rare anyway since she had a home in the Hamptons, where she would go most weekends.

There was an ongoing dispute between John and Ed Schlossberg about what to do with the furniture and the significant family memorabilia at the Kennedy compound in Hyannis Port. "Ed became very obsessed with the value of the material at Hyannis Port because of what it was," the friend said. "There was this battle over all this stuff, and John and Caroline didn't actually speak for almost an entire year." But that summer, with things between John and his wife becoming increasingly tense, he picked up the phone and called his sister. "They had this really, really good conversation," the friend continued. "And I knew about it because he told me about it . . . and all I can say is fortunately for fucking her, because they hadn't spoken for almost a year." (Caroline Kennedy declined to be interviewed.)

With a cast off his leg for the first time since Memorial Day weekend, John was hobbling around the *George* office on Friday, July 16, on crutches. He met with Kliger, the Hachette magazine executive, to discuss ways to revitalize *George*. "He and I agreed that there had not been a well-thought-out business plan," Kliger told the *Times*. "So we said, 'Let's figure out how to go forward.'" Kliger said

John left the meeting feeling "fairly positive" about the outlook for *George*.

At around one o'clock, John spoke by phone with an employee at the airport hangar in New Jersey, where he kept his Piper Saratoga, confirming that he wanted to fly the plane later in the day and that he planned to get to the Essex County Airport between 5:30 and 6 p.m.

Shortly thereafter, Blow popped into John's office and asked him if he wanted to grab lunch. "Sure," he said. "I'm starved." It was obvious to Blow that John's ankle was still tender, and that he was using the crutches to judge how much weight, if any, he could put on his leg. "With every step, John looked as if he was assessing how much pain his ankle caused," Blow recalled. They went off to Trionfo, a small Italian restaurant near the *George* offices. The owners loved it when John came in, and quickly ushered him and Blow to a private room in the back of the restaurant where John wouldn't be bothered. "John was in a contemplative mood," Blow remembered. "We spoke about the magazine's future, and he sounded confident and upbeat." John told Blow that, following their meeting at the Yankees game the night before, Lachlan Murdoch had called Gary Ginsberg asking about *George*'s circulation and "how involved John was" in the day-to-day operations of the magazine. They spoke about whether there would be staff changes if *George* changed publishers. John said there would be. "You know," John told Blow, "for a while I hired people because I found them entertaining." That had made the office fun, John continued, "but it hadn't always helped the magazine." That would have to change.

As they headed back up to *George*'s forty-first-floor offices, Blow asked John what he was doing for the weekend. He said he was flying up to Hyannis Port for his cousin Rory's wedding. "I glanced at John's foot—even the short walk from the restaurant had tired him—then gave him a skeptical look," Blow recalled.

"Don't worry," John told him. "I'm flying with an instructor."

"Just don't crash, O.K.?" Blow replied. "Because if you do, that speech about all of us having jobs at Christmas goes right out the window."

"Not to worry," John said. "I'll be fine."

At around 4 p.m., John popped into Blow's office to ask him his opinion about the possibility of publishing a poem by Jack Kerouac. But they both agreed the poem wasn't much good. They passed on it, and John returned to his office to write a rejection letter. Five minutes later, he sent an email to his friend John Perry Barlow. Barlow's mother had just died. He commended Barlow for being at his mother's side. He knew something about that kind of loss, too. "I will never forget when it happened to me," John wrote, "and it was not something that was all that macabre. . . . Let's spend some time together this summer and sort things out." Barlow did not open the email until later the next day.

John's initial plan to get to the Essex County Airport by around 6 p.m. was, of course, foiled and he ended up leaving 1633 Broadway at around 6:40 p.m., along with Lauren Bessette, who had put in a full day at Morgan Stanley; together he and Lauren would drive in John's white Hyundai convertible to the airport, near Caldwell, New Jersey. Normally, the trip from Midtown Manhattan to the small airport could be accomplished in around forty minutes. But not on a warm summer Friday. John and Lauren left the *George* offices and encountered heavy traffic along the way, especially as they made their way through the Lincoln Tunnel. At 8:10 p.m., with the light beginning to fade, John and Lauren pulled into the West Essex Sunoco gas station across the street from the airport. Wearing a light-gray T-shirt, John went into the store and bought a banana, a bottle of water, and six AA batteries. When they arrived at the airport a few minutes later, Carolyn was not there. By prior arrangement, she was to come to the airport separately in a black sedan.

Where was Carolyn? Following her sister's intervention at the Stanhope two days earlier, Carolyn had reluctantly resolved to join John at Rory's wedding in Hyannis Port. On Friday afternoon, she went to de-

signer boutiques on the third floor of Saks Fifth Avenue to find a dress
that she could wear for the wedding the next day. For $1,640, she found
what she wanted: a short black dress by designer Alber Elbaz. From
there, Carolyn decided to get a pedicure. According to Colin Lively, a
haircolorist and stylist, "it was late at the end of the day on Friday, and
Carolyn Bessette Kennedy was right next to me, sitting in the same
line of people getting pedicures. She had a little piece of sheer fabric—
about three inches square, almost white with a hint of lavender—and
she wanted her toenail polish to match the swatch. The pedicurist
would apply the polish, and Carolyn would go to the window and put
her foot up and put the fabric next to it. Meanwhile, her cell phone
kept ringing, and she kept answering it. '*What?*' she said impatiently
into the phone. 'I told you—I'm getting a pedicure.' She made the
pedicurist re-do her toenails, and the phone rang again, and she said,
'The more times you call me, the longer it's going to take!'" She had
the pedicurist do it three times. "She wasn't overtly bitchy," Lively
said. "But she was so self-involved. If this was a key to her personality,
then I would say she was obsessive about a lot of things." Carolyn's
phone rang a third time. It was her driver. "If you can't park, circle the
block," she told him. "I'll be down in a few minutes."

At around 8:30 p.m., Carolyn arrived at the Essex Airport. Moments
later, she, John, and Lauren climbed into the Saratoga and strapped
themselves into the comfortable leather seats. At 8:38 p.m., twelve minutes after sunset, the airport tower cleared John and the Saratoga for
departure, and they were off.

John had told Blow that he would be flying with his flight instructor, and not to worry. But in the end, primarily because of how late the
hour had gotten, John told the flight instructor he would go it alone.
Ed Hill recalled: "That night, there was a flight instructor. He said to
John, 'You're taking off late. There's cloud cover over the Vineyard. Like
most Americans, I'm willing to inconvenience myself out of my love
for you. I will fly up there with you and bring the plane back or get my

356   FOUR FRIENDS

ass back to New Jersey somehow. Don't go without me.'" But John told
the instructor to go home and be with his family. He would fly alone.
"He did [go alone]," Hill said. "It was magnificently stupid that he did."

According to a subsequent report by the National Transportation
Safety Board, John told the flight instructor that he "wanted to do it
alone." Two weeks earlier, the same flight instructor had flown with
John up to Martha's Vineyard for the Fourth of July holiday weekend.
That flight, too, was at night, and the instructor later reported to the
NTSB that an instrument landing was required, although John was
not certified for instrument use. On July 1, John had a "non-plaster
cast on his leg," according to the NTSB, and had proven competent
using the autopilot in flight. But on the taxiing for takeoff and for the
landing, the flight instructor was in control of the Piper Saratoga. He
told the NTSB after the July 1 flight that he thought John "had the
ability" to fly the plane "without a visible horizon" but "may have had
difficulty performing additional tasks under such conditions." He also
said that John was "not ready for an instrument evaluation" as of July 1,
1999, and "needed additional training." He said he was "not aware" of
John "conducting any flight" in the Piper Saratoga "without an instructor on board." He had told the NTSB that he "would not have felt
comfortable" with John "conducting night flight operations on a route
similar to the one flown on, and in weather conditions similar to those
that existed on, the night" of July 16, 1999.

John flew the Piper Saratoga with three different flight instructors.
One of them had taken "six or seven" flights with John to Martha's
Vineyard in the previous year or so. Most of the flights were conducted
at night and, he told the NTSB, John "did not have any trouble flying
the airplane" and "was methodical about his flight planning and that
he was very cautious about his aviation decision-making." He said John
"had the capability to conduct a night flight to [Martha's Vineyard] as
long as a visible horizon existed. Still, John was not a particularly experienced pilot, especially when it came to flying at night when visual

flying conditions were impaired." In the fifteen months before July 16, John flew to or from Martha's Vineyard about thirty-five times, seventeen of which were John flying without an instructor along and five of which were at night. By July 16, John had completed about half of a formal instrument-training course. John told other pilots at Essex that the instrument training was "very confusing" to him and "tough sledding."

The night was hazy, hot, and humid. And it was difficult to see the horizon as the haze accumulated and the light faded. John had not filed a flight plan with the FAA, nor was he required to do so. He also had not engaged a private tracking service to monitor his flight—nor was that a requirement, either. At least one other pilot at the Essex Airport that night had decided not to fly because of the hazy conditions. Kyle Bailey told *Time* that he canceled his planned flight because of "a troubling haze that had already reduced visibility" and that when he "looked off in the distance" he could not see a familiar mountain ridge. "That is a test that most pilots use at the airport," he said.

The idea was for John and Carolyn to drop Lauren off at the Martha's Vineyard Airport and then to fly on to the Barnstable Municipal Airport, in Hyannis, just across Vineyard Sound from Cape Cod. At 8:34 p.m., John contacted the tower: "Saratoga niner two five three november ready to taxi with mike . . . right turnout northeast bound." The flight controller instructed him to go to runway twenty-two, which John acknowledged. Four minutes later, John informed the tower he was ready for takeoff. He was then cleared. The controller asked John if he was heading north toward Teterboro Airport. "No sir, I'm uh actually I'm heading a little uh north of it, uh eastbound," John replied. He was then instructed to "make it a right downwind departure then." John confirmed the instructions: "right downwind departure two two." There were no further conversations between John and air traffic controllers.

John flew the Piper northeast across the Hudson River, at an altitude of around fourteen hundred feet. Then he started climbing. He reached an altitude of fifty-five hundred feet about six miles northeast of the Westchester County Airport. He then presumably put the plane on autopilot: it remained at an altitude of fifty-five hundred feet; passed Bridgeport and New Haven, Connecticut; and then, flying parallel to the Connecticut and Rhode Island coastlines, passed Port Judith, Rhode Island, and flew across the Rhode Island Sound. At about thirty-four miles west of the Martha's Vineyard Airport, John began to descend at a rate of between four hundred and eight hundred feet per minute, at an airspeed of 160 knots.

At around 9:38 p.m., John turned the plane to the right, heading in a southerly direction. Thirty seconds later, John leveled the plane out at an altitude of twenty-two hundred feet and began a climb that lasted another thirty seconds. At 9:39 p.m., the plane leveled off at twenty-five hundred feet and headed in a southeasterly direction. About a minute later, John climbed the plane to twenty-six hundred feet and made a left turn and then began descending at a rate of nine hundred feet per minute. "It's unclear why the plane was descending so quickly," Jeff Kluger and Mark Thompson wrote in *Time* a few days later, "but Kennedy may have been trying to drop below the haze. For nearly five minutes, the plane's descent continued at this relatively steep rate, losing about two-thirds of its altitude until it was just 2,300 ft. above the Atlantic wavetops. Martha's Vineyard was by now only 20 miles away, but if the Piper kept dropping at this rate, it would hit ocean well before it reached the landing strip. For a pilot flying in better conditions—even an inexperienced pilot—the next step would be obvious: look out your window, get your bearings and level out your plane. J.F.K. Jr. didn't have that option. No matter how low he flew, there was still haze. Kennedy, who had earned his pilot's license only 15 months ago, now found himself flying a plane that might as well have had no windows at all. The first rule pilots are taught in a vertiginous situation like this is to ignore the signals your body is trying to send. The inner ear is equipped with an exquisitely well-tuned balance mechanism, but it's a mechanism that's meant to operate with the help of other cues, particularly visual ones. Without that, the balance system spins like an unmoored gyroscope."

Then John, increasingly disoriented and "apparently flummoxed," according to *Time*, turned right; the speed of the plane increased and it was descending rapidly, at a rate of forty-seven hundred feet per minute. "Perhaps he was still searching for a break in the haze, or perhaps merely stumbling about," Kluger and Thompson continued. "If he followed his flight training—and his reputation as a generally cautious pilot suggests he would have—he would now have performed what's known as 'the scan,' a quick survey of half-a-dozen key instruments that would reveal his plane's altitude, attitude and direction. But his brief experience with instrument piloting—he was certified to fly only under eyeball conditions—left him ill-equipped to handle a confusing situation. As the dials on the panel and the signals in his brain told him two different things, his eyes probably bounced back and forth between the instruments and the windows in a frantic attempt to reconcile the two. 'He was like a blind man trying to find his way out of a room,' a Piper Saratoga pilot surmises. And like a blind man, he now completely lost his way."

According to the NTSB, the last recorded radar position for John's Piper Saratoga occurred at 9:40 p.m., at an altitude of eleven hundred feet. The Piper's airspeed, vertical acceleration, bank, and dive angle continued to increase, and the right turn tightened until the plane hit the water, at about 9:41 p.m. "Trying to guess the atmosphere in the cockpit during the last 15 sec[onds] or so before the plane hit the sea will always be speculation—and grim speculation at that," *Time* concluded. "It was probably terrifying as the trajectory steepened. It was almost certainly quick—mercifully quick—when the last bit of sky ran out and the water met the plane like an asphalt runway. Death, at that speed, is instantaneous, and well before the wreckage of the Saratoga could descend the 116 ft. to the bottom of the darkened Atlantic, its three occupants were gone." In its report, the NTSB claimed that the "probable cause" of the accident was John's "failure to maintain control" of the Piper "during a descent over water at night, which was a result of spatial disorientation. Factors in the accident were haze, and the dark night."

AT AROUND TEN O'CLOCK that Friday night, the couple who had been waiting at the small Martha's Vineyard Airport to meet Lauren Bessette had grown restless, wondering where she was, and asked Adam Budd, a twenty-one-year-old intern at the airport, for help in locating her. Five minutes later, Budd called the FAA, in Bridgeport, Connecticut, and asked whether John's plane could be tracked. Budd was told that this was not the kind of information that could be shared over the phone. A few minutes later, John's uncle Ted called John's apartment on North Moore Street. Senator Kennedy had learned that John's plane was overdue and was hoping that perhaps John had decided to stay in New York City for the night. RoseMarie Terenzio answered the senator's call. The air-conditioning in her apartment wasn't working, and John had agreed to let her stay in his place for the weekend. Terenzio had similar conversations for the next few hours, including one with Carole Radziwill, the wife of John's first cousin Anthony.

At 2 a.m., the family alerted the Coast Guard about the Piper's disappearance, kicking off a full-scale search-and-rescue mission in the waters off Martha's Vineyard. Soon enough, CNN was broadcasting that John's plane was missing and showed the military helicopters circling the water, looking for any sign of a missing aircraft. John's disappearance was news all around the world. I remember returning from a run near my farmhouse in upstate New York that Saturday morning when my wife shared the news with me. I sat glued for hours to the CNN broadcast.

For the next four days, the Coast Guard, the navy, and the Massachusetts State Police together searched for the plane's wreckage at the bottom of the Atlantic Ocean. Around noon on July 20, a group of state police divers, in an envoy of three small boats, headed out of Menemsha Harbor, on Martha's Vineyard, as part of this search. Three hours later, they returned empty-handed. It was looking increasingly grim. "We are filled with unspeakable grief and sadness by the loss of John and Carolyn and Lauren Bessette," Senator Kennedy said on behalf of his family. "John was a shining light in all our lives and in the lives of the nation and the world that first came to know him as a little boy."

John's closest friends were in shock. "I spent a couple of hours trying to convince myself that what they'd done was to run away," John Perry Barlow said. "So I thought, *Gosh, maybe they've pulled this off. Maybe they'll go off and get plastic surgery and disappear from the face of the earth, and*. . . . But that was a pretty optimistic view." Sasha Chermayeff shared Barlow's fantasy. "I held out hope for a while that he would be stranded somewhere, like swimming there, or whatever," she said. Rose-Marie Terenzio refused to believe what had happened. "Not in a million years did I think there was any way possible that plane had gone down," she said. "I just thought, 'He's somewhere else.' You know, to be honest, I don't think I'll ever grasp what happened." When Gary Ginsberg heard from a friend that John's plane had gone missing, he called RoseMarie, who he knew was staying at John's apartment. "Rose, this is not true," he said to her. "And she broke down and said, 'Yeah, it's true. They can't find the plane.' And that's how I found out."

LATER THAT NIGHT, AROUND TEN FORTY, US Navy divers from the recovery ship USS *Grasp* found the plane in about 120 feet of water, some one-quarter mile north of John's last-known radar position. There was a debris field on the bottom of the ocean. The main cabin of the plane was found in the middle of the debris field. The plane's wreckage was brought up from the ocean floor, placed on the *Grasp*, and transferred to Newport, Rhode Island. It was then transferred again, to Otis Air Force Base on Cape Cod, where John had once pleaded, in vain, to join his father on a trip aboard Air Force One.

ON JULY 21, DR. JAMES WEINER, in the office of the chief medical examiner for the Commonwealth of Massachusetts, examined the bodies of John, Carolyn, and Lauren found inside the wreckage and determined they had died as a result of "multiple injuries" caused by an "airplane accident."

On July 22, in keeping with John's request, John, Carolyn, and Lauren's bodies were cremated and their ashes were strewn into the Atlantic Ocean from the fantail of the USS *Briscoe*, a navy destroyer that had been anchored between Martha's Vineyard and Hyannis Port. "We commit their elements to the deep, for we are dust and unto dust we shall return," a navy chaplain prayed. Only seventeen family members attended the ceremony aboard the *Briscoe*, but millions more were glued to their television screens. NBC's coverage featured the eerie observation by John's father, from September 14, 1962—during a toast to the America's Cup sailing team—that "it is an interesting biological fact that all of us have, in our veins, the exact same percentage of salt in our blood that exists in the ocean, and, therefore, we have salt in our blood, in our sweat, in our tears. We are tied to the ocean. And when we go back to the sea, whether it is to sail or to watch it, we are going back from whence we came."

ED HILL REMEMBERED BEING in bed at 6 a.m. on Saturday in Portland, Oregon, when his phone rang. It was 9 a.m. on the East Coast, and his father had been battling cancer. He thought the phone call was likely to be about how his father had taken a turn for the worse. It was his sister.

"Ed, it's Meg," she said.

"Yeah. What's up?" he replied.

"Um, well I have some bad news," she said.

"Well, I figured this phone call was bad news," he said.

"No, it's not Dad," she said. "The thing is, John Kennedy's plane is missing."

He thanked her and said he had to go. "I hung up the phone and all the air went out of my life," he said. "I walk[ed] back across the room, back to the bedroom. I got in bed and I lay down with my back to my girlfriend. She said, 'Who was that?' I said, 'That was my sister.' She said, 'Oh my God. Is it your dad?' I said, 'No. John's plane is missing.' God bless her, she didn't say a fucking word. . . . All I could think of was, *You fucking idiot.* I knew there was going to be a bad reason why that plane was gone, and there was. It was like, *Couldn't you just fucking listen to me just fucking once?* Dumb-ass motherfucker, fucking did that to the whole fucking country. I just wish that he hadn't had so many enablers. I think he had reached the point where I don't think he needed enablers anymore. . . . He died in a way that was sadly predictable. I was furious."

After John's death, Terenzio called Hill and insisted that he come to John's apartment on North Moore Street to help her. By then, hundreds of people had been gathering on the street in front of the apartment building and had placed all sorts of memorials of John—candles, cards, flowers—on the stoop leading into the building. (I visited the shrine, too.) "I flew into New York and went to his apartment," Hill recalled. "There was a Macintosh computer sitting there as he left it, open to flight simulation software. Oh, nice effort, John, but it's a little more complicated than that. A glancing relationship with some software when you've got fucking three hours of documented instrument time is not going to save your life; in fact it might end it, and it did. It was stupid."

The memory got Hill thinking. "So why was he so fucking stupid?" he wondered. "Did he want to die? Did he want to climb out of his skin because he wanted death? Did he want to climb out of his skin because it felt like it was crawling with vermin? Did he want to climb out of his skin because he couldn't live in that skin with his dead father? I don't know, but he couldn't stop himself from being reckless. As he got older and he's meeting these fucking investment bankers or these corporate lawyers or whomever, you know, guys who would cut their fucking balls off to be able to hang out with him just so they can impress their girlfriends—'I rode a snowmobile across the North Pole with John Kennedy,' or whatever. Those guys are legion. 'I rode a mountain bike across the floor of the Atlantic Ocean with John Kennedy'—he would have no trouble finding anyone to go along with any goddamn reckless amusement that he could conceive. Fortunately, those of us who were close to him, having pushed the envelope enough, had reached the point where we were like, 'No, fuck this shit.' The last time I was in a plane with him, we take off from Barnstable, which is the Hyannis airport. We fly to Logan. We get in this fucking airplane. Not only are we flying ahead of a serious storm—you could see it, it was right behind us—but the radio was fucked up. I don't know how the hell he got back home. I don't think he flew back. I think he had to leave the plane there or something. I don't remember the whole story, but it was reckless. I mean general aviation in general is reckless. I've been in the air with three friends, Jerry Gerber—that's Gerber knives—John Kennedy, and Tiger Warren, Geraldine Pope's first husband, who crashed his plane into the Columbia River, killing himself and his three sons. But anyway, I've sat next to three friends of mine in their putt-putts, and two of those friends died in those putt-putts. Jerry Gerber is still around. It's stupid. General aviation is a fucking—

they call them 'doctor killers' for a reason, but if you want to be totally reasonable you should call them 'stupid doctor killers.' Yes, John, airports are a drag if you're John Kennedy, but this has nothing to do with privacy, bro. This has to do with notching your belt—'I'm a pilot, too.' Fuck that."

AT JOHN'S MEMORIAL SERVICE, on Park Avenue, John's eulogy fell to his uncle Teddy. He started by thanking President Clinton, Hillary, and Chelsea for coming to the service and for their "extraordinary kindness" through the course of the week, which included Clinton's secretary of defense, William Cohen, signing off on the use of the navy ships and the burial at sea. "Once," Senator Kennedy began, "when they asked John what he would do if he went into politics and was elected president, he said: 'I guess the first thing is call up Uncle Teddy and gloat.' I loved that. It was so like his father. From the first day of his life, John seemed to belong not only to our family, but [also] to the American family. The whole world knew his name before he did. . . . But John was so much more than those long ago images emblazoned in our minds. He was a boy who grew into a man with a zest for life and a love of adventure. He was a pied piper who brought us all along. He was blessed with a father and mother who never thought anything mattered more than their children."

He spoke about John's love for his mother, his sister, and his new bride. He described John's support for the Institute of Politics at Harvard, which was named after his father, and about his founding of Reaching Up, a program to train caregivers for the mentally disabled. And he spoke about John's quiet but significant support for the Robin Hood Foundation, in New York City. "He was still becoming the person he would be, and doing it by the beat of his own drummer," he said. "He had only just begun. There was in him a great promise of things to come." He said that like his father before him, John had innumerable gifts but not the gift of a long life.

Then he paraphrased "In Memory of Major Robert Gregory," a 1919 poem by William Butler Yeats lamenting the loss of a friend's young son: "What made us dream that he could comb grey hair?"

Acknowledgments

This was a particularly challenging book to report and to write. My four friends were not around to be interviewed and, except for John, they had each led lives of relative anonymity. They also lived (and died) in an era before having an online presence was even a possibility. So, again except for John, typical Google searches, and other typical journalistic research techniques, yielded little, if anything, of substance.

But to my enduring appreciation, that is where their friends, girlfriends, brothers, sisters, and children played such an important role in the writing of this book. I will be forever immensely grateful to them for agreeing to speak with me and for sharing both their memories and memorabilia of their loved ones. They could have easily said no and that would have been that. But they did not.

To that end, I would like to thank specifically Bruce MacWilliams, Doug Buck, Beau Poor, Jamie Lustberg, Alison Spear, Michael Neuman, Bill Van Deventer, Hugh Jones, Iain Day, Justus O'Brien, John T. Davis, Joshua Rothman, Bobby Cohan, Norman Berman, Alan Cantor, Carol Kingsley, Zach Berman, Steve Bache, John Barber, Jim Horowitz, Ilyse Levine-Kenji, Brooks Klimley, Allen Bennett, Ray

Rickman, Steve Sposato, Richard Stratton, Clif Daniel, Thomas Daniel, Phil Balshi, Benji Swett, Mark Bodden, Mike Boschelli, Cha Cha Hartwell, Ezra Susser, Sarah Conover, Miriam Cytryn, Daisy Douglas Savage, Steven J. Donovan, Richard Riker, Terry Gruber, Will Iselin, Marc Wallis, Melissa Bank, Michaeline Bresnahan, Mimi Gaber, Mark Opler, Peter Begley, Will Zogbaum, Giles McNamee, Karna Bull, Mary Ellen Bull, Pam (Bull) Garvin, Rick Bull, George Bull, Tim Kyros, Ken Cera, Kathy Roach, Marty Koffman, George Lombardi, Sasha Chermayeff, Brian Steel, Peter Blauner, Christopher Randolph, Meredith and Nancy Price, Jeff Strong, Ed Hill, Gary Ginsberg, Mark Three Stars, Michael Gross, Nancy Haberman, Chris Oberbeck, John Pucillo, William Bradford Reynolds, Jim Spader, Santana Goodman, and Richard Weise. I couldn't have written this without you.

I'd also like to thank especially Paige Roberts, the Andover archivist who was extremely helpful to me throughout, and to Diane Silvia, at the *Brown Daily Herald,* who was incredibly generous with her time in rooting out obscure reviews of John's acting roles while at Brown. Thanks also are due the archivists at the Massachusetts Institute of Technology for allowing me to pore over the records of David Buck's father, Dudley, during the years he worked at MIT before his untimely death. I would also like to thank Gordon Goldstein, my friend and fellow Andover graduate (Class of 1982), who provided ongoing wisdom and counsel throughout this project. There were many others who were also extremely helpful to me as sources in the writing of *Four Friends* but who would prefer to remain anonymous. You know who you are and I thank you immensely.

I owe a massive debt of gratitude to Noah Eaker, my editor at Flatiron Books. He did a masterful job editing and shaping this book into what I hope is a first-rate narrative. He was a beacon through some rough seas, and always found a way to bring me safely into port, as needed. He did a fantastic job. I would also like to thank Bob Miller,

Flatiron's president and publisher; Colin Dickerman, now at FSG; Amy Einhorn, Flatiron's executive vice president; Marlena Bittner, Flatiron's director of publicity; and especially Lauren Bittrich, at Flatiron, who worked tirelessly to bring this book to fruition.

As usual, Joy Harris, my literary agent, was crucial in making this book happen. She has been by my side throughout and I am tremendously fortunate and thankful to have her there. Her wisdom and wise counsel are peerless. I would also like to thank Adam Reed who works with Joy and who makes sure everything that needs to be happening, does happen.

My parents, Paul and Suzanne Cohan, as well as my brothers, Peter and Jamie, and their families, have always been steadfast in their love and encouragement. There would be no *Four Friends* without them, if for no other reason than it was my parents, in their infinite wisdom, who decided the three Cohan brothers should go to Andover in the first place. Big thanks are also due my in-laws, especially Ellen Futter, Jeff and Susan Futter, and their families. And, as always, to Gemma Nyack.

Sometimes I marvel at how lucky I am to have my extraordinary wife, Deb Futter, and my two incomparable sons, Teddy and Quentin, in my life. Their love and friendship has been invaluable to me for what seems like forever. I can't imagine life without them. At the end of writing a book about the unexpected loss of four of my high school friends, their essential roles take on even more importance.